Library of
Davidson College

The Work of the Science Film Maker

LIBRARY OF FILM AND TELEVISION PRACTICE

THE WORK OF THE FILM DIRECTOR
A. J. Reynertson
THE WORK OF THE SCIENCE FILM MAKER
Alex Strasser
THE WORK OF THE MOTION PICTURE CAMERAMAN
Freddie Young and Paul Petzold
THE WORK OF THE INDUSTRIAL FILM MAKER
J. Burder

The Work of the Science Film Maker

by
ALEX STRASSER, F.R.P.S.

With a Preface by
SIR ARTHUR ELTON, Bt.

COMMUNICATION ARTS BOOKS
Hastings House, Publishers
New York, N.Y. 10016

© FOCAL PRESS LTD. 1972

All rights reserved. No part of this publication may be reproduced, stored in a retrieval system, or transmitted, in any form or by any means, electronic, mechanical, photocopying, recording or otherwise, without the prior permission of the Copyright owner.

Library of Congress Cataloging in Publication Data
STRASSER, Alex.
　　The work of the science film maker.

　　(Library of Film and Television Practice)
　　Bibliography: p.
1. Cinematography—Scientific applications.
2. Moving pictures in science, I. Title.
TR893.S75　　　　778.5′38′5　　　　77–38311
ISBN 0–8038–8051–0

Filmset in Baskerville and printed by Page Bros (Norwich) Ltd., Norwich

Contents

	ACKNOWLEDGMENTS	9
	PREFACE	11
	INTRODUCTION	13
1	THE MEDIUM	15
	The Cinema's Family Tree	15
	The Range of Film-Making	20
	Science and Education	21
	Conception of a Film	22
	Visualisation	23
	Components and Style	24
	Scripting and Editing: Cornerstones of Film Language	25
	The Image	27
	Human Eye and the Camera Eye	27
	Visual Truth and Deception	31
	Function of the Single Scene	36
	Scene Length	37
	Lenses as Creative Tools	37
	The Field of View	39
	The Close-up	41
	Sharpness and Softness	41
	The Unshackled Camera	43
	Light and Lighting	44
	Exteriors	45
	Interiors	46
	Colour	47
	Sound	49
	Speech	50
	Music	51
	Sound Effects	53

2	**THE SUBJECT**	55
	Our Visible and Invisible Worlds	55
	Explaining Science	59
	Filmed Lecture	59
	The Invisible made Visible	61
	Complex Themes	66
	The Interpretive Film	67
	Making the Message Clear	68
	Aiming at an Audience	70
3	**SPECIAL TECHNIQUES**	72
	Photographic Methods	72
	Effects in Science Films	72
	Camera Optics	73
	Cinemacrography, cinemicrography	73
	Manipulating the Image	75
	Pepper's Ghost	77
	Masks and Mattes	79
	Infrared Cinematography	81
	Ultra-Violet Cinematography	84
	Filter Effects	86
	Schlieren Process	87
	Cinematographic Methods: Time Dimension	89
	Special Cameras	91
	Under-running	92
	Single-frame and Time-lapse Methods	92
	Over-running	93
	Intermittent Slow-motion Cameras	96
	High-speed Cameras	97
	Freezing Action	97
	Reversing Action	98
	Optical Printing	98
	Preparation for Optical Printing	99
	Models and Scenic Effects	100
	Models	102
	Engineering, Architectural and Scientific Models	102
	Do-it-yourself and Commissioned Models	105
	Unit-produced Models	107
	Professionally Made Models	109
	Atmospheric Effects	111
	Graphics and Symbols	113
	Symbols as a Code	114

Animation	116
Graphics	117
Commissioning Animation	118
Cost of Animation	118
Do-it-yourself Methods	119
Titles	121
Jump Animation	123
Simulated Animation	129
Analogies	130
Unfilmable Analogies	136

4   FILMS IN THE MAKING   139

Film Work is Team Work	139
The Work of One Team	141
Three Science-Education Films	142
Science in the Orchestra	142
PART 1: Hearing the Music	145
"V for Vibration" (Production of Sound)	145
No Air—No Sound (Transmission of Sound)	146
Lightning and Thunder (Speed of Sound)	148
Lend me your Ear (Hearing Sound)	151
PART 2: Exploring the Instruments	152
Chimney into Flute (Vibrating Air Columns)	152
Ta-ti, Ta-ti (Pitch)	156
Seven Times Ta-ti (Musical Compass)	157
PART 3: Looking at Sound	160
Harmonics	160
Oboe into Flute (An Experiment)	162
Editing Schedule: High Notes and Low Notes	163
Transference of Heat	164
Convection	165
Conduction	177
Radiation	182
Electro-Magnetic Waves	186
Working with Scientific Apparatus	196
Problems with Diffraction and Interference Photography	198
Two Films on the History of Modern Science	203
Historical Personalities	204
Historic Equipment	205
Mirror in the Sky	206
Introduction: a Signal Across the Ocean	206
Discovery of Radio-Waves by Heinrich Hertz	209
Marconi's Experiments	212

Ionisation (an Animated Diagram)	213
Discovery of the Ionosphere by Appleton	218
Further Research	222
Radio-astronomy	223
Conquest of the Atom	224
Synopsis	225
The Shrinking Atom	225
J. J. Thomson finds the Electron	226
Rutherford's Shooting Range	228
Rutherford Splits the Nucleus	233
Cockcroft–Walton Atom Smasher	237
Chadwick Discovers the Neutron	240
The Neutron in Action	242
Summary	247

5	FILM MAKING PROCEDURE	249
	Sponsors	249
	Finance	250
	Technical and Educational Advisers	251
	Production Routine	252
	Pre-production	253
	Chart for Production Routine	254
	Filming and Editing	259
	Recording, Track-laying, Dubbing	262
	Completion	266

6	AUDIO-VISUAL AIDS	269
	The AVA Scene	269
	8mm Film in Education	270
	Loop Films (Cassettes)	272

APPENDIX	275
Guide Lines for the Evaluation of Science Films	275
Film Libraries and Catalogues	279
Scientific Film Associations and Societies	282
Educational and Popular Science Films	283
Film Running Time to Footage	285
Bibliography	286

GLOSSARY OF FILM TERMS	289

INDEX	300

Acknowledgments

I AM obliged to all those sponsoring organisations and production companies which have given me permission to reproduce stills and scripts from their films, particularly to the Central Office of Information, the Educational Foundation of Visual Aids, Mullard Ltd., the Gas Council, Shell International and the Realist Film Unit.

Likewise I am grateful to all who have contributed valuable suggestions, checked the manuscript or supplied technical diagrams, foremost amongst them Sir Arthur Elton, Mr. Gerald Garratt, Dr. George Wilkinson and my colleagues Adrian Jeakins and Denys Parsons.

Further individual acknowledgments are given within the text and in the captions of the illustrations. In the case of quotations I have stated source and author.

The technicians' credits for most of the films discussed in this book will be found on pages 283–5.

Finally, I wish to thank my wife and life-long working companion Sesu whose practical help and moral support have been indispensable to the writing of this book. A.S.

Grateful acknowledgement for illustrations is due to the following:

1 Royal Library, Windsor Castle, by gracious permission of H.M. the Queen. *2* Philadelphia Museum of Art. *3* British European Airways, London. *4* Peter Keen, London. *8* Captain M. W. H. Day, R.E., The British Nepalese Army Annapurna Expedition 1970. *9* Alte Pynakothek, Munich. *10* National Gallery of Art, Washington D.C., Rosenwald Collection. *11* Museo del Prado, Madrid. *13*, *14* Marlborough Fine Art Ltd., London. *17* ICI, London. *18* Unilever, London. *19* Mullard Ltd., London. *21* From K. Philipp: "Der Film im Dienst der Wissenschaft", Göttingen. *22* Prof. Dr. H. M. Peters, Zoophysiologisches Institut der Universität Tübingen, Abtlg. Physiologische Verhaltensforschung. *23* Shell International, London. *25–27* Kodak Ltd., London. *28*, *29* EMI Electronics Ltd., Hayes. *31*

National Physical Laboratory, Teddington (Crown Copyright). *32–35* Anni Rita Scheibel, Ober-Mörlen. *36* as 116. *37* as 18. *38* Prof. M. H. S. Wilkins, F.R.S., King's College, London. *39–42* Central Office of Information, London (Crown Copyright). *43–45* The Gas Council, London. *46* Midland Bank Ltd., London *49, 51–57* as 43. *58, 59* Shell-Mex Ltd., London. *61, 62* The Royal Society, London. *63–73, 75–77, 81–92* as 39. *94, 96–100, 102, 103, 106–109* as 43. *116, 120, 122, 124* Educational Foundation for Visual Aids in Association with Mullard Ltd., London. *127* Marconi Ltd., Chelmsford. *128–130* as 116, *131* as 127. *132–134, 141, 146, 148, 150, 151, 153, 154, 157, 160* as 116.

Preface

IN A FILM world dedicated to the support of false values it is a pleasure to introduce a book by an author at once so modest, and so professional as Austrian-born Alex Strasser, a man who has worked in films all his life, and who has added a kind of elegant simplicity to almost everything he has touched. For the past twenty five years or so, he has concentrated on the production of science films, and the book that follows unfolds for the younger generation the mass of specialised experience he has acquired, and the various special techniques and methods he has used and developed. Strasser started his film career in Germany in 1927 on the camera at the UFA Studios, but he soon switched to direction. After making some experimental films on his own, he produced a series of educational and documentary films for TOBIS. These included a number illustrating the circumstances leading up to the Weimar Constitution, commissioned by the then democratic German government. Hitler's government must have found these incompatible with their less than democratic aspirations. In any event, Alex Strasser came to Britain in 1934.

His talents were soon recognised. Among other films he shot *Birth of a Robot* in 1935/36, an early film by Humphrey Jennings and Len Ley. After a stint of teaching cinematography and a year's war service, he was taken on by the late Richard Massingham whose films combined wry humour with a mastery of scintillating and at that time revolutionary techniques of montage. For Massingham was one of the first to realise that the elaborate subterfuges of conventional film editing to get you from one place to another were often a waste of time. The obvious way was to jump the gap, and the devil take the continuity. Strasser carried into his later work some of Massingham's disregard of convention to attain an effect.

In 1944 Strasser joined Basil Wright's Realist Film Unit, directing and later producing a whole series of factual and scientific films, each as lucid as it was penetrating. The titles speak for themselves: *Your Children's Eyes, Your Children's Meals, Science in the Orchestra, Transference of Heat, Conquest of the Atom, Electro- Magnetic Waves.* Many received international awards. Strasser worked with Realist till 1964 when he set up a company of his own.

The Work of the Science Film Maker

The first part of this book is an exposition of theory and practice from which Strasser engagingly strips away the clamour and the froth that usually obscure even the simplest film operation, and sets out what happens with his accustomed lucidity. The second part is of particular importance for its analysis of a number of his own films, starting with *Your Children's Eyes*. Beginning production with cows' eyes as models (for Strasser always takes a direct approach) and finding they were reduced to formless jelly before he could film them, he took a characteristic short cut. Oranges, he discovered, resemble eyes, not only in shape but in substance. So, oranges it had to be, even though it was necessary to defeat wartime rationing to obtain them in sufficient numbers. To make oranges behave like eyes required deft manipulation, so to the cast was added a conjuror. Strasser's direct approach combined with an imagination peculiarly his own led to a memorable teaching film.

Strasser's methods, frequently relying on analogy and animated models, are described, film by film, often accompanied by a section of the script. They reveal as no words of mine can reveal, principles that made Strasser one of the leading makers of films inculcating scientific principles.

When people look back on our age and find it as garish to the eye as it is deafening to the ear and pretentious to the mind, they may see through the clamour and the froth to more profound things below. Among them they will surely find the films of Alex Strasser.

Arthur Elton

Introduction

There are several types of science film. Many scientists use the film as a medium for analysis or as a record of their research and their practical work. For this kind of cinematography, a working knowledge of certain camera techniques, such as high-speed photography, is sufficient. The resulting 'films' may consist either of single scenes—some of them no longer than a few feet or even frames—or of short sequences; others may show a particular process in successive disjointed stages as is often the case with micro cinematographic material. Sometimes, not even a print is required and the negative is thrown away after evaluation. Others are kept on file for future reference. These films, made purely for research and scientific investigation, do not come within the scope of this book, most of them being films in name only.

The second type embraces all films which present scientific ideas, facts and events in a truly cinematic form. Their aim is usually to impart and spread scientific knowledge. Some of these films, too, might be very short, but whether they are three minutes or thirty minutes long, they demand a thorough understanding of the art and technique of film making.

The term 'science film' is rather arbitrary and open to individual interpretation. Science films may range from the strictly scientific film to the factual film dealing with a great variety of subjects on the fringes of science. Some technological and industrial films, for instance, can rightly claim to be science films whether they are made by a scientist, a professional film unit, a teacher, a university film society, an in-plant unit or any other kind of film maker and whether they are shown on the conventional screen, cassette viewer or T/V set.

Thus, science films vary greatly in their purpose and intended audience. They are made for education, instruction and information, for the promotion of new ideas or products and for many other reasons. Some may be simple demonstration films, others teaching films (from the 'single concept' loop to the elaborate background film) or popular science films for general audiences. Films of this kind often deal with unfamiliar topics, with intricate concepts and theories, with visible and invisible phenomena.

Much of their subject matter cannot be illustrated by ordinary camera techniques but needs interpretation by means of animation, models, special effects or analogies.

Many science films are not concerned with science only, but often spread over a wide area of life in general. Science films are classed as films of facts but this is of no great significance as far as their production is concerned; the difference between making fiction and non-fiction films is a matter of degree; the methods are the same. There are, however, differences of style within every category of films. Just as in science literature a distinction is made between handbooks, textbooks and imaginatively written monographs, so science films can differ widely in character and mood. A film maker must be sure of the objective of his film and of his own intentions; at the same time he must have a sound knowledge of the rules and methods of film making so that he can make best use of them for the ends he has in mind.

Film-making forms a pattern made up of principles, techniques and matters of routine. This book traces that pattern. In addition, it tells how one team of film makers of which I was a member has tackled particular problems which presented themselves in the course of two decades of work. These descriptions are not intended as instructions but rather as pointers and they will leave the reader to draw his own conclusions.

Some basic knowledge of the mechanics of film-making in the departments of scripting, camera work and editing is assumed. If the reader has no practical experience at all, he is advised to study one of the books written on the subject of film-production in general. Some are listed at the end of the book.

1

The Medium

THE CHARACTER OF to-day's film is deeply rooted in the cinema's nature and history. No matter in which form or style a motion picture sees the light of day, it carries with it the inherited features, the 'genes', of a long line of ancestors.

The cinema's family tree

The first show copy of a film is called a 'married print' because the picture track and the sound track which have led more or less separate lives up to this stage have now been combined in a single track—been married for better or worse.

Picture and sound can be regarded either as technical components concerned with lenses and emulsions, wires and circuits or as manifestations of creative expression. In the first case, their lineage is of fairly recent origin, in the second it reaches right down to pre-historic times.

Picture

All pictorial art, as far as it can be traced back, began with the images drawn some 30,000 years ago on the walls of the caves of primitive man; these pictures might be looked at as the first visual documentations ever. The same is true of the wall paintings and graffiti of later civilizations which, 5000 to 7000 years ago, developed into means of communication—picture language. The first record of science, the zodiacs and calendars of ancient Mesopotamia and Egypt, all appeared around that period.

Cave paintings show the first awareness of *motion in art* in the lively attitudes of some of the animals and hunters. The problem of presenting movement in a static image has since then occupied the mind and brush of every artist. (Figs 1, 2).

Related to motion in art is the *art of motion*, cultivated long before our calendar started, in the Eastern temple dance and the Greek dance drama, the forebears of the modern theatre. In addition to these stage plays, many

Fig. 1. (above): *Leonardo da Vinci*, 1452–1519, has given his *Rearing Horse* six or seven legs and enveloped its head and tail in a whirl of lines.

Fig. 2. (opposite): *Marcel Duchamp* in his *Nude Descending a Staircase*, 1912, has achieved a vivid impression of motion by stratification of the moving figure.

Motion in Art; the conventional technique of presenting movement is to catch a frozen image of the moving subject, equivalent to an instantaneous exposure in photography. But painters of all periods have broken through this convention by trying to add a third 'stroboscopic' dimension.

other kinds of staged action took place in the amphitheatres, sport arenas and fairgrounds of the distant past.

All these ancient art forms, rites and public spectacles exerted their influence on the cultural and not so cultural activities of later periods, and necessarily also on the film.

The Work of the Science Film Maker

The technical ancestry of the picture track originated, of course, at a much less remote age. Although the earliest known means of mechanical reproduction of visual images, the Chinese woodcut, seems to date back to the seventh century, it was not until 700 years later that this process was put to practical use in Europe for the manufacture of religious designs and even more so of playing cards. The invention of the printing press and engraving on metal in the middle of the fifteenth century and the great advances in papermaking techniques between 1630 and 1800 made communication techniques in to-day's sense possible. The mass dissemination of news and of thought was, at first, mainly confined to the printed *word*. *Pictures* illustrating both actuality and fiction, appeared on the scene much later and they came into their own after 1798, the year lithography was invented.

In the nineteenth century, the sciences of optics and chemistry in combination with the skill of instrument makers created a new visual medium—photography. It brought with it the fresh breath of adventure by creating the 'instant art' of the lens in its many hundred ramifications.

But this art is, at least in one respect, not so different from that of the painter. They both record a chosen subject at a chosen point in time and in both cases the result is—in to-day's parlance—a 'frozen' image.

Fifty years after the introduction of still photography, the cine camera, evolved from a number of optical animation toys, arrived to 'defreeze' this image—adding to photography the dimensions of time and motion. And since motion in this context equals action, cinematography provides the means of re-creating on the screen the world in which we live. True, it is a curiously twisted world, full of artificial time-and space-values and other distortions, and more often than not shot through with hocuspocus and make-believe, but still a world accepted by our senses as 'real'. Moreover cinematography is able to present a world on the screen in which motion is not recorded but synthetically *created*—the world of the animated diagram in the factual field and the cartoon world in the realm of phantasy.

More than anything else, it is the element of *movement* in picture making which has brought about the distinct character of the film language. To say this seems to propound the obvious, but nowadays subsidiary elements such as colour and sound are often regarded as of equal, even of primary importance. Yet, if they were suddenly to disappear from the arena of the cinema, good films could still be made. The dynamic and gripping pictures of the pre-colour, pre-sound period are ample proof of this. Colour and sound are powerful means of aesthetic and emotional impact and often of specific significance, but whenever they try to usurp a dominant position, the film loses the intrinsic qualities of its language and becomes either a photographed stage production or a lecture illustrated by moving photographs.

The Medium

Sound

On the sound side, the film's pedigree is similarly chequered. Expressions of the human voice: oratory, chant and song are as old as recorded history. Music developed over the centuries in step with the appearance of the various instruments; the earliest group of professional music makers in Europe were the minstrels of the Middle Ages and the first orchestra on the lines of a modern one probably came into being about 1620.

Sound recording and transmission techniques have their beginnings, like cinematography, in the nineteenth century. The first mechanical recording and reproduction instrument was Edison's parlophon of 1887. It signalled the birth of the gramophone industry but for the purpose of the film a purely mechanical system proved unsuitable. All modern sound processes, used in film and TV, are combinations of mechanical, electrical and electronic methods; they owe their existence to pioneers of science such as Faraday, J. J. Thomson, Lee de Forest and many others. The *magnetic* sound track was commercially introduced in the early fifties. It was followed by the magnetic picture track in the form of videotape which has replaced film stock as the main medium for making television pictures.

One might ask what influence purely technical innovations have on the creative and aesthetic side of filming. The answer is, sometimes little and sometimes much. In editing, for instance, it is possible that the use of scissors will sooner or later come to an end. This has already happened in TV where editing is often done by vision mixing.

As in vision mixing, the future film editor will probably sit in front of a control panel surrounded by monitoring screens. Sound and picture will be lined up on various tracks and tapes which are then played backwards and forwards for the selection of the material. The chosen scenes will be electronically transferred in the required lengths to a final track without any physical cutting taking place at all. This system resembles somehow the making up of a goods train by remote control from a signal box where trucks are picked from several trains, shunted and re-assembled into a new train.

An increasing use of videotape is bound to bring about new editing techniques. Since editing is one of the most formative processes in film-making, a change in its technique is apt to change the art of film-making as a whole. New effects become possible, old ones have to be discarded and film language will certainly be affected. Similar developments are at work in all departments of film-production where the creative side is conditioned by technical methods.

This shortest of monographs will give an idea of the intricate process of cross-breeding which took place in the ancestry of the film. Each 'parent medium', whether artistic or technical, has helped to shape the film's nature, character and language by giving it some of its own life blood, its traditions and its laws of conduct.

The range of film-making

The film as an industry is divided into the spheres of speculative and sponsored film-making. Squeezed between the two, the subsidized film leads a precarious existence.

The speculative field is mainly concerned with producing films for entertainment to be shown in cinemas. It includes such subsidiaries as newsreels (where they still exist), film magazines, interest films, travelogues, cartoons and similar short programme fillers. The producing companies finance themselves by way of bank credits, backers and distribution agreements, and they make their films exclusively for profit.

A newcomer to the speculative field is the 8mm teaching loop which is produced for sale to schools and universities. More will be said about this type of film later.

In the subsidized field interest centres mainly on the experimental and avant-garde type of production. Most of these films are not accepted by commercial distributors and must find their finance from private sources which do not expect a return. They are sometimes supported by an organization such as the British Film Institute which wants to encourage new talent or wishes to identify itself with a particular project. Films of this kind are made on a shoe-string and their economics are of no consequence as they are mainly shown at festivals, in art cinemas and by film societies. Some are now finding their way into commercial cinemas. Within the general scheme of things, such films are of importance, concentrating as they usually do on new and often revolutionary ways of treatment and technique. Many well-known film directors such as Karel Reisz, John Schlesinger and others have started in this way.

Sponsored productions are mostly factual films. They are made with an enormous diversity of purposes ranging over advertising and sales-promotion, training, education and information. The sponsors can be government departments or large industrial concerns, professional bodies or educational organizations and hundreds of such films are produced every year in the English-speaking world alone.

Companies making sponsored films call themselves specialized film producers but colloquially they are still referred to as documentary film units. This is a misnomer because the term 'documentary' should be associated with the type of film produced in England in the thirties by John Grierson and his school. Few of the present-day factual films have any resemblance in form and motive to those original documentaries; this kind of filmic approach is now largely in the hands of television.

Film-making is concerned with the presentation of facts and ideas.

The Medium

This is common to both fiction and non-fiction films but the problems in these two categories are very different.

The expenditure involved in a full-length feature production can be several hundred times that of a quite lavishly made sponsored film. Everything is on an elevated plane: the fees and salaries, the technical and artistic facilities, the cost of studios and travel and the profits and losses. Problems of presentation which, due to their expense, can be a great headache to the maker of a sponsored film, hardly exist in the feature field where the producer and his creative staff have the complete range of expensive cinematic processes, such as travelling mattes, etc., at their disposal.

This difference in production levels does not mean, however, that the sponsored film offers less scope to a creative mind. On the contrary, because the available facilities are more limited, an inventive approach is all the more necessary and it has often been proved that its impact can be greater than spectacular gimmicks or technical gloss. The presentation of scientific facts and ideas, for instance, invisible or unsubstantial as they often are, poses particularly exciting problems.

Science and education

Informational, technical, educational and science films account nowadays for the majority of sponsored products. Our age of highly specialized sciences and technological methods has brought with it a complete re-orientation of our lives, thinking and work, and this in turn has had a profound effect on the film scene.

The cinemas are flooded with science fiction films and to-day's educational conference halls offer a bewildering variety of optical and electronic audio-visual aids. In this profusion of instruments and gadgets the film stands out as a powerful tool for the modern educator. As we are only at the beginning of the audio-visual teaching era, scientists and teachers must be anxious to know as much as possible about the educational potential of the film and its allied media.

Although this book deals essentially with film-making, much of what it says applies to television, the other most prominent medium of the audio-visual field.

Film and television have much in common. Both are means of mass communication but can serve small audiences equally well. Both make their impact mainly by force of the visual image, and both can easily include material which an actual lecturer would be unable to bring before his audience. Television is a fusion of cinematography and radio and, as anybody working on the creative side of television is automatically forced to make use of film-production methods, knowledge of the film's language is indispensable to him.

Both film and television have, each in their own way, contributed—

if not yet adequately—to the demands of the broadened educational scene. Up to the end of the fifties there was a steady, though slow, increase in the production of science teaching films. In the sixties, television took the numerical lead in the output of programmes for use in classrooms and further education. These programmes are bound to be built up still further to supply the "open universities". Closed circuit television, too, will have a great future in education.

It has, however, become clear that not all educational television programmes are able to do the job of a well-produced film. Although television has the advantage over an actual classroom lesson in that it can assemble heterogeneous and widely dispersed material and can integrate it with classroom demonstrations, it still needs a teacher or demonstrator appearing in person on the television screen to present the material and to develop the argument. In essence, an educational television programme is a filmed lecture with the lecturer explaining the more difficult concepts by word of mouth as he would do in an actual lecture. This technique is necessary because educational programmes are treated as Cinderellas by the television companies; costly and time-consuming production devices, such as good diagrammatic animation and special cinematic effects, can only be used sparsely.

Well-conceived and imaginatively executed educational films, even if they use a lecturer on the screen, are entirely different in scope and character from educational television programmes. The possibility of making the best use of *cinematic* devices as well as less hectic production methods gives a film producer the chance for a much stronger visual interpretation, particularly of scientific facts and problems. Films are more likely to present intricate subjects in depth and clarity. Films are also more flexible in use, they can be shown in parts or screened repeatedly as often as is necessary.

There is much virgin territory in the sphere of the educational and science film and adventure in its exploration. And because the visual presentation of scientific ideas is often difficult, it offers great scope to an inventive mind.

The conception of a film

There are many ways of treating a film subject, and it is this treatment which determines the character, type and style of a film.

Most science films are short. They usually run for about 2 to 30 min. Short films are not short long films just as short stories in literature are not mini-novels. Both short stories and short films have their own laws; for instance, there is no time for an elaborate build-up of the theme or of a given situation; we have to plunge straight in.

The first step is to visualize the project in your mind. Every film

The Medium

maker has his own methods which depend on his personality, his outlook on life, his technical and artistic abilities and on his understanding of film language.

Visualisation

How does one visualize a film? Many factors must be considered—content, purpose, the audience to which the film will be addressed, and the available money, time and facilities.

Then there are the technical and artistic elements: the action, the spoken word, music and sound effects—all these have to be taken into account. The visuals may require exterior and interior shooting, either on location or in a studio. There may be some animation, or a number of models or special effects. The spoken word could consist of commentary, dialogue or of spontaneous interviews and conversations. Sound effects could be an important part of the story or just a desirable tonal background. Music also can be incidental or integral; only a small group of musicians may be needed, or a full-blown symphony orchestra.

Since the subject determines the content and, to a degree, the style of a film, it is intimately bound up with the question of finance. A shoestring budget obviously gives less scope to the film maker's imagination and range of action than a liberally financed prestige production, and before he lets his creative energies run wild, he has to know how much money will be at his disposal. There might be a rare case where a sponsor tells the producer, 'Make the film the way you feel about it and blow the expense.' In an equally rare case, the producer might convince his sponsor that the subject requires twice the earmarked amount. Miracles like these have actually happened but in the ordinary run of film financing such chances must be ruled out.

Whatever the scope, visualizing a film is never a tangible piece of work like scripting, shooting and editing which, as concrete stages of filmmaking, can be calculated and turned into budget items. Neither does visualization take the form of a sudden flash of inspiration emerging—like Aphrodite from the foam—in splendid and perfect finality. It is a process which, depending on the complexity of the subject, consists of hard work, sweat and headaches over shorter or longer periods—a process of continuous fermentation.

The first rather vague ideas take shape during the investigation and, assisted by subject expertise, build up into a visual framework that can be roughly outlined in the treatment, or synopsis, submitted to the sponsor. If approved, this treatment is the starting point for the scripting. The visualization process continues, and it does so not only during scripting but throughout the production.

Stage by stage, detail by detail, the sketch becomes a complete picture. Ideally, the finished and approved shooting script should be a blueprint of the film to be made, but this never happens. The *contents* of a film are communicable on paper, its *form* very much less so; it remains to the last in the mind of the director and finds his ultimate shape only on the cutting bench. It is often when the first show print has left the laboratory that the film maker gets his most brilliant ideas!

Components and style

The use to which the various technical and artistic resources of film-making are put, as well as the space and priority given to each of them, are again determined by the subject. The film of to-day is a complex piece of work but basically it is a union of just two components: picture and sound. In this union the picture is the constant, and the sound the variable. Sound can be dispensed with in a film for long periods of time or be omitted altogether, but a film without a continuous visual presence is unthinkable.

This makes it clear why the visual image is the most important element in the language of the film. There is great need to stress this point because numerous films, particularly in the factual field, miss their chance of reaching the audience and of making an impact through uninspired visualization or by flogging a once good idea to death. Good camerawork helps but photography is, after all, only a record of a concept and it is the concept itself that counts. This is one of the first necessities of film visualization, no matter what type of film is contemplated.

There is another side to visualisation. The rhythm and character of our ways of life are changing rapidly. Our senses have become more blunted, tastes are getting coarser, we need sharper stimuli. Many of to-day's films reflect these conditions. Colour has become more violent, the sound track is deafening. The pace of most films, as expressed in the editing, has quickened; continuity is often dispensed with, story and action are fragmentized, providing a kaleidoscopic firework display which is dazzling to look at but does not always make sense and often leaves us no time to assimilate what we see.

This trend is an expression of the new social and artistic consciousness and as far as fiction films or television commercials are concerned, one can either accept or reject it. But on the educational scene, a visually overcrowded and restless film can be as useless as a visually sterile one; there is a saturation point which must not be exceeded. Visual ingenuity and gimmickry are entirely different things.

The same goes for sound. A negative example is the interviewing practice now often seen on television where even the most scholarly individuals are expected to walk, run, cycle or drive while they answer the interviewer's questions, or are made to talk surrounded by the din of main road traffic or of a factory hall. All this is done in the name of greater realism but it certainly makes comprehension more difficult.

The Medium

Scripting and editing: cornerstones of film language

The language of the film developed slowly. The 'flicks' in their infancy were a sort of side-show at the funfair and nobody took them seriously. D. W. Griffith was the first film maker to realize the potential of film and to formulate a language in which films could and should speak to us. He initiated the specific criterion of cinematic art, not least by introducing the Close Up shot. Griffith's ideas are still regarded as the fundamentals of all serious and inspired film-making.

The vocabulary of film language differs from that of words in that it has always to be created *ad hoc*. Each film-shot is part of an existing situation; there is no past or future in an image. Each such shot is, as it were, part of a jigsaw puzzle; it is in the sum total of these single images that the whole situation reveals itself. That is why planned shooting is so essential.

The script, the first concrete document in the visualization chain, not only guides the shooting in relation to the story content and the sequence of events, but also gives detailed technical instructions. But during both scripting and shooting, editing requirements must be considered as well. Thus, there seems to be a straight linear progression from scripting via shooting to editing. Yet, things are not quite so straightforward.

Editing procedure, as far as its mechanics are concerned, varies slightly according to the habits and practices of individual editors. The object of editing, however, always remains the same: it is to pick and arrange the material so that it corresponds both with the film maker's intentions and with the nature of the cinematic language.

The film maker's intentions are laid down in the script but even a detailed script can only be regarded as a master plan which indicates the story content, the style of the film and its continuity. Now, on the cutting bench, this paper document has to become a document written on celluloid. Thus, editing is a means of transposition and recreation.

Real time and real space have to be turned into film time and film space. This may mean squeezing 5 real minutes into 5 screen seconds. This transformation of time values is one of the foremost features of the film language; it may be done in terms of hours, days, weeks, months, years in any condensation, and it may reach into the past or the future in any chosen order.

On the other hand, real time can also be extended. Events which happen simultaneously must be dissected to form a quick cross-cut sequence, and to a momentary occurrence, such as a staged explosion or a car smash, added dramatic force can be given by breaking the happening down into a short series of flashes which give the illusion of being instantaneous (page 98). All such editing effects must, however, be anticipated either in the script or, at the latest, during the shooting, so that the necessary material is available.

Space can be manipulated much like time. One or two establishing shots of well-known landmarks will imply that the action takes place in London or New York, and a screen character might consist of the parts of several actual people shot in close-up.

The conventional means for the separation or bridging of time periods and for switching from one place of action to another are optical dissolves, wipes and fades. One of the positive contributions that television has made to the film is that it does not bother too much about time- and space-transitions but uses straight cuts instead of the usual optical devices. This speeds up the progress of the story and the money saved is made available for more essential matters. But some confusion can result from this practice and it must, therefore, not be used at points where orientation is vital.

There are various categories of film in which shooting with a minimum of scripting is legitimate and even unavoidable. When setting out on an expedition, we are confronted with unknown factors and have only a general idea of what we intend to film. On such trips, a great amount of footage is normally expended on scenic and episodic material. In order to use this footage later to best effect, the film maker should regard each phase of shooting as an intrinsic link in the envisaged theme. He must also procure enough related close-up material; this is indispensable for creating a filmic reality at the editing stage.

Films of animal behaviour, of human conditions such as portrayed in the film *Warrendale* and of certain kinds of industrial activity belong to the same category. The hoped-for actions and events are often unpredictable as to the exact moment they occur and the course they take. We may have to run roll after roll of film through the camera before getting, if ever, what we are after. Visualization can only keep to the overall idea; the aim must be to translate the actual happening into the best film terms obtainable under the circumstances. It is, again, later in the cutting room where most of the creative work takes place.

The compilation film must also be mentioned. The object is to produce a film on a given subject by assembling scenes or sequences from existing films. The first step is to find these films; there may be five, or there may be twenty five. After viewing these films you have to negotiate with their owners. The required scenes are then marked and in good time, after weeks or months, the material arrives, often from all over the world, in the shape of dupe-negatives or 'lavenders' from which rush prints have to be ordered from your own laboratory. Compilation is entirely an editing job and, as one might realise, such films can sometimes eat up more time and cause more headaches than making two or three films from scratch.

Editing has other functions as well and an almost unlimited number of devices and tricks are available to assist the editor in his work. Yet, lack of even a single scene, vital for the build-up of a particular effect, can be very

The Medium

frustrating, and this is only one of many things that can go wrong at this stage; hence the need for continuous cross-reference, for re-thinking, re-editing and often for additional shooting.

All this indicates that the relationship between scripting, shooting and editing is triangular rather than linear. Each of these components is able to put its own powerful stamp on the film even to the extent of making or unmaking it—and each has to work in perfect co-ordination with the others. They are dependent on one another for achieving unity of purpose and for successfully linking the visualization with the realization.

The image

In order to make full use of the possibilities offered by photography and cinematography, we should briefly consider the mechanism peculiar to human vision.

The human eye and the camera eye

Our eyes can recognize motionless shapes and objects as well as movement. Many animals can perceive only movement; they would starve if their prey did not move. Our eyes can perceive colour; dogs and cats see the world in monochrome.

Our eyes have an angle of sight of about 120°. The angle of a dog's vision is about 80°, that of fish or birds can approach 360°. We now have 'fish-eye' lenses in our camera arsenal and the pictures they produce appear distorted and unreal to us whilst they would appear quite real to fish. All living creatures' experience of reality is certain to be determined by their particular systems of vision.

The *focusing* angle of the human eye is narrower than 120°. Depth focusing is operated by the accommodation mechanism of the eye, and that of width by a split-second scanning process. Animals have different accommodation systems if they have any at all.

Our binocular vision creates for us a world of three dimensions. It is strange that in the age of moon-landings and mechanical brains we have come nowhere in sight of a practical solution to the need for three-dimensional cinematography.* Perhaps this is because we have from childhood been conditioned to read the third dimension into two-dimensional pictures and screen images.

The similarity of the eye and the photographic lens is often stressed but this similarity is confined to certain optical features. Behind our eyes, and stimulated by the optical nerves, is our ceaselessly working brain which interprets what the eyes see and completes our vision system by adding the psychological element to the physical and physiological one. Our three-dimensional perception is the result of this combination.

---

* The newest development, holography, is still in the experimental stage (see glossary).

The Work of the Science Film Maker

The Medium

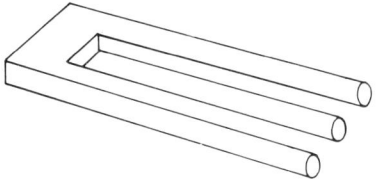

Optical Illusions. FIG. 5. A strange object.

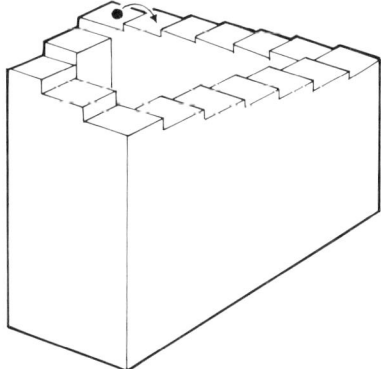

FIG. 6. The ball jumps up a never-ending staircase.

FIG. 7. Converging lines destroy our ability to judge the proper size of objects.

The camera eye merely obeys the laws of optics. It is 'objective'. Behind it is just a sheet or length of film which records the information sent to it by the lens. What it records must be fed back to our eyes and brain for interpretation. We can anticipate the feed-back process to some extent by putting our brain behind the camera to teach its lens how to see. This is what every photographer and film-maker has to do.

There are other differences between our eye and that of the camera. We have, for instance only *one* lens in each of our eyes which covers at any

---

FIG. 3. (opposite top): *Interior of a Turkish Mosque.* The hemispherical effect of a fish-eye lens.

FIG. 4. (opposite bottom): *Parking Meters in a London Street.* The bunching effect of the telephoto lens.

particular moment *one* field of view. Our eyes can do what no camera lens can do—rove from point to point, near or far, at split-second speed. Yet they cannot do what the camera lens does, which is to register instantly every detail within their field of view.

Our eyes are flexible but they are fixtures. The camera has dozens of interchangeable eyes at its disposal, which are different in focal length, resolving power and other characteristics. Thus, cameras are flexible in a different way. They can supply a multitude of images where our eyes give us only one, and they can isolate areas or objects from their surroundings.

Our angle of sight, combined with our binocular vision and supported by empirical and psychological factors determines our sense of perspective. Photographers are aware of the fact that the geometrical perspective seen by

Fig. 8. *Captain G. Owens below the Summit of Annapurna*, 1970. Through tilting the camera upwards, the steep mountain pyramid appears almost like a flat arctic ice field.

the lens is different from the retinal perspective seen by our eyes. The grandeur of a distant mountain panorama shrinks to insignificance in a photograph taken with a lens of normal focus. We have to resort to a long focus or telephoto lens, but this reduces the field of view.

Environmental experience is one of the determining elements of 'seeing'. If a man is the last and lowest member of a climbing party scaling a vertical cliff, his experience tells him that the wall is, indeed, perpendicular.

The Medium

But if he takes a photo from his position at the bottom of the cliff, it will show the other climbers crawling like beetles across a horizontal area of rock. There is no psychological point of reference in the picture.

Visual truth and deception

The fact that the eye is often deceived is proved by the great range of optical illusions.

Fig. 5 shows a perfectly believable drawing of a perfectly impossible object.

Fig. 6 shows a winding staircase which one could climb and climb until doomsday. A computer-made loop film of this illusion in which a ball jumps upwards from step to step without ever 'arriving' was produced by Dr. E. Zajek in the USA, and was shown at various exhibitions.*

Fig. 7 is particularly interesting for film makers because it demonstrates that a system of converging lines can destroy our ability to assess sizes in their proper proportions. Use can be made of this illusion for films by building film sets in false perspective in order to achieve either more realistic or exaggerated and weird effects. The famous *Cabinet of Dr. Caligari*, made during the German expressionist period, was the first full-length film using this technique and owes much of its powerful impact to the special scenic designs.

An interesting experiment was made a few years ago by the American, Adalbert Ames. Its object was to test the part that psychological factors play in seeing and perceiving. He built a trick room with sloping walls, floor and ceiling and with differently angled corners. This unaccustomed architectural arrangement of lines and spaces confuses our eyes to such an extent that one and the same person appears unnaturally dwarfed or elongated in height according to his or her position in the room. This room was filmed and has been shown on TV.

Painters often use exaggerated perspective in order to express their own ideas of reality. In photography, false perspective can be produced by the use of lenses of certain focal length or curvature. Long-focus lenses produce quite different perspective effects than wide-angle lenses (see page 39 and Figs 3, 4).

The resolving power of the human eye is relatively poor. This seems to be of advantage to us. If it were much stronger, all textures and surfaces would look very strange. We could, for instance, not read printed text because the ink distribution on the paper would not form letters but would appear as a pattern of minute dots uneven in tone. We would clearly see

---

* A similar *aural* illusion was produced by Professor Ch. Taylor in Cardiff, also by means of a computer. He calls it *Music of the Spheres*; it consists of a tonal scale which climbs endlessly higher and higher without ever getting out of range of our hearing.

FIG. 9. *Perspective: Albrecht Duerer: The Lamentation for Christ*, circa 1500 (detail). This fortified city is a small background detail within a hugh canvas. The strongly compressed depth of this long-distance view anticipates the bunching effect of the telephoto lens. (Fig. 4).

FIG. 10. *Giovanni Battista Piranesi*, (1720–1778) from his series: *Carceri d'Invenzione*. The web of intersecting diagonal lines produces a strong dynamic effect. 'This imaginary prison scene would startle geometry' (Horace Walpole).

FIG. 11. *Persistence of Vision: Velazquez: The Spinners* (Las Hilanderas), circa 1655. *Persistence of Vision* was first recorded pictorially some 350 years ago in the above painting of a spinning wheel. No spokes are discernible; the wheel is shown as a transparent disc. This phenomenon is the physiological basis of all cinematography.

the pigments in paintings but could not recognise the paintings themselves. We would be like people who do not see the wood for the trees.*

Photography and cinematography only exist in their present form because of the imperfections of our seeing mechanism and because our eyes are so easily deceived. The exaggerated 'dottiness' in a film or photograph, caused by the image-forming emulsion grain, often becomes a nuisance in dupe negatives and enlargements.

The illusions involved in cinematography are familiar to us: the transport mechanism in the cine-projector—as in the cine-camera—holds each frame in the gate for about 1/50 sec and then pulls it down to make place for the next frame whilst the blade of the rotating shutter obscures the gate. In this way, 24 images, each slightly different from the preceding one (unless the subject is static) pass the gate every second.

Our brain fuses these 24 separate frames, each of which is exposed three times in the projector gate by the shutter, into a single image in

---

* Was it Professor Philip Morrison who once said in a Christmas lecture that we perceive the world as we do because of the size we are?

The Medium

which the movement of objects appears quite natural and without flicker. The phenomena which are involved in this process are known as 'persistence of vision' and 'phi-phenomenon'. There are many opportunities to observe them in our daily life.

If we turn a bicycle upside down and spin one of the wheels, the spokes disappear and we can see through the rotating wheel as through a veil. A torch swung rapidly in a circle appears not as a light point moving round but as a complete luminous circle. Numerous pyrotechnical effects are based on this illusion. Many more examples could be mentioned.

The stroboscopic nature of the rotating shutter often results in undesirable effects. Movement can reverse its direction; this is most often noticeable in filmed scenes of moving vehicles where the wheels sometimes appear to turn backwards (see also pages 200–201).

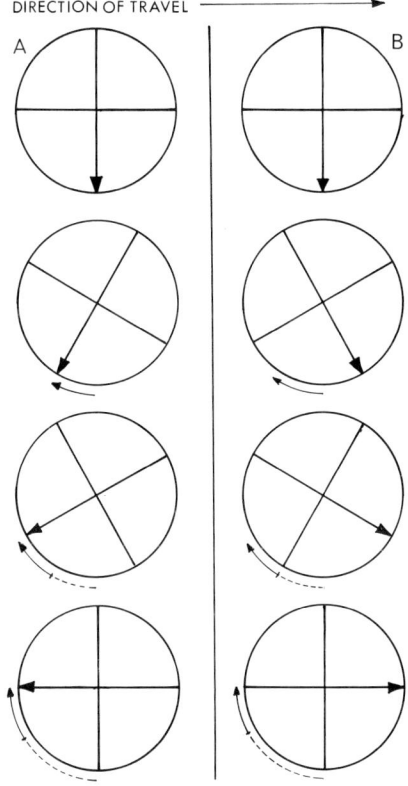

FIG. 12. *Persistence of Vision.* Why do spoked wheels of cars moving across the screen often appear to turn in the direction opposite to that of the car's movement? In row A of this drawing each successive film frame shows the spokes of the wheel only slightly turned from its previous position and the eye fuses these single steps into a forward motion. But if the car travels at a speed in which every successive frame shows the spokes turned almost full circle, as in row B, the eye fuses the different positions into a backward motion. See also Fig. 124.

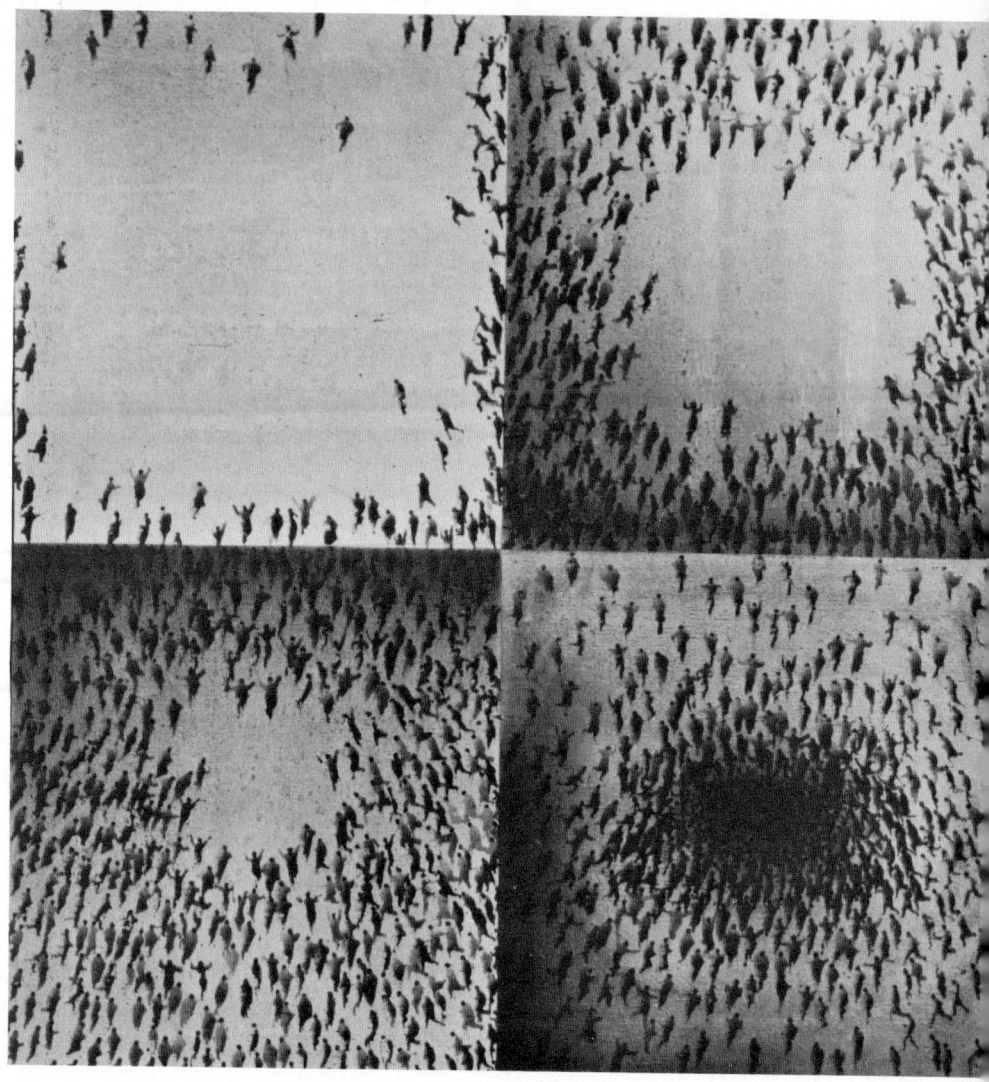

Fig. 13. *Composition: Juan Genoves: Grouping*, 1966. The pictures shown here are not frames from a film but paintings. They show the role of symbolism in picture making.

Function of the single scene

No image can stand on its own in a film, it is always part of a sequence. According to the context in which it is used, one and the same image can evoke different responses in different audiences or in different members of one audience, from sober appraisal through indifference to delight or revulsion.

Each film scence has two aspects: one addressed to the viewer's reason and one directed toward his emotions. This twin nature of a scene means

The Medium

that the right balance between the two values must be found. The film maker might want to induce either of these forms of audience response but what he does not want is a reaction opposite to the one he is trying to achieve. He may, for instance, wish to give a clear matter-of-fact account of a technological process and therefore avoids what he considers to be pictorial trimmings. That could, with good intentions, result in a sequence of stereotyped, uninspired visuals. Pictorial monotony can easily allow the attention of an audience to wander whereas an imaginative visual approach is more likely to keep it alert.

Again, suppose in a road safety film, the director wants to point out the folly of overtaking at the wrong moment. To make his point, he accentuates the actual incident by a montage sequence of smashed metal and shockingly injured people in close up. The sensational nature of these scenes may have a stimulating rather than a cautionary effect.

The symbolic significance of sometimes quite common objects and actions can be exploited without distracting from their factual meaning. Men and machinery, traffic in streets, the flight of birds or planes can be filmed in such ways that their symbolic aspect is emphasized. Compositional features such as high or low camera positions, unusual angles, symmetrical or asymmetrical arrangements, perspective effects, hard or soft lighting and so on, create certain emotional responses. Every filmgoer is by now sensitive to symbolic undertones in the images he sees and he accepts them, often quite unconsciously, as metaphors of the film language and filmic convention.

Figs. 13 and 14 are not stills from a film but paintings by the Spanish artist Juan Genoves. They show the role of symbolism in picture making, and they also show the influence which the film nowadays exerts on paintings (See also Figs 9, 10).

Scene length

How long should a scene be held on the screen? There can be no norm. In educational and science films, the lengths of scenes must be determined mainly by their factual content. The flow of the visual material is naturally slower than that in slapstick comedy or sporting events.

Lenses as creative tools

Camera optics are generally divided into four rough categories: short-focus (wide-angle), normal focus, long-focus and telephoto lenses. But actual measurements of focal length mean nothing unless related to the picture format. What we call a lens of normal focus (say 40mm) for the 35mm camera is a long-focus lens for the 16mm camera and almost equivalent to a telephoto lens for the 8mm camera.

The difference between our eyesight and that of the camera becomes most evident when we consider the respective angles of view. Whilst we

Fig. 14. *Juan Genoves: Labyrinth*, 1966, detail. The 'split-screen' like appearance of this painting with its narrow strips of high menacing walls surrounding the diminutive running figures help to create the impression of claustrophobia and panic.

have seen the horizontal lens angle of our eye to be about 120°, the angle of the widest wide-angle lens available for 16mm is only about 80° and for 35mm 90°. The angles of 'normal' lenses are about 30° for both 16mm and 35mm. Long-focus lenses have an angle of about 12° for 16mm and 17° for 35mm. And telephoto lens angles range from about 4° to 0·5° for 16mm and from about 8° to 1·5° for 35mm.

When filming, we must therefore forget how *we* see and must take account of the sight mechanism of the camera. We usually have to break down the reality in front of our eyes into a series of separate scenes, or we must approximate the eye's view by panning or tilting the camera. The material thus obtained when assembled at the editing stage should create a film reality which either corresponds to the actual one or is a subjective interpretation of it.

The lens determines not only the angle of view but also the quality

The Medium

of the image. When using telephoto lenses which are indispensable for shooting distant subjects such as wild life and aircraft at a reasonable scale of reproduction, the two main characteristics soon become apparent. They have a shallow depth of focus which makes accurate focusing essential, and they tend to compress both space and movement.

The definition of telephoto lenses is easily impaired; haze or mist can play havoc with it; clear translucent air conditions are best for filming at a great range. Camera vibration is another bugbear, and an extra solid support for the camera fitted with such a lens is advisable. The focal length, or magnifying power of telephoto lenses can be increased further by fitting special lens-extenders but these make it necessary to stop down the aperture considerably to obtain reasonable quality. All in all, shooting with telephoto lenses needs experience and skill.

Wide-angle lenses have the opposite effect. They give an exaggerated perspective in that any parts of the subject near the camera appear disproportionately large and—often comically—distorted. Distortion occurs also near the edge of the frame. Movement along the axis of the lens appears speeded up. Wide-angle lenses are handy for special effects and they are indispensable in the field of architecture and for filming in cramped surroundings. Stopping them down too much must be avoided because it can produce a vignetting effect.

The science film as far as concrete objects and processes are concerned, deals mainly with hard-and-fast facts and the selection of a lens must be determined by prevailing conditions and chosen if possible not to distort those facts. However, wide-angle lenses *must* be used in small rooms and in locations where the camera can only just be squeezed into a narrow gap between machinery or laboratory equipment. Telephoto lenses *must* be applied to bridge long distances and long-focus lenses are necessary for filming small objects. Lenses of normal focus are the most universally useful ones for all ordinary conditions.

Nowadays, there is a tendency among many film-makers to rely almost exclusively on zoom lenses. Several 16mm and 8mm cameras can only be obtained with a non-interchangeable zoom lens fitted. Such lenses are very convenient but under certain light conditions their optical quality is inferior to that of individual lenses. The film-maker is also tempted to use the zoom effect excessively. This can become very irritating to an audience.

The field of view

We said that a film-maker must break down the 'eye view' into a multitude of 'lens views'. The film script indicates these lens views by marking each scene as long-shot (LS), mid-shot (MS) or close-up (CU). Often, even more detailed instructions are given.

The LS establishes the 'geography' of a scene, the MS goes into its

Fig. 15. a, b and c. *Field of View*. Long-shot (LS), mid-shot (MS) and close-up (CU). (a) The long-shot establishes the 'geography' of a scene.

(b) The mid-shot goes into details and clarifies the action.

(c) The close-up isolates and highlights the essential. In addition, it is an important stand-by for the editor in moulding the shape of a sequence.

details and the CU highlights the essential though the shots do not always appear in that order. In a laboratory, the LS would probably include as much of the length and width of the room as can be covered by a normal or wide-angle lens. The MS can show a person working at a bench, surrounded by some apparatus. A CU would include the head of this person peering attentively at a flask with a chemical solution in it. A 'big CU' would show the flask with the liquid only, and an 'extreme CU' the single drops falling from the dripping device at the bottom of the flask.

If, in a nature film, the scene shows an ant-heap, the LS would include the whole of the heap and would thus cover an area which in the laboratory would correspond to a CU. Long-shots in one situation are close-ups in another and *vice versa*.

A small piece of equipment, invaluable for both investigation and

The Medium

actual shooting is the so-called director's viewfinder. It gives the field of view of almost every lens; the latest types can zoom as well. These viewfinders are not cheap but they may save valuable time by quickly establishing the appropriate camera set-ups. They are equally useful for rehearsals.

Another aspect, connected with the field of view, is the camera angle. We differentiate between objective and subjective angles. Shots taken from overhead or from below ground level with the camera pointing steeply down or up, or shots taken from a moving vehicle create *subjective* viewpoints and they are often used to express emotions, ranging from fear or terror to joy or fun. In films of science subjects, the *objective* uninvolved camera angle usually prevails.

Of all the possible fields of view, the close-up comes first in importance.

The close-up

The close-up is of great significance in all film making, but it is the very essence of the science film. We can summarize its main tasks as follows:

A close-up can magnify a small object so that it fills the screen and it can make the smallest details recognizable; comparison with familiar things such as coins or matchsticks can indicate the sizes of the objects shown. A close-up can isolate an object and can exclude unimportant or disturbing features within a set. Distant objects can be moved near for close inspection; small features of machinery can clearly be demonstrated.

But close-ups are also essential for saving screen time. They can replace unnecessarily lengthy action and can effectively suggest moods or conditions which would otherwise need elaboration. A cobweb across a doorhandle is instant proof that the door has not been opened for a long time; the wheels of a train thundering past the camera can replace a whole travel sequence; they can also, in the right context, stand as symbols of speed, danger, flight, and other concepts.

A close-up serves as a means of transition to the scene or sequence which follows it. In juxtaposition with other close-ups, particularly in montage sequences, close-ups can bring about associations of ideas, and by emphasizing similarity or contrast, they can make critical or amusing comments. We must, therefore, make sure that a sufficient number of close-ups are to be available to the editor. What use he eventually makes of them, and in which form, will depend on the emerging shape of the film.

Sharpness and softness

Depth of field, that is, the field of sharpness in front of the lens (depth of focus is the field *behind* the lens) when the lens is focused on a given point is not only a technical 'by-product' of the focal length and aperture of a lens but also a means of readily creating visual and emotional effects. Normally, you focus on the object or person which ranks as the centre of interest and choose a lens stop to suit the light conditions. The depth of field then takes care of itself. But one can reverse the process and intentionally create a given depth of field and then arrange the light conditions to suit the chosen lens stop.

Depth of field can vary enormously. A lens aperture of $f0·9$ which is about the largest available today, gives a field of sharpness at close range of almost hair's breadth; on the other hand, the depth of focus of an extreme wide-angle lens even if not stopped down covers the whole length of a large factory hall almost from the camera to the far wall 50 m away when focused on a mid-point. Sharpness in such depth is called 'deep focus' in technical language.

Deep focus increases the sense of spaciousness or expansiveness in a scene. It is valuable in locations where movement is along the lens axis and where following focus (gradually adjusting the focus to keep a moving subject sharp) is ruled out because everything has to be rendered completely sharp. The disadvantage in interior locations is the need for greatly increased lighting which is expensive, time-consuming and cumbersome. With restricted budgets, the deep focus technique can only be practical in halls well lit by skylights.

A compromise between all-over sharpness and individual focusing can be achieved by setting the focus at the hyperfocal distance. This method is particularly appropriate for rapid outdoor shooting since everything between approximately half the distance set and infinity appears acceptably sharp. Tables and calculators, showing the depth of field for lenses of various focal lengths usually give the hyperfocal distance for any chosen lens stop.

Differential focusing, where one object is deliberately picked out sharply against the others is used to shift interest alternately from one person or object to another in the same take. This is of value whenever attention is drawn to details discussed in turn in the commentary. As the interest switches, the focus is 'pulled'. Focus-pulling also becomes necessary if either the subject or the camera is moving. Focusing points must be determined in advance and marked on the rim of the lens.

Factual films usually require crisp and sharp rendering of the subject but now and then an impressionist sort of image might be wanted in which either the whole picture or large areas are to be soft or unsharp. All-over softness or out-of-focus effects can easily be achieved by one of three methods: by racking the lens out, by using wide open apertures in combination with neutral density filters, or by putting gauze or diffusion filters in front of the lens.

Sometimes, you might want to create a small sharp central area within an otherwise blurred image in order to emphasize a particular detail. To get this effect you have to use gauze with a hole cut into it.

Another effect is achieved if you set the focus on a distant point so that while the background is sharp objects in the foreground appear out

The Medium

of focus. A dynamic impression is achieved particularly if the foreground consists of cars or people moving across the field of view. Various other effects can be produced by manipulating the focus.

The 'unshackled' camera

There is a widely held belief that, as the cine-camera is a medium for recording movement, the more movement it records the better. Hence the urge for continuous panning, tracking, zooming and zipping. Not all compulsive panners are amateurs; many professional cameramen, particularly in TV, are just as guilty. Much is to be said in favour of the 'unshackled' camera (an expression used at the time when it was first discovered that cine-cameras did not *have* to be cemented to the ground) but like so many new modes of expression, the roving hand-held camera often turned from an exciting, fresh approach into a mere gimmick, used indiscriminately and giving the audience a headache. It seems, therefore, necessary to stress the obvious: camera movement of whatever kind should be employed only where it serves a definite purpose.

Where precision of movement, accuracy of framing and steadiness is essential, a good tripod or some other firm support is indispensable.

Shooting from a tripod is not necessarily synonymous with pedestrian camera technique. Exciting and lively films can be shot with the camera attached to its support, liveliness arising from the choice of viewpoints and the rhythm of editing.

A tripod allows for any number of camera angles. 'Baby legs' or a 'top hat' (a small round metal stand) can put the camera low on the ground, a crane can lift it high into the air (camera cranes, like any type of equipment, can be hired by the day). In studio or factory halls, where tracking shots are needed, the camera is usually fixed on a dolly or Velocilator; even ordinary goods-trolleys can sometimes be used on a smooth floor. A zoom lens can often, but not always, obviate the need for a wheeled camera support.

One problem with panning is that where the subject contains vertical features, such as pillars or windows, the pan movement must be slow enough to avoid flicker or other disturbing stroboscopic effects. Sometimes over-running the camera slightly (i.e., using a higher filming speed) might help. You must also bear in mind that panning shots are, at the editing stage, often found to be too long, yet cannot be shortened without jump-cutting which is a very unsatisfactory solution. An optical dissolve *within* the scene is then the proper cure. When panning is used to lead from one object to another, a fast zip-pan is often effective.

There are, of course, many situations where hand-held cameras *must* be used. Obvious occasions are shooting in lively crowds, in crammed surroundings, from small craft in agitated water, on expeditions and whenever there is a need for minimum weight of equipment, great mobility

The Work of the Science Film Maker

and rapidity of work. Even with a hand-held camera relatively steady pictures can be obtained; there is certainly no need to wave it about continually. A unipod is often helpful.

Light and lighting

Light is necessary in photography firstly for producing the latent image on the film and secondly for illuminating the subject in the desired way. You are once more up against the dual nature of film-making as a technique and an art.

In our everyday life, light greatly influences our mental disposition: we speak of a face lighting up on hearing good news, of somebody appearing in the light of a saint or of shedding light on a subject if we want to explain something clearly.

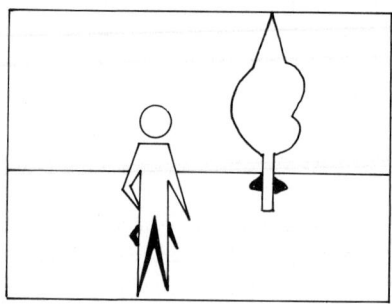

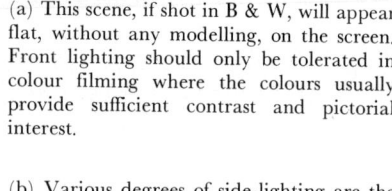

Fig. 16. a, b and c. *Direction of Light*. The above drawings show the same subject shot with the sun behind, at the side and against the camera.

(a) This scene, if shot in B & W, will appear flat, without any modelling, on the screen. Front lighting should only be tolerated in colour filming where the colours usually provide sufficient contrast and pictorial interest.

(b) Various degrees of side-lighting are the norm for both B & W and colour photography. The shadow parts of the persons in the foreground will have to be lifted by means of reflectors (light wooden boards covered with aluminium foil). Their use controls the quality of modelling of the details in the scene. In indoor filming, the reflectors are replaced by light units called flood lamps or booster lamps.

(c) Back-lighting provides strongest contrast. Again, reflectors are useful for lightening the deep shadows in the figures if pure silhouette effects are not wanted.

The Medium

In film-making, lighting throws the essential into relief and determines the key or mood in which a scene or a sequence is visualized by its maker.

Technically speaking, it is only the intensity of the light falling on the emulsion which matters for obtaining a printable negative. The necessary intensity can easily be assessed by experience or with the help of an exposure meter. A sufficiently exposed negative does not, however, necessarily form a satisfactory image. We need contrast as well, and modelling, which is the way in which light describes solidity of objects by the interplay of light and shade across its outer surface.

Exteriors

In outdoor photography, contrast normally takes care of itself if the best use is made of prevailing light conditions. If they are unsuitable, you have to wait for them to be right. Most important is the *quality* of the light and its *direction* relative to the subject and to the camera. Both depend largely on whether the sun is high or low in the sky. Quality is also greatly influenced by atmospheric conditions which play a major part in long-shots of landscapes and in many other types of outdoor photography. When we speak of the 'atmosphere' in a scene, we usually mean the mood created by the quality of the light.

In the main we differentiate between crisp (or hard) and soft light and between high key and low key. When referring to the direction of the light, we speak of flat (front-lit), well-modulated (cross-lit) and contrasty images (often shot against the light).

In a cloudless sky, the sun provides the key light, and to soften the shadows (raise shadow density), reflectors with silvered surfaces of various strength are used. If the sky is overcast, there is no key light or very little. The light is diffused and although it can be quite strong, produces an image with little or no contrast. To counteract this, artificial light sources (usually arc lights) are sometimes used for an outdoor scene to provide an artificial key light.

Sharp deep shadows can be a nuisance but they can also be effective and often made into a special feature. The American film *A Time to Play* (1967) showed a children's game filmed from immediately overhead in the late afternoon. The result was that the children themselves were only seen as small points on the ground, but their long sharp shadows created a uniquely exciting pattern full of movement and fun.

In outdoor shooting, filters provide an extra means of light control. They can be placed either in front or behind the lens. The ideal place is in the matte box. Many kinds of filter are available for use in black-and-white and colour filming but for general purposes only about a dozen need to be carried. Some of them should be graduated in density across the surface for partial control of the image area. Colour correction, tonal contrast and neutral density-filters are the most frequently used. There are also a great number of special purpose filters (see page 86).

Interiors

The principles governing the quality and direction of light are much the same for indoor as for outdoor photography. The main difference is that indoors you have more control over the lighting.

The compact tungsten–halogen lamp is still the most popular type with small film units. Since the introduction of the Colortran lighting sets working with overrun lamps, lighting equipment generally has become much smaller and lighter, thus making it easier to control and faster to handle. A set of Colortrans, together with the necessary cables and junction boxes, is now often part of a science film unit's gear, but every type of lighting equipment can be hired with or without personnel.

Lamps, according to their function, are divided mainly into two forms; the spot light (with a focused beam) and the floodlight (an open but diffused lamp). There are many types of floodlight known by special names. The key light in the set comes from the spots; the filler light, equivalent to that from the reflectors used outdoors, can be from either spots or floods. A photoflood outfit is useful as a standby. In very small rooms, photoflood lamps can be hung on walls or even fixed to them by camera tape.

Another advantage is that their bulbs can be put into existing lamp fittings appearing in the scene, whereas the usual 60 or 100 W bulb would be too weak to film by or even to register on the film.

For table-top sets and bench experiments, the smallest spots, known as 'inkie-dinkies', are a great help. They allow several small objects to be lit individually with pools of concentrated light where larger lamps would tend to flood the whole set more or less uniformly.

To prevent stray light from spilling into the camera lens or falling on areas of the set which should remain dark, shading devices are needed. These are either fitted to the lamp housing or on to separate stands and positioned nearby. Foremost among them is the so-called barndoor (with movable flaps) which can carry diffusers, gelatines and other means of controlling the light. Black pieces of cardboard or metal in all sizes and shapes, known as 'gobos' or 'flags' can also be placed in the beam of the lamps. There are also dimmers which alter the power either of a single lamp or of the whole lamp set-up and so provide additional light control for specific effects (see examples on pages 78 and 245).

Abstract lighting effects such as haloes and out-of-focus light patterns, particularly when shooting in colour, are now very much in vogue. In science films they should be considered as effective expedients to suggest conditions, such as radiation, which are not in themselves visible.

A few points about lighting for colour are discussed in the next chapter.

The Medium

Colour

Films in colour show us the world more or less as we see it. The emphasis is on *more or less* because all colour rendering depends on the degree to which it can be controlled.

The aim of colour photography is to reproduce what the manufacturers claim to be natural colours. There are, however, too many technical elements involved in colour cinematography which militate against achieving this aim fully.

To start with the film stock is bound to vary in quality. A certain safeguard against inconsistent colour quality is to use the same manufactured batch number of material throughout a production.

There is also the problem of colour temperature. This is an expression of the tonal 'warmth' of lighting conditions, which vary from the relatively cold normal daylight (with its high blue content) to the relatively warm artificial light (with its high red bias). These variations are calibrated in a system based on the absolute temperature to which a theoretical black bodied radiator is raised to give out light of a particular colour quality. For photographic purposes the temperatures on the absolute scale are referred to as kelvins (K). Colour emulsions are manufactured to give correct colour rendering under certain colour temperature conditions. They are matched, or 'balanced' for a given light source.

Tungsten lamps have a colour temperature of about 3400 K; so an emulsion balanced for this temperature must be used with these lamps. The various shades of daylight (according to the time of day, year, etc.) have rather different colour temperatures and if film stock balanced for tungsten light is used it must be exposed through an appropriate compensating filter for outdoor work.

It follows that daylight and artificial light cannot be mixed if you shoot in colour. When filming indoors, windows have either to be blacked out completely or you can film after dark. Or again, if you are working in daytime and windows form part of the scene, they must be covered with orange gelatine sheets to correct the colour. Alternatively blue gels (gelatine sheets) or the more effective and expensive dichroic filters can be placed in front of the lamps to alter the light quality at source. In this connection it is also important to maintain the right voltage. It must not fluctuate or drop, as is often the case where long extension cables are used.

For ordinary purposes, cameramen usually cope with colour by relying on their experience. This results in quite a wide hit-or-miss margin as far as naturalness is concerned but as long as the colours are aesthetically satisfying or exciting, audiences do not worry too much about their accuracy. If the colours must be true-to-nature or very definitely correct as often happens in science films, a special colour temperature meter must be used to take actual readings while working.

In the film laboratory the film passes through many chemical and optical processes which again can cause variations in the rendering of colours. It is astonishing how much the colours in re-prints often differ from those seen in the original rushes. Even after the final grading of the cutting copy, the colour quality in the follow-up prints is not always consistent.

On the other hand, the laboratory has a great number of colour correction methods at its disposal, mostly in the form of filters; it can also alter the colour of a scene completely for certain effects such as sunsets, moonlight and so on.

The acceptability of colour values is a subjective matter. In professional film-making, unrealistic colours are often intentionally created for greater dramatic effect but inaccuracy has its limits in factual films. The colours of well-known objects, of flowers, of faces, etc., should be kept within a believable range of hues.

In the field of educational, instructional and science films colour has two main functions apart from its aesthetic and emotive aspects. Correct colour rendering is imperative if you have to compare blood samples, show symptons of skin diseases, reproduce the hues of chemical solutions, of spectra or of flames. Certain species of animals and plants can only be identified on the screen if shown in their true colours. Further examples can be found in any other sphere of science.

To render *one* colour correctly is perhaps not particularly difficult; the trouble starts where two, three or more colours have all to be rendered accurately in the *same* scene. A skilled cameraman knows whether and to what degree this is feasible and where a compromise is unavoidable. If you can send samples of the photographed materials to the film laboratory together with the rushes, they will give the grader a valuable clue when he estimates colour quality. The usual grey scale, shot at the beginning of each roll of film, is not a very reliable guide.

The other important function of colour in the factual film is its value as a code. In animated diagrams, models, flow charts, maps, etc., colour as a distinguishing medium is much more effective than anything that can be devised in black-and-white. You can use coloured liquids, gases, light rays or materials such as threads or flags, to denote or isolate visually the functions or motions of various objects or processes. The question of natural colour rendering does not arise here but good contrast is essential.

Odd things can happen. Once, in one of my instructional films, I took great care to follow the directions of the commissioning films officer with regard to the colours to be used. At the first showing of the completed film, the instructor for whose use the film was made turned out to be partially colour-blind and he could not tell the difference between some of the colours in the film which were specially ordered. This is perhaps an extreme example but it illustrates how the best intentions can come to

The Medium

nought in film-making—in this case through lack of liaison within the commissioning organization.

Sound

Although the picture—the image—is the chief vehicle of communication in "film language", sound long ago established itself as a co-ordinated medium. There are three forms of sound in film: speech, music, and noises from various sources which are grouped together under the name of sound effects. When considering the use of sound, you must differentiate between sound which is *vital* to the understanding of the happenings on the screen and is, therefore, an essential part of the presentation of a subject; sound which is *desirable* for lending atmosphere to a sequence or for heightening dramatic effects; and sound which is *neither essential nor desirable*. This last kind of sound is sometimes the unavoidable by-product of sync-shooting.

Sound can also be assessed from the audience's angle. There is sound of which the audience is very much aware and to which it reacts either positively or negatively. And there is other sound which often does not even register with an audience although people may be unconsciously stimulated or irritated by it.

Expressed in a nutshell: there can be good and bad sound (not to be confused with good and bad sound recording and sound projection).

Sound is a very tricky medium which, clumsily handled, can easily militate against the purpose of a film. Both the entertainment film and TV offer countless opportunities for observing good and bad sound manipulation. We may notice that sound often runs counter to the picture instead of supporting it as when a speaker's voice is drowned in the noise of a factory hall. Often it is used to obtain well-worn effects such as the artificial frenzy of the commentator's voice during a horse race or the transition from an assaulted person's scream to a police whistle.

An interesting example of how a director can make good and not so good use of sound in one and the same production is Lord Clark's TV series *Civilisation*, directed by Michael Gill. A few sequences of this otherwise outstanding series are somewhat spoilt by the too frequent singing of choirs laid over pictures of church interiors and filling the pauses in Lord Clark's discourse. The singing itself is good but 'out of tune' with the character of the film; it also interrupts the flow of the argument instead of giving it added impetus. At other points in this series, sound is used to splendid effect: Offenbach's and Mozart's music integrates poetically and wittily with the visuals of the rococo period. The sequence of the surging sea breaking on Britain's rocky coast to the rhythm of a Beethoven symphony is breathtaking.

In Basil Wright's film *Waters of Time* a recurring musical theme, overlaid with the slow tick-tock of a clock, surfaces at various points of the film from below the commentary to mark the passage of time: a beautiful, lyrical, haunting effect.

Joseph Losey's film *Accident* starts with a visual of an empty stretch of road and the sudden sound of a car crash. The volume and quality of the sound suggests a head-on collision of two lorries but the following scene reveals a sports car which had run into a tree. One consequently felt a little bewildered. Here, the sound effect amounted to an unfulfilled expectation in an otherwise exciting film.

These few examples, chosen at random, show that sound, with all its frequent clamour and noise, is a very sensitive medium of film making.

In science films, the *creative* use of sound is as important as in any other type of film but is limited to the more ambitious kind of production. The sound track of a straightforward teaching or information film usually carries only speech, mostly in the form of a commentary and perhaps a few vital effects.

Speech

The main attributes of a factual commentary are clarity of thought and simplicity in expression. Short words are preferable to long words and brief sentences to long ones. The voice must be alive, monotony of sound is as unbearable as visual dullness. The talk should complement the picture, not describe it and its rendering should be neither too fast nor too slow, neither pompous nor dramatized. A professional commentator under good direction will do the best job. Many scientists believe that they are well suited to speaking commentaries because they know the subject and are probably used to lecturing, but in practice this seldom works out well. There is a great difference between giving a lecture to a live audience, and speaking a given text in the box of a recording studio trying to keep pace with the film which runs its inexorable course, matching the voice to the picture, observing the cue signals of the director and getting used to disregarding slips of the tongue which have to be corrected later by re-takes. In addition, many good lecturers have bad recording voices and preliminary tests would be necessary.

You can, of course, record a commentary 'wild' but the voice often loses the inflections associated with the picture. Recording wild also adds considerably to the editing time, and the whole exercise may prove a costly failure if the speaker talked too slowly. Experience still counts in film-making and whilst amateurs often break new ground on the creative side, do-it-yourself jobs in specialized film methods can become very expensive in the long run.

Speaking in sync is quite different from commentary reading. The talk is not that of a disembodied voice which must be word-perfect, but of an actual person seen in the picture, and this person, in the case of a science

The Medium

film probably a scientist, can remain his natural self. He can talk freely; occasional hesitations or brief pauses to find the right word do not matter, they even convey a greater feeling of spontaneity. Moreover, as the speaker will usually give a demonstration or make an experiment whilst he speaks, the attention of the audience is drawn more to the visual than to the aural aspect. A strong personality or a good camera presence will naturally add to the quality of the presentation.

As in all filming, it is advisable to break down a lengthy sync-scene into several shots; every shot must be rehearsed. As the microphone and the lights have to be adjusted for each new camera angle, you should take as many shots from each set-up as are admissible from the action point of view. This means that the scenes are not shot in their natural order but out of sequence, whilst the action continuity must be preserved. The proper order is reinstated in the cutting room.

Often, close-up inserts are later cut into a sync-scene with the speaker's voice running on. These are the points where alterations in the speech can be made by retakes, shot wild. If the shooting of a sequence with the same speaker is spread over several days or locations, the voice quality and sound levels are bound to change. This can confuse the audience when they see and hear these scenes cut in sequence. It is the sound mixer's job during the dubbing session to minimize these disturbing effects.

When shooting in sync, many incidental noises are often recorded as well. Sometimes they are necessary features of the scene but more often they are irrelevant to the action and the recordist must make sure that they do not interfere with the speaker's voice. Each sound take should be played back immediately for checking.

Two effects must be mentioned in connection with speech: the distorted voice and the echo-effect. They are both well-known from animated cartoons and science-fiction films. They can be quite striking or amusing but should be used with discretion. These effects are now all done electronically; the old echo-chamber is largely outdated.

Music

If a film is *about* music (as in the case of *Science in the Orchestra* (pages 142–163)), the music must be treated like any other film subject in accordance with its purpose.

What we are concerned with here is music as part of a film's style and presentation. For such music the term *incidental* is often used, an expression which dates back to the times when a musician accompanied the 'flicks' on a piano in front of the screen. Nowadays music is not expected to be incidental but very much integrated with the theme of the film.

We also talk of *background* music, an expression which is correct only when it is played under the commentary or dialogue, often to the detriment of both music and speech. Also, a background should remain at the back and music which weaves in and out of speech and effects and often gains ascendancy over the spoken word is anything but background music. However we define it, film music has to be descriptive of the mood and atmosphere of the visuals; it must instil a greater sense of drama or humour, of poetry or violence; it must accentuate certain points of the action and should sweep the audience emotionally along.

For any film in which music is used as an integral medium of presentation a musical director should be engaged. Again, only a fraction of documentary or science films can go to such lengths.

Many educators are against any kind of music in teaching films. From their point of view they may be right, yet to put music at least over the title is not only an embellishment but serves a useful purpose in that it helps the audience to settle down and the person who acts as projectionist to adjust the sound level before anything vital is said in the commentary. Industrial sponsors of science films, on the other hand, are very keen on a good musical score for prestige reasons. Thus, whether to use music or not in a science film is not so much a matter of the director's preferences as of academic and commercial expendiency.

The sources from which music is obtained vary. A generously financed film can have music specially composed, or existing copyright-free music can be arranged (most classical music is free) and played by an orchestra engaged for this purpose.

Music can also be selected from any of the numerous music libraries by listening to dozens of discs and tapes with tunes recorded to suit every mood, contingency or situation from high drama to slapstick. Under such headings as *Wheels of Industry* or *Scientific Adventure* you will probably find more items than you could use in a lifetime of film work. Music libraries make a modest charge for every minute of music eventually used in the film. They are the main source of music for small-budget films, TV productions and commercial spots. To find what you want is a nerve-wracking task and it is quite obvious that such music is more often than not a run-of-the-mill affair.

If the orchestra itself forms part of the film's visuals, the music is recorded in sync. Alternatively, you can reverse the process, pre-record the music and play it back in the studio, shooting the picture with the players going through their motions. The method chosen depends on individual circumstances (see page 163).

Many directors are fond of using electronic or concrete music whenever the scene suggests something scientific. This was alright when that type of music was new but, as so often happens, it soon became a gimmick. The pendulum now seems to swing the other way and the music of Bach and Vivaldi has become fashionable as an accompaniment to visuals showing bacteria, refraction patterns or nuclear reactors. What is so irritating is that each new idea is bound to be aped and aped again until it becomes a dreary cliché.

The Medium

Sound effects

In the old days, these used to be called 'natural' sound effects because they were mostly recorded on location. But 'natural' sound often sounds unnatural on the screen and it was found that to simulate certain sounds on the studio floor gave a better effect. There are effects artistes who are experts in producing noises in synchronism with the action seen on the screen. They can, for instance, quickly open and close an umbrella before the microphone to suggest the flapping of the wings of large birds. They can reproduce any kind of water noises, whistles, shouts, footsteps and so on.

Scientific effects such as cosmic noise, etc., can be introduced electronically during dubbing. Many other distinct sounds (e.g. gunfire, crying babies, traffic noise) can be obtained from effects libraries which work on the same lines as music libraries. You can find any of a thousand common, and even quite a few uncommon, noises such as the clanging of an old tram car or the sneeze of a horse.

Like music, effects can be integral or incidental. Integral effects fall into two categories: those which are seen to be emitted in the picture and which are often synchronized with some action, and others which are used to *replace* visual action or are otherwise vital to the presentation of an occurrence.

The first category comprises sounds created by machinery or apparatus which are part of the scene. Such sounds may come from sources like electrical or electronic equipment, machinery, motors, etc., or from experiments which produce specific sounds. Theoretically, such scenes ought to be shot in sync. with a blimped camera. A blimp is a clumsy piece of equipment, it slows down the work and is not worth carrying around for the sake of one or two effects. It is often more sensible to shoot the sound effects wild with a tape recorder and to do the synchronizing later on the cutting bench. If this procedure is adopted, picture and sound must be shot separately; in the case of an experiment this means repeating it. Again, if the sound is typical, one will often find it in a library.

The second category consists of effects which usually suggest happenings that occur off-screen. An example of this type was Losey's car crash (page 50). Such use of sound is not only a filmic and artistic device but it can also save much time and money. For instance, the sound of a car crash can be laid over an appropriate visual; next, the sound of an ambulance siren is heard over a street scene, and then we can go straight into the operating theatre in which the vital action begins. Two preliminary cumbersome and expensive visuals which would have to be specially laid on—the cars colliding and the ambulance weaving through the traffic—are replaced by two easily obtainable scenes and two sound effects acquired from a library. There are endless possibilities to use sound in this way.

Sound effects can also make an important contribution to the atmosphere of a scene. They can signify suspense, shock, drama, finality.

Subtlety is usually more effective than brute noise. There is an unforgettable scene in Arnold Fanck's film *Mont Blanc*. A lone scientist, stationed in a small meteorological observatory near the top of the mountain, has to abandon his post due to an emergency. It is a dramatic moment, full of tension and foreboding, when the man is seen leaving the hut during a terrific storm in a desperate effort to reach the valley. After he has disappeared on the mist-shrouded glacier, the camera tracks into the hut with the door banging in the storm and a radio set playing a gay Viennese Waltz in the deserted room. The sounds of the music, the wind, the banging door combine to produce a masterly effects sequence.

Too many films and TV programmes, particularly factual ones, use uninterrupted background noise, supposedly to make the action appear more alive and realistic. Actually, too many film-makers are afraid of even a moment's silence in their films. Moments of silence are, however, necessary to give sound its full impact. Furthermore, unnecessary background noise is very irritating and whilst it adds nothing to the meaning of the film, it certainly adds to its cost.

When sound effects overlap, two or more effects tracks have to be made up as is the case with music tracks. Continuous repetitive sound is put on a short loop which runs on a separate channel during dubbing. In feature films, intricate effect-patterns may need as many as 15 or 20 tracks which are gradually reduced by pre-dubbing to four or five tracks for the final dubbing session. Most science films do not need an elaborate sound build-up but only a few definite effects and one or two tracks will usually be quite sufficient.

2

The Subject

THE COMPASS OF our vision, measured by everyday standards, is extensive. The normal naked eye can identify objects or dots smaller than a pinhead. At the other end of the scale, the curvature of the earth limits the view to about 40 km at sea level, but high mountains can be seen from other high mountains over a distance of 200 km. Above us we see the stars, or rather the light emitted by stars, some of which might be billions of kilometres away. Actually, the stars themselves might be extinct but their light still reaches us after travelling perhaps for millions of years. Thus, 'seeing' involves not only the dimension of space but also that of time.

Our visible and invisible worlds

The diameter of the known part of our universe is estimated at 10,000 million light years (10^{28} cm). The diameter of the proton, said to be the smallest measurable particle, is in the neighbourhood of 10^{-13} cm, giving a ratio of 10^{41} between the two extremes.*

Many models exist of atoms showing the orbits of the electrons round their nuclei, and there are clockwork models of the solar system, the orreries, in which the planets are made to move round the sun. But it is easy to realize that there can never be a scale model of the cosmos. Even if the earth in such an assumed model were represented by a sphere the size of a pinhead, the model would have to be much bigger than our entire solar system.

If we consider those parts of our universe which can be observed *optically*, either by the naked eye or by means of instruments, then we have three clearly defined spheres of action for the cine camera:

1 the range covered by the human eye, measured in millimetres, metres and kilometres,

2 the micron- and millimicron region which is the field of cine-micrography,

---

* From *Man Measures the Universe*, published by UNESCO.

The Work of the Science Film Maker

	18 —	Nearest stars
	17 —	
	16 —	
	15 —	
	14 —	
	13 —	Distance of sun (1.5×10^{13})
	12 —	
	11 —	
	10 —	Distance of moon (4×10^{10})
	9 —	$\emptyset$ of earth (1.3×10^9)
	8 —	
	7 —	
	6 —	A distant view
Radio Waves	5 —	Kilometre, a long street
	4 —	Height of a tower
	3 —	Width of a street
	2 —	Metre, a chair
	1 —	A hand's breadth
	0 —	Centimetre, Thickness of a pencil
	−1 —	Thickness of a card
	−2 —	A hair's breadth
	−3 —	Bacteria
Infra-red Waves	−4 —	(One micron unit)
Visible Waves	−5 —	
u.v. Waves	−6 —	Molecules
	−7 —	
X-rays Gamma Rays	−8 —	Atoms (One angström unit)
	−9 —	
	−10 —	
Cosmic Rays?	−11 —	
	−12 —	
	−13 —	Atomic nuclei
	−14 —	

From *The Universe of Light* by Sir William Bragg*

'This table shows the relative magnitudes of various objects which we observe and measure. It is like a set of shelves on which we place specimens of objects and magnitudes from the very great to the very small. On a middle shelf, marked zero, we have the centimetre and the thickness of a pencil to represent objects of that order of magnitude. On the shelf above we place an object of about 10 cm in size; the width of a hand will serve. The shelf above takes objects of about 100 cm, for example smaller objects of furniture. The width of a street will represent the thousand centimetres, the height of a tower might be 10,000 cm or 100 m and so on.

Below the zero shelf comes first a shelf holding something of the order of a millimetre in thickness, as a card. Then the hair's breadth on the next shelf and so on. Bacteria are at various heights on the third and fourth shelf down; molecules on the sixth and seventh, atoms nearly down to the eighth.

On the other side of the vertical line the various wavelengths are shown in the same way. Distances are sometimes given in figures. The sun's distance is 15 million million centimetres or, in symbols $1.5 + 10^{13}$. This goes, therefore, on the thirteenth shelf up.'†

---

* Published by G. Bell & Sons, London 1962.

† Professor George Porter has during his Christmas lectures 'Time Machines' at the Royal Institution demonstrated a similar scale for time values, reaching from millions of years down to a picosecond (10^{-12} sec) which is the smallest time unit measurable with present-day 'clocks'. Wavelengths are here replaced by frequencies.

The Subject

3 the domain of astronomy in which cameras have to combine with telescopes to explore the worlds measured in light years and parsecs.

This last-mentioned field is the prerogative of optical observatories and hardly ever comes within the scope of film-making with which this book is concerned. If scenes filmed through telescopes are required many observatories will oblige by supplying dupe negatives of existing material. An even more exclusive field is that of space-cinematography and television carried out from manned and unmanned spacecraft.

Cinemicrography, too, is a matter mainly for experts such as biologists or medical research workers whose chief concern is microscopy and not cinematography. A great number of spectacular biological and medical films have been made but the revealing medium is the microscope, not the film camera which is for the most part only a means of recording and occasionally speeding up movement. There are few creative elements involved in cinemicrography. The problems are technical, concerned with the degree of magnification, the lighting of the specimens and with time-lapse methods. Nevertheless great expertise is necessary for filming live organisms through microscopes and special expensive accessories are often required. A few companies producing factual films, such as the Shell Film Unit in London, have developed their own techniques of cinemicrography with excellent results. But it would be uneconomic for a small film unit to go into this field if micro-material is only rarely needed. You can obtain it either by subcontracting the work to a specialist company or by buying existing scenes from research laboratories.

Sir William Bragg's chart on page 56 provides a kind of measuring scale for our observable world. The most common manifestations of science and technology, visible to the unaided eye, occupy the range from -1 to about $+6$. It is in this area that man's material experiences, his main areas of activity, his reality, are encompassed. Above and below this range begin the worlds of the telescope and the radio-telescope, the microscope and the electron-microscope.

Objects, events and phenomena which are invisible to the naked eye could perhaps be categorized in the following way.

They are, or take place, in the dark, in fog or under water.

They are situated behind material obstructions which act as irremovable screens.

They are too small, too large or too remote. (Figs 18, 37, 38)

They happen too fast or too slowly.

They are too intricate in their nature or behaviour for visual comprehension.

They are unsubstantial and can be detected only by specific scientific methods. (Fig. 19)

They exist only in our mind as thoughts, theories, hypotheses, dreams or hallucinations. (Fig. 17)

A number of these categories can be made visible by what are termed 'special techniques'. For a long time now, our sight has no longer been dependent on the visible spectrum alone; to-day we can see and photograph by the 'light' of infra-red, ultra-violet and X-ray radiation, even by the medium of electrons. The cine camera has, on a different level, contributed time-lapse and high-speed photography to the world of supra-natural vision.

Yet, there is still much that remains truly invisible. The spoken explanations of a lecturer seem here the only solution. Film and television often record lectures and thus make them available to millions. In such case, film is a mere medium of 'broadcasting' such lectures though, sometimes, the film can put its own interpretation on the filmed event. But film has also the power of *creating* a picture of obstinately invisible matters, resorting to such methods as animation, models, effects and analogies.

Special effects—and there is usually more than one involved in a film—are time-consuming and films incorporating such techniques cannot

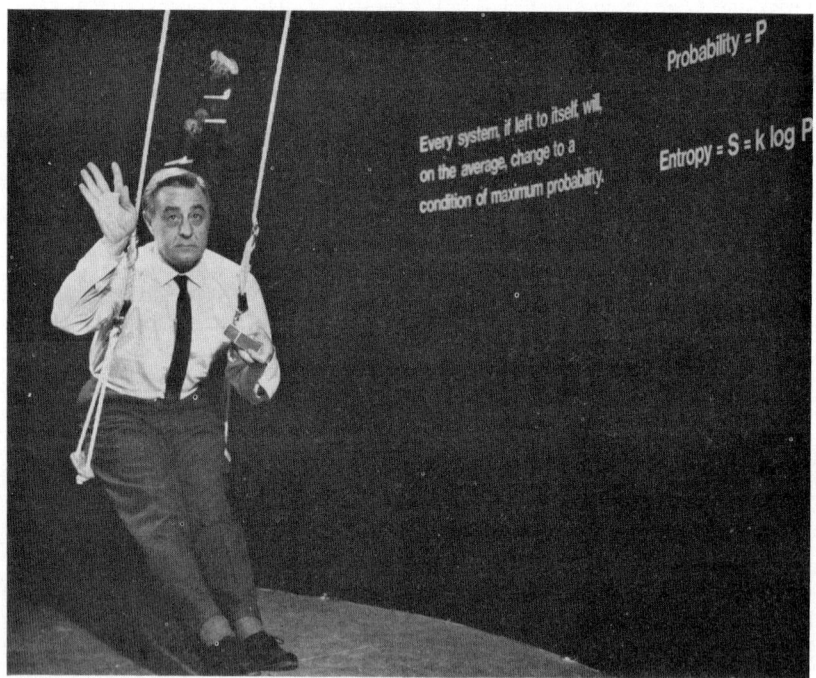

FIG. 17. *Reversing Action.* Prof. George Porter, F.R.S. uses a box of matches to illustrate his statement that 'the increase of entropy with time is one of the few ways we have of telling the direction of time'. When the scene is printed tail to head, the matches return to their ordered arrangement in the box and so we know that time has been reversed.

Still from *The Second Law of Thermodynamics*, the second film in a series for schools produced in association with the Royal Institution of Great Britain.

The Subject

be produced in a day or a week but may need many months and are therefore expensive. Yet, many such films have been made, and the results have usually justified the trouble and cost involved because of the enhanced teaching value and impact on the audience.

Whatever type of film we make, we have to produce a screen image and this brings us back to the terms of the visible world and its photographic problems.

Explaining science

When filming lectures and scientific demonstrations it makes a great difference whether we must shoot what goes on without disturbing the routine, whether facilities are provided and extra time is allowed for filming or, finally, whether the event is specially laid on for us.

Filmed lecture

The demonstration-lectures given by eminent scientists in the Royal Institution in London are a case in point. BBC TV has filmed many of them while they were actually in progress, and the filming lasted exactly as long as the lectures themselves: about one hour. The ensuing television programmes, sometimes shown in the *Horizon* series, are well-produced true-to-life screen-reproductions of the actual occasions.

In contrast, several of Sir Lawrence Bragg's Christmas lectures, given to schoolchildren, were reconstructed by Anvil Films in the Royal Institution with Sir Lawrence appearing in the films. Each one-hour lecture was condensed into a film of 20 min for use in schools. The filming of these 20 screen minutes took about one working day, with a number of close-up inserts subsequently shot in Anvil's studio.

There is, thus, a great dissimilarity in the methods employed by the BBC and by Anvil, both in the actual filming and in the editing. The BBC used the 'multicam' (multi-camera) method, placing 4 cameras at different vantage points in the lecture hall. The shooting was done on videotape. There is no waste with videotape because the takes can be erased and the tape used again and again; furthermore, no laboratory work is necessary at all. It therefore matters little from the cost angle how much tape is consumed during the filming and all 4 cameras could run simultaneously almost throughout the lecture, dividing the angles and fields of view between them. Editing was done electronically by the vision-mixing system (page 19), only a few cuts had to be made with scissors. But, being an electronic, not an optical medium, videotape can only be used in connection with television screening.

Anvil used the conventional film technique in which the cost of stock, processing and labour plays a great part. Shooting a 20-min film of this type in a day or two is very fast work indeed and probably the limit of

The Work of the Science Film Maker

The Subject

what is possible in the way of economizing in time. The films were mostly shot with two cameras on 16mm Ektachrome and then edited in the usual way. The surprising thing is that the difference in production methods is hardly noticeable on the screen. This shows that one and the same aim—in this case the recording of a lecture—can be reached by widely varying methods such as are best suited to the purpose in question. The purpose in the first case was to show the lectures on television to general audiences and in the second case to distribute them to individual schools for teaching. Live television transmission or closed circuit TV could have been employed as still other possibilities.

Neither the BBC nor Anvil intended to go beyond recording what the audiences of the actual lectures experienced. Lecturing scientists usually present their facts and theories to audiences by demonstrating effects as they talk about causes. Thus, in these films, the audience watched the lecturers carrying out their demonstrations by means of scientific apparatus and bench experiments and heard their verbal explanations of the phenomena which caused certain visual and aural effects. The phenomena themselves remained invisible.

The invisible made visible

Film-making presents us with both technical and intellectual problems. This becomes most obvious when a film deals with the invisible. Getting images on to celluloid is a matter of technique; dreaming up visuals supposed to show something one cannot see is an intellectual exercise. The invisible worlds are in the main made up of dynamic interactions, of continuous change in both space and time. This activity can be fast or slow; the half-life of radio-active isotopes vary from less than a millionth of a second to more than a million years.

Although modern high-speed photography is now almost approaching the light barrier, there is a limit to what the cine camera by itself can achieve in the way of direct illustration. Optics cannot show events lasting a million millionth of a second, nor can they produce an image of a million years. There are countless concepts like these in science; this is where interpretation by indirect methods has to replace those of illustration.

Popular and educational science films, as opposed to research films, are more often concerned with a chain of interlocked patterns and events than with single functions. Such a chain sometimes forms a straight line and the progress of the film is predetermined by the sequence of those events. At other times there is a complicated interplay of processes and

---

FIG. 18. (top): A model of a myoglobin molecule showing all 2500 atoms. Still from *The Structure of Protein*, produced in collaboration with the Medical Research Council, Laboratory of Molecular Biology, Cambridge.

FIG. 19. (bottom): Iron filings make the invisible magnetic forces visible. Still from the Mullard film: *The Invisible Force*.

The Work of the Science Film Maker

phenomena and their presentation and continuity must be built up arbitrarily in the film since there is more than one way of presenting the subject. The scriptwriter is, therefore, confronted not only with the problem of understanding scientific details (in which he must inevitably be guided by his technical advisers) but also with the task of welding bits and pieces of information into a logical and organic whole which in turn must make the subject visually understandable to the audience.

The measure of understanding varies, of course, with the subject and the audience. A complicated scientific topic can rarely be understood at a single screening; usually we get an idea of the underlying principles and miss out on the details, or it is the other way round. Now and then, however, either the subject or its treatment makes complete and instant understanding possible.

In 1960 the Shell Film Unit made a film to mark the tercentenary of the Royal Society. This film, called *A Light in Nature* is an ambitious production, centred round a meeting of the fellows of the Society and branching out into a survey of the present-day scientific scene. Part of the script, concerning an investigation into the living cell, is produced below as an example of perfect co-ordination of illustration and interpretation.

A LIGHT IN NATURE
"A View of World Science at the Frontiers of Knowledge"
produced by SHELL FILM UNIT

16mm footage:	*Picture*	*Sound*
70·6	Crowd walking past close to camera.	SOUND OF CROWD *2nd voice:* What makes us as we are? What makes us alike as a species? Different as individuals?
75·2	Mix to swarm of fruit flies.	SOUND OF BUZZING The geneticist attacks this problem—why we're alike and why we're different . . .
79·6	Jars containing fruit flies on shelf. Geneticist takes one.	SOUND OF LABORATORY BACKGROUND . . . by studying fruit flies.
81·0	Geneticist takes further jar.	SOUND OF LABORATORY He's been studying them for fifty . . .
82·2	Geneticist walks to bench and sits down.	SOUND OF LABORATORY . . . years. They breed fast. In a year or so . . .
84·8	Face of geneticist as he puts his eyes to the microscope. Camera moves down to microscope stage where he sorts anaethetized fruit flies.	SOUND OF LABORATORY . . . he can examine the equivalent of seven hundred years in man. He sees that peculiarities appear, making the flies different from each other. Variations in the colour of . . .

The Subject

16mm footage:	Picture	Sound
92·4	View through microscope of the heads of four fruit flies, showing different coloured eyes.	... the eyes, for example. Why? In every tiny cell ...
96·8	Camera moves in past man holding slide to close view of chromosome slide.	... of the fly's body ...
97·4	Photographic enlargement of a chain of chromosomes. Camera moves in to close view then left along chain and in again to an irregularity.	MUSIC ... are strings of chromosomes—carriers of hereditary instructions. And each peculiarity is due to some change in one of these strings. An irregularity *here* ...
105·6	Fruit fly with bar-eye.	MUSIC ... and a bar-eye results.
108·8	Cell division. (*Mytosis in Endosperm*—Dr. A. Bajer, Jagiellonian University, Cracow, Poland)	MUSIC Life maintains itself by cell division. Thousands of cells in your own body are dividing—like this—now. And the chromosomes of the parent cell divide also—passing to each daughter cell an exact copy of the hereditary instructions. But how?
121·2	Bottom of test tube as thymus from a rat is dropped in and pounded up.	The chemist takes a mass of living cells from a freshly killed ...
125·8	Man homogenizing thymus in test tube.	... rat. He separates out, in the centrifuge, the material within the ...
129·0	Man places material in centrifuge.	... chromosomes that carries the hereditary instructions.
130·8	Close view of test tube as it starts to spin.	SOUND OF CENTRIFUGE
133·2	Centrifuge spinning.	SOUND OF CENTRIFUGE
134·8	Mix to man stirring rod in test tube. He lifts it out coated with white material.	MUSIC This is it. The stuff that somehow ...
139·6	Close view of the rod carrying white material.	MUSIC ... governs what we are.
141·6	Liquid being stirred in a flask.	SOUND OF CHEMISTRY LAB. What is it made of? Fundamental chemical research revealed ...
145·8	Chemist carries flask from bench and lifts it.	SOUND OF CHEMISTRY LAB. ... phosphate groups, and four compounds—nucleosides ...
147·4	Chemist lifting flask to fix on stand.	SOUND OF CHEMISTRY LAB. ... made up of bases combined with a rare ...

63

The Work of the Science Film Maker

16mm footage:	Picture	Sound
148·8	Camera moves down side of benches as chemist moves to look at apparatus.	SOUND OF CHEMISTRY LAB. sugar, deoxyribose. So they called the substance...
151·2	Camera moves down from flask to dripper feeding moving test tubes.	SOUND OF CHEMISTRY LAB. ... this stuff that determines life— Deoxyribo Nucleic Acid. D.N.A. The chemist sees it as a chain of different groups of atoms. But under the most...
158·4	Mix to electron micrograph of D.N.A. chain.	MUSIC. SOUND OF CHEMISTRY LAB. ... powerful electron microscope the molecule is seen only as a mere thread.
163·2	Mix to camera moving over benches to group of chemists discussing D.N.A. over coffee.	SOUND OF CHEMISTRY LAB. How can we get closer? Find out how the chains of atoms are arranged...
168·8	View of group watching a colleague drawing a diagram	SOUND OF CHEMISTS' VOICES ... along the thread-like molecule? They puzzled out a chemical sketch.
172·0	Hand drawing chemical sketch of D.N.A. molecule.	SOUND OF CHEMISTS' VOICES Sugar and phosphate atoms along the backbone. The four compounds forming side-links. SOUND OF CHEMISTS' VOICES But a sketch on paper's one thing. What does it look like in reality?
184·4	Eye peering through lens.	MUSIC Here, the physicist can help.
187·4	Physicist looking at drawing of D.N.A. thread through lens.	MUSIC He draws...
189·4	Glass rod drawing D.N.A. thread.	MUSIC ... the D.N.A. into a fibre. As it lengthens...
191·8	D.N.A. fibre being drawn.	MUSIC ... so the thread-like molecules align themselves in a regular pattern that allows him to use his most powerful tool....
196·2	Dissolve to D.N.A. being prepared for X-ray.	SOUND OF GENERATOR HUM ... X-ray crystallography. His method is to make the...
199·2	D.N.A. preparation placed in X-ray 'box'.	SOUND OF GENERATOR HUM ... fine atomic structure of the D.N.A. reveal its shape by scattering the even finer X-rays.
203·6	X-ray 'box' is carried to apparatus and fitted.	SOUND OF GENERATOR HUM He plays the X-ray beam on the D.N.A. for four to six weeks...

The Subject

16mm footage:	Picture	Sound
207·2	Mix to physicist playing geiger counter over X-ray equipment.	SOUND OF GENERATOR HUM Makes it break up the beam, to reveal on a photographic plate an image which he . . .
210·2	Mix to X-ray photograph of D.N.A. structure. Camera moves in to close up.	MUSIC . . . can mathematically relate to the atomic structure of the molecule. And so, by intricate calculation . . .
215·2	Mix to D.N.A. model	MUSIC . . . and a brilliant guess, we get a model of something no one has ever seen—of the giant molecule of D.N.A.
219·6	Hands working on model. Camera moves down its length.	MUSIC And we find, in this enormous complexity, not one chain of atoms, but two. Two chains, with up to thirty thousand atomic links, coiled around each other—suggesting a template mechanism of reproduction.
231·8	Mix to bottom of molecular D.N.A. model. Camera moves up its length to close view of groups of atoms.	MUSIC We know now that it's the different order of arrangement of the atoms along these chains that spells out the code dictating the character of life—man or mouse, you or me—as the chains unwind, . . .
242·8	Mix to close view of revolving D.N.A. model showing spiral formation.	MUSIC . . . as the chromosomes part, as the cells divide, to make a new living creature.
251·2	Mix to cell division. (*Mytosis in Endosperm*—Bajer—Poland)	MUSIC Why are we as we are? The questions Darwin and Mendel first posed, we're beginning to answer . . .
262·2	Mix to overhead shot of crowds walking beneath camera.	MUSIC, SOUND OF CROWD . . . precisely. One day—who knows?—we may break the hereditary code itself.
267·8		

This film was shot in 35mm colour and reduced to 16mm. Its running time is about 35 min and that of the above sequence $5\frac{1}{2}$ min. These $5\frac{1}{2}$ min span a century of research and an immense scientific pattern in breadth and depth. In this film, the proportion of the technical and intellectual contribution to the presentation of the subject is well balanced but proportions can vary greatly.

The Work of the Science Film Maker

Complex themes

Generally speaking, the broader the subject and the deeper the penetration into theories, the greater is the demand on the intellectual capacity of the film maker. As already mentioned, it would be absurd to expect that all invisible phenomena, all theories and ideas can be visually expressed. If all direct means of illustration prove unworkable or too expensive and if no convincing indirect method of interpretation can be found, then the scene must of necessity shift to an expert presenting the argument by talking to the audience in sync. The cinematic film will use this solution only as a last measure except where it intends to introduce a famous personality in the flesh. Some scientists are great showmen.

In 1960, the Shell Film Unit made another visually exciting film, *The Revealing Eye*. It starts with the experiments of Eadwaerd Muybridge in 1870 in which he used 20 still cameras in a row, successively recording stages in the movement of animals. His separate stills were later recorded on cine film to give an effect Muybridge himself could never have witnessed except perhaps crudely in a Zoetrope. This sequence is followed by the chronophotographs of Marey. The film then leads us through the whole range of cine techniques: high-speed and time-lapse methods, cine-microscopy, X-ray amplification by electronic image intensifiers, infra-red and ultra-violet photography, underwater and astronomical cinematography, interferometry and methods used in medicine by such means as the bronchoscopic and laparocinescopic cameras.

The film shows, amongst a host of other phenomena, the mortal struggle of two plants in which one of them strangles the other, cell division by mitosis, a chick developing within the egg, the digestive tract of a house fly, a man sawing a log of wood as seen through the multiple lens of a fly, time-lapse studies first of the movement of a glacier and then of the aurora borealis, the rotation of Mars, the mixing of hot and cold water made visible by the Schlieren method, views of the inside of the lungs and abdomen, a human foetus in the womb, earth and moon seen from rockets (now quite familiar sights), and finally the movement of the sun from sunrise to sunset: an entire day concentrated into one minute by the time-lapse method and filmed with an all-sky camera.

Thirty-one research organizations all over the world contributed to the production of this film. Since it was made, new cinematographic techniques and new styles of presentation have developed but *The Revealing Eye* will remain a pioneer work of filmic thinking and filmic execution.

More recently, Agfa-Gevaert have produced a film *Magic Light*. It is a promotional film telling the story of a new type of film stock from the initial market research to the last production stage. Blatant advertising of the sponsor's products is omitted and the film deals entirely with scientific and technological aspects. It is both visually and cinematically a remarkable piece of work discussing such topics as infra-red and ultra-violet

The Subject

photography, oscillography, holography and other techniques. There are wonderful colour effects created by the glow of fluorescent materials in ultra-violet light but the most memorable sequence is that of the emulsion-coating process shot in complete darkness by means of infra-red film and infra-red filters which, put in front of the lamps, cut out all visible rays. Every stage of the process is clearly visible as if it had been shot under normal conditions, yet a quaint sense of unreality creeps in whenever workmen appear in the scene. Their eyes are wide open and have the sightless expression of blind people. One sees them cautiously groping about trying to avoid bumping into things.

Years ago, Mary Field used a similar technique to show the reaction of children to a film while they were watching it. Here, the children looked more normal because the light from the screen was reflected in their eyes. Highly interesting psychological conclusions could be drawn from these scenes.

Zoologists use infra-red film for studying the nocturnal habits of animals. In all these last-mentioned films, illustration outweighs interpretation.

Two other films should briefly be mentioned: *The Structure of Protein* (Unilever), and *Carbon* (Morgan Crucible Company).

These two films, though different in intent and treatment, both set out to explain visibly natural forces of enormous complexity. The first film deals with the same subject—the living cell—as the sequence from *A Light in Nature*, but whilst that sequence gave a sort of bird's eye view of the subject, *The Structure of Protein* explores it in depth. Both films make use of all possible cinematic techniques, particularly of models and animation, and both manage to reveal the staggering beauty and perfect order of crystalline structures and molecular chains, of forms and colours found in nature as manifestations of their functions. Everything falls into place, and from an aesthetic and filmic point of view, these two factual films put many art films into the shade.

The directors and technicians of the above mentioned films are not scientists but professional film-makers and it is notable that every one of these films has received festival awards not only for their cinematic treatment but also for their scientific value.

To sum up: the camera takes care of the 'picture'-side of the script, in other words: of illustration and documentation. The structure of a film, the presentation of the argument, the integration of picture and sound are matters of interpretation. These two functions support the edifice of a film, particularly of a film concerned with the invisible.

The interpretive film

Too many films are plodding and stodgy where they should be crisp and adventurous. This goes for industrial and general interest films, too.

The Work of the Science Film Maker

Whenever we make a film which sets out to explain or interpret a difficult concept, we should remind ourselves of the hours of boredom in our school days when we were the victims of humdrum and arid methods of instruction; but we should also remember the relief we felt when a particular teacher, through his stimulating personality, managed to break through deadening inertia and turned learning into an exciting discovery. What a film—any sort of film—needs is a fluent and inspired presentation and authoritative but comprehensible exposition.

The subject of a film, its aim and its intended audience, have, of course, much to do with the way in which a film can be presented. Many subjects are by their nature so clear and fascinating that they can make their point with a minimum of elucidation. Others need a great deal of it. We might review a few productions where the treatment is of particular interest in this respect.

Making the message clear

Not long ago, three films were made on themes in which *water* formed either the subject or the background. Each of these films is a prototype of its kind. Each is different in purpose but similar in achieving it by filmic means; all are beautifully photographed in colour, and all have the distinction of a highly personal handwriting.

Physics and Chemistry of Water (Unilever) is a 20-min teaching film showing how hydrogen and oxygen combine to form water. It examines the atomic structure of the water molecule and demonstrates how the properties of water can be explained by the electrical forces in the molecules and the resulting hydrogen bonds which form between them. The behaviour of these bonds explains the three states of water as liquid, solid and gas. The film makes use of almost the whole range of cinematic techniques, from animation and micrography to models and simple but fascinating laboratory experiments. There are no fussy tricks and the exposition is clear.

The film *The River Must Live* (Shell Film Unit) is about river pollution and what is done to counteract it; it is probably mainly addressed to ecologists but is of interest to general audiences, too. It contains many interesting micro-shots. There is a memorable scene in this film. A director is usually hard pressed for visual variety when the subject is specific. In a film about water there are bound to be dozens of references to water in the commentary and in hackneyed types of film hackneyed scenes of water would be shown every time water is mentioned. In this film, quite suddenly, a beautifully photographed close-up of a horse urinating makes the point that water carries away the body's waste. It is the unexpectedness of this scene, following a micro-shot of blood pulsating through an artery, which makes the impact. Surprise stirs our consciousness whilst the predictable dulls it. It took a whole day to film this scene but it is this sort of approach,

The Subject

the willingness to take trouble and the readiness on the part of the sponsor to back such an attitude which lifts a film out of the ordinary.

Between the Tides was made by British Transport Films. This Unit mainly produces training films for railway staff but it also makes films for general audiences with the purpose of encouraging railway travel by presenting various aspects of British life and scenery—in this case a stretch of coast at low tide. Impressionist, lyrical, poetic, the film is yet highly informative about the many forms of animal life at the tide mark.

All three films could in less ingenious hands easily have become trite and pedestrian because the subjects, apart from the last one, do not *a priori* consist of attractive visual material.

Other subjects are exciting in themselves, as for example are many animal films. The Russian film *King Solomon's Garden* discusses the communication systems, the languages of various species of insects, fish, birds, apes. The French film *The Animals*, directed by Frederic Rossif, demonstrates the evolutionary chain from the protozoa to the present-day animal world, found between the equator and the poles. Both films are straightforward records of animal behaviour, brilliantly shot and presented in a matter-of-fact manner. The creatures themselves are so entrancing and their habits so interesting that no form of 'directing' could have improved the films. The commentary of the French film is unfortunately somewhat whimsical and often keeps to generalities instead of giving the expected factual information. The music, however, is beautifully integrated with the visuals.

Exploring Chemistry is a Unilever film forming part of the Nuffield Science Teaching Project. A class of children is set the task of finding out what makes copper black when heated. An intriguing study of the children's faces intent on their work is combined with a lively play of give and take between class and teacher. The film then broadens out to include other aspects of chemistry and we see such details as VanGogh's 'Sunflower' superimposed over the benzol ring to show similarities of natural forms; we see an excellent mathematical model which resembles a piece of abstract sculpture and we see a bubble raft (page 131) to suggest a diffraction pattern. This film certainly serves its purpose of giving an insight into modern teaching methods.

Visual Aids, made for the Ministry of Defence, is an introduction to the range of visual aids now in use. This could have become a catalogue of instruments and gadgets but the director managed to provide 20 min of highly entertaining information.

The film *The Violent Universe*, made and compiled for BBC Television and shown as a two-and-a-half hour non-stop programme is an example of how science films should not be made. Its length alone militates against itself; it is too much to expect a lay audience to concentrate on an unfamiliar subject for some 150 min. Less would have been more: if the film had been cut by an hour much repetitive and highly esoteric material would have been eliminated. No doubt, the film contained fascinating details of various phenomena on the earth and in the heavens. A large studio model, however, showing part of the Milky Way, seemed slightly naïve; the stars resembled not so much stars as peeled potatoes. The film was shot in colour but since the majority of TV sets at the time of showing were not yet adapted for colour, there was really no point in devising visuals which might have been effective in that medium but were unattractive and even confusing in black-and-white. A number of scientists talked—sometimes rather too technically for a non-technical audience—on the various aspects of astronomy and on their own particular fields of work. The connecting commentary sounded somewhat pompous but the concluding talk of one of the astronomers was excellent, relating the drama of the universe to the humbler problems of humanity.

Aiming at an audience

The foregoing examples provide an opportunity to talk about one or two important points:

Sir Arthur Elton, Head of Film Centre International Ltd wrote in an article *How We Make Films at Shell*: 'Each film or series of films is specialized in the sense that it is made for and aimed at a particular audience. Paradoxically, it has been found that films made within rigid audience terms of reference sometimes achieve a much more general success than the so-called general interest films; these, aimed at everybody, may sometimes fail to capture the imagination either of the specialist or of the man in the street.'

This has a bearing on what was discussed on page 37. Most audiences, even children, are nowadays conditioned to the film language whose symbolism and conventions are no obstacle to the comprehension of a film.

If there are obstacles, they lie mostly in the technicalities of the subject. This is natural enough considering the differences in national environments and habits, in levels of knowledge and intelligence, in professional and occupational spheres of interest. Defining the envisaged audience is sometimes easy, as in school- and training-films, but not so easy in the case of films made for 'non-theatrical distribution.' All non-theatrical audiences are, in terms of the film trade, 'specialized' (as opposed to those in cinemas) and it is with regard to these audiences that Shell's experience is of such importance.

When it comes to teaching films, no child or student can be expected to get a grasp of complicated notions in a single showing and rarely can a film explain them fully in ten or twenty min. It is, therefore, customary and indeed essential that a sponsor of such films issues either 'teaching notes', handbooks or other forms of informative literature which elaborate on the contents of the film. Also, several showings of a film or of sequences from it will often be necessary.

One of the less satisfactory features attendant on factual films is the

The Subject

appalling conditions in which such productions are sometimes screened. The projection equipment in schools and halls is often very poor and out-of-date, and many effects and subtleties in pictures or sound, to which the producer has devoted much time and care, are lost or ludicrously distorted. This should not deter us from making the best job we can. We must hope that with the increasing recognition of film as an important teaching medium, the projection facilities will gradually improve and that eventually films will everywhere be given a fair chance of appraisal.

3

Special Techniques

FOR THE PURPOSE of discussion the special techniques in film production may be considered in two broad categories: photographic, or space-dimensional and cinematic where the dimension is time.

Photographic methods

There is no rigid borderline between the techniques used to film the visible and the invisible worlds. The instruments designed to make some of the invisible subjects visible (microscopes, spectroscopes, telescopes, etc.) are *scientific* devices and the cine camera's role, as stated before, is mainly that of a recording medium. In cinemicrography and in high-speed cinematography it is the *degree* of time- and space-magnification rather than the technique itself which leads gradually from the visible to the invisible. No camera methods can claim to be *exclusively* concerned with the invisible, but certain optical and chemical processes, used in cinematography are more suitable than others to illustrate or interpret invisible phenomena. The term 'special effect' is unfortunately ambiguous. A simple lap-dissolve or an intentionally overfiltered scene are special effects but would hardly rank as such in the eyes of a special effects technician. In the highly departmentalized field of the entertainment film the special effects team, in co-operation with the director of photography, is mainly concerned with process photography which includes glass- and mirror-shots (often in conjunction with foreground miniatures), travelling mattes, front-and-back-projection and other sophisticated methods for the production of split-screen and superimposed composite images. Most of these methods are usually far beyond the resources of the ordinary factual film unit.

Effects in science films

But there are also special optical effects which can be achieved by quite simple means. The present and the following chapters will select and describe some which are relevant to the type of work encompassed by this book. A selection like this cannot be exhaustive nor insist on distinctive

Special Techniques

methods; new apparatus and new cinematic methods are devised year by year which will certainly enlarge the scope for special effects for the filmmaker who keeps himself up-to-date.

Photographic methods can be divided into those which take place within the camera and those which make use of equipment placed in front of the camera. As these methods must often be combined, they will be dealt with together.

There is a third and very important way for creating both photographic and cinematic effects: the aftertreatment of the filmed material in the laboratory by means of the optical printer. This will be described later on.

Photographic effects are based either on the optical system of the camera, on the properties of the film emulsion or on special types of lighting. Again, more often than not, one medium is dependent on the other: emulsions on filters, filters on the prevailing light, the prevailing light on emulsions and so on.

Camera optics

The lens, apart from producing an image, determines the image-to-subject ratio. This ratio refers to the area covered by the camera frame mask, not to that seen on the cine- or television screen. The magnification of the film image by projection is a different story altogether.

Some reference should first be made to a special field of close-up photography which is concerned with filming very small animals such as ants and flies or other objects of miniature size. This technique does not reach into the region of invisibility but it magnifies the hardly visible so that it becomes perceptible for investigation.

Cinemacrography, cinemicrography

In cinemacrography, magnification ratios of up to 10:1 can be achieved with ordinary and long-focus lenses which must either be racked out by extension tubes or bellows or must be combined with diopter lenses (positive supplementary lenses). Commercially manufactured macro-lenses are also available. Since the depth of field is usually very shallow, absolute rigidity of all components is essential. High magnification seemingly speeds up movement and this must be compensated for by slightly overrunning the camera.

Exposure time is very critical and the lens aperture has to be opened up in step with diminishing the distance between camera and subject. The exposure factors must be carefully calculated or measured by an incident exposure meter with a diffusing hemisphere attached to it, or by one of the special light meters available for cinemacrography.

Since the light has to be strong and concentrated, the heat caused by it may incapacitate or kill living specimens. Heat-absorbing glass sheets (such as the Kodak 500/00/HRI non-photographic filters) should therefore be put in front of the lamps.

Where the distance from lens to subject is so short that front-lighting becomes difficult, the subject can be lit by reflecting light onto it from the side through a semi-transparent mirror. Such a mirror must be angled at 45° to the camera as in the Pepper's ghost technique (page 79). As mirrors transmit only part of the light falling on them, the light loss must be taken into account.

A great variety of instrumentation exists which is specially adapted for cinemacrography such as optical benches, special lenses, low-voltage lamps powered by batteries, cooling devices (cuvettes), etc. In order to keep living specimens in place in front of the lens, the following method was adapted and described by K. Philipp, Göttingen:

> Small 'cells' to contain the animals were made up of optically true glass such as can be obtained from photographic plates from which the emulsion had been removed. After accustoming the creatures to these cells, the glass plates were gradually slid nearer to one another until the necessary narrow depth was achieved and the animal's movements were sufficiently restricted. Some animals were so little disturbed that it was even possible to remove some of the glass plates altogether in order to eliminate light reflections.* (See Fig. 21)

For still higher magnifications, up to about 2000:1, we have to turn to cinemicrography which opens our eyes to almost invisible worlds. Camera lenses are no longer required, the camera has to be attached by tubing to

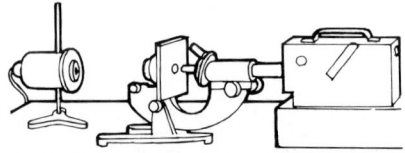

FIG. 20. *Cinemicroscopy*. This drawing shows a camera attached, without its lens, to a simple school microscope. Only static material can, of course, be filmed through a microscope of this type. The slide of the fly's proboscis (Fig. 23), was shot by the above combination.

the optical system of the microscope. Cinemicroscopy of living bodies and tissues is a highly scientific discipline and a matter for experts. This applies even more to ultra-violet and electron-microscopy. Since the wavelength of an electron beam is about a hundred thousand times smaller than that of a light-beam the resolving power of an electron-microscope is so great that large molecules become visible. When micro-material of a specific nature is required for a film it can, as explained before, be sub-contracted

---

* From: *Der Film im Dienste der Wissenschaft*, (1961) Institut für den Wissenschaftlichen Film, Göttingen.

Special Techniques

to one of the specialist cinematographers working in this field. Microscenes of a general character can often be purchased from film libraries.

Manipulating the image

The importance of the image-forming properties of various lens types was mentioned earlier. The distorting effects of the wide-angle and the telephoto lens are well known. There are, however, a number of methods by which an image can intentionally be distorted or given some other unusual appearance such as may be necessary for dream sequences, in 'subjective' photography and for a variety of other purposes. Most of such effects are produced by accessories and gadgets placed in front of the lens outside the camera.

Certain types of supplementary lenses, but also prisms, pieces of ordinary curved glassware, cutglass and even bits of broken glass held closely in front of the camera lens, might distort or break up the image in various ways. A small transparent plastic sheet, heated until it buckles or becomes pliable, gives the same kind of effect. Highly polished curved metal sheets (such as seen in 'Halls of Mirrors') will reflect persons or objects so that they appear squeezed or elongated. The bending of such sheets during shooting can produce a variety of useful effects.

A mirror, submerged under water in a dish, reflects objects like any mirror provided the surface of the water remains undisturbed; but if the water is agitated, the reflection starts to wobble and eventually dissolves.

Reflections on glass or metal are often troublesome but they can be put to good use for suggesting abstract or concrete phenomena such as stars or star clusters, etc., or moving patterns as mentioned on page 152.

Individual areas of blur or softness in an image can be obtained by shooting through glass smeared with vaseline or by stretching some gauze in front of the lens (see also page 42).

All these methods, used singly or in combination, lend themselves to endless permutations but some experimenting is necessary in order to get what is wanted.

Distorting lenses and factory-made lens attachments of various kinds are often available for hire. One of them produces ripple effects; others contain prisms which can either turn the image upside down or at any other desired angle, as well as double or multiply an image or rotate it in all sorts of ways, often fragmentising it or producing kaleidoscopic effects.

Matte boxes are very useful. In essence, they are just bellows, attached to the front of the camera by means of two horizontal metal rods on which the front part of the bellows slides. Matte boxes are fitted with filter holders and frames and they can hold differently shaped effect gadgets including transparencies showing cloud formations or other pictorial features. Matte boxes make it easier to position lights without fear of lens

The Work of the Science Film Maker

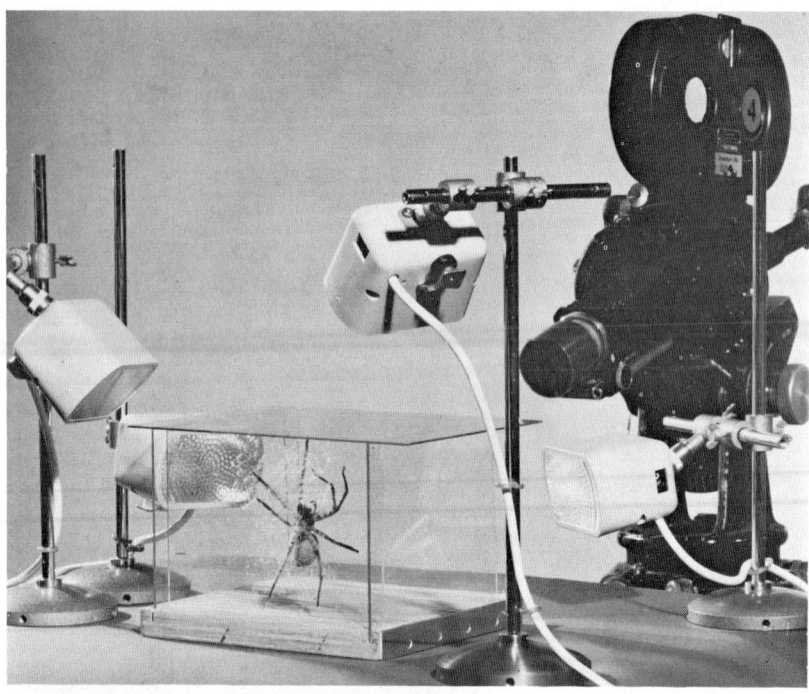

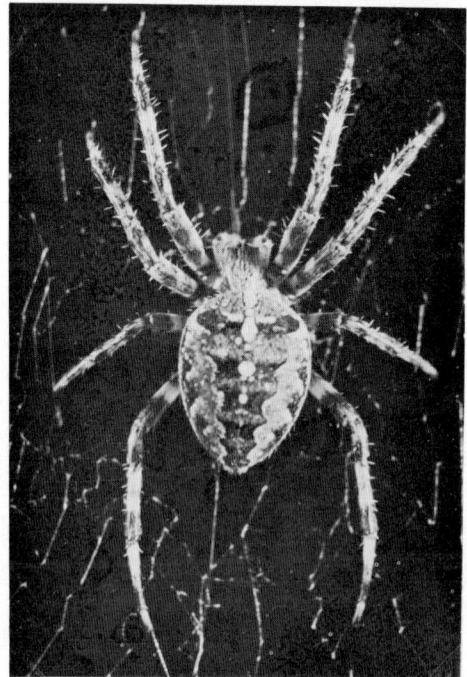

Fig. 21. *Cinemacrography.* (above): The lighting (special synchronized flash equipment) and caging arrangement for the filming of living specimens, as developed at the 'Institut für den Wissenschaftlichen Film', Göttingen, Germany.

Fig. 22. (opposite): A garden spider *(Arancus diadematus)* lying in ambush in its net.

Special Techniques

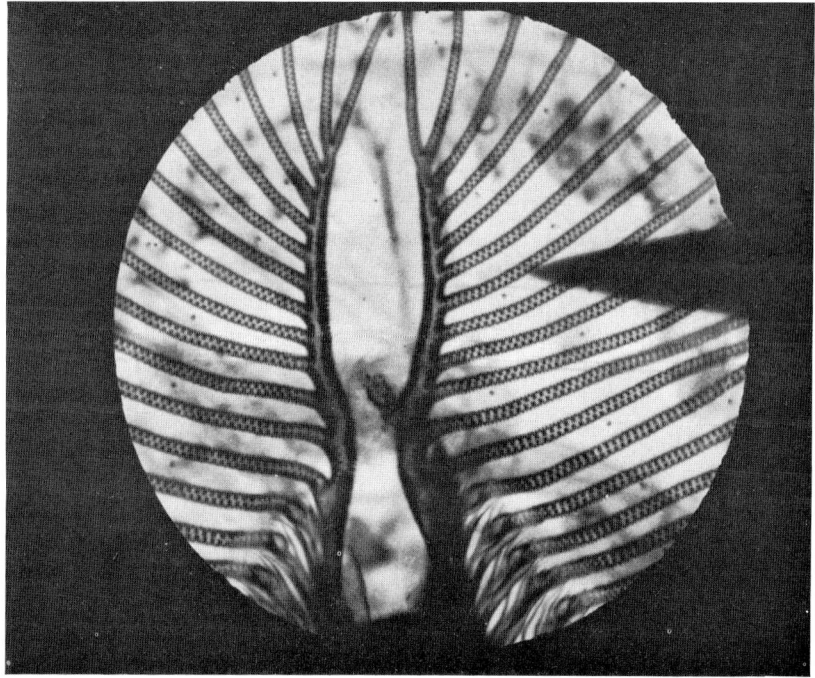

Fig. 23. *Cinemicrography.* Micro slide of the proboscis of a fly filmed by the method shown in Fig. 20. Still from the film *The Microscope.*

flare. If used in conjunction with wide-angle lenses, care must be taken that the front edges of the matte box do not intrude into the picture area.

Pepper's Ghost

A hundred years ago, the illusionist H. Dircks invented a trick device by means of which an apparition could suddenly appear on a theatre stage as if by magic. This trick was improved and made popular by a stage exhibitor called Pepper. The illusion was created by a mirror which reflected the image of an actor *off* stage on to a point *on* the stage. The principle of this trick is widely used in films for techniques allowing in-the-camera superimpositions of two independent sets or objects situated on the studio floor. The effect is the same as that obtained by double exposure or in optical printing, but where the situation permits its use, the Pepper's Ghost method has several advantages. It is relatively simple and inexpensive and the director and cameraman can watch the visual effect whilst it is created and filmed. The name Pepper's Ghost may now sound somewhat archaic but there is no other unambiguous name which refers to this particular method. The term 'mirror shot' can mean more than one technique.

Basically, the Pepper's Ghost process requires only a small semi-transparent (half-silvered) mirror, placed at 45° in front of the camera lens. The camera then films the main set, immediately in front of it, through this mirror. At the same time it photographs the *reflection* of the second set which is put at the side of the camera at right angles to the optical axis of the lens (Fig. 24). If both images are to appear sharp, both sets or objects have to be at equal distances from the mirror.

The Pepper's Ghost method can be used in quite small studios. The maker of science films will find it of great value for many purposes. Even in its simplest application, it can replace costly techniques such as optical printing or animation. Diagrams, art work, titles, live-action or abstract effects can be superimposed on the main scene with equal ease. Later, applications of this technique will be described.

The two separate sets have, of course, to be lit individually and it is easy to verify the light balance of the two images by direct observation or measurement. If the lamps used for lighting each set are connected to dimmers, the light balance can be altered during the shooting. One of the component images can be faded in or out or kept subdued for part of the shot—a fact of special importance when scientific phenomena have to be explained.

The simple arrangement described above can be greatly elaborated as is the case in the Schufftan process and other effect methods used in feature production. A more recent development is the Multiplexer system in which movable half-silvered mirrors reflect images from several projection sources into the camera.

For better definition, a prism can replace the mirror. This was done for the film *How the Motor Car Works*, made by the Shell Film Unit. The shooting arrangement is described below as an example of the type of subject suitable for the Pepper's Ghost method.

The exploded model of a motor car engine, such as is sometimes displayed in motor showrooms, was set up at right angles to the camera. This engine contained no pistons. In front of the camera was a skeleton model of the pistons, made in the Shell Engineering workshop to exact specifications, so that the pistons precisely fitted the model engine in size and arrangement. The pistons were held in position by an inconspicuous plastic rod structure which allowed for their motion.

When only the motor was lit, the camera photographed it without the pistons; similarly, the piston model could be shown without the motor. When both models were lit, the images superimposed themselves on each other so that the pistons seemed to move within the motor. The transition from one set to the other as well as the composite picture could be modulated in any desired strength or length by means of the lighting. Both sets could be either front- or back-lit, allowing for four lighting stages and requiring sixteen light units in all. The light was controlled by two dimmers. This scene took two days to prepare; a test shot made during this time was

Special Techniques

Fig. 24. *Pepper's Ghost Set-up.* The camera points towards the main set (SET 1) which is often a static chart or drawing but can also be a model and it shoots this set through a semi-transparent mirror (M) which is placed at an angle of 45° in front of the lens, normally quite close to it. Alternatively, a prism can be used. The side set (SET 2) is positioned at right angles to the lens axis in such a way that its image falls on the mirror. The side set usually consists of moving parts or of an effects mechanism and the effects produced by it are superimposed by the mirror on the image of the main set. For both images to appear sharp both sets have to be equidistant from the mirror. This time- and money-saving device does away with the need for optical printing work in the laboratory.

actually usuable. No such flexibility could have been achieved by any other means.

Glass-, mirror- and prism methods have various other functions some of which are described later. Mirrors are also used in connection with lighting. An example was given on page 74.

In all mirror techniques, particularly where superimpositions are involved, the camera, the mirror and the sets have to be rigidly locked and kept in positions until the rushes have been seen and approved. Cameras with a rewinding mechanism are a great advantage for all double-exposure methods. We must also remember that the focus of mirror images is at the apparent distance of the reflection, i.e., camera to mirror, plus mirror to subject.

Masks and mattes

Technical literature is often rather vague when describing the difference between masks and mattes. As is so often the case in film parlance, terms can have identical meaning if used in one context, and are at variance if used in another one. Without prejudice to a different interpretation, the following definitions are suggested here:

Masks are black pieces of metal, cardboard or film, cut to different shapes and inserted in the gate of the camera in order to shade off part of the image which the lens is projecting on to the negative. Masks are essential for split-screen photography. Some cameras are supplied with a set of gate masks which divide the image horizontally, vertically or diagonally but cameramen have often to cut their own masks for particular screen-splitting effects.

Most masks make double-exposure necessary, and exactly matching countermasks are needed for the second exposure which completes the composite picture. No double exposure is necessary with cut-out masks which are used to obtain apertures such as keyholes, slits or circular openings. These last imply views as seen in microscopes or telescopes. With a cut-out mask, the masked-off part is not replaced by another image but remains black on the screen.

All gate masks create a sharp dividing line on the negative. If a soft line is required or where one half of the split-screen image is to merge into the other, masks must be put outside the camera in front of the lens. The degree of the softening effect depends on the distance of the mask from the lens. Such masks must be much bigger, of course. They allow for greater flexibility but the placing of the countermask is more critical. A matte box (page 75) is a most desirable accessory where masks are used in front of the camera.

Split-screen effects can be a great asset to the science film maker. He can show a long shot and a close up of the same object in one and the same image; he can demonstrate an object in different stages of development or under different conditions; or he can place different objects side by side for comparison. Masks can also be used for pictorial effects.

Mattes are lengths of exposed film containing picture components to be inserted in or superimposed upon the main image. The length of a matte must correspond to the length of scene for which it is intended. In general, mattes are of two types: masking mattes and effect mattes.

Masking mattes are used for much the same purpose as the masks described above: to block out certain areas within existing scenes when elaborate composite images are required. Masking mattes are usually made on the optical printer and are thus part of laboratory technique. Complicated composite effects may require half a dozen or even more separate printing stages and a corresponding number of mattes. Masking mattes are of little interest to makers of low-budget films and can be disregarded here. The same is true of travelling matte processes which are still more complex and expensive.

Effect mattes are different in character. They may consist of shots of artificially produced rain- or snow-fall, filmed against a black background for straight superimposition on live scenes. Mattes with lightning effects can be prepared to be used in connection with night shots. Still other mattes can be made of such scenes as raindrops running down window panes, reflections from neon lights, flickering fires, etc. Many other

Special Techniques

concrete and abstract effects can be dreamed up, filmed and superimposed on the principal scene in the optical printer.

Most effect mattes can be shot by the film-maker himself and they have proved their value on many occasions.

Infra-red and ultra-violet cinematography

The emulsions and filters available for ordinary cinematography are sensitive to light rays which form the visible part of the electro-magnetic spectrum. The image, seen by the camera lens is, therefore, basically the same as that seen by the human eye.

A number of film emulsions are, however, sensitized to record certain types of invisible radiation. Infra-red film, available in both black-and-white and colour, belongs in this category.

Infra-red

The visible spectrum covers the electro-magnetic waveband from about 400 nm to 700 nm; the radiation on either side of this range cannot be seen by the human eye. Infra-red rays are longer than light rays and their range extends from 700 nm to beyond 1300 nm, gradually merging into the spectrum of radio waves.

Infra-red cine film is sensitive to only a small part of the entire infra-red waveband, responding to wavelengths from 700 nm to about 900 nm.

The importance of this type of photography lies in the fact that substances such as the chlorophyl in green plants or certain dyes and inks absorb a great part of the visible radiation but strongly reflect infra-red rays. In combination with suitable filters, infra-red film often alters the normal appearance of objects and landscapes considerably. It is used for both pictorial effects and for revealing features which our eyes are unable to perceive. Consequently infra-red film serves many purposes.

Outdoors it is used for penetrating strong haze in landscape scenes, producing moonlight effects, for rendering green fields and woods white so that they appear snow-covered, or for generally creating unusual and dramatic pictorial impressions. Aerial survey and star photography are two of several specialized applications.

Indoors, infra-red film is needed—in combination with special lighting or by covering the lamps with light-opaque infra-red-transmitting gelatines—for photography in the dark as described on page 67, and for scientific, forensic and medical purposes. Infra-red film plays an important part in the detection of forgeries, in the examination of works of art, in the diagnosis of skin diseases and particularly in cinemacrography.

Thermal photography is the photography in absolute darkness of hot objects which emit invisible heat rays but no visible radiation. This type of photography is often necessary for the study of thermal phenomena and for the analysis of surface temperature distribution. Exposure times

THE WORK OF THE SCIENCE FILM MAKER

Special Techniques

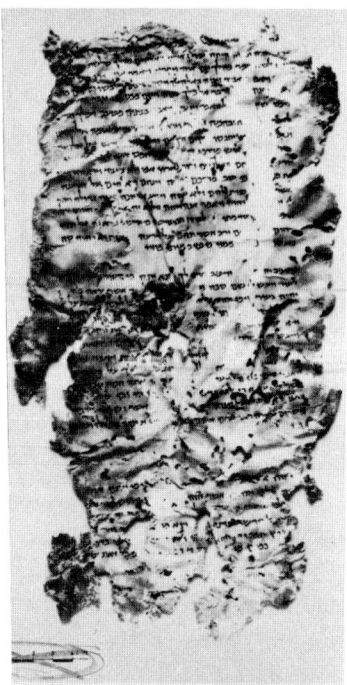

Fig. 25 and Fig. 26. (opposite) *Infra-red Photography*. The same landscape shot on ordinary film (top) and on infra-red film (bottom). The lower picture shows greater haze penetration, greater detail in the distance and the characteristic rendering of the green foliage as white.

Fig. 27. (above): A fragment of the Dead Sea Scrolls photographed (left) by ordinary methods, and (right) with infra-red film and special filter.

have normally to be so long as to put this technique outside the scope of the cine camera. If the object can be kept at a *steady* temperature, one can perhaps use a time lapse method and expose each frame for long enough. A safer method is to use a still camera, loaded with a high-speed infra-red film and then to film the resulting photograph (see pages 182–3). The EMI Thermoscan and the Barnes* Infra-red Camera are specially designed for this type of photography. (Figs 28, 29)

Focusing is critical in infra-red photography because infra-red rays focus in a different plane from light rays. Focusing by eye is therefore of little use. Charles C. Clarke† recommends 'to focus forward of the actual distance $\frac{1}{4}$ of 1 % of the focal length of the lens. With a 50mm lens the values are:

---

* EMI Electronic and Industrial Operations, Hayes, Middlesex, England; Barnes Engineering Co, 30 Commerce Road, Stamford, USA. Both these firms have published literature containing detailed information.

† Charles C. Clarke, *Professional Cinematography*, published by American Society of Cinematographers, Hollywood 28, California.

Infinity	50 ft
25 ft	20 ft
10 ft	9 ft
5 ft	$4\frac{3}{4}$ ft

Other distances and lenses would be focused proportionally'.

Exposure also is a problem. Normal meters are unreliable as they measure visible radiation. The ASA speed rating for ordinary infra-red film in combination with a Wratten 25 filter is: daylight 50, tungsten 150, requiring an aperture of about 5·6 for distant landscapes.

Full information about exposure factors, filters and lighting are contained in the American Cinematographer Manual and in the Kodak Advanced Data Book M3: 'Infra-red and Ultra-violet photography'.

Ultra-violet cinematography

Violet rays have the shortest wavelengths of the visible spectrum, about 400 nm. The still shorter rays adjoining the violet waveband are called ultra-violet (u.v.); again, they are invisible. The 'photographically effective range of u.v. radiation reaches down to about 250 nm. Strong sunlight contains much of this type of radiation which can become a nuisance to ordinary photography wherever the atmosphere is very clear as in high altitudes, and u.v. filters become necessary to suppress the amount of blue which reaches the lens from the sky.

But u.v. radiation can also be useful in photography. There is no such thing as an u.v. emulsion; most panchromatic high speed emulsions, even colour films, can be used, but the visible light has to be cut out by special filters. For artificial u.v. illumination of objects in darkened rooms, special lamps are needed. Most of them have their output at 366 nm (long-wave lamps), and again, special filters are required. The output of short-wave lamps is at 258 nm. For photography which uses such short wavelengths special quartz lenses are necessary and the eyes have to be well protected.

There are two different methods of u.v. photography: the reflection method and the photography of fluorescence produced by u.v. radiation as is sometimes used in the clothing of road workers or for stage effects. This second method is of interest from a pictorial point of view. The scientific applications of u.v. photography are much the same as those for infra-red and are a matter for experts working in these fields.

Fig. 28. (top): A person examining an electric blanket heated by a 0·5 V current.
Fig. 29. (bottom): A good example of the analysis of surface temperature distribution. The nose is the coldest part of the face and therefore the least exposed in the picture.
These are examples of Thermography, the photography in complete darkness of hot objects, illuminated by their own heat radiation.

Special Techniques

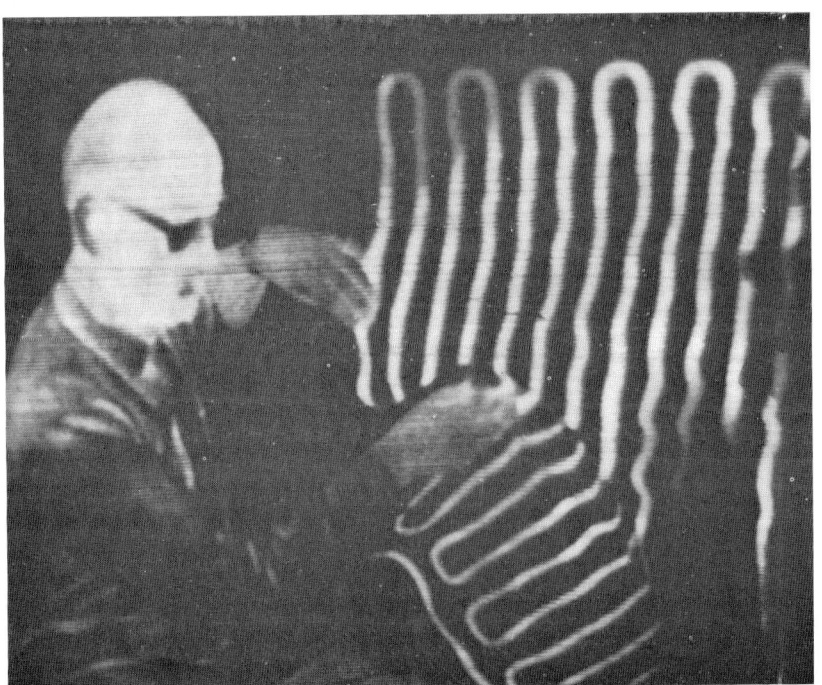

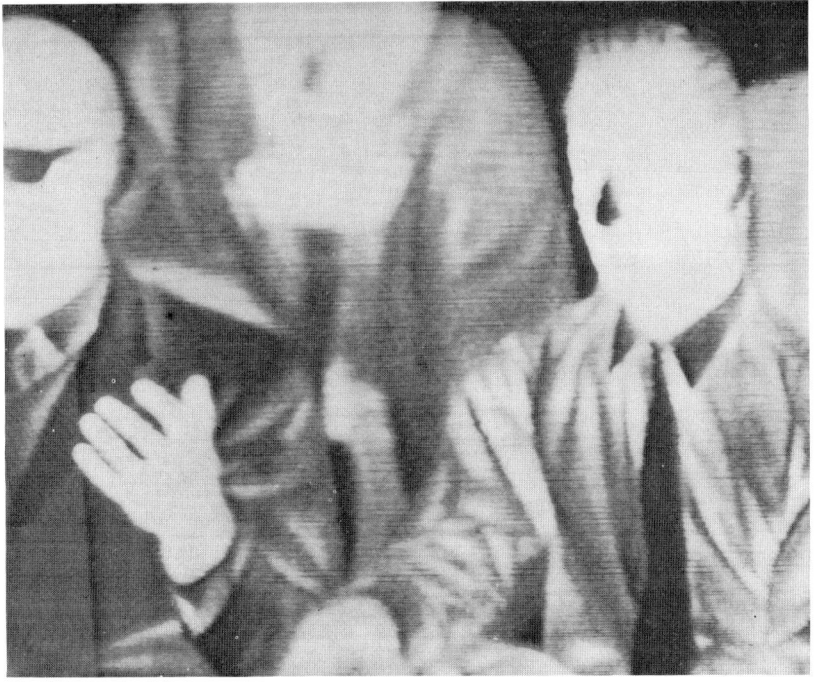

The Work of the Science Film Maker

Filter effects

Although filters have been referred to in a general way elsewhere, a few specific filter effects which are often needed in factual film making must now be mentioned.

Dramatic cloud effects are achieved by using heavy graduated contrast filters such as yellow, green or even orange or red for monochrome work giving increasing contrast in that order. With colour, certain polarizing filters can be used. Under-running the camera will speed up the movement of the clouds and thus increase the pictorial impact.

Day-for-Night photography: most night effects are shot in bright sunlight. Suitable filters must be used and slight under-exposure is recommended. This alone, however, will not be sufficient. You must try to catch the typical night atmosphere by making the absence of light a positive feature. This is an art in itself in which the position of the sun, the colour of the sky, the type of background, the tonal values of the faces and dresses of people all play a part. Also you must decide whether you want darkness as such, or a moonlight effect. Too often, so-called night scenes look like nothing on earth even in million dollar productions. There are almost as many methods for creating night effects as there are cameramen and the following notes can only serve as a general guide.

The main aim is to darken the *blue* sky (a white sky is unsuitable for producing night effects). With monochrome film, a combination of a red and light-green filter, both perhaps graduated, can prove effective. A neutral density filter might be added to suppress foreground detail. The filter factor should be disregarded or an appropriately smaller lens stop chosen. Shooting with the sun is not advisable; shadows should fall towards the camera.

Infra-red film, exposed through a dark-red filter, will produce striking moonlight effects.

With colour negative film, the tendency now seems to be to expose as for ordinary daylight scenes through the filter normally used with such emulsions and to leave the creation of the night effect to the laboratory. With colour reversal film, no filter at all need to be used. The laboratory will print the scene through a blue filter.

It pays to consult the laboratory before shooting night effects because developing and printing methods differ considerably, and the cameraman should know what sort of negative the laboratory prefers for getting the best results. The shots should be clearly marked 'Night Effect' on the camera sheet.

Night scenes in town with street lamps, shop windows and neon lights do not come under the heading of day-for-night photography but should be regarded as subjects for straightforward photography in artificial light.

Reflections in glass, particularly in shop windows, can be cut out,

Special Techniques

reduced or increased with polarizing filters (or screens). Laboratory glassware, too, is apt to produce irritating reflections which can prevent a clear view of what is going on inside retorts, etc. Either pola screens or glass equipment with flat fronts must be used. Pola screens are put in front of the lens like filters and must then be turned until the reflections disappear in the camera's viewfinder. They are only effective for this particular camera position and must be re-set for each subsequent one. For panning along a shop window, pola screens are therefore of little use. Sky and cloud reflections in water can also be eliminated with pola screens but they are not effective in the case of flare and reflections from metal surfaces.

Haze filters. A haze filter is designed to destroy or reduce aerial haze, it should not be confused with a fog filter which *produces* a mist or fog effect. They therefore have opposite functions.

All filters meant to cut down the effect of ultra-violet radiation are haze-penetrating—they range from yellow filters for light haze to orange and red filters for strong haze. The greatest penetration is achieved with infra-red film and a red filter, but this method changes many tone values contained in the landscape and may produce an unnatural though interesting appearance. All these filters are also used in aerial survey photography from air to ground.

Emulsions used without filters intensify the haze effect because they record more haze than is visible to the eye.

Fog filters are obtainable in various grades: at one end of the scale grade 1 produces slight mist effects. At the other grades 4 and 5 give strong fog effects. The trouble is that all these filters reduce visibility not in depth but evenly; they cannot simulate the increase in the atmospheric density towards the background as is the case in real mist or fog. Thus, there is always something artificial about these effects which a visually alert person can spot. Yet, fog filters have their uses as a feasible alternative to the real thing. It is rarely possible to wait for actual fog. Layers of white mist can be produced in the middle distance by means of smoke candles which, in combination with a fog filter, will create a more realistic effect but this is usually only practical outside built-up areas.

With all filters, the filter factors to compensate loss of effective film speed recommended by the manufacturers must be taken into account when estimating exposures. The only exception are *diffusion* filters which do not absorb light but scatter the rays so that a softening effect is created. These filters, too, are made in various grades. A matte box (page 75) is a most useful accessory for fitting and manipulating filters.

Schlieren process

'Schliere' is a German word meaning a defect in glass such as a streak or striation which causes a change in the refractive index. The Schlieren technique was originally evolved for testing the quality of glass but it

THE WORK OF THE SCIENCE FILM MAKER

developed into an important means of observing and illustrating various kinds of invisible phenomena where changes of refractive index take place in transparent solids, liquids and gases. Later, reference is made to the film *Convection* in which this method was used to show up the hot air rising from a heated body and from a chimney stack (page 172). Likewise, it can be used to demonstrate many other things, such as aerosol sprays, shock waves emitted by flashing sparks, mixing liquids of different density and so on.

Because of its ability to reveal areas of changing air pressure, the Schlieren technique has become one of the most important tools in aerodynamic research. The National Physical Laboratory in Teddington, one of the pioneer institutions in this field of science, developed a system by which the Schlieren effect could be recorded on 16mm colour film. The Shell Film Unit in London extended and improved the technique by the use of 35 mm film for its film *High Speed Flight* made in 1956. In 1959 this unit made a highly instructive film on the Schlieren method as such, under the title *Schlieren*.

'Basically, a Schlieren set-up arranged for photography consists of a light source, two large concave mirrors placed, slightly angled, at a given distance opposite each other, a knife edge device put in the focal plane of mirror 2, (in the case of b/w photography), and a camera (Figure 30). The most commonly used light source is a tungsten lamp with a small filament. It is placed at the focus of mirror 1 which directs an (almost) parallel beam of light towards mirror 2. This mirror in turn reflects the beam towards the lens of the camera, converging the rays at the same time. The 2 mirrors together with the camera lens make up the optical system necessary for Schlieren photography.

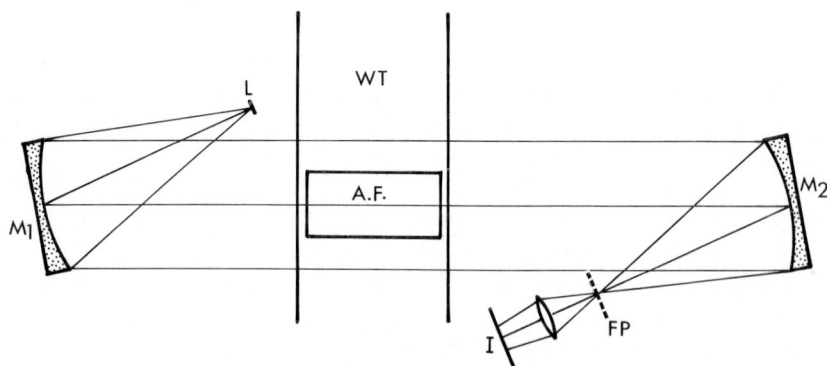

Fig. 30. *Set-up for Schlieren Photography* L = light source, M_1 and M_2 = large concave mirrors, FP = focal plane of M_2, I = Image focused on film. The object photographed in this diagram is the aerofoil AF, positioned between 2 windows in the wind tunnel WT. The knife edge or, in the case of colour filming, a special colour filter is placed at the focal plane FP. (Text and diagram from: "A Note on the Schlieren Method" published by Shell, London).

Special Techniques

Any solid object placed in the path of the light beam between the two mirrors appears on the film in silhouette. If the object is an aerosol can, its spray has a different refractive index to that of air and the light rays are slightly bent. The knife edge is now placed in the focal plane of mirror 2 so that it cuts off half of the main source image. The result is that the intensity of the background light is also halved. All density gradients caused by the aerosol spray having a component in the direction at right angles to the knife edge will become visible on the film; they will appear darker than the background. (Fig. 31)

For aeronautical research, a wind tunnel is placed at right angles across the path of the parallel light beam, with 2 round glass windows to let the beam pass through. An aerofoil or a model of the aircraft whose airflow characteristics are to be tested is fitted in the centre of the tunnel between the windows. Again, all density gradients caused by the varying pressure of the air stream on the foil become visible.

When photographing in colour, the knife edge is replaced by a colour filter made up from strips of coloured gelatine sandwiched between thin glass plates about 2 in. square. The narrow centre strip is green; on one side and in close contact with the green strip is an area of red, on the other side an area of blue. With this filter positioned so that the undeflected image passes through the central green strip, the background of the picture will appear green, the density variations red and blue. In the case of the aerofoil, for instance, the shock waves will show up as red and the expanses as blue. The cutting and positioning of the coloured strips needs some skill and experience. Recently, commercially manufactured filters have come on the market for this purpose.'

Schlieren equipment exists in several large university- and research-institutions and permission can be obtained to use it. The cooperation of the laboratory technicians is indispensable for solving any problems.

The Schlieren apparatus in these laboratories is usually large, intricate and expensive; the cost of the mirrors alone may run into four figures. Some time ago, Mr. M. G. Keen, then Chairman of the Research Group of the British Industrial and Scientific Film Association demonstrated in a meeting of the Royal Photographic Society a 'shoe-string' Schlieren set-up in which ordinary convex condenser lenses, taken from photographic enlargers, replaced the expensive mirrors. A razor blade provided the knife edge. This demonstration was perhaps the first step towards do-it-yourself Schlieren Cinematography. Thus, a highly specialized scientific research process might one day become a routine technique for the maker of low budget factual and science films.

Cinematographic methods

It was shown in an earlier chapter how actual time can be transformed into film time by means of editing techniques. Since editing is concerned with the creation of a filmic reality, achieved by appropriate assembly and juxtaposition of single scenes and transitional devices (fades, mixes, etc.), the creation of film time by way of editing is a psychological process. But as we know, there are also physical means of altering time values in films.

A scene has to be projected at the same speed at which it was shot in order to reproduce actual movement truthfully. In the case of sound film, the speed is 24 frames per sec. If you film a moving object at less than that speed—if you under-run the camera—and then project the scene at 24 fps, the action is speeded up. The most extreme form of under-running the camera is stop motion (or time lapse).

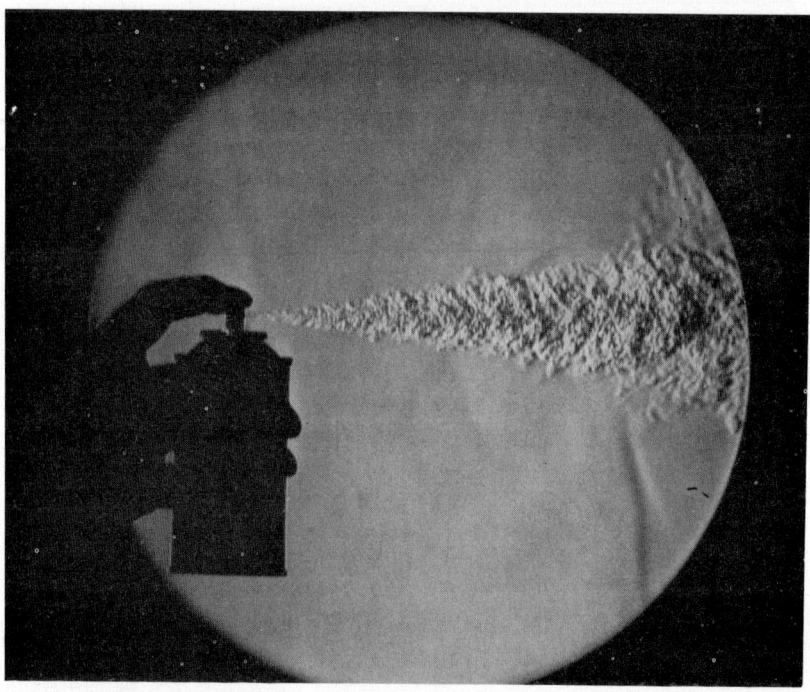

FIG. 31. *Schlieren Photography.* Any solid object placed in the path of the light beam within the Schlieren set-up appears on the film in silhouette. The example shown here is of an Aerosol can and its spray.

Under-running results in the *compression* of actual time. The opposite effect is achieved by over-running the camera. The action is then slowed down and we speak of slow-motion or high-speed photography in which the camera *expands* or magnifies time. Slow-motion stretches a given period of actual time in the manner of an elastic band, yet it retains the same amount of action within this lengthened period. The magnification factor is arrived at by dividing the taking rate by the projection rate. A scene shot at 48 fps

Special Techniques

and projected at 24 fps slows down all movement to half its actual speed. At a shooting speed of 480 fps, the magnification is tenfold. If a timing device (such as a clock designed for the purpose) is included in the picture area, the *actual* time passed since the beginning of the shot can be read off at once in each frame of the film. This is an essential feature for the subsequent evaluation of the scene.

Every cinemagoer and TV viewer is familiar with both under-running and over-running techniques which are often used in entertainment films for creating amusing or weird effects. Their scientific importance is that they can present very slow or very fast natural, technical or biological processes in a way which allows us to interpret, decipher or analyse them with ease. Time-lapse and high-speed techniques are, therefore, widely used in scientific and research cinematography.

Special cameras

Most of the usual production cameras can be under-run and over-run only to a very limited degree, though some models provide for single-frame photography by means of special mechanisms. But generally, special time-lapse and high-speed cameras must be employed. A point to be aware of is that the trend in scientific film-making leads increasingly away from the expensive 35mm format. The 35mm film retains its importance for certain kinds of production, such as films to be shown at festivals and in cinemas, but the general run of science and research films is now mainly produced on 16mm. In fact, high-speed cameras are now almost exclusively of the 16mm size, and there are also several 8mm high-speed models on the market. The 8mm film has made tremendous headway in recent years and has long ceased to be regarded as a plaything for amateurs.

It is not possible to list here even the most popular makes of time-lapse and high-speed cameras. New and modified models appear on the market all the time; it seems that more research goes into the development of high-speed cameras than into any other field of cine camera production.

An ideal camera would obviously be one which could take pictures at any desired speed from 1 fps to, say, 600 fps and which could also be used for single frame and time-lapse photography. Such an instrument does not yet exist and the choice of camera is, therefore, conditioned by the main purpose it has to serve. Broadly speaking, there are three categories: (a) ordinary production cameras with variable-speed motors providing speeds down to about 6 fps, or with high-speed motors for up to about 128 fps. Several cameras give a number of fixed speeds* (b) single-frame and time-lapse cameras; (c) high-speed cameras.

---

* The *American Cinematographer Manual* names a number of 35mm and 16mm cameras with the available motors.

The Work of the Science Film Maker

Under-running

With the type of camera mentioned in category (a), action can be speeded up, say, two-fold or four-fold. This might be sufficient for slow industrial processes—a crane lifting a load up a high building or a ship docking, also for giving a more vivid impression of trains and cars travelling at high speed. For scientific purposes and for pictorially interesting effects, however, these speed increases are rarely sufficient and you have to resort to cameras such as mentioned under (b). In addition to ordinary production cameras several single-frame cameras also permit continuous running both at slow speeds and at 24 fps.

Speeding up techniques are almost as old as cinematography itself. They were the most popular effects in Keystone comedies and similar films produced in the time of the old 'flicks', and to-day they are still much in vogue, particularly on TV. Hans Hass, for instance, made a TV series, probably filmed at 1 or 2 fps, called *Man* in which he explored the behaviour of crowds, groups and single people working, eating, playing, courting. In this case, the 'squeezing' of the people's movements was an excellent means of social investigation and satirical comment.

Under-running effects can also be produced in the laboratory on the optical printer (page 98) by what is called the skip-printing process. Scenes, shot at normal speeds may in the editing stage be found to require speeding up. In such cases the laboratory can be instructed to print only every second, fourth or sixth frame of a scene, and the effect will be almost the same as if shot that way in the first place. Cloud movement, for instance, is often speeded up optically as an afterthought to fit in with a dramatic situation. But optical printing is expensive and always results in a slight loss of photographic quality since an optical negative is a duplicate. Thus, skip-printing should only be used in an amergency.

There are one or two *variable speed projectors* on the market which allow films to be run at any speed from 1 to 24 fps without creating flicker. Such projectors widen the scope for analysis in many fields of research. Originally designed for X-ray cinematography, they have proved their value in other scientific and industrial fields. They allow an instant switch from forward to reverse motion and can, therefore, repeat sequences in quick succession. They also have all the features of a normal projector and can be used as such with either an optical or magnetic sound track.

Single-frame and time-lapse methods

If the camera does not run continuously at a given speed but exposes only a single frame and then stops until it receives a new impulse, then we speak of stop-motion photography. This is divided into single-frame and time-lapse methods.

In the first case, the exposures are made at irregular intervals as required. This procedure is essential in all animation work and for a few

Special Techniques

special effects. Several 16mm cameras have a single-frame mechanism incorporated. Of course, not only one but as many frames as desired can be exposed each time.

Time-lapse photography in conjunction with either synchronised flash or tungsten lighting works mainly automatically. Once the special trip-gear mechanism is pre-set and the synchronizing motor connected with the light-source so that the lamps are switched on before each exposure and off again after it, the system works day and night of its own accord, exposing one or several frames every two seconds, minutes, hours or at whatever other time-interval is planned. The exposure time itself can be varied as in still cameras. Time-lapse photography is perhaps the only field of cinematography (nowadays one should say: terrestrial cinematography) which does not need the presence of the cameraman during actual shooting. The main component of the set up is an intervalometer. This controls the lapse and works in combination with special power-units and other accessories. The instrumentation differs with the various models and many cameramen have modified existing equipment to make it more suitable for their particular type of work.

Time-lapse studies of a scientific character are legion. Orginally they were mainly used in popular nature films to show the unfolding of flowers, the growth of a seedling surfacing from the soil or hatching of birds. In the twenties and thirties, Percy Smith's *Secrets of Nature* films were masterpieces of this technique and Walt Disney also used it in his True Life Adventure series. Crystal-growing, too, was and still is an obvious subject for time-lapse cinematography.

The main applications of time-lapse photography are in the fields of biology, chemistry and cinemicrography. It is also useful for time-and-motion experiments, traffic flow research and many other purposes; some book-makers are said to use it for fixing the exact time of betting.

Over-running

The range of continuous mechanical under-running is normally limited to 1 fps at its extreme; this corresponds to a time compression ratio of 24:1. The extent of over-running, on the other hand, has become almost limitless, with time magnification ratios of up to many millions to one.

A few ordinary production cameras can be over-run to about 36 to 48 fps. This results in a 50–100% slowing-down of movement which is often not very noticeable but might do to smooth out, say, the fidgety motion of miniature models and mechanical toys (page 103). It might also be handy,

---

FIGS. 32, 33, 34 and 35 (pages 94, 95). *Time-lapse Photography. The Opening of a Tiger Lily Blossom,* shot with automatic trip-gear and intervalometer, coupled with Synchro-flash equipment. $f/22$, 1/30 sec. on Agfa Isopan film. The four shots are part of a longer series taken over a period of 50 hours; the intervals between these four exposures are about 17 hours each.

The Work of the Science Film Maker

Special Techniques

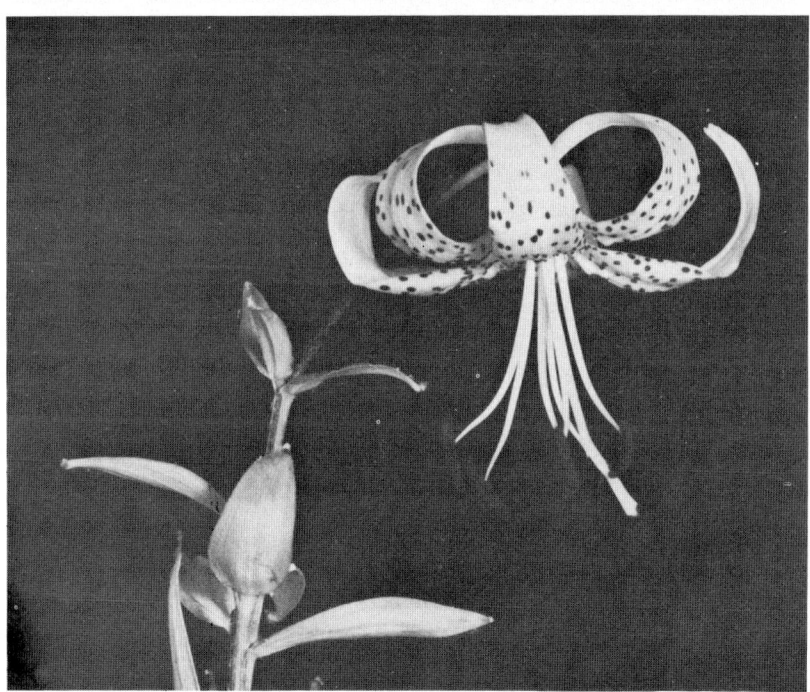

for instance, for scenes which at normal speeds would be too short for covering vital commentary. For all serious and striking slow-motion or high-speed effects, high-speed cameras with special film gates, motors and transport mechanisms must be used. The term 'slow motion' usually applies to speeds of up to 600 fps. Above this we speak of high-speed photography.

Because of their visual attractiveness, slow-motion effects are much used in films dealing with athletics, ski-ing, diving, horse racing and other sport events. They are, of course, an excellent means for the study of human or animal movement, of scientific or industrial processes, of natural phenomena such as water currents or avalanches, and they are much used in cinemicrography.

Intermittent slow-motion cameras

The transport mechanism of this type of camera resembles that of the ordinary model. The film is held stationary during exposure and is pulled down by a claw (or two claws) whilst the rotating shutter obscures the gate. The highest speed obtainable with such mechanical systems are 500–600 fps, corresponding roughly to a time magnification of up to 25:1. An advantage of such cameras is that they often allow under-running as well.

Due to the progress made in the manufacture of film emulsions, most makes of film stock, black-and-white or colour, of the negative–positive or reversal type can be used in slow-motion cameras. Some of them, however, require film with special long-pitch perforations to avoid tearing.

When lighting for work at these speeds the usual types of lamps are suitable. It was pointed out earlier that, where a great amount of light is concentrated on a small area, the heat becomes excessive and may affect the condition of the filmed object. In such a case, heat-absorbing filters should be placed in front of the lamps. The sensitive photo-cells of exposure meters should be similarly protected lest they be damaged by the heat.

With speeds upwards of 100 fps, time registration by clocks becomes inaccurate or impractical, and timing-light devices, marking the edge of the film at short regular intervals, are used for both time-base and event recording.

As with under-running, slow-motion effects can be produced to a very limited degree in the laboratory *after* the actual shooting. The method employed is called multiple printing and is also done on the optical printer. Instead of missing out frames as in skip-printing, each frame is printed twice or three times, thus lengthening the scene to the equivalent of shooting it at 48 or 72 fps. Stretching the slowing-down process still further by optical printing is inadvisable because the eye can no longer experience the sensation of continuous movement. The scene flickers during projection and action appears jerky.

Special Techniques

High-speed cameras

Slow-motion cinematography up to about 600 fps is probably the limit for an ordinary production unit. Much higher speeds are within the reach of cinematographers or units specializing in this type of work for research purposes.

High-speed cameras with rotating prism- or lens-devices can produce up to 10,000 fps. In these 'special' cameras the film is not held static in the gate during exposure but passes the gate in a continuous movement. The rotating prism device, moving in step, serves as a shutter and prevents the image from appearing blurred. Such a taking rate is the limit of what can be regarded as filming in the accepted sense. Films taken at higher speeds are unsuitable for projection and are evaluated by different methods.

Streak- or smear-cameras can take up to 40,000 fps (of quarter-frame size). The image is created by a special prism- and slit-device.

Rotating mirror cameras with special barrel- or disc-shutters can produce up to 120 8mm pictures at a rate of several million fps.

Image dissection cameras magnify speed up to 600,000 times and *image converters* 20–30 million times; the expression frame-per-second has lost its meaning. These cameras are operated for extremely short periods each time. Some use short lengths of film, others plates, 4×5 in. in size on which the filmed phenomena are recorded in the form of micro-dots. Special printing processes can turn the image on the plate into a cine strip but usually the plate itself is sufficient for analysis and remains the end product.

Summing up: high-speed cinematography acts as a magnifier of time much as cinemicrography does of space. Actual events and processes which in duration are far below the threshold of human perceptibility are presented to us so that they can be observed and analysed. High-speed photography and cinemacrography often go hand in hand. This combination is probably the ultimate in making the invisible visible by direct illustration.

Freezing action

As reference has been made to time manipulation by means of the optical printer, a method called 'stop-printing' must be mentioned. It means holding one particular frame for any desired length in the gate, thus stopping the action at this particular point. This has become a well-worn gimmick, often used in TV for no apparent reason.

There are, however, one or two valid grounds for holding a single frame for a few seconds. In instructional films you may wish to demonstrate a particular technical phase or the stance of a person. Freezing of live action in a film can only be done either on the optical printer or by stopping the film in the projector. Its drawback is that the emulsion grain is apt to show. In TV it is possible to freeze action by an electronic device.

The Work of the Science Film Maker

Reversing action

This also is mainly a matter for the optical printer. An example: the script may state that a pedestrian is run over by a car. This has to be staged in a way which excludes any risk to the person in question but still looks convincing and even dramatic, and it can be accomplished by a combination of camera technique and editing.

Scene 1: the person steps out into the road. Scene 2: a car approaches. Scene 3: big CU of the person's face. The eyes stare horrified and mesmerized in the direction of the approaching car. Scene 4: the car, seen from the person's position, bears down on him at great speed, getting out of focus as it comes closer and closer. The screeching of the tyres intensifies the feeling of terror. Scene 5: (midshot) the person under a wheel of the car or in any other suitably ghastly position.

All scenes except No. 4 are shot normally. Scene 4, however, is under-cranked with the car *backing away* from the camera as fast as it can. This shot is then reversed in the optical printer so that the first frame becomes the last one when projected in the ordinary way. The effect on the screen is that the car seems to run right into the person.

This technique has many applications in the science field as can be seen in the examples on pages 150, 234 and 244.

Reverse action can also be effected by putting the camera on its head when shooting. This is cheaper than optical printing but not always feasible, and it is useless where parts of the same action are alternatively to be shown straight *and* in reverse. When filming with the camera in the upside-down position we must remember that the space allotted to the sound track will show as a black strip on the right side of the screen and that the picture area becomes correspondingly smaller. If this is undesirable, you have to reverse the gate where this is possible, or fit another one.

Optical printing

The optical printing department in the film laboratory has taken over much of the effects work which had to be done in the early years in the camera by means of fading devices and external gadgets. The first optical printers were home-made affairs used for routine transitional effects such as fades, dissolves and wipes, for certain kinds of superimposition, for reversing action and speed alterations.

The modern type of optical printer is a highly complicated commercially made piece of equipment (though often custom built) which is capable of producing every conceivable effect and many inconceivable ones. A new development is the aerial-image system which can combine optical printing and animation and widens the scope of optical effects technique still further.

Much optical imagery has now become so familiar to cinema audiences

Special Techniques

and TV viewers that the usual types of effect are hardly noticed by them. It is only when an audience sees something out of the ordinary on the screen such as people travelling on a magic carpet high above the ground that they become aware of some trickery. Many effects, real or phantasy, can still be dreamed up, and no film-maker can nowadays ignore the possibilities offered by the optical printer. The director of science films will often find in them a solution for a visual problem which could not, or not easily, be achieved by any other means.

The variety of optical effects is endless. They can be divided into those for which there exists standardized procedure and those which must be created, often for the first time, for a particular situation. The technician who is in charge of the optical printer is not only a skilled craftsman but, like a good cameraman, an artist with an inclination towards experimenting along unusual and untried lines.

The main categories of optical effects can be summed up as follows:

Transitions and image replacements of every description;
Speeding up, slowing down or reversing action, holding ('freezing') frames or eliminating unwanted sections of a scene as already described on previous pages;
Blowing up 16mm negative to 35mm or reducing 35mm to 16mm or 8mm;
Enlarging or reducing image size, repositioning part of the image for split-screen effects;
Superimpositions of live scenes on each other, combination of live scenes and art work (as in titling) or of live scenes and effects mattes (rain, snowfall, lightning, clouds, etc.);
Creating rotating, rocking, zooming images, caleidoscopic effects, distortions and image disintegration;
Blacking out a given area in an image (if this was not already done in the actual shooting) and filling this area with live action material, for instance in scenes containing TV sets;
Change of mood (day into night), adjusting colour and tonal values for matching adjoining scenes.

Some of the more elaborate effects, for instance those connected with travelling matte systems are, unfortunately, for financial reasons out of bounds for the short-film maker.

Preparation for optical printing

The instructions given to the laboratory relating to optical printing must be absolutely unambiguous. For standard effects it is sufficient to fill in the printed forms available from the laboratory. The film's edge numbers are of vital importance and should be double-checked on the instruction sheet.

When there are no clear edge numbers, the corresponding section of the cutting copy must be marked up and handed to the laboratory. This must also be done for multiple or otherwise complicated effects which should, in any case, be discussed with the head of the optical department. If a special effect is envisaged before shooting, the laboratory should be consulted in advance so that the cameraman can provide the most suitable negative.

A loss of photographic quality is sometimes inevitable, particularly when enlarging an image from, say, 16mm to 35mm. In such cases, a certain tolerance must be allowed for; the optical department can advise on this and perhaps suggest a short test. If much optical work is contemplated, it is best to use slow fine-grain stock for the principal photographic work. Reversal film is quite suitable.

Optical printing is expensive. Special effects may need time-devouring preparations and laboratory labour charges are high (there are no reduced rates for non-feature productions). In addition much material may have to be duplicated, re-printed and re-duped; the final optical negative of an intricate effect may be three or four steps removed from the originals. This material has to be paid for. Most laboratories have fixed rates for standard opticals such as fades and dissolves but these charges do *not* include printing the 'inter-material'. This is sometimes overlooked by film makers who get a shock when they get the bill. The cost of providing the interpositives and internegatives can be a multiple amount of that charged for the optical itself.

It is a wise precaution to arrange that only the *minimum* length of each original negative, necessary for an optical, should be used for the preparation of the intermediates. It is hardly worth bothering about short scenes but with scene lengths of 50 or 100 ft the saving can be considerable.

Some laboratories have devised auto-printing systems which saves printing and duping intermediate material for standard optical work. This involves, however, dividing each reel into A and B rolls, and the cost of the additional editing time, negative cutting and printing is correspondingly higher.

For special opticals, the charges are worked out on a time-plus-material basis and an approximate estimate should be obtained beforehand.

Although optical work is expensive, it can still work out cheaper than other methods such as special effects photography or animation. Also, optical printing is often the only possible method for obtaining a particular visual effect, or for remedying errors made during shooting; it can save a whole sequence from having to be reshot. A reasonable amount of money should therefore be set aside in the budget for optical work, whatever the film.

Models and scenic effects

Effects achieved by optical means do not exist in a tangible form, they manifest themselves only on the screen. There are, however, a great

Special Techniques

number of 'mechanical effects' which make use of *concrete* processes and devices. Such effects are not executed *in* the camera but *for* the camera. They are usually meant to simulate actual situations, from artificial cobwebs to intricate miniature or life-size-models of rockets and spaceships, from rain- and snow-effects to shipwrecks, earthquakes, explosions and other assorted natural or man-made catastrophies.

According to their nature, these mechanical devices and effects are filmed either by straightforward cinematography in the same way as any normal set or live subject, or they are combined with optical effects either in the camera during shooting (as by the Schüfftan process) or later by optical printing.

In feature production, the preparation and construction of mechanical effects is the responsibility of the special effects department or is subcontracted to units specializing in particular branches of effects photography. Out of the 1001 mechanical effects only few are of practical interest to the maker of factual and science films. Foremost amongst them are models because with these you can cut your coat according to your cloth; quite a few models and scenic effects can be produced with a few sheets of cardboard and some paint, or with the help of liquids and powders. But it needs somebody in the unit who has the dexterity and know-how to create something out of almost nothing.

A good reason for using models is that we are accustomed to seeing our world in three dimensions and that three-dimensional models are often more telling than animated diagrams. They convey a sense of reality to scenes showing objects or processes which, for one reason or other, cannot be filmed as they actually are.

Static models can be made more interesting—where this is practicable—by changing light effects or by putting them on a turntable so that they can be seen from all sides. Other models can be taken to pieces or assembled from parts, still others can be animated. Many models are in themselves mobile or they contain moving parts.

Models can be shown in isolation or as part of a set built around them. The possibilities are limitless.

In combination with certain camera effects, models can often replace animated diagrams in order to make *invisible* phenomena visible or to show complex action. Animated diagrams are perhaps more 'accurate' but if they are to be imaginatively executed and pictorially interesting, the cost is very high and usually beyond the means of a modest budget. If done on the cheap, animation can be very dull whilst a model sequence is usually not only less expensive but also more enjoyable to watch and often more informative. Take the 'Brownian Movement' for instance, that perpetual random motion of small particles in liquids or air. It can actually be filmed through a microscope but since this is a matter for experts, the choice for the ordinary factual film unit lies between an animated diagram and a three-dimensional model such as you find in science museums. These models are fascinating and leave a stronger impression than animated drawings.

Vibration in musical instruments is another example. The paragraph 'V for Vibration' (page 145) shows how convincingly this phenomenon could be demonstrated by the simplest and cheapest type of model.

Models can be divided into three categories:

(*a*) objects which are mass-produced and are available from stores or direct from the manufacturer;

(*b*) models which had once been made for an exhibition or for some other purpose, often as a prototype for a particular project, and since then stowed away in some showroom or museum. Models of this kind are either discovered by sheer good luck or by wearisome investigation;

(*c*) those specially made for the film in hand, either by members of the unit or by a professional model-maker.

FIG. 36. A 3 ft high engineering model of the radio-telescope in Jodrell Bank, shot against a moving cloud background. It was necessary to resort to a model scene because at the time of filming the actual radio-telescope was not yet completed.
Still from the film: *Mirror in the Sky*.

Models of every type are of greatest importance in the making of science films. A diversity of models is shown in many of the following illustrations.

Engineering and Architectural models

Technical and engineering models are either full-size or smaller, made to scale. Examples are mentioned on pages 78 and 102. Generally speak-

Special Techniques

ing, the larger a model is, the easier it is to handle. Very small models, such as miniature cars and trains, should not be filmed in a big close-up because various factors combine to make such BCU shots unattractive. Particular attention must be paid to the *movement* of such miniature models. Frank P. Clark* gives precise formulas for working out the size-and-motion relationship where movement is involved. The gist of it is that the speed of a miniature car or train, moving over a given distance, must be transposed from miles per hour to feet per second in order that real speed and screen speed correspond. Clark, using a conversion factor of 1·4667, calculates that a car of 1/12th the real size will have to move about 4 ft per sec in order to simulate a speed of 35 m.p.h. of the full-size vehicle.

Not every kind of motion in or of models can be calculated by such a given formula. The general practice is to film all moving small-scale models by over-running the camera so that a slight slow-motion effect is obtained which makes the movement appear more realistic. This applies also to models in the process of collapse (houses, bridges, etc.) or to free-falling objects. The degree of over-running must be determined by the effect wanted. If the film-maker lacks experience in this field, a certain amount of experimenting is unavoidable.

Architectural models belong to category (b) mentioned above; they can certainly not be bought in shops. If you need a precision-made model of a single building or of a housing estate to illustrate a general point, you must try to borrow one from an architect, a building firm or a town council which commissions buildings on a large scale. For any particular purpose, architectural models have to be made to specifications; they are very expensive and should only be considered if they can be used for a long sequence or repeatedly at various points of a film in combination with special effects.

Architectural models can sometimes be built in false perspective to heighten their effectiveness (see page 31).

Scientific models

Anatomical models are made of plastic or Perspex. Most models of the human body or of organs such as the eye or the ear, can usually be taken completely apart but they are not very suitable to demonstrate those organs' actions or motions. For the film *Science In The Orchestra*, a special large-size model of the inner ear had to be built to show the movements of the ear drum and of the three little bones behind it (Fig. 75). It depends on the purpose and depth of the demonstration whether ready-made anatomical models can be used.

Human skeletons are nowadays also made of plastic. They can be

---

* Frank P. Clark *Special Effects in Motion Pictures*, published by the Society of Motion Picture and TV Engineers Inc., New York 10017. This book is mainly concerned with mechanical effects.

THE WORK OF THE SCIENCE FILM MAKER

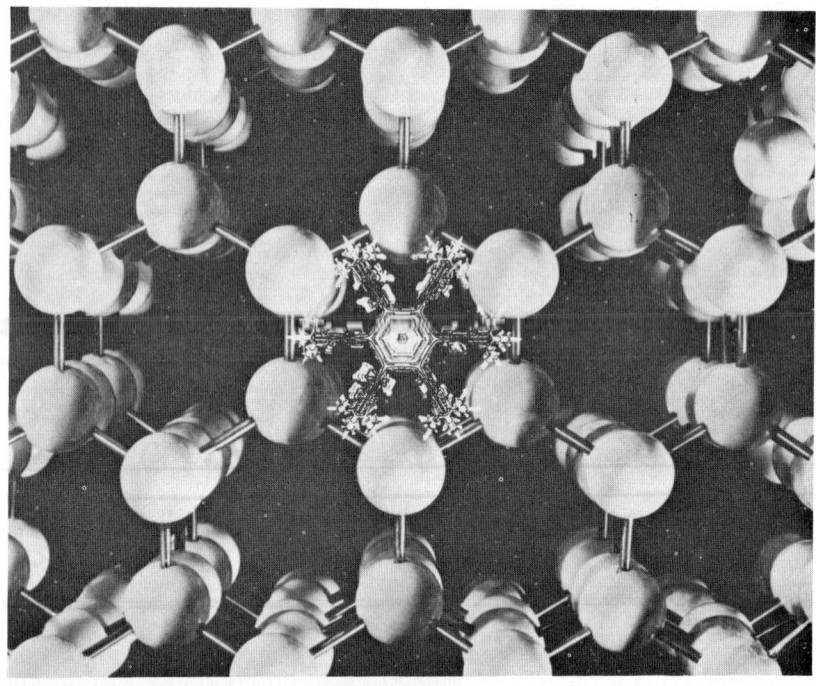

FIG. 37. *Molecular Model.* (above): A crystal lattice type model of an ice molecule (see also Fig. 18). From the film: *Physics and Chemistry of Water.*

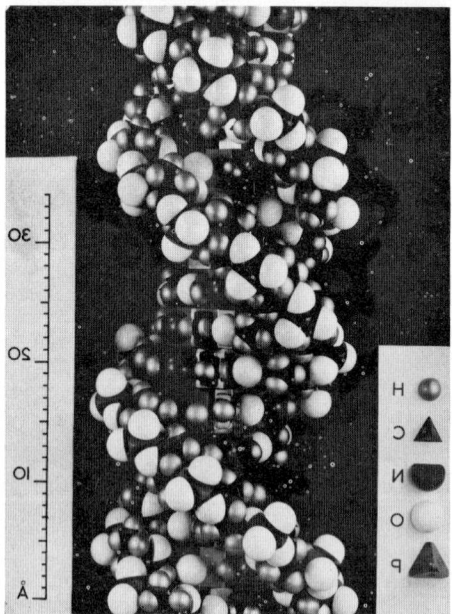

FIG. 38. (left): A Colette type model of the DNA molecule. From the film: *Electro-Magnetic Waves.*

Special Techniques

taken apart for the demonstration of single bones and of joint-movements. But being the wobbly and dangling things they are, full-figure skeletons cannot be properly animated by means of wires or threads, certainly not without long preparations and an army of assistants.

Molecular models are either of the Calotte type or of the Crystal Lattice variety. Both use coloured spheres for the atoms. The first represent the spatial arrangements of atoms in molecules of chemical compounds. The second show the geometry of molecular (crystal) lattices. Here the spheres are connected by metal rods and the latticed structure can be recognized at a glance. Both types are very rigid and can easily be held in place by clamps, etc., for single-frame filming. These models can be assembled to form complicated molecules such as that of myoglobin or ice (Figs 18, 37) or of a giant molecular chain like DNA (Fig. 38).

Rigid lattice models can be made flexible by using spiral springs instead of metal rods. In the ICI Millbank film *The Second Law of Thermodynamics*, Professor George Porter demonstrates the 'State of Disorder' by whirling such a model around in his hands so that the spheres execute a wild chaotic dance.

Mathematical models can also be assembled and taken apart. They are made of Perspex and so they can become troublesome because of reflections. A pola screen may help to reduce these.

Quite a number of toys can be used as models, whether naturalistic or stylized. To mention just a few: balls, tops, hoops, building bricks and all sorts of mechanical toys from prams to bulldozers and fire engines. Scenery can be built up with the help of farm buildings, dolls' houses, petrol stations, traffic signs, etc. Puppets and articulated figures designed for the use of artists may come in handy. In the right context, any of these things can lend atmosphere or put a scientific fact over. It was with a simple child's kite that Benjamin Franklin proved the electric nature of lightning, and scientists lecturing at the Royal Institution often use toys and everyday objects if, through them, they can illuminate a certain point.

Do-it-yourself and commissioned models

Later in the book actual case histories where such models were used are discussed and illustrated in detail. Information here, therefore, is of a more general nature and should be regarded as a preliminary to the following chapters.

One feature which purpose-built models and animated diagrams have in common is that you have the freedom—within the possibilities of the chosen medium and the budget—to do what you like. The first thing is to decide about the nature of the model in its basic form, then to look at it from a practical viewpoint. Must it be entrusted to a professional model maker or can you make it yourselves? The answer depends on the talent and facilities available within the unit and whether it is financially worthwhile

The Work of the Science Film Maker

Figs. 39, 40 and 41. *Do-It-Yourself Models.* (left): These simple 'models' were devised to emphasize pictorially the necessity for regular meal times. The clock motive was used to time the stages from the start of cooking to that of the meal.

Fig. 42. (opposite): An actor is made up for his role as the face of a grandfather clock to call out the meal time. From the film: *Your Children's Meals*

to spend your own time on model-making. Often it is. And if the talent of a member of the unit lies in a particular field, be it metal work, woodwork, electrical work or a knowledge of chemicals, you would naturally try to adjust the basic idea to the skill of this particular person. Often, a freelance artist can be engaged on a fee basis. To keep model-making within the unit is particularly useful when the models have to be manipulated or touched up during shooting.

Special Techniques

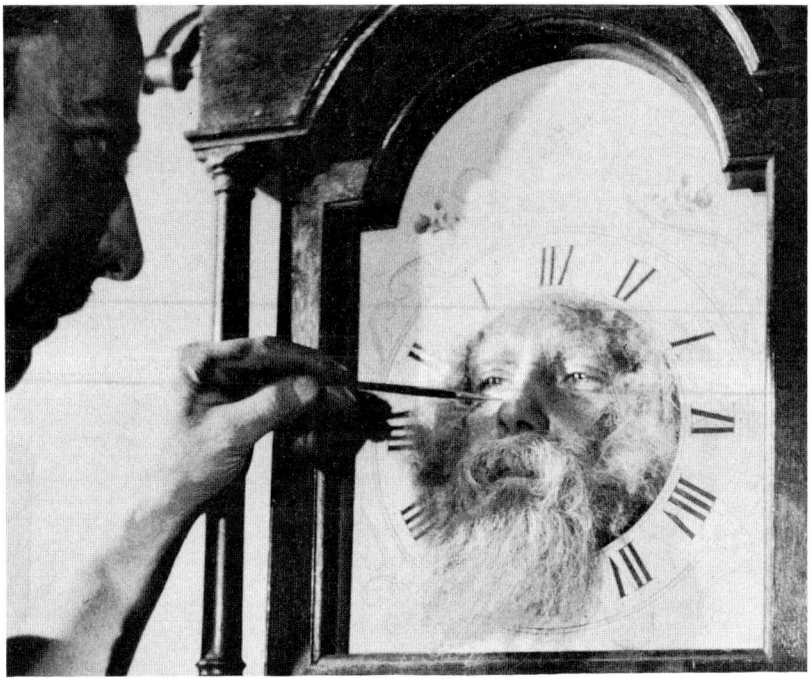

Unit-produced models

The following examples describe some models of the kind that have been made by film unit personnel.

In my film *Your Children's Meals*, commissioned by the Central Office of Information on the subject of children's health for the guidance of mothers, a sequence stresses the importance of the regularity of meal times. A 'clock-motive' puts this point over in a light-hearted way. Figs 39–42 show that the lids of pots and pans and the plates were made up as clock-dials. A grandfather clock with an actor's face within the dial called out the hours, and finally a family of twelve was sitting at a round table, the scene itself now forming a clock pattern. This was an easy piece of 'model-making' requiring only some good lettering.

In another film, the effects of the sun's radiation on glass houses was explained. As the film had to be produced at an unfavourable time of the year, a scale model of a section of a glass house was built with flower pots in corresponding size. This scene dissolved into itself with plants now seen fully grown (Figs 43, 44). The plants were made up from artificial flower material. The scenes were shot in reversed order because removing the plants from the pots was less likely to disturb the set than putting them in.

In a Gas Council film about air pollution, a smoky townscape was needed as a background for the titles which were drawn on glass. A reality

The Work of the Science Film Maker

Special Techniques

shot was undesirable because there were already too many in the film. What was wanted was a dramatically stylized scene symbolizing the threat of illness caused by the polluted air which hangs over every industrial community. Thus, a set was built with three-dimensional rooftops and chimney-pots for the foreground and a cut-out town silhouette for the background. Some of the chimneys were joined to tubes at the back so that smoke could be blown into them which then poured out of the chimneys. The dramatic character of the shot was intensified by making it a night scene. A dark effect was in any case necessary to make the white lettering of the superimposed titles stand out well. (Fig. 45)

With work of this type, it is very important to have a good knowledge of the nearest sources from which to obtain the necessary materials such as display items, wood of all kinds (not to forget balsa wood), cardboard, stationery articles, glass, plastics, slotted angle iron and other metal parts, polystyrene in all its forms, cloth, string and cotton threads, wire, chemicals, electrical gadgets, plasticine, etc. A good assortment of tools is a matter of course. A little knowledge of display methods is a great advantage and you should keep yourself up to date by visiting appropriate exhibitions, design-centres, showrooms and department stores, by studying window displays and last, but not least, by watching other people's films which contain models and effects.

Professionally-made models

There are many types of model which you cannot possibly attempt to make yourself and which have to be commissioned from professional model makers or artists, from specialists such as glass blowers, scientific instrument makers, precision engineering works or makers of architectural models. Also, sometimes models are too big to be made in the unit's own workshop. An example is the 'giant stave', illustrated on page 158. Large relief maps also belong to this category as well as mock-up sets of historic or modern scientific apparatus. The presence of an expert adviser during shooting is often required for supervising the proper working of such models.

If you have not had previous dealings with individuals or firms specializing in the type of work you need, it is worthwhile shopping around. One supplier can be twice as expensive as another for exactly the same model or product. Also, it is advisable to visit these people in their place of business and not to let them come to your own office. The condition of their workshops is often, though not always, a tell-tale sign of what you can expect.

FIG. 43. (opposite top): Model of the section of a glass house with artificial tomato plants to show the effects of the sun's radiation. The pots with the seeds dissolve into the figure below.

FIG. 44. (opposite bottom): the same pots with the fully grown plants. Models instead of reality scenes had to be used because the film, as often happens, had to be shot at the wrong season.

From the film: *Radiation* (page 182).

THE WORK OF THE SCIENCE FILM MAKER

FIG. 45. (above): Model of a typically Dickensian roof-top scene with smoking chimneys, which was used as a title background to introduce the theme of air pollution.
From the film: *Window to the Sky*.

You also gain an impression of the existing facilities and attitudes. It is of the utmost importance to get full understanding and co-operation from a subcontractor.

Once you are satisfied that you are in good hands, then you must give the model maker every chance to make a good job by providing him with written specifications, including a colour scheme. Illustrations copied from books and exhibits in museums or showrooms can give valuable guidance to a model maker. He must also be told whether special effects will be used in connection with the models because that may require quite a different technical approach on his part. He should send a preliminary sketch along with his quotation. When you have approved the sketch and the work has been taken in hand, you should not ask for alterations unless it is vital and you must be prepared to pay for them. With intricate models, inspection of intermediate stages is advisable.

Model-making is an art and craft like any other in which the personal handwriting of the artist must be acknowledged. You should not be disappointed, if the end result does not quite conform to your own ideas. As long as a model is functionally satisfactory and of pleasant appearance, all is well.

Special Techniques

The animation of models and simulated animation effects are discussed on pages 128–130.

Atmospheric effects

Rain, snow, fog, etc., are often required for scenic effect. In the big studios, they are produced by special machinery. In connection with table top sets, the problem is one of bringing such effects into proper proportion to the small set and controlling them. A natural raindrop would look much oversized in a miniature set. For a *rain* effect, a very fine water spray must be used and lit from behind. Some water should be seen dripping from objects in the foreground; a trough with tiny holes, fitted above these objects, will do the trick. Although models, used in successive scenes, should normally be of the same scale, it might be possible to add a realistic touch to a model sequence by inserting a CU of say, an actual puddle or a dripping branch.

Snow lying on the ground or clinging to house walls, etc., can be simulated by various means; common salt-and-plaster or artificial snow sprayed from aerosol cans are satisfactory for small sets; for bigger ones finely ground polystyrene can be recommended. Factories in which polystyrene sheets are cut to size, produce heaps of waste in the form of chips and powder which is there for the taking. *Snowfall* can be produced by sifting such finely ground chips through a sieve above the set; a fan intensifies the effect by blowing the flakes slantwise. Falling snow should be lit from the front, otherwise the flakes appear dark.

Fog can vary from a slight mist to a 'pea souper'. Fog filters can simulate these conditions but they have their disadvantages (page 87). There are again various methods for producing fog mechanically for small sets, such as dry ice (solid carbon dioxide) for white mist to smoke, or vapourized oily liquids for the denser varieties. The problem is not so much to create the fog as to keep it suspended in or over the set without motion. The slightest draught, even the movement of persons, may agitate the vapour and destroy the illusion wanted. It may help to enclose the set between glass sheets. You have to work rather quickly because the layers of dry ice or smoke remain only for a short time.

Smoke is not only used for scenic effect but just as often for making scientific phenomena visible. For instance, smoke boxes are used to study the behaviour of light rays (page 183). The National Physical Laboratory in their film *River to Cross* used smoke to represent the wind currents blown against a model of the Severn Bridge. In the film *Convection*, smoke was used to show the ventilation of rooms and coal mines (page 174).

Smoke is easy to produce by means of cigarettes, smoke candles, smouldering rags soaked in saltpetre, smoke machines, etc., but it can be an awkward medium to control if applied to a specific condition. We may need static smoke, drifting smoke, rising smoke, whirling smoke;

smoke *above* small sets or smoke confined *within* glass boxes or tubes for demonstrations. Some experimentation is almost unavoidable.

Flames, particularly gas flames, can be made brighter by sprinkling lycopodium powder on to the rim of the burner. For a blue flame effect, cupric chloride can be used. To make things burn brightly, wood alcohol and paraffin wax is recommended.

Flow phenomena in liquids, though not strictly atmospheric in character, should be mentioned in connection with lycopodium powder. (There is now an artifical variety available which is much cheaper.) This substance produces good streak effects in water. Other means are oak dust and potassium permanganate (see also page 172). The last-mentioned chemical can be sprinkled into a water tank and will sink slowly to the bottom. With the camera turned upside down, the effect is reversed: the powder particles appear to rise to the surface simulating a convection current.

All these and other methods of producing atmospheric effects are described in greater detail in Frank P. Clark's book, mentioned on page 103.

Fig. 46. *Graphic Symbols*. Great play can be made with animated letters and graphic symbols to enliven stodgy mathematical, financial or scientific concepts. An example of such a graphic technique is shown. This type of effect can only be fully appreciated on the screen in animation. (See also Fig. 149).
Still from the film: *Money Talks* (Midland Bank).

Special Techniques

Graphics and symbols

Charts, diagrams, maps and other graphic material is often an integral part of a factual film. The requirements for static art work are simple: it should be clear and well designed, with bold lines, large lettering and good colour contrast. The same applies to titles. You always have to keep in mind the conditions under which many films are shown: on badly reflecting small screens in insufficiently blacked-out rooms or halls by unsteady projectors. What makes a marvellous visual on a good cinema screen may be quite unacceptable in 16mm and 8mm projection or on TV screens. Text should be terse and the lettering well within the area of the *projected* image; most sub-standard projectors cut off part of the picture near the edges and, with it, often parts of the words. The shots should be kept long enough on the screen for the content to be taken in but not so long that the audience gets bored. Some film makers regard graphics as a cheap means to illustrate a lengthy commentary. This method should be discouraged. When the commentary requires a long written explanation, such as a formula or an equation, it is better to use a blackboard and write the words or draw the graphs while shooting the scene in step with the commentary.

For self-drawing graphs and diagrams and for animated lettering see pages 119, 122 and 129–30.

Graphic symbols play a prominent part in films. According to their nature, they can be divided into those which form part of the language of science, those common in animation, and those which are specially devised for a particular purpose.

The symbols, signs and formulae used in technology and science are shorthand notations. They are understood by members of the same discipline all over the world. The use of these symbols is essential in films which have to explain a given science subject in the shortest possible time to the widest specialized audiences. A teaching film about electronics could not be made without resort to the graphic symbols used for valves, tubes and circuits. Simple mathematical symbols and those of weight, measures and money are familiar to every man, woman and child in the land.

Many symbols and glyphs used in certain spheres of interest are still not internationally recognized and a UN committee has been set up trying to standardize all glyphs so that their adoption becomes world-wide.

What makes symbols in films different from symbols in textbooks is that they can be made to move. An example of the animation of symbols representing chemical elements is illustrated on page 236 describing Rutherford's first atom-splitting experiments. By no other means could the transmutation of nitrogen into oxygen have been shown as briefly and convincingly. Countless other examples spring to mind.

The use of symbols is not restricted to science subjects. The Midland Bank made a series of advertising filmlets which were shown in cinemas to

The Work of the Science Film Maker

promote the bank's Personal Cheque Scheme. They consisted of simple word-play in which the symbols for money (£sd) were animated to form amusing word patterns (Fig. 46). Ordinary letters were also transposed into symbols for cars, trains, bridges and tunnels; they were used to form and re-form words associated with saving, spending and other money transactions. All these effects were filmically brilliant but cannot be described by words or by static illustrations. It was one of the producers' biggest problems to convey their idea to the sponsors. Eventually they decided 'to show the visuals on slides with persons describing the action of the words and producing the associated sounds by "home-made" effects'. These highly amusing filmlets gained many festival awards.

Symbols as a code

The last group of symbols uses familiar objects, substances and situations to stand in for unfamiliar ones. Abstract ideas can also be expressed by them. A red signal is not only an order for traffic to stop but is the general symbol for danger. Victory over an adversary is often symbolized in films by the time-worn device of showing a chessboard with a hand making the checkmate move.

In science, symbols of this type can act as a code. The film *Distillation*, made by the Shell Film Unit, makes brilliant use of playing cards to show the separation of hydrocarbons in crude oil. Here is a short extract from the post-production script:

DISTILLATION (*Extract*)

35mm footage	Picture	Sound (*Narration*)
655	Move down a row of playing-cards arranged numerically in suits.	The range of hydrocarbons is rather like the range of cards in a pack . . . from one to fifty-two . . .
665	Dissolve to cards moving about, shuffled together.	. . . but all shuffled up together.— Instead of isolating . . .
	At 671 one card becomes stationary, while the rest continue to move.	. . . each hydrocarbon. . .
	678 Stationary card starts to move with the rest	. . . for our main products we separate only . . .
681	Three complete, separate suits appear	. . . groups of hydrocarbons whose boiling points are ranged together. These groups are called 'fractions' We can suppose that the first fraction is from the Ace to the King of Spades.'

Special Techniques

35mm footage	*Picture*	*Sound (Narration)*
		The next fraction, all boiling at points above the first, may be represented by the Ace to the King of Hearts. And so on.
	Dissolve to:	We can see . . .
755	Drawing of bench-stills	. . . how distillation can split up crude oil into these fractions, if we look at these rather old-fashioned bench-stills.
977	Move quickly in to show vapours rising through tray. Dissolve in bubble-cap and the bubbles of vapour can be seen passing through the condensed fraction of the tray.	Caps called 'bubble caps' force the rising vapours to bubble through the liquid in the trays. Let us go back to the cards.
997	The liquid and vapours dissolve into playing cards.	
999	Tray and bubble cap fade out, leaving playing cards only. The cards in the tray are with one exception—Spades.	Any hydrocarbon in the tray which ought not to be there . . .
1009	The exception, a Diamond, is circled. Diamonds, representing hot vapours, pass through the Spades, and one 'carries' with it the circled card.	. . . is boiled off by the hot vapours passing through . . .
1024	Tray and bubble-cap fade in, and liquid and vapours, as before.	
1031	The tray, bubble-cap, liquids and vapours dissolve back to the cards.	
1043	A Spade card, circled, rises up with other cards. As they all pass through the 'liquid', the other cards go on, but the circled card remains in the tray.	. . . while any hydrocarbon in the vapours which ought not to be there, is condensed in the tray by the cooler liquid.
1049	Cards dissolve back to tray with liquid and rising vapours, as before.	
1056	Sectional drawing of entire fractionating tower with oil being heated, vapours rising and condensed fractions collecting on trays.	

The film (between 755 and 977) demonstrates in live scenes and animation the process of distillation and the vaporization of the crude oil in the fractionating tower of the refinery. As the vapours pass up the tower, they cool and trays catch the various fractions as they turn into liquids. Only the lightest fraction of all remains as vapour. This is drawn off and condensed separately. The trays help to separate the fractions by their construction.

The film ends by referring to the products resulting from the distillation process. This film was first made in 1940 and was recently re-made in colour. It shows that films dealing with principles can retain their value for decades.

Animation

The creation of movement by stop motion (single-frame) photography has established itself as an indispensable technique in the field of the factual film. There is hardly a technological or science film made to-day which does not contain one or several animation sequences. Many instructional films, up to 5 or 6 reels, consist entirely of animation.

There are several reasons for the breakthrough in this medium. One of them is the rapid cine-technical progress in recent years; there is now such a variety of animation methods available that any degree of simplicity or sophistication can be attained from a simple line diagram to the complicated figurative multi-layer cartoon. Almost the only feature which animation lacks is the third dimension. Another drawback is the cost: good animation must, of necessity, be expensive.

Many hidden or invisible mechanisms, processes and phenomena can be made visible, explained and analysed in simplified, time-saving and often amusing terms. Aesthetically, there is complete freedom of expression in form, colour, movement and speed. Thus, the animation sequences can adapt themselves easily to the style of the live part of the film. Timing is accurate: animation can synchronize perfectly with the wording of the commentary or the rhythym of the music.

The language of animation makes intensive use of symbols, of visual conventions derived from static drawings and strip-cartoons. The best-known of these are the speed-lines attached to a person, animal or vehicle to suggest a quick get-away or a lightning dash across the screen. Other such conventions are 'squash' and 'drag' used to represent physical force and inertia. 'Squash' is a squeeze, which compresses a figure or shape for several frames to convey an impression of weight or force. 'Drag' is another impressionistic effect. In reality a person walking against a stiff wind bends forward. In animation, a similar bending of a figure or an object, but in a reversed form (centre leading, ends dragging), stresses the reluctance to overcome inertia. The bow-shape also helps to prevent jitter. Halation and

Special Techniques

flashing effects have similar symbolic functions. All these graphic features, together with the various kinds of distortions, exaggerations and simplifications form the mainspring of cartoon reality. Without them, the animated figurative film would be lifeless. The animated technical diagram naturally offers fewer opportunities for the use of these symbols but even here the degree of skill and imagination to which the conventions of animation are exploited decide whether the result will be forceful and interesting or pedestrian and boring.

Film audiences are no longer conscious of these symbolic effects; they have been conditioned to them as they were conditioned to the conventions of the film language in general. But the people working on the creative side of animation have to know the exact significance and nuance of every symbol and convention used in this medium if their work is to be articulate and effective.

Every film maker who considers the inclusion of animation in his film, must have some basic knowledge of the principles and techniques which are involved. John Halas's book* provides detailed information on every aspect of this topic. As with model work, quite a few forms of animation can be carried out by a non-specialist film unit, time and talent permitting. In order to come to a decision on this point, it is best to examine first those categories which can *not* be done by such a unit.

Graphics

All graphic work, whether in the form of diagrams or cartoons, is nowadays animated by means of cells.† Cells are transparent plastic sheets on which the drawings are made. Cell-animation is precision work of the highest degree, and the preparation, handling and photography of these cells requires a specialist team: producer, director, designer, lay-out man, animators, tracers, checkers and cameramen. Several functions are sometimes combined in one person but even a small animation unit consists of six or eight artists and technicians. All these people need specialized and expensive work benches, rostrums and cameras. The electronically

---

* John Halas and Roger Manvell *The Technique of Film Animation*, London: Focal Press.

† We must disregard here the type of animation in which the images are painted directly on to the film. This technique was developed long ago by Len Lye in England when he made his famous Post Office trailers; to-day, Norman McClaren in Canada is the undisputed master in this field. The visuals of such films are purely abstract and this technique lends itself, therefore, mainly to art films: for instance, to bring abstract painting to life or to express music. Films of this type have been commissioned by commercial organizations for publicity purposes.

What is interesting from our point of view is that McClaren often leaves one or two blank frames between the drawings on the film. In this way, he saves himself a considerable amount of time and trouble, letting the brain of the viewer do the work of connecting the painted patterns so that they form flowing and continuous motion. The eyes' persistence of vision is instrumental in bringing about this effect.

The Work of the Science Film Maker

controlled Oxberry Aerial Image Animation Camera provides enormous versatility in the relationship between lens, camera, animation board and back-projection devices, making it possible, amongst other effects, to superimpose graphic material in the process of animation over existing live action scenes on the rostrum without the need for optical printing. But even less ambitious work requires skill, experience and equipment far beyond that available to a unit which is mainly concerned with live photography.

It follows that all graphic animation work, with a few simple exceptions to be discussed later, must be handed over to an animation unit whenever professional finish and quality are required.

Commissioning animation

The procedure to be adopted for commissioning animation work resembles that described on page 109 in connection with models, but it has to go further because animation involves the dimension of time. Exact timing is essential. Good liaison between the film director and the producer of the animation unit—call him the 'animator'—is therefore of greatest importance.

The sort of information an animator requires is shown on pages 175–9 but this has to be preceded by a personal discussion about style, lay-out, cost and other points. The opinion and advice of the animator should be sought. He might be able to suggest better and cheaper ways of doing things. Generally, all cartoon work, requiring several cell layers for fore-, middle- and back-ground, and all work with figures or shapes which recede, advance, bend, turn and whirl is much more complicated and therefore much more expensive than diagrammatic line work done in a single plane and with sideways movement only.

The animator should be given the relevant part of the script to read, and if the live scenes, adjoining the animation sequence, have already been filmed, they should be shown to him. Rough sketches, blueprints or diagrams, either existing or specially prepared with the assistance of the technical adviser, should be enclosed with the instructions. With complicated work, it is advisable to put the work in hand as early as possible because any but the simplest kind of animation takes time.

Cost of animation

The cost of animation is based on the commissioned footage but it varies with the intricacy of the job. It is usual to order the finally required footage in finished form. Therefore, all editing and optical work is done by the animation unit. The only drawback of this procedure is that it leaves no margin for small adjustments in length found necessary when the animation is cut into the film. To be on the safe side, each scene in the animation sequence which is static or shows repetitive action, should have

Special Techniques

one or two feet added for 'juggling'. This extra footage is usually supplied by the animator at a nominal charge. In the case of a 100 ft edited sequence, the actual length will probably be between 110 and 120 ft.

As a first step, the animator produces a storyboard showing drawings of the key situations. This should be approved by the technical adviser. Animation tests are often made as the next stage. The greatest dangers in animation are strobing, jitter or focusing defects, and since these cannot easily be detected on a Moviola, the tests should be viewed on a proper screen. The presence of the technical adviser is again desirable: he may find some movement too rapid or too slow and now is the time for corrections. The rough cut of the finished diagram should be viewed immediately after completion and shown to both the adviser and the sponsor to forestall any future arguments. It is, by the way, very rare that an animated sequence has gone so completely wrong that it has to be done all over again. There may be one or the other detail which looked all right on the story-board but seems odd when animated. Usually, such a defect can be put right by replacing the offending part by a close-up insert which has, of course, to be paid for if the defect was not the animator's fault.

Do-it-yourself methods

What type of animation can be tackled by a non-animation unit? We said that *most* graphic animation is out of the question. So what remains?

Lines and graphs which draw themselves can be done by one of two methods. One method will be described later in its proper context (pages 129–30), the other is to draw the *complete* line or graph with a white or yellow grease pencil on a glass sheet or on a cell fixed rigidly upside down in front of an evenly lit dark-coloured (or unlit) background and then erasing the line bit by bit, photographing each stage by the single-frame method. Reversing the negative before printing will make the line appear to draw itself. Similar effects can be done with words writing themselves, with symbols appearing and disappearing, etc. How much you have to erase each time depends on the size of the cell or glass, on the length of the line or graph and on the time in which it is supposed to grow to its full length. If a line is 60 cm long, removing 5 mm between each exposure produces a take of 5 sec. Shooting every frame twice, which will still ensure smooth movement, makes the scene 10 sec long.

For such work a single-frame camera is needed, with a frame-counter and preferably a wire release, and some sort of rostrum or bench on which camera and object can be rigidly positioned.

A rostrum on which the camera shoots *vertically* downwards, has the advantage that the drawings can be made on the glass or cell as you would normally do them on a drawing board. The disadvantage is that both the distance from camera to object and the size of the cells are limited: the maximum field of view is usually 12 × 15 in. (Fig. 47)

119

A *horizontal* bench with a sliding device for the camera has the advantage that it can be used for many other purposes such as for filming models, charts, maps, magnetic boards, etc., of all sizes, and also a number of effects which require tracking. The usual commercial type of bench (called 'titler') is as limited as regards object size and movement as a rostrum. It is better to construct such a bench to suit your own requirements (Fig. 48).

The main point is that the camera must be in true alignment with the centre of the vertically fixed glass sheet, cell or board and the cradle on which the camera is mounted must slide easily and without jerks if you want to track with a continuously running camera. A worm-gear device with a handle for manual operation or with a gear-wheel connected to a motor can assure smooth movement. Absolute rigidity of all parts is essential.*

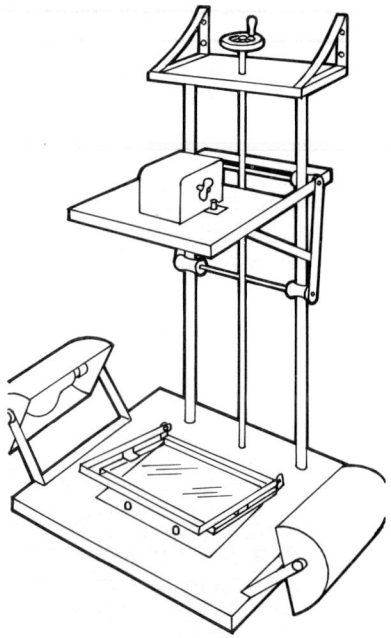

FIG. 47. *Simple Vertical Animation- and Title-Rostrum.* The camera is mounted on a sliding platform. The metal bracket on the bottom board engages with the register pins. All drawings or cells must have corresponding holes so that their accurate positioning is ensured. The metal frame contains a glass sheet which acts as a pressure pad. The two lamps at the sides provide even illumination; they can be connected to a dimmer for fades and mixes. There are various models of such animation tables on the market.

---

* Some people may be sceptical of the usefulness of home-made equipment. They may be interested in what a newspaper reporter wrote about the outfit used by Oliver Postgate, the creator of the well-known *Pogle* puppet films: 'He is loath to buy what can, with a little

Special Techniques

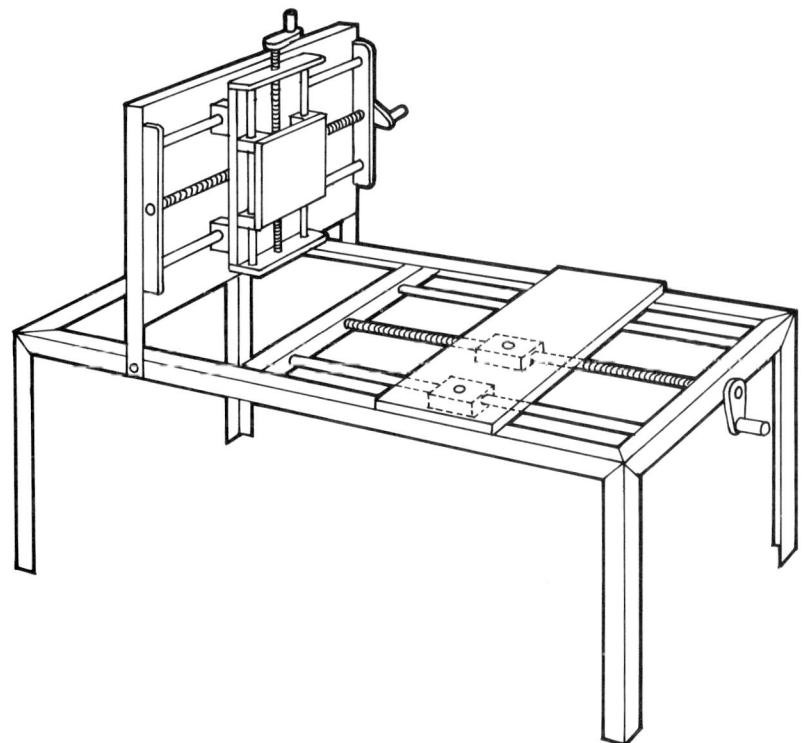

FIG. 48. *Horizontal Animation-, Title- and Effects-Bench.* This was constructed in our unit's own workshop from angle iron, metal rods, worms, handles and boards of wood. Measurements of the bench frame: 6 ft × 2 ft 6 in. × 2 ft. The camera is screwed on to the camera platform which can be wound forwards and backwards. The board on which art work is mounted can be moved horizontally, vertically or diagonally. The whole upper structure with the board can easily be taken off to allow three-dimensional models to be shot.

Titles

Professional title makers have benches with various refinements but a self-made bench as described is very suitable for simple work. The title card can be any size: small with type-written wording or large for stylized lettering. The easiest way, perhaps, is to use self adhesive transfer letters such as Letraset. To line up the titles so that the lines are absolutely horizontal and parallel with both the upper and lower edge of the frame is a little tricky; they always seem to slant one way or the other. It is advisable to prepare a 'lining-up chart' the size of the title cards with many parallel, vertical and diagonal lines which ensures that you can line up the camera

---

ingenuity, be made. An animation table constructed from odds and ends, including parts of a bicycle, a tape measure and an assortment of shop-window lights loomed up in a corner. . . . It cost about £70 to build against £5000 to buy one, and in spite of the appearance, it works. Proof is the production of one successful TV series after another.'

The Work of the Science Film Maker

squarely and quite vertically. Kodak focusing boards are suitable but they are only available in one size.

Animated titles can either be written and erased bit by bit by the method described before, or letters made from plastic, cork, wood or metal can be 'jumped' in one by one. Again, it is easier to line up the full title first and then jump the letters out. This must be done on a rostrum with the title card in a horizontal position; if a magnetic board is used to which the letters stick, a horizontal bench is satisfactory.

A magnetic board is a very useful piece of equipment to have around the studio, it permits all sorts of effects, including flat-figure animation. Figure animation is usually a matter for an animation unit; for a short scene, however, an articulated figure, 8 in to 10 in high, made of cardboard, can be manipulated by any sufficiently dexterous person. Small metal discs fitted to the back of each part of the figure's body, will keep it in any desired position on the magnetic board, even if this is covered with thin paper on which a scenic background is painted or drawn. A little crudeness in the movement does not really matter as long as the effect as a whole does not look amateurish; it can even heighten the visual attractiveness as evidenced by the charming silhouette films of Lotte Reiniger.

Fig. 49. A sectionized model of a skyscraper (about 5 ft high) which erects itself on the screen in rapid jumps. See Fig. 50 for details of its construction.
From the film: *High Speed Building*.

Special Techniques

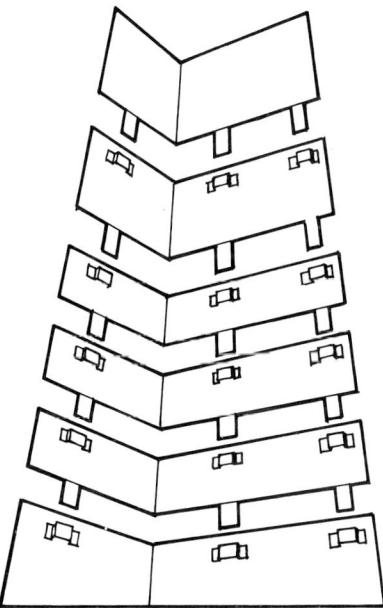

Fig. 50. *Model Construction.* This drawing shows the back of the cut-out model illustrated in Fig. 49 and the simple provision for sliding the six sections apart or together. (See pages 125–6)

Jump animation

Quite a different type of animation is the jump- or bump-technique. The 'action stills', often seen on TV, are a good example. The idea is based on the strip cartoon, and an action-stills series resembles the storyboard for an animated cartoon sequence. The key situations of the story are photographed with a still camera or drawn in cartoon form. Under the title: 'Rush Hour', for instance, a man is shown leaving his house; next, he has joined a bus queue; next, the queue is now twice as long; next, a bus passes by without stopping; next, the man is inside a bus squeezed-in amongst the crowd; next, he stands on the station platform with his train just disappearing, and so on and on until he finally is seen sitting dishevelled and exhausted at his office desk.

The stills are filmed, one after the other, about 2–3 ft at a time, but probably cut shorter in the editing and the result is a sort of film strip projected as a film. The above example could be a rapid and effective introduction to a film about traffic problems in big cities.

The bump technique is suitable for many varied ideas or facts which have to be put over quickly. Here are two more examples:

In a film which I made about modern building-methods, a short sequence had to imply the great speed with which buildings can be erected

The Work of the Science Film Maker

Special Techniques

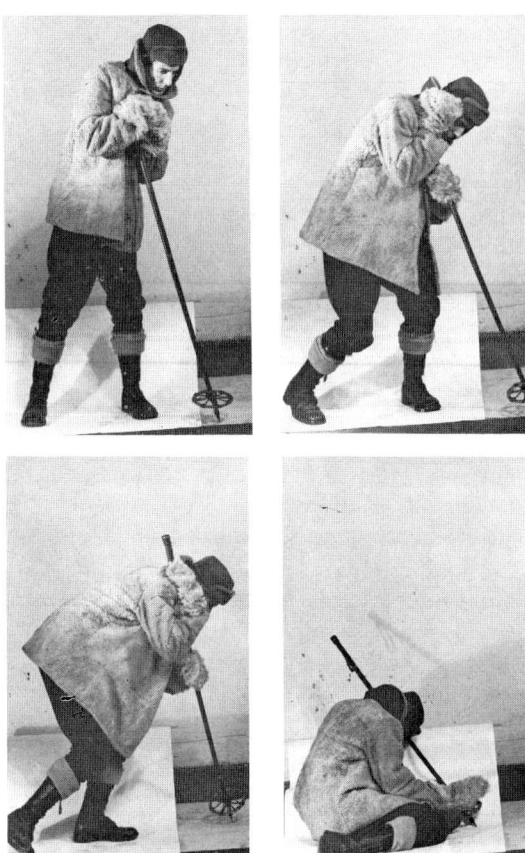

FIGS. 53, 54, 55 and 56 (above): Stages of the explorer's collapse (page 113). From the film: *Creatures of Comfort* (Gas Council).
Bump Technique. These figures, cut out from photographs of a dressed-up actor, were used on a table-top set to show the explorer's collapse and death as described in the text (page 126).
FIG. 51. (opposite top): An actual film frame: the explorer in an arctic blizzard.
FIG. 52. (opposite bottom): The insert of the thermometer shows that his body temperature is far below normal.

by means of pre-fabricated wall units. The sponsor wanted a symbolic, yet fairly naturalistic effect of a building going up in almost no time at all.

Filming a real building in the course of construction for this type of effect was out of the question. It had to be a model. So, a suitable negative was selected from the sponsor's stock of photographs, showing a twelve storey block of flats seen from a low angle, and a 4 ft enlargement was made from it. This was mounted on some hardboard, the building's surroundings were trimmed off and the remaining cut-out photograph was sliced horizontally into six sections so that each part contained two storeys. To the back of each section, a slot device was fitted so that the parts could be easily and neatly slid together again.

This model was set up on a table in a garden against the sky. The camera was put low on the ground and this, together with the false perspective of the model itself increased the impression of seeing an actual building standing out against white clouds. To obtain a still greater effect of realism, a model of a tower crane (obtained from a crane-hire company) which happened to be of the right scale was put behind the building. Each stage of erection was filmed, starting with the complete building and dismantling it section by section. In this way, there was less danger of shaking the model, which would have been fatal. With the scenes, each 2 ft long, cut together in the proper order, the sequence gave indeed the impression of an actual building magically jumping out of the ground in quick stages. (Figs. 49, 50)

In a physiological classroom film, the influence of environmental conditions on the body had to be shown. Amongst other scenes, the script provided for a man freezing to death in the arctic. To hire a studio, build a set and produce a blizzard for a live scene was, of course, much too expensive. It meant using models again.

The completed scene shows an icy spot in the arctic waste at night, with a blizzard blowing. The figure of an explorer in his snow-covered fur-coat stands in the centre of the screen leaning on a stick. In a CU-shot, a hole appears in the fur-coat, showing a thermometer inside the figure. The blood temperature is far below normal. The thermometer disappears and the man is again seen in full figure. Gradually he collapses until he lies in a heap on the ground. (Figs. 51–56).

For this scene an actor was dressed up and stills were taken of him in various stages of his collapse. The filming procedure was much as described in the previous example. The cut-out figures were about eight inches high, except the one for the thermometer shot which was twice that size. The polar scene was a table top set with a salt mixture representing the snow. The night effect helped because we did not need to bother about a background. The blizzard, however, needed some experimenting. In the end the best result was obtained by pouring water on a block of dry ice at the side of the set and blowing the resulting vapour across it with a small fan. The various cut-outs were one after the other put in exactly the same spot. Two dissolves were necessary for the thermometer-insert. No attempt at realism could be made due to the thermometer shot but a strange naturalistic effect was unintentionally achieved.

The bump technique can also be used for assembling or dismantling in stages any three-dimensional structures built from toy bricks, wooden

FIGS. 57 and 58. *Model Animation.* Len Lye animating a toy car and the 'robot' in a desert set.
From the Shell film: *The Birth of a Robot.*

Special Techniques

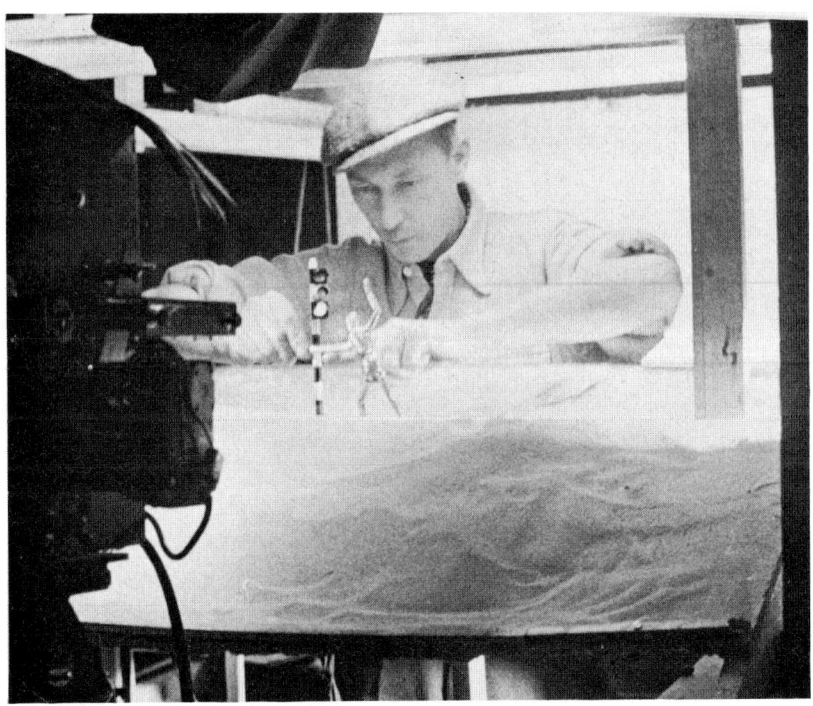

blocks or from Lego, Meccano or other construction kits. The main thing is not to move the structure or any part of it even by a hair's breadth during manipulation; glue, cellulose tape and modelling clay are often necessary to keep things in place. By using small models and scenic sets, the future appearance of estate projects, the spread of urban developments, road systems, etc., can be shown. Elevations in the ground can be produced with sheets of hessian, painted with mat colours or covered with the artificial turf used in window displays.

Abstract objects such as cubes, pyramids, cones, but also models of vehicles or ships which are to move around must be animated from one position to the next in very small stages. The degree of shift varies according to the size of the object, the desired speed of movement and the length of the scene. Francis Rodker, Head of the Shell Film Animation Unit during the war, states that in a film involving ships moving at their natural speed, a model one inch long, took 240 frames to travel its own length. Obviously, this is an extreme case, but it shows how much pain must be taken in technically, and scientifically exact animation. A technician who is inexperienced in this field, will have to achieve his ends by trial and error. In order to reduce cost, positive film or the short ends of negative rolls can be used for such tests. As a rule, the smaller each move, the more likely it is to avoid strobing effects, the bane of all animation. Also white objects are more likely to strobe than darker ones.

If models of human figures are animated, the articulated joints must be tight enough to keep the figure and its limbs in any necessary position. Figs. 57 and 58 show stills from the Shell-Mex film *The Birth of a Robot*, in which the star was a metal figure about 6 in high.

Puppet animation is a technique in itself. Puppets are not discussed here because it is very unlikely that they would be required in the type of films with which this book is concerned. The various techniques of puppet animation are described in several books exclusively concerned with that field.

For subjects or shapes which are supposed to grow or shrink the method described for the arctic figure should be adopted. Many different sizes of the same model have to be made and then one exchanged for the other between each shot. How many sizes are necessary depends on whether the object is allowed to grow in visible bumps or whether the movement must appear continuous.

Whatever the type of animation, a chart must be prepared in which the total running time of the scene is broken down into a frame-by-frame count. After each exposure, the corresponding entry in the chart is ticked off and compared with the frame counter on the camera. This system makes it easier to avoid mistakes; errors usually mean restarting the whole scene.

Animation is time-consuming work. Even with the simplest type of

Special Techniques

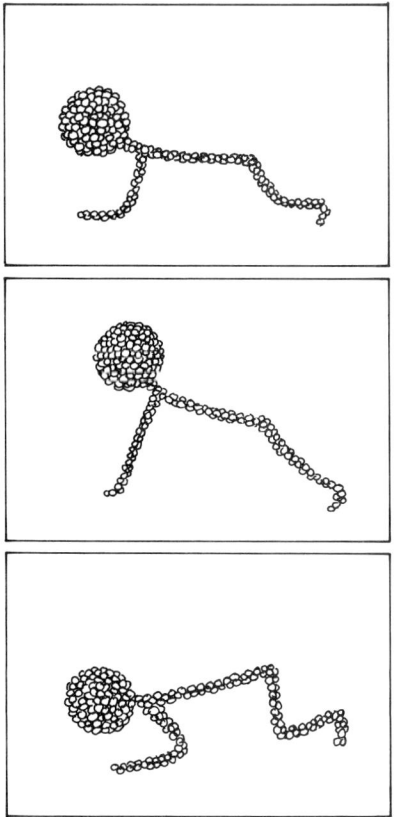

Fig. 59. *Confetti Baby.* The above drawings, reproduced from the "Film User", show quite a new and original method of do-it-yourself animation. Confetti was used to create the figure of a small child and the little paper discs were then moved in successive steps to animate the child from a prone position into a crawling one. Inventive film-makers might think of similar simple and unorthodox ways to overcome, where appropriate, the problem of cost of subcontracted animation.

model animation one cannot hope to obtain more than a few feet per hour, not counting the preparations of the models, the setting-up and any repair work which has to be done during the filming. But animation is worth the time and effort if certain facts or phenomena cannot be made visible or elucidated by any other means.

Simulated animation

This provides an alternative to the single-frame method. The idea is to obtain animation effects with a continuously running camera. As an example, again take a line, drawing itself. This does not necessarily demand the single-frame method discussed previously. You can cover a glass sheet or cell with two pieces of black paper so that they do not join each other but leave a narrow gap across the width of the glass. Lit from behind, the gap appears as a white line within a black area. All you have to do now is to cover this line at the back of the glass with another strip of black paper, mounted on a piece of hardboard for easier handling, and to slide it along the gap in order to expose it. The line thus seems to draw itself while the camera is running. The sliding can be done at any speed but it must be even throughout (see page 211).

Numerous other effects can be obtained by means of sliding cells, glass sheets or other materials on which scenery or diagrams are drawn. Once, on location, a 10 ft long canvas painting, showing a housing estate, had to be slid across the camera field. Tracking the camera was not possible in that particular case and a sliding mechanism had to be improvised. A wooden board to support the painting was fitted by clamps across two trestles. Two battens were fastened to it to form a groove. The painting was mounted in a wooden frame and was held upright by another board at the back. All parts of the frame which came into contact with the groove and the board at the back were well greased. An old coffee grinder, found on the spot, was fitted to another trestle at the side. A piece of string was attached to the bottom corner of the frame and wound round the revolving drum of the grinder. By turning the handle of the grinder, the string was wound up on the drum and the canvas slid smoothly in its groove across the camera field. The effect could not have been better if an elaborate motor mechanism had been prepared.

All kinds of other simulated animation effects can be obtained by many means, often in combination with special effects such as Pepper's Ghost. All these effects need a certain amount of preparation but usually less than is necessary for single-frame animation. The saving in time and labour when replacing stop-motion camera work by straightforward filming is very great. Naturally, the field for simulated animation is restricted, but wherever this method is suitable it should be considered because surprising effects can be achieved for little cost. Dreaming up new ways of doing things is one of the satisfactions that a film-maker derives from his work.

Anologies

If a concept or a phenomenon cannot be demonstrated or illustrated by any of the aforementioned methods, you have to find an oblique way of explanation. Scientists often use an analogy to explain their theories. You can do the same.

FIG. 60. *Analogies.* (top): A perfect bubble raft. Molecular phenomena can be demonstrated by means of the bubble raft method;
FIG. 61. (bottom): bubble raft showing how dislocations can be demonstrated with the use of this technique.
A film *Experiments with a Bubble Model of a Metal* has been produced in co-operation with Sir Lawrence Bragg (see page 284).

Special Techniques

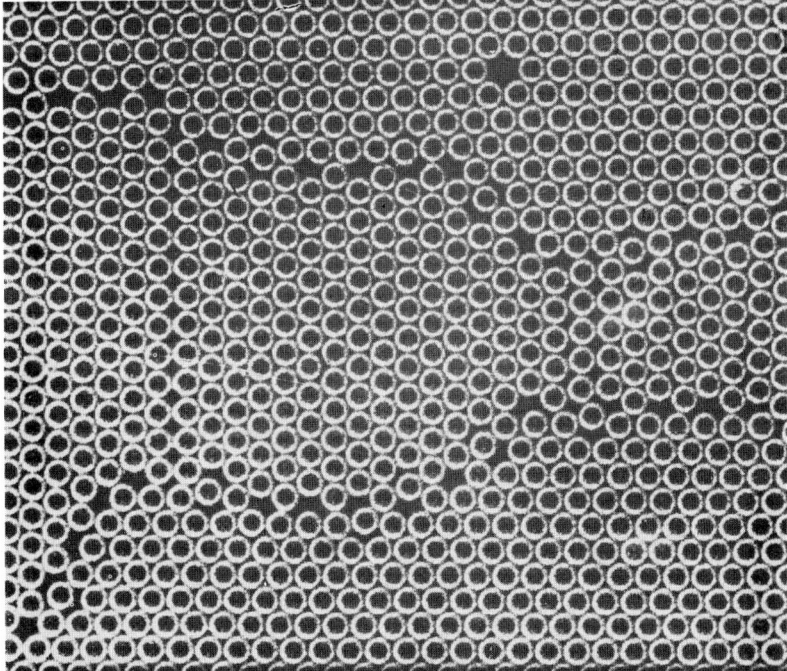

The Work of the Science Film Maker

Not every analogy which is of use to a scientist is, however, suitable for a film-maker. Scientists might explain a new hypothesis by comparing it with an established concept, but this may be as abstract and intangible as the new one. The film needs analogies, similes or metaphors which can easily be translated into visual images.

An amusing and very photogenic analogy was used by Professor J. Maynard Smith in the Granada TV programme *Evolution* to explain the hereditary mechanism in Darwin's theory. Here is an extract from the Granada programme notes:

> A bicycle represents the body, and the book of instructions from which it is made represents the hereditary material. The effects of natural selection are represented by a bicycle race. The book of instructions is carried during the race. All but the first few bicycles past the finishing post are eliminated. At the end of the race those books of instructions, carried by bicycles which were not eliminated, are copied twice and new bicycles made from each copy of the instructions. There is then another race and the process continues. Thus, only the books of instructions which have led to the making of an efficient bicycle will tend to be perpetuated. . . .

Professor Smith proceeds to show how errors in the copying process lead to mutations: a bicycle may be made with square wheels; in living organisms a biological defect may result. The programme then deals with the question of sex, cell division, etc. This analogy was both lucid and pictorially vivid.

Another striking analogy was used for Rutherford's first atom-splitting experiment. The small apparatus he had built for this experiment was called his 'shooting range'. The target (the atomic nucleus) was a fly buzzing around in the dome of St. Paul's, and in order to show the proportional dimensions which were involved it was implied that Rutherford had to hit the fly from a firing stand situated on the moon.

Scientists at different periods of history have compared the atom successively to a solid ball, a currant bun and a planetary system. Another analogy is the Nelson's Column representing the radius of the atom (page 234). All these examples are to the point, easy to understand and they can be visually well expressed.

A useful and filmically effective model for the demonstration of molecular phenomena by analogy is the 'bubble raft', a favourite device of Sir Lawrence Bragg. It consists of a shallow tray, 2 in. deep, which contains a solution of a soap-and-glycerine mixture. Some detergents are also suitable. The bubbles on the surface of the liquid can be produced by various techniques; they must, however, be blown from a fine orifice under constant pressure to make them uniform in size, about 1 mm in dia.; this is essential for the success of the demonstration. The perfect bubble raft

Special Techniques

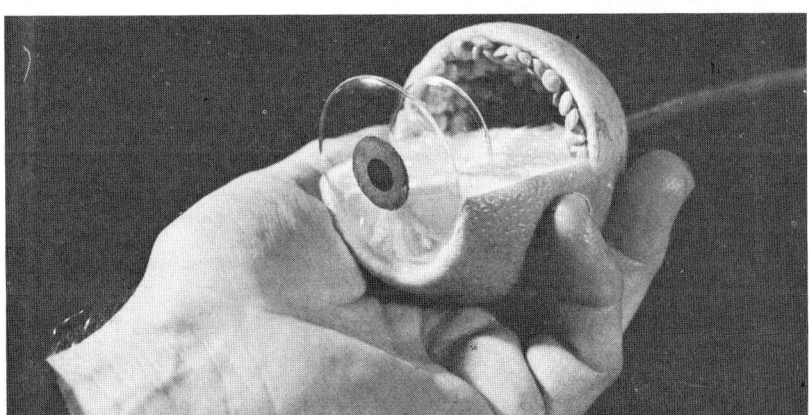

Figs. 62, 63 and 64 show the different stages of the orange-eye model. Three separately prepared models were needed for the complete sequence.
From the film: *Your Children's Eyes*.

The orange was used as an analogy for an eye-ball and a conjurer was called in to transform the fruit from its natural state into a complete three-dimensional cross-section of the eye.

shows the uniformity and regularity of crystalline structures but the bubbles can also be made to reveal dislocations and other structural imperfections (see Figs 60, 61). This method can, of course, only be filmed in a physics laboratory under the guidance of a crystallographer. For a film on this method see page 284.

During the war, I had to make a film for the Central Office of Information, called *Your Children's Eyes*. It was part of the children's health series mentioned on page 107, to be shown to mothers of young children. The film was to contain a demonstration of the working mechanism of the eye. In view of the intended audience, a didactic approach was ruled out, and with my preference for three-dimensional models a black-and-white animated diagram was not to my taste.

I consulted an eye specialist who told me that for dissecting practice in anatomy classes the students use cows' eyes. In war-time London it was not easy to come by that commodity. Everything was rationed and cows' eyes were listed under the heading of 'meat'. After lengthy official procedure, involving several ministries, I at last procured a permit authorizing the purchase of two dozen cows' eyes which I obtained from one of the municipal abattoirs without further ado. An amused attendant put them in a tin for me and added a preserving fluid which was supposed to keep them fresh for several days. This was on a Friday. I put the tin with the eyes in a cool corner of my garage and left them there over the weekend.

I had arranged for a medical student to come and do some dissecting tests for me early in the following week. When I opened the garage door on Monday there was a suspicious smell, and looking into the tin I found a disgusting-looking jelly which I buried in the garden as fast as I could. And so, cow's eyes were out!

Thinking of possible alternatives, I remembered having once seen in a book an illustration showing the model of an eye-ball made up from an orange. After some frantic search, I found the book* and looked again at the 'orange-eye'. It seemed indeed a very convincing analogy and, both in size and substance, a much more manageable object than an actual eye, cow or otherwise. But oranges, too, were rationed and I had to do the ministerial round once more. This time it was something of an obstacle race as the various officials could not readily understand why I needed oranges for demonstrating eyes. In the end, however, a permit again arrived.

The question now was how best to stage the demonstration. My general idea was to start with the orange as it came from the fruit basket, to dissect it before the camera, to add such unorangy bits and pieces as the cornea and lens and to end up with the complete orange-eye *in situ*. The manipulation had to be done quickly and elegantly; thus, a professional

---

* F. Kahn: *Das Leben des Menschen*, Stuttgart: Franckscher Verlag.

Special Techniques

magician was the most obvious choice. Mercifully, there were no war-time restrictions on magicians and I was lucky in finding a man who quickly grasped and enjoyed the idea and was able to perform his juggling act perfectly. After a promising rehearsal I put down the various stages of the action in a short script, wrote the commentary for each scene and timed the lengths of the single shots. With this as a guide, we prepared several orange models in progressive stages of completion and then filmed the whole sequence in one afternoon. On the screen, the dissecting and building-up takes place, of course, in continuous action.

The sequence runs as follows:

YOUR CHILDRENS EYES (*Extract*)

		Picture	Commentary
1.	MS	Magician's hand takes orange from basket.	An orange is very much like an eye.
2.	CU	His magic wand circles round the orange.	The outer skin represents the white of the eye; it keeps the eyeball together.
3.	CU	By sleight of hand a knife appears.	Now, a knife—
4.	CU	Knife cuts a one-inch hole in the outer skin.	—to cut a hole into the outer coat; this becomes the opening for the *eye window*.
5.	CU	White inner skin pointed out, and a smaller hole cut into this.	Underneath is a second coat.—In its centre is another hole. This is the *pupil*.
6.	CU	Hand produces a grease-paint stick from the air.	Next, a stick of grease-paint such as actors use.
7.	CU	Grease-paint stick stamps a round mark on to inner coat.	With its help, the *iris* which gives the eye its colour can be marked.
8.	MCU	A watch glass appears in the hand and is inserted in the outer skin in front of the iris.	A watch glass represents the window of the eye, called *cornea*. It is actually a transparent part of the outer coat.
9.	CU	*Change to second orange model* Hand removes front of orange to reveal its inside.	The inside of the eye is filled with a sort of jelly, just as the orange is filled with its fruity part.
10.	MCU	A small magnifying glass is passed across a printed page enlarging the letters behind it.	The *lens* is one of the most important parts; it looks like a small magnifying glass.
11.	CU	Lens is inserted in orange behind the iris.	It is suspended behind the iris and throws an image onto the back of the eye. There, at the back

			is a layer of nerve cells which is sensitive to light and picks up the image.
12.	CU	Hand picks up an umbellate flower with a long stalk.	This flower looks somewhat like this layer. It has many nerve cells attached to tiny nerve fibres which combine and form a cable, called the *optic nerve*—represented by the stalk.
13.	CU	*Third model: half an orange with the fruity part removed.* The stalk is pushed through the skin so that the flower cluster covers the inside of the skin.	The system of nerve cells and fibres which lines the back of the eye is called the *retina*, and it records a picture much as a photographic film does.
14.	CU	The second orange model with the lens, etc., is put in front of the third model containing the retina.	And here is the complete seeing-mechanism of the eye: the cornea—the iris—the pupil—the lens—the retina—and the optic nerve which transmits the picture to the brain.
15.	MCU	The orange-eye is held in the magician's right hand; with the left he puts a mask in front of the orange. Only one half of the mask, with its one eye in position behind it, is in the camera's field.	If a mask is put in front of the model, then the eye is in the position in which we normally see it.

These fifteen scenes, shot in four hours, make up a sequence of two and a half minutes running time. The preparations and experiments for such a model sequence might require seven or eight working days. This compares very favourably with the time and cost which would be involved in the production of an animated diagram of the same length. Such a diagram would perhaps be more 'accurate' but would certainly leave less of an impression on the audience.

The orange sequence, supplemented by two more sequences in a similar style, was very popular with the sponsors, the audience and the critics alike.

Unfilmable analogies

But things are not always so obliging. There are many scientific theories (often called models) which come within a hair's breadth of the filmically impossible. What is one to make, for instance, of the following

Special Techniques

analogy which the physicist Sir James Jeans uses to explain Einstein's model of the universe?*

'A soap bubble with corrugations on its surface is perhaps the best representation in terms of simple and familiar materials, of the new universe revealed to us by the theory of relativity. The universe is not the interior of the soap bubble but its surface and we must always remember that while the surface of the soap bubble has only two dimensions, the universe bubble has four: three dimensions of space and one of time. And the substance out of which this bubble is blown, the soap-film, is empty space welded on to empty time.'

Although this analogy conjures up a visual image of sorts, it is difficult to see how this could be filmed without a whole string of further analogies.

One of the main difficulties with Einstein's universe is how to express the fourth dimension—time—in visual terms. Although this dimension is part of everybody's daily life and experience, and although the film itself can only exist in this dimension, we cannot yet produce a tangible model of time. Several films have tried it, not very successfully.

It is interesting to compare Sir James's soap bubble with another analogy—or rather a set of analogies—contained in the book *Flatland*†, published in 1884 when Einstein was only 5 years old. In it, the author, who writes under the pen name A Square, uses the analogy of an assumed two-dimensional world whose inhabitants are as little able to visualize our third dimension as we are able to grasp the idea of a fourth dimension.

A Flatlander's sense of perception is restricted to seeing shapes as *lines*. In his two-dimensional world there are no elevated viewpoints and no matter whether the creatures in Flatland exist in the form of triangles, squares, pentagons, hexagons or circles, the Flatlander can only perceive the edge of these shapes as straight lines. If a three-dimensional sphere would descend on Flatland and pass through it, the inhabitants would see it as a mysterious line expanding from nothing and shrinking and disappearing into nothing. Thus, they would 'attribute to growth in time what to us is solidity and motion'. And like the Flatlanders, we ourselves can evolve various theories about the fourth dimension, but the limitations of our own sense of perception are such that we can only dimly comprehend the essence of it.

If we use an analogy and so create a new reality, the whole point is that we do not expect the result to be a blueprint of the concept we want to explain. We just want to help the audience to understand the unfamiliar by comparing it visually with something familiar. Some teachers dislike analogies in classroom films because they are afraid that the similarities will be taken too literally and establish themselves in the mind, thus

---

* Lincoln Barnett, *The Universe and Dr. Einstein*, London: Comet Books, Collins.
† *Flatland*, A Square (E. A. Abbott), (re-issue 1926) by Basil Blackwell.

preventing the child, or even an adult, from realizing the differences. This objection is surely open to question. No child or adult who has viewed Professor Smith's demonstration, will henceforth believe that the evolution of living organisms takes place by means of bicycles. Now and then, misconceptions may arise but they can surely be put right without difficulty. The advantage of using well-chosen analogies is that their language is more powerful and more immediate in effect than strictly accurate but lengthy and pedestrian explanations.

4

Films in the Making

Film work is team work

Now AND THEN, one meets a lone wolf amongst film makers who directs, shoots and edits his films single-handed. This is feasible when only straightforward photography is required, as is perhaps the case on safaris or in scientific research work. Stobart, on the Everest Expedition, shot a full-length film himself but he was assisted by his colleagues and porters with humping and other non-technical chores. Where, for example, a science subject involves time-lapse technique it would be both impracticable and uneconomic to engage a camera unit to carry it out. There are one or two other fields of work where single-handed filming might be unavoidable.

By and large, however, films are made by more than one person and good team work and team spirit is as essential here as in any other art or trade where a group of people is closely united by a common purpose or motive. Team work assures a reasonable distribution of the various technical tasks amongst those who, by their specialized training, are best able to obtain good results. The emphasis must be on *reasonable* because a narrow interpretation of the team idea often creates a rigid demarcation mentality such as is found in many industries and which is bound to lead to friction. It is not unusual in feature-film production for the shooting to be interrupted by long delays while some disputes of a trifling nature, often only concerning working etiquette, are thrashed out on the studio floor. Such problems seldom arise in the factual field. Although labour agreements must also be observed here the whole atmosphere within most non-feature units is generally more like that of a large family.

Division of work is not the only reason for banding together in a team. Even the most imaginative film-maker needs both stimulation and constructive criticism. This is often supplied by the producer of the film if he exists as a separate person. But producers are usually busy people, often burdened with much administrative work; they are not always available for scrutinizing details such as a particular notion which a director has dreamed up during the night and which he is eager to discuss. Therefore, a congenially assembled 'field team' is the most helpful instrument for the exchange of ideas which crop up in day-to-day work.

A survey by the University Film Foundation of the USA* deals with the activities of some sixty university film units. Talking about the composition of these units the authors say that 'their most impressive experience during their survey was to see a small but highly motivated unit . . . produce a film that would be a credit to a large generously budgeted commercial production company.' But they also remark: 'One imaginative film-maker can raise a unit to superior calibre, loss of one man can reduce a small unit to mediocrity or worse.' This is equally true of commercial film units.

The 'field' team of a film unit, working in the factual field and capable of tackling any job that may come its way, however complex or out of the ordinary, should consists of at least four to five people: the producer, the director (their functions are sometimes combined in one person), the cameraman, the assistant director and assistant cameraman and perhaps a production- or unit-manager.

If the unit owns a small studio, there must be a technician in charge of it. He is usually an electrician but in addition he is expected to be a jack-of-all-trades. In his workshop, equipped with a carpentry bench and a lathe, he quickly produces the many mechanical odds and ends called for during shooting. Such a factotum is particularly important if the unit specializes in scientific subjects. Everyone who is familiar with the routine of a science laboratory knows what an essential part the laboratory assistant plays. On his ingenuity, technical know-how and manual skill depends the smooth performance of the lecturer's experiments and demonstrations. He prepares and manipulates the implements of science like a magician. Lucky the film team which has a similar magician amongst its members.

For simple routine jobs, to be shot on 16mm film, three or even two technicians would often be sufficient. Additional personnel, such as a sound crew or extra electricians, are hired as the occasion demands. Specialized teams like animation units, etc., have, of course, different set-ups.

When it comes to editing, however, there are two schools of thought. One school believes that the director should also edit the film himself with the help of an assistant. The other school sees the director only as a supervising element in the cutting room while the actual work is carried out by a separate film editor and his assistant. Both ways of thinking have their pros and cons. Often there is no choice, for instance when the director has other commitments following on at once.

Everything said up to now refers to *professional* film teams in the

---

* D. G. Williams and L. V. Snyder, *Motion Picture Production Facilities of Selected Colleges and Universities*, US Dept. of Health, Education and Welfare.

Films in the Making

usual sense. But it looks as if the whole structure of factual film-making is at present going back into the melting pot. Great changes have come about in recent years. Documentary and current affairs films are now mainly in the hands of TV departments and many technical films are made by works photographers or small in-plant units.

In addition, there are now many non-professional film-makers: film groups in schools, universities, research institutions as well as single scientists, doctors, teachers and so on. Excellent films have been made by such groups and individuals in the fields of environmental study, local geography, animal life, travel, medicine, science and other spheres. The present improved standard of 16mm and 8mm equipment, emulsions and laboratory facilities encourages this development.

Thus, while professional teams will always be needed for the more intricate or ambitious types of film, much of the simpler work, particularly in the educational field, may well become uneconomic for such units in the future and it might pass into the hands of a generation of non-professional film-makers.

The work of one team

For two decades I belonged to a team which formed part of the Realist Film Unit in London, one of the oldest documentary units, established by Basil Wright and John Taylor before the Second World War in the heyday of the documentary movement. A number of distinguished producers guided the fortunes of the company at various times, many directors of originality contributed to its reputation as a pioneer company and countless young technicians found in it a practice ground and springboard for their careers.

But there was also a permanent nucleus at Realist, the mainstay of which was—and still is at the time of writing—the cameraman Adrian Jeakins. He photographed probably 200 of the 250 films or more which this unit has made to date. One could not have had a better man, both as a person and as a creative technician, at one's side. His righthand man, George Cooper, is an electrician by training and a magician by attitude and aptitude.

I and Sesu, my wife and assistant, joined Realist during the Second World War and our work brought us into permanent close contact with Adrian Jeakins and George Cooper, particularly after I began to specialize in directing scientific and technological subjects which require the very know-how and skill which these two technicians possess. We remained together for almost 20 years and tackled films of every description. Our most rewarding work was in the field of science education because it necessitated the presentation of many visible and invisible processes by techniques in which we were all similarly interested.

The Work of the Science Film Maker

If I now describe how our team set about making its films, it is not my intention to teach how such films ought to be made. Every film-maker has his own methods. The methods we used are neither revolutionary nor jealously guarded trade secrets; we only tried, for reasons discussed in previous chapters, to find a visual presentation for a variety of tricky problems for which the animated diagram seemed an obvious, but not always the best solution. Everyone with a flair for experimenting can do likewise if he is so minded.

I admit that, occasionally, we had to bend over backwards in order to obtain the results we were after. It would have been so much easier to sub-contract one or the other ticklish job to an animation unit and let them worry about it. Also, with the wisdom of hindsight and with present-day facilities, we would probably tackle some of the problems differently now. But as a whole, I think, our methods did succeed in giving our films some added visual interest and it helped us to achieve what every film-maker regards as his most cherished asset: an individual style. That our team was able to develop such a style was due mainly to two or three appreciative sponsors whose continuous support kept us together as a working unit for such a long time.

By chance, all our subjects were related to physics, but any other branch of science can be tackled in much the same way. In describing our work it was sometimes necessary to explain certain scientific facts in order to show the problems for which we had to find the solutions. Since this is not a book about science, all such references are to be regarded as incidental.

Much of the substance of our particular production techniques is as valid today as it was when we made these films, and they will be valid tomorrow and for a long time to come because they simply make use of the unending variety of facets of which our world is composed. Thus, it is hoped that the following pages will be taken less as a course of instruction than as a source which will both inform, and stimulate the imagination.

Three science-education films

SCIENCE IN THE ORCHESTRA

This film in three parts was commissioned by the Central Office of Information. An earlier C.O.I. film, the well-known *Instruments of the Orchestra*, directed by Muir Mathieson and with the late Sir Malcolm Sargent in the dual role as conductor and compère, illustrates the structure of an orchestra and the character of the various instruments in a performance of music by Benjamin Britten, played by the London Symphony Orchestra. Intended as a film for schools, it was of great interest to adult audiences as well.

Science in the Orchestra which I was asked to direct is complementary to the above film by demonstrating various aspects of the physics of sound

Films in the Making

FIG. 65. *Science in the Orchestra.* Muir Mathieson talks to the children who take part in the film.

FIG. 66. Part of the orchestra and some of the models which were used in the film.

in general and of those of music in particular. Its running time is about 40 min.

In this film, Muir Mathieson took on the part of conductor and compére. His engaging personality and showmanship make him the ideal 'teacher' for children. He was supported by two character actors playing the parts of a science demonstrator and his assistant. The music, composed by Malcolm Arnold, was again played by members of the London Symphony Orchestra.

As the budget did not allow the hire of a big studio, we had to look around for alternatives and after a long frustrating search we found a sympathetic headmistress of a girl's school who was willing to give us the freedom of her beautiful school hall for a couple of weeks during the holidays.

The stage was not quite large enough to accommodate the orchestra and we had to extend the apron at the front. Our art director did this by putting up a number of movable rostrums which together added some eight feet to the depth of the stage. This arrangement allowed for some of these rostrums to be taken out when the camera had to move right into the orchestra for close-up shots. At that time, zoom lenses did not exist. To the right and left of the orchestra, near the front of the stage, we placed the smaller models and the scientific apparatus needed for the demonstrations.

Additional sets and props were held in readiness in another part of the hall. We shot all the orchestral sequences of the film in this location but a great number of inserts and special effects were filmed in our own small studio later on.

There remained one problem. As it was our intention to give, throughout the film, the impression of a lecture-concert taking place before a live audience, we did not wish to switch repeatedly from live action to 'abstract' cinematic effects and vice versa. This would have interfered with the idea of attending an actual concert. Television has overcome this problem by the simple expedient of not bothering about the apparent inconsequence of mixing live action with effects or animation, but the cinematic convention of the time made such mixing inadvisable, particularly in view of the very critical attitude of school children.

After some consideration we decided to use traditional lecture procedure by putting a cine-screen up beside the orchestra on which all cinematic effects were to be shown. In the following examples this screen will be referred to as the 'side screen'.

The C.O.I.'s concurrence with our recommendation to use, as far as possible, three-dimensional models made the film an exciting assignment and a challenge to our team. At that time, Brian Smith was Realist's producer, and in view of the company's expanding teaching-film programme, Realist had previously taken on two resident scientists: Dorothy Grayson and Denys Parsons. The first, in her capacity as co-producer and co-scriptwriter was very much a 'back-room boffin', but Denys worked with us throughout on the practical side of the job. Being himself a flute- and piano-player, he was a great asset for this particular film. He has also a profound knowledge of London's resources and can put his finger at a moment's notice on the very shop, market stall, junk joint or science laboratory from which even the most improbable item can be obtained, often at a moment's notice. (He later wrote a famous London Shopping Guide.*)

The sets were designed by an art director, a temporary but indispensable addition to any unit that has to work in a big studio or whenever large sets are required. We also had to call in a specialist model-maker because the many models that were required exceeded the capacity of our own workshop.

Science in the Orchestra was an intricate and lengthy job. Conceived as a 'visual unit' it involved not only making the film but also several film-strips and in addition writing handbooks for teachers (which Dorothy Grayson undertook); from its inception to the delivery of the first show copy, the production lasted for more than three years. Most of this time was spent on preparatory work: on scripting, and numerous meetings with

---

* Denys Parsons. *What's where in London with B.P.*, a 'must' for all British film makers.

Films in the Making

the C.O.I.'s subject advisers, on composing the music and on a great many other details.

As mentioned before, certain cinematic effects, due to their nature, are perceived only on the film screen—they do not exist off it. Many of the visuals in this film can, therefore, only be described rather inadequately in words or drawings. But, where production stills and other photographs have been available, they should help to illustrate the various points.

Part I Hearing the Music

'V for Vibration' (Production of Sound)

One of the first sequences of the film demonstrates that making sound is a matter of vibration.

To show the vibrations of solid instruments as well as of strings and drum skins proved simple. We did it by cutting the letter V out of stiff white paper in different sizes and glueing them to the ends of thin wires.

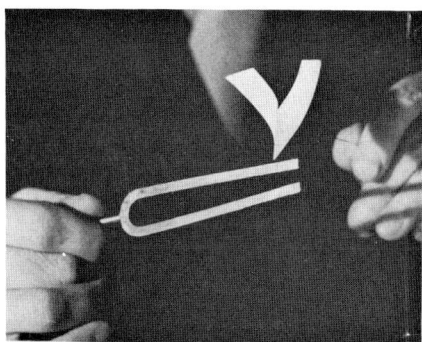

FIG. 67. 'V for Vibration'. Dancing paper letters held on wires against tuning fork and instruments demonstrate that making sound is a matter of vibration.

Held by the children against cymbals and triangles, strings and drum skins while the orchestra played, these paper letters danced vigorously up and down. A fast montage of close ups of these Vs gave a lively impression of the quivering agitation on the surface of the instruments.

Quite a different type of vibration is that of the *air* contained *within* the bodies of the string instruments and drums, and of the *air columns* in the tubes of the wind instruments.

To show vibrating air was not quite so easy; we needed two separate negatives for each scene for later superimposition, and it involved masking parts of the images.

We started with the kettle drum. The film showed the percussionist playing a roll on it. Now, the camera panned on to the side screen on which a close up of the same drum appeared. Within its outline the effect of vibrating air became visible.

The shooting procedure was as follows: first the actual drum was shot,

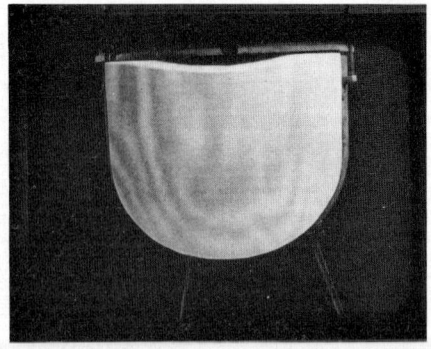

Fig. 68. This model shows that both the drum skin and the air inside the kettle drum vibrate.

its outline fully lit by side lighting, but with its body kept dark by shading it from the light. This produced a sort of silhouette effect. Using a frame from the negative of this scene as a 'register' (see glossary), we cut a mask with an opening in the exact shape of the drum body and put it behind the gate in the camera.

Meanwhile, a small table-top set had been prepared consisting of a ground glass sheet, 2 ft square, which was to stand in front of two perforated metal sheets of similar size. When this arrangement was lit from the back and the metal sheets moved against each other, an interference pattern was produced on the glass, giving, after a few trials, the desired effect. This moving pattern was put slightly out of focus and shot so that it fitted the opening in the mask.

In addition, the up-and-down vibrations of the drum skin also had to be made visible. A small piece of black cardboard, (a 'gobo' or 'flag') was suspended in front of the set so that its lower curved edge protruded slightly from the top into the field of view of the lens. This gobo was slightly agitated by hand while taking the shot and produced the impression of the vibrating surface of the drum, seen in profile.

The two separate scenes, the first showing the actual drum, the other the vibration effect, were then superimposed over each other on the optical printer in the laboratory.

A similar demonstration showed the air movement within the sound box of the double bass. The vibrating air columns in the wind instruments, with the flute as an example, had to be represented by a different method. This is described on pages 154–156.

No Air—no Sound (Transmission of Sound)

Having demonstrated that sound is a matter of vibration, produced by banging, bowing and blowing, the film now showed how the music reaches the audience.

For this sequence, the orchestra's percussionist lent us his gong. It was hung on a stand downstage and a big transparent bell-jar, made of

Films in the Making

Perspex (Plexiglass) was placed over it. This bell-jar had seen better days; it was once part of a wartime fighter plane. A striking-mechanism, driven by a motor, beat the gong throughout the scene.

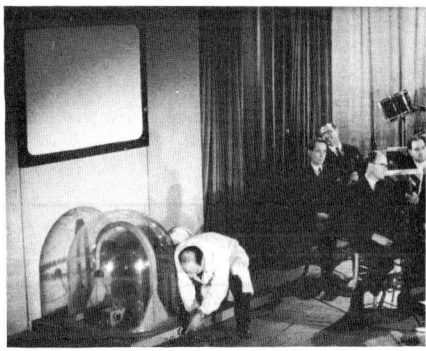

FIG. 69. The 'gong-in-the-bell jar' experiment shows that air is necessary for sound to travel.

The next sequence showed how the bell-jar was connected to an air pump. Whilst the air was slowly pumped out, the sound of the gong became fainter and fainter although the striker continued hitting the gong. Finally, the sound ceased altogether. (This is a well-known classroom experiment. It had to be included here because it demonstrated an important point of the argument. Also, many schools have no such equipment. In our case, the air pump was a dummy and the sound was faded out in the dubbing session.)

Muir, next to the now inaudible gong, pointed out: 'No air ... no sound ... Obviously, air has something to do with sound getting to us, but how?' While he explained that air is made up of lots of separate tiny particles, too small to be seen, the following sequences appeared on the side screen:

A ping-pong ball bounced repeatedly against a mirror colliding with its mirror image. The ball represented an air particle and the scene demonstrated the *elasticity* of such particles.

Next: a hand, holding a thin metal rod, by stabbing at various points in the air above, 'picked up' and collected on it a number of 'ping-pong air particles.'

For this scene, a score of perforated balls were slid on to the rod beforehand. With the camera turned upside down, the balls were then filmed dropping one by one from the rod which was waved about, pointing downwards, by a person standing on a table. The background was black velvet. This scene was later cut into the film tail to front.

Now, the gong appeared again and the rod with the row of balls was held horizontally against it so that it touched its surface.

The 'gong' consisted of a round frame with a metallic-looking rubber sheet tightly stretched across it to form the beating surface. This rubber gong could be caused to bulge out and cave in—i.e., to 'vibrate'—at the desired speed by means of a bicycle pump, and the bulged or caved-in surface of the gong could be held static for any length of time.

The nature of a sound wave was now demonstrated on the side-screen. Oscillating air particles created forward travelling 'bumps' and 'gaps'; the balls on the rod show how this happens.

In the first part of this sequence the balls were shifted to and fro by hand. We did it this way because the action of the fingers which made the balls collide and separate emphasized strongly the phenomena of *compression* and *rarefaction* which Muir explained in the commentary.

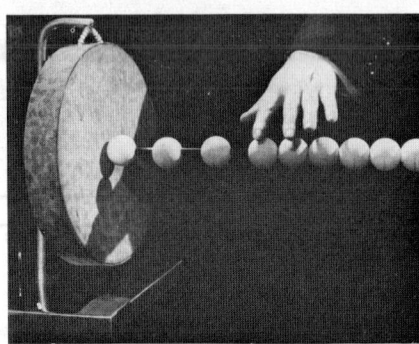

Fig. 70. Ping-pong balls on a rod touching a pulsating rubber gong demonstrate the nature of a sound wave. The hand disappears after the first few feet and the balls now move to and fro on their own.

Having done its job, the hand disappeared and the balls continued to move to and fro on the rod under their own steam, apparently activated by the vibrations of the gong. By increasing the speed of the oscillations, a distinct impression of an outward travelling movement was created.

For the 'unaided' motion of the balls we needed a wave-machine of the type which demonstrates longitudinal wave motion by means of little oscillating metal prongs. The ping-pong balls were fixed onto the ends of these prongs, facing the camera; they hid the prongs which were sliding to and fro. The wave-machine itself was concealed behind a backcloth of black velvet and the prongs protruded through a slit in the cloth. The set-up needed a certain amount of experimenting but worked well in the end.

As Muir now pointed out that sound waves spread through the air in all directions, the scene changed to show curved lines, each representing the crest of a wave, following each other closely across the screen.

This effect was produced by exchanging the balls on the wave-machine for slightly curved vertical rods which oscillated in the same way as the balls.

This scene led into the next sequence dealing with the *speed* of sound.

Lightning and Thunder (Speed of Sound)

At the beginning of this impressionistic sequence, shown on the side-screen, was seen the silhouette of a 'celestial' percussionist hitting a gong as lightning streaks across the screen. Waves in the shape of expanding

Films in the Making

spheres emanated from the gong. As the first wave reached the frame line, the sound of the gong was heard. The point made here is that lightning and thunder occur simultaneously, but while we see the lightning the moment it happens, we have to wait for the noise of the thunder to reach us. At the end of this scene a 'lightning and thunder' motive, played by the doublebasses and drums, started up.

The scene now mixed into a night sky seen through a window. Flashes of lightning illuminated the swaying branches of a tree outside. The corresponding gong sounds of thunder, heard after the necessary intervals were reinforced by effects in the music. The sequence ended by showing once more the 'celestial' percussionist hitting the gong and dissolving into a reality shot of the orchestra with a close-up of the actual percussionist finishing his performance at the gong.

The gong player scene involved superimposing three shots over each other:

(*a*) First a close-up of the orchestra's percussionist was filmed against a white background, underexposed to get a silhouette effect. A dupenegative of this shot was used in the superimposition to show the gong player as a white silhouette like an ethereal being.

(*b*) For the effect of the concentrically expanding spheres travelling

FIG. 71. Percussionist in front of a white background.
The effect sequence 'Lightning and Thunder' required some elaborate model photography and processing work as described in the text.

FIG. 72. The negative image of the percussionist, surrounded by clouds and lightning flashes, suggests a 'celestial gong player'. Expanding spheres, emanating from the gong, represent the sound waves (see Fig. 73).

towards the camera, we again used balls. The camera was mounted some 8 ft above the floor pointing downwards. A few inches below it, a small plywood square was fitted with a hole dead in front of the lens. By means of a chute, a number of balls were fed through the hole and fell to the floor. The floor was covered with black velvet and shaded off so that the balls disappeared into darkness at the end of their fall. The resulting shot was optically reversed in the laboratory. Superimposed on the gong player scene, these balls looked like spheres rushing out of the gong towards the camera.

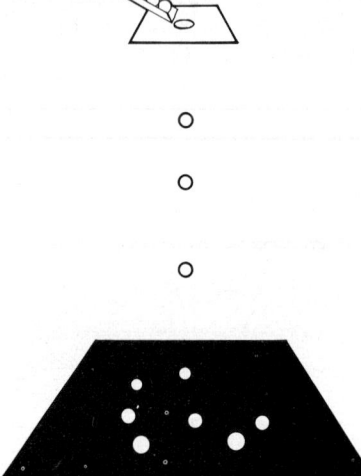

FIG. 73. *Set-up for filming 'Expanding Spheres'.* The camera is pointing vertically down. Ping-pong balls were fed into a hole in a board fixed in front of the lens. The balls dropped onto a sheet of black velvet which was shaded from light so that the balls disappeared into darkness. Optical reversal of the scene made the balls rushing up to the camera giving the impression of rapidly expanding spheres.

(*c*) A few clouds were painted on glass and this glass sheet set up in front of a black velvet cloth. Then, two or three other glass sheets were coated black on one side, and varying lightning patterns were scraped into the paint, again in register with the gong surface. These sheets were successively put between the first glass and the piece of velvet leaving room for backlighting. In order to get the flashing effect, this scene was shot in singleframe, switching the lights on and off as desired. Of course, the start of the flashes and their lengths had to be timed to synchronize with the action of the gong player.

All this sounds more complicated than it was. The three scenes were not shot on the same day but at various times as convenient. The secret of all work involving multiple superimposition is to give the optical department of the laboratory precise frame-by-frame instructions in the form of an 'optical printing schedule'. The edge-numbers on the negative make this easy.

Films in the Making

For the scene with the window, we built a little set in our studio. The swaying tree branches, billowing curtains and a flickering candle, all agitated by a fan, gave the desired impression of a stormy night. We could shoot this scene 'straight' with flashes of sheet-lightning illuminating the sky. Timing was important, but again not difficult. The script envisaged the sequence to last for about 1 min and we had asked the composer to give us music of that length with 5 or 6 'thunder crashes' at uneven intervals. After the music was recorded, we measured the footage between the sound modulations of the crashes, and all we had to do now was to cut in the visuals of the flashes correspondingly.

The following sequence concerns how we hear.

Lend me your Ear (Hearing Sound)

'Sound waves pass through the air to our ears', continued Muir, 'but what then?' He signalled to one of the children. 'David will lend us his ear. We'll go right inside it to look at the organs of hearing'.

On the side-screen appeared a big close-up of David's ear. The camera tracked onto and into it. One after the other, the ear drum, the organs of the middle ear, and the labyrinth of the inner ear were demonstrated, with Muir explaining their functions.

For this sequence, several models were made. That of the outer ear canal was simply a slightly curved tube, wide enough to track into, and at its far end closed by the ear drum, a taut piece of rubber vibrating to the puffs of a bicycle pump.

The model of the middle ear was more elaborate. We made it about 5 ft long because the bigger a model is, the easier and smoother is its manipulation. The bones—hammer, anvil and stirrup—were made of stiff paper and connected by articulated joints. The end of the hammer pierced the ear drum and provided a convenient handle for 'vibrating' the bone mechanism from outside the model by pushing and pulling. On the opposite side of the model the stirrup touched the oval window which communicates with the inner ear. This window, and the round window below it, were activated by two bicycle pumps, working in rhythm with the vibrations of the bones.

The inner ear model was also some 4–5 ft long. It had to show the electric nerve currents which we decided to represent by streams of light. This model consisted of a stiff paper spiral—the labyrinth—fixed by one edge to a sheet of parchment. Behind it, we fitted a faceted mirror-glass sphere such as is sometimes used in ballrooms. When this sphere, lit up by a strong beam from a spotlight, was made to spin, a fluctuating travelling light effect was reflected from it onto the back of the semi-transparent sheet of parchment.

On one side of the model, a few feet away and out of focus, we fixed a transparent glass sphere, covered with tufts of cotton wool and lit from

The Work of the Science Film Maker

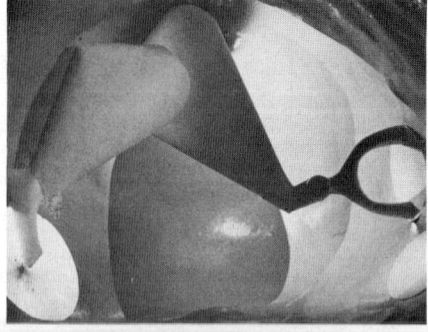

Fig. 74. Working model of the middle ear showing the vibrating ear drum and the movements of the hammer, the anvil and the stirrup. On the right, the 'fenestra ovalis' communicates with the inner ear.

Fig. 75. Effects model of the inner ear ('labyrinth'). Streams of moving light represent the nerve currents leading to the brain.

within. A switch device made this luminous body blink, suggesting that the sound signals were received by the brain.

This inner ear model made no pretension to being functionally accurate. Since nobody yet knows in detail how our brain works, an analogy involving electric currents was the given solution for a film.

The sequence, and with it Part One of the film, ended with a scene of the entire orchestra playing a swinging tune. In front stood a dummy figure with its skull lighting up in rhythm with the music. David, sitting nearby, enjoyed this effect. Muir smiled at him: 'Well, there aren't any lights in your head but the vibrations set up currents in your nerves which go to your brain. And so you hear.'

Part II Exploring the Instruments

This part dealt with the question of how the instruments are sounded and how notes of different pitch are produced. A short reference was first made to banging and bowing, then blowing was examined in detail.

Chimney into Flute (Vibrating Air Columns)

The film at this point is concerned with air eddies and vibrating blocks of air. On the side screen, the roof and chimney stack of an old house

Films in the Making

appeared silhouetted against the night sky. The flutes of the orchestra played a 'windy phrase' which changed into the natural sound effect of wind howling in the chimney.

A close up shot of the chimney model dissolved to an insert showing air eddies swirling around the rim of the chimney.

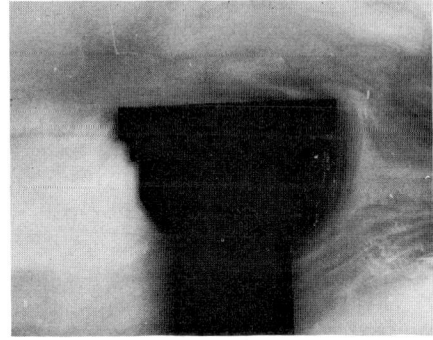

FIG. 76. Model trick shot suggesting 'wind howling round a chimney stack' showing the air eddies.

The problem of making these swirling eddies visible gave us a headache at first but finally we hit on a workable idea.

A bas-relief replica of the chimney model was made and inserted into a shallow glass tray standing slightly tilted on a table covered with black velvet. The camera was mounted above the tray, pointing downwards, and the bas-relief put in register with the chimney in the preceding scene. We filled the tray with water and, after starting the camera, added some milk at the raised side of the tray; this made the water overflow at the lower side. Milky streaks swished against the chimney rim, curled around it and flowed on. We continued pouring water and milk alternately into the tray until we had sufficient footage to cover the length of the scene. The camera was under-cranked to speed up the swirling. On the screen the streaks of milk gave the desired effect of turbulent air.

The CU shot of the chimney rim with the eddies dissolved back to the static scene of the chimney stack seen before. Muir asked: 'What has wind to

FIG. 77. *Set-up for Swirling Air Eddies.*
The bas-relief model of the chimney in the glass tray had to be put into register with the chimney model seen before. Milk was then injected into the water which was poured into the tray on the right. The mixture swirled round the bas relief and overflowed on the left. The effect on the screen was very 'atmospheric'.

153

do with music?' The camera panned down the chimney stack and within it appeared the effect of a standing wave.

The movement of standing waves can best be demonstrated with the aid of a rotating Crova disc the lines on which give an illusion of a concertina movement. The disc was set up behind the chimney stack. A section of the front and back of the stack was removed exposing the to-and-fro movement of the lines on the Crova disc. Black velvet surrounded the outline of the chimney and hid everything which was not meant to be seen.

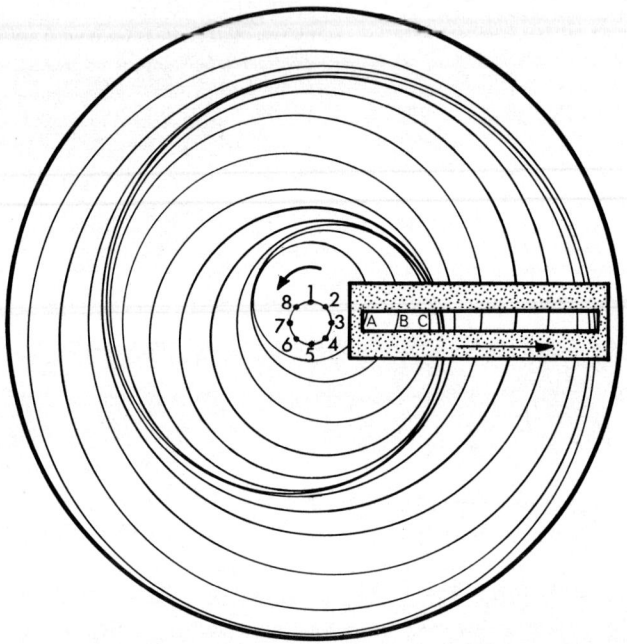

Fig. 78. *Crova Disc.* Circles of different radius are drawn with their centres marked by numbers 1–8. A piece of cardboard is then placed in front of the rotating disc with a slot exposing small parts of the circles. These parts or lines, marked ABC, etc., move to and fro, giving the illusion of successive compression- and rarefaction-waves travelling along the length of the slot. Crova discs can usually be obtained from firms selling scientific equipment. But these commercially available discs are too small for filming and it is best to draw one's own disc. The minimum size should be 60 cm across so that the operative slot is about 25 cm long.

Muir: 'The disturbances at the top of the chimney make the block of air inside it vibrate. This creates the howling sound. Much the same goes on in the wind instruments which allow the players to control the air columns so that they produce musical sounds instead of hisses and howls.'

To illustrate this similarity, the chimney dissolved into the close-up of a flute. Since the chimney was upright, the flute too was shown upright. This close-up was followed by a medium-long shot which included the

Films in the Making

FIG. 79. *Chimney into Flute.* An effects sequence referring to vibrating blocks of air in wind instruments.

1. The chimney shown in Fig. 76 dissolves into the model of a similar chimney. The camera tracks on to narrow the field of view to the frame marked by the arrows.

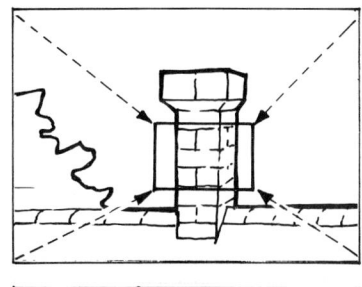

2. The inner part of the brickwork dissolves into a standing wave, produced by means of a Crova disc. (Fig. 78). The standing wave moves to and fro.

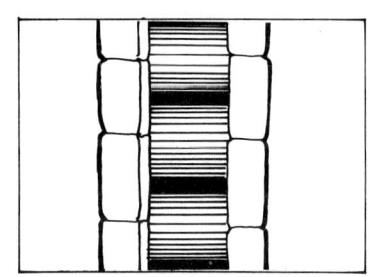

3. The standing wave remains but the brickwork around it dissolves into the outline of a section of a flute. The scene now resembles the one shown in Fig. 80 except that the flute is here in a vertical position.

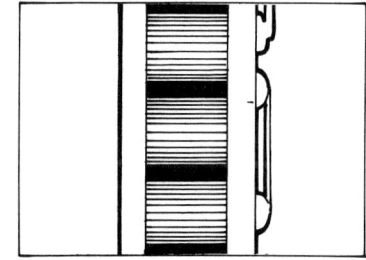

4. This is a live scene, played for a laugh. Since the flute in the previous scene is vertical, it is logical to show the flute player in a horizontal position. He was therefore filmed through a prism.

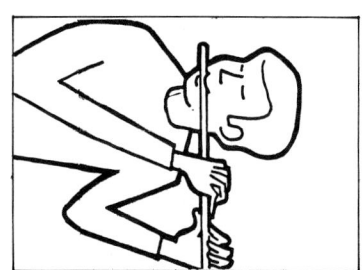

5. The prism is turned by 90° and the flute player spins round into his normal upright position. Fig. 80 is a short insert within this scene.

flautist. We played this scene for a laugh. With the flute in an upright position, the flautist had to appear 'floating' horizontally across the top of the screen; muffled in a blowing scarf, he could be taken as an impersonation of the wind.

FIG. 80. Effects scene showing the vibrations of the air column in a flute. (A Crova disc shot, superimposed on a CU reality shot of a section of a flute).

This scene was shot through a prism fitted to the front of the lens. Turning the prism through 90° while the camera was running, the flautist and flute swung round into their normal position.

During this scene, the sound changed from howling to a tune played by the flute. The lights went up over the orchestra where our flute player just finished his tune.

The film now continued by demonstrating the technical characteristics of flutes and reed instruments, and then by discussing *pitch*.

Ta-ti, Ta-ti (Pitch)

The orchestra played a short piece of music ending on three sets of low and high notes, an octave apart. Muir repeated the notes: 'Ta-ti, Ta-ti, ... 'What,' he asked, 'makes this difference? The answer is: long length—low notes, short length—high notes.' A boy demonstrated this with the help of a ruler.

The effect was repeated on the harp, the glockenspiel and on a pan pipe: these instruments have separate lengths for each note. 'Others' says Muir, 'give many notes from the same actual length because the *vibrating part* can be altered.' This was shown by a double bass and a flute. The flute led up to a scene demonstrating how changing lengths of air columns change the pitch of the notes.

One of the boys, Tom, blew a penny whistle. It gave the lowest note when *all* the holes of the pipe were covered. But as Tom took his fingers off the holes one by one, the notes got higher and higher. Muir now took a pair of scissors and cut the pipe off at the hole nearest the mouthpiece. Tom could still play the highest note on the remaining bit of his pipe. This proved that the sounding part of the pipe ends at the nearest uncovered hole and the rest of the pipe no longer matters.

Films in the Making

FIG. 81. (top) and FIG. 82. (bottom): The demonstration of Pitch. 'Long lengths—low notes; short lengths—high notes', shown by means of a ruler and a harp.

Now, the brass instruments; the French horn with all its coils forms a tube of 16 ft in length. The horn player played the lowest note on it, the fundamental. An 'uncoiled' horn, 16 ft long, descended from the ceiling and remained suspended above the heads of the orchestra. Again the horn player blew the fundamental on it, it was the same low-pitched note as before. He then blew the notes of the harmonic scale. Muir demonstrated how these higher notes are produced in brass instruments by the player's lip movements which split the air columns in 2, 3 or more sections.* Muir ended by saying: 'In the old days, only the notes of the harmonic scale could be produced but there are gaps in the scale. With to-day's instruments it is possible to fill in these gaps. Let's look at the full range of a modern orchestra.'

Seven Times Ta-ti (Musical Compass)

This sequence on the musical compass opened with a shot which included the whole orchestra. From the side, a giant transparent stave slid in, showing all the notes of the musical compass. The stave, almost as

---

* A Melde string apparatus (see page 162) makes this splitting process visible. Strictly speaking, this apparatus only demonstrates the production of harmonics in string instruments but the splitting of air columns occurs in a similar manner.

The Work of the Science Film Maker

Fig. 83. An 'uncoiled' French horn, 16 ft long, descends and comes to rest above the orchestra. The player's lip movements 'split' the air column and produce low and high notes.

Fig. 84. Muir Mathieson demonstrates the whole compass of the orchestra: 7 octaves.
The range of each instrument is demonstrated by means of a giant stave, slid in front of the orchestra. As each player plays a scale from the lowest to the highest note, the notes on the stave light up in synchronization.

wide as the stage, came to rest in front of the orchestra, with the conductor and players still clearly seen behind it.

Muir turned round: 'An orchestra has a range of about 7 octaves. Most instruments only play about three of them but the harp covers almost the lot. For the very lowest notes we need a double-bassoon, for the very highest a piccolo.'

The lights dim, leaving a faint view of the stave and its notes. At the beat of a gong the flute player, spot-lit, appeared in front of the stave and started playing a scale from the lowest to the highest note of the flute's range. As the scale was heard, the corresponding notes on the stave lit up; these lighted notes showed the complete range of the flute.

The demonstration was repeated by the rest of the woodwinds, the brass and the strings. The very lowest and the very highest notes of the musical compass were shown and heard in a duet, or duel, between the double-bassoon and the piccolo, the one growling lower and lower, the other squeaking higher and higher. The corresponding notes on the stave twinkled in rhythm.

This sequence is a good illustration of how an expensive, animated diagram, many hundred feet long, can be avoided by the use of a model which allows the integration of live action with simulated animation in a natural and enjoyable way. Although the model mechanism was fairly elaborate, its cost was not half that of conventional animation.

Films in the Making

Fig. 85. The range of the trumpet: about 2½ octaves.

Fig. 86. The range of the cello: about 3 octaves.

The stave-model itself consisted of a wooden frame across which a sheet of theatrical gauze was stretched. The stave lines were depicted in white tape. Fifty-two small light bulbs, representing the notes, were fitted on a black batten running diagonally across the frame. This framework was built in a carpenter's workshop.

The electrical mechanism was designed by our 'magician' George Cooper and was one of his masterpieces. He wired each bulb on the stave to the corresponding key on a dummy piano. Every time a piano key was touched its note lit up on the stave. This dummy piano stood next to the camera in a position from which the pianist who worked the dummy could see the orchestra members in front of the stave and could keep time with them on his keyboard.

This sequence, including a few re-takes, was shot in two consecutive days.

The sequence ended with the harp. It played a glissando which turned into the tune of *Oranges and Lemons*, the notes on the stave doing their trick again. The tune was now taken up by the whole orchestra and, the stage lights come on again while the stave slid back into the wings. Finally, the scene faded out.

The Work of the Science Film Maker

Part III Looking at Sound

This part goes further into the question of loudness and pitch and then explains the differences in musical quality.

No specially made models were needed here because the whole action centred round an audio-spectrometer. This instrument analyses sound and translates it into a visual record which appears in the form of the familiar electronic tracings on the screen of a cathode ray tube. Variations in loudness are shown by expanding and contracting horizontal lines, pitch by the height of these lines on the screen, and quality by the pattern which these lines, one above the other, form and which indicate the harmonics of which each note is made up.

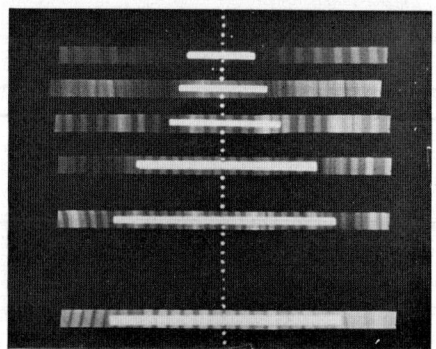

FIG. 87. An audio-spectrometer pattern showing the fundamental (bottom line) and the overtones (harmonics) of a musical note.

Denys Parsons discovered this unusual research instrument in the laboratory of a large electronics firm and persuaded the management to lend it to us complete with an operator. Denys and this man had to make many mysterious adjustments before the instrument responded to our particular requirements.

Harmonics

Muir opened this sequence by saying that each sound from a musical instrument is composed of the fundamental note and of various overtones, called harmonics; these differ according to the characteristics of the instrument. He chose the woodwinds to prove this. Four players: flute, oboe, clarinet and bassoon, standing in a row near the audio-spectrometer, blew the same note on their instrument, and each of these notes produced a different pattern on the audio-spectrometer screen.

To show the significance of these patterns, a demonstration on a Melde string apparatus was given. It showed that a string can vibrate either as a whole, or in two or more sections (simple vibrations). It can also vibrate simultaneously as a whole *and* in sections (complex vibrations). Such complex vibrations occur in all musical instruments, that is why all instrumental sounds contain harmonics, which the audio-spectrometer

Films in the Making

Fig. 88. Four different instruments successively playing the same note.

Fig. 89. The fundamentals and overtones of the above four instruments are represented on the audio-spectrometer by a pattern of vibrating blocks of air, produced for the film by means of a Crova disc (see Fig. 79). Each Crova disc scene had to be shot separately and individually superimposed on each of the four patterns. The position of the lines indicate pitch, their width loudness.

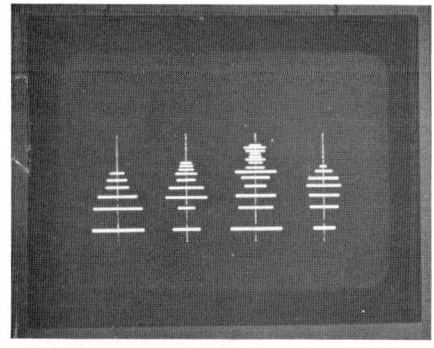

Fig. 90. By manipulating the controls of the audio-spectrometer an oboe can be made to sound like a flute. The transition from one stage of the harmonic pattern to the next can be distinctly seen on the screen of the A.-S. and heard in the loudspeaker.

Fig. 91. The audio-spectrometer shows the fluctuating sound pattern of the whole orchestra.

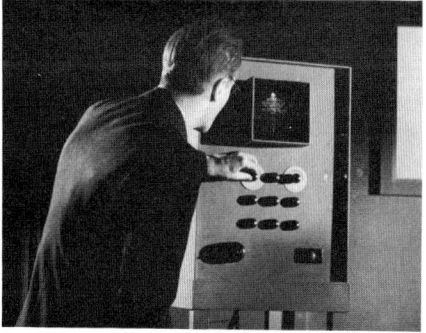

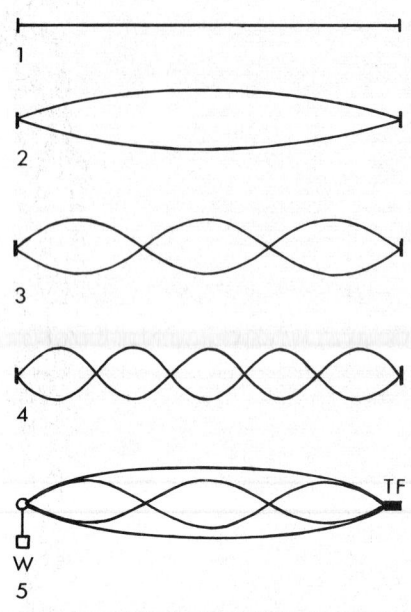

FIG. 92. *Melde String Apparatus.* A stretched string or wire (1) can vibrate as a whole (2), denoting the fundamental of a musical note, or in several sections (3, 4), denoting its harmonics. These are simple vibrations. The string can also vibrate as a whole and in sections at one and the same time (5). These complex vibrations occur in all musical instruments. Part 5 of the diagram shows the principle of the Melde string apparatus. One end of a stretched string is attached to an electrically vibrated tuning fork (TF), the other end runs over a wheel and is fixed to a weight (W) which keeps the string taut. The film shows this apparatus in use and all kinds of simple and complex vibrations can clearly be observed.

screen records as varying patterns of multiple lines. Each line represents a different wave frequency.

Having demonstrated all this, Muir smiled: 'Since harmonics make such a difference, tinkering with them ought to change the quality of the instrument. We are going to make an oboe sound like a flute.'

Oboe into Flute (An experiment)

This sequence showed the oboe-player in a sound-proof box playing a sustained C. The sound was filtered through a special amplifier which could suppress or boost any harmonic. Our science demonstrator worked the controls of this amplifier and cut out the harmonics one by one: the oboe's pattern on the audio-spectrometer screen slowly changed to that of the flute. At the same time, the *sound* of the oboe assumed that of the flute. Muir: 'Changing the pattern of harmonics does change the quality of the note.' The orchestra loudly applauded this tour de force. (Since the amplifying equipment was not available at the scheduled time, we had to make up a dummy and film the actual experiment later.)

The film ended with the whole orchestra playing the main theme of the music which appeared as a fascinating fluctuating pattern on the screen of the audio-spectrometer.

The fluorescent light pattern on the audio-spectrometer screen was not bright enough to register on the stock we used if the camera had been run at normal speed. We had to under-run the camera to get the necessary exposure.

Films in the Making

As the camera was under-run the music, played on a record player from a pre-recorded disc, also had to be under-run at exactly the same rate. Denys Parsons and Adrian Jeakins did some rapid calculations, the turntable speed was adjusted accordingly and Malcolm Arnold's lively finale echoed through the hall at the slow beat of a funeral march. Miraculously, when projected, sound and visual were in perfect synchronization, well visible and running at normal speed.

A few final notes about this production. The film was shot in 35mm black-and-white and reduced to 16mm for distribution. The shooting in the school hall itself took about 7 working days but a few players had to come to our studio later for close-up shots and retakes. The preparing and shooting of various inserts, models and effects took place over a period of several weeks.

The sound was recorded and dubbed by Anvil Films. All of Muir's speech was recorded at the school hall without the need for further sessions. The music was partly recorded in sync, and had partly been pre-recorded and was played back during the film. For certain scenes, a guide track only was recorded during filming and later post-recorded; in addition, wild tracks were recorded where necessary. All these varied methods had to be adopted due to some acoustic problems in the school hall and because of the non-availability of some players on certain days.

Editing took several months. A page from the editing schedule, prepared for the guidance of the editors, is reproduced below.

Editing schedule: High notes and Low notes

Code: S = Sync; M = Mute; RT = Retake; PB = Playback; GT = Guide track;
  PR = Post-recording; WT = Wild track.
  ③ = printed take

Shot No.	Date	Code	Takes	To be used	Contents	Comments
247	31	S	1 ②	2	M.M. conducting, turning, talking	Includes 249; speech covers 250 and 251
248 RT	29 6	PB	1 ② ①	2 RT 1	Whole orchestra, Nearer shot	
249	31					Contained in 247
250	30	S	1 ②	2	CU Harp	
251	7	S	①	1	CU Glockenspiel	Cut out whisper
251a	4	GT	①	1	Peter blows Pan pipe	For PR
251b	4					Contained in 262a; use if needed
253a	30	S	1 ② ③	Use best take	M.M., Peter, Tom	Take 2: false start; Use last part for 261b

The Work of the Science Film Maker

Shot No.	Date	Code	Takes	To be used	Contents	Comments
261	7	S	①	1	CU Ruler	Insert for 253a
261a	4	M	①	1	Peter watches Tom	Use as cut-away for 261
261b					Boy getting up from kneeling	This is last part of 253a; to precede 262
262	7	S	1 ②	2	M.M. talking	
262a incl. 251b	4	M	①	1	Tom and ruler; Tom watches Peter	Keep for reference
263	6	S	1 2 ③	3	Cellos and D.-basses	Use second action
267	3	GT	①	1	Pan along orchestra	WT 267 contains commentary
268	7	WT	1 ②	2	Flute explained	
271	7	M	1 ②	2	Horn demonstration	WT 268 covers this
273	30	M	1 2 ③	3	Long horn descends on orchestra	To be cut up for use in 273, 276a, 281.—Zip-pan to right at end.

TRANSFERENCE OF HEAT

This teaching film for lower age groups in three parts was shot in 35mm colour and reduced to 16mm for distribution. Commissioned to Realist by the Gas Council, it was designed to assist in the teaching of children, aged 12–15, and it is made up of the three one-reelers: *Convection*, *Conduction* and *Radiation*. Each of the three films consists of an introduction, followed by 4 or 5 examples (experiments or cinematic demonstrations) of specific teaching points, and ends with a brief summary.

The methods of presenting the subjects in these films had, therefore, to be very different from those in *Science in the Orchestra*. That film had been conceived as a lecture-demonstration, shot in sync. The presence of a 'teacher' on the screen, talking directly to the audience and unfolding the story step by step, relieves the actual teacher in the class of much groundwork, leaving to him mainly to answer questions or elaborate on certain points *after* the films are shown.

Transference of Heat, on the other hand, does not deal with the subject comprehensively. This film is meant to illustrate certain self-contained aspects of it. The teacher can thus adapt the screening of the three parts to his teaching routine: he can run them as an introduction to, or a summary of, his lesson, or show them in sections stopping the projector after each sequence to discuss its contents, much as is nowadays done with single-concept film loops. This type of film is therefore more flexible than the

Films in the Making

previous one. Being an integral part of the lesson, it requires the teacher to be 'film-minded'; he must respond actively and sympathetically to the idea of teaching with the help of visual aids.

After the educational adviser determined the contents of the series, the general framework was discussed, the details fixed and the script written in close co-operation between all parties concerned.

The main technical problems consisted of making water-currents in pipes and vessels and air-currents in rooms visible and translating heat conduction and heat radiation into visual terms. The following pages describe how we filmed some of the more interesting effects.

Although each of these three films was to be complete in itself, we tried to think of a 'common denominator', a sort of 'black body' symbol, which would serve as an introduction to each of the films. Since almost every hot body convects, conducts and radiates heat, the problem boiled down to finding an abstract object rather than a utilitarian article. After some deliberation, we decided on a ball of iron.

It is strange how difficult it is in a city the size of London to buy a ball of iron. It had to be about 10 centimetres in diameter to fit the ordinary type of bench tripod. No shop seems to stock iron balls that size. At last, an idea: what about an old cannon ball? I went to the Imperial War Museum and returned with £1's worth of Crimean War munition, ideal for our purpose.

The cannon ball, resting on its tripod and heated by a Bunsen burner, was the desired 'leitmotiv' to appear at the beginning and end of each film. We had now to think about how best to show its function as a convector, conductor and radiator.

Before going into the details of our work, it may interest the reader to look at one of the scripts in this series. It is short and shows where the various effects which we are going to describe, have their place in the eleven minute film and how they are linked to the rest of the material.

Convection:

POST-PRODUCTION SCRIPT

Sc. No.	35mm footage	Visual	Commentary
1.	0	(*Fade in*) Main and Credit Titles (*Fade out*)	
2.	28	(*Fade in*) Iron ball on Bunsen burner tracking on to CU (*Mix*)	A hot body or substance warms the air around it. Heated air becomes less dense and is forced upwards causing air currents. We have used a special process to make these currents visible.

Sc. No.	35mm footage	Visual	Commentary
3.	53	Same ball with Schlieren effect.	This is a picture of the actual air rising from the ball, pushed up by the heavier cool air coming in from the sides.
4.	71	Hot-air currents, Schlieren effect.	Here is another picture of hot air rising. This transference of heat by air-currents is called *convection*.
5.	86	MS Glass tank on Bunsen flame; water currents are shown.	The same happens in liquids. This vessel is filled with water which contains some metal powder to make the currents visible. The water nearest the flame becomes hot first, less dense and lighter.
6.	110	CU of water currents in tank.	The cooler water above falls and pushes the warm water up. Here again, convection currents carry the heat upwards. These currents cause different temperatures within the vessel until all the water reaches boiling point.
		(Fade out)	
7.	135	*(Fade in)* Title: CENTRAL HEATING *(Fade out)*	
8.	144	LS Central Heating Glass-model. The water is seen to circulate.	The gravity-fed system of central heating works entirely by convection. Again, powder is used here to show up the currents.
9.	159	CU Model-boiler on flame.	The water is heated in the boiler:
10.	164	Real boiler in an outhouse.	Boilers usually stand in the kitchen or outhouse.
11.	170	Pan up model-pipe	The hot water rises.
12.	179	Real pipe in room.	The pipes get warm and some of their heat is given up to the house.
13.	186	CU Model expansion pipe	At the top of the system, there is an expansion pipe which takes care of any overflow.
14.	197	Real expansion pipe in loft.	This is usually in the loft.
15.	202	Pan along model to radiator.	The water continues round the system, flowing through the radiators.
16.	211	Real radiator in room	Radiators have large surfaces—
17.	216	Other real radiator.	—so that they can heat the rooms as much as possible.
18.	222	Model: pan from radiator back to boiler.	Having passed through all the radiators, the water flows back

Films in the Making

Sc. No.	35mm footage	Visual	Commentary
18.			to the boiler to be heated up again.
19.	233	LS Whole model again. (*Mix*).	In this way, there is continuous circulation.
20.	242	Chart of c.h. system with forced convection.	In some modern central heating systems, the heated water is forced through the pipes by means—
21.	253	Chart as above: pump jumps in.	—of a pump.
22.	256	Chart: CU of pump.	The pump enables the pipes to be of a smaller size and the water circulates more quickly.
23.	267	Chart: CU of pump and arrow.	The direction of flow—
24.	269	ditto: arrow reversed. (*Fade out*)	—can be varied.
25.	276	(*Fade in*) Title: VENTILATION (*Fade out*)	
26.	285	(*Fade in*) Glass model designed to show smoke currents. On the left: a candle inside the model.	Air can be made to circulate by convection just as well as water. The model will show how
	285	Smoke issuing from a tube held above model. The smoke goes up.	The air movement will be made visible by smoke. As smoke normally goes up, it would not flow through the glass channel. The air in the channel remains stationary.
27.	320	CU, candle being lit.	But if the candle is lit—
28.	323	Glass Model as in 26. The smoke is drawn through the model.	—the heat sets up convection currents. The lighter warmed air above the flame is pushed up by the cold air which is streaming in from the side, causing the air to circulate. Many years ago, coal-mines were ventilated simply by lighting a fire at the bottom of one of the shafts.
29.	355	(*Fade out*) (*Fade in*) Room with a fire in the fireplace with two children in front of it. (*Mix*)	In the house, open fires create convection currents.
30.	366	CU Model fireplace with draught-effect.	These currents are often so strong that they amount to a draught.
31.	376	LS Model room with fireplace and draught-effect.	This draught chases most of the heat up the chimney.

167

The Work of the Science Film Maker

Sc. No.	35mm footage	Visual	Commentary
32.	385	CU Model of chimney with Schlieren effect, showing fierce hot-air currents.	Using the special process again, we can see the heat carried upwards by the convection currents, warming the air *above* the house rather than the air *in* the house.
33.	403	Real gas fire (convector-radiator)	Modern heaters, such as this one, provide good ventilation without draught.
34.	413	Model room with model gas fire and circulation-effect	The warm air circulates gently round the room and distributes the heat evenly.
35.	427	CU Chimney-model with Schlieren effect, showing only a little hot air escaping. *(Fade out)*	Very little heat is now escaping by the chimney.
36.	436	*(Fade in)* Title: AERONAUTICS *(Fade out)*	
37.	446	*(Fade in)* Classroom with master pointing to a painting showing Montgolfier balloons.	The fact that hot air rises was used as far back as 1783 by the French brothers Montgolfier to lift balloons into the air.
38.	465	CU. The painting	Huge fires on the launching platform heated the air which filled the balloons.
39.	477	As 37. Master displays 2 more small pictures of balloons.	
40.	486	CU. First small picture.	Later, braziers, suspended from the balloons, provided them with heat during their flight.
41.	496	CU Second small picture.	These balloons were able to carry aeronauts who had to look after the fire continuously.
42.	503	Master walks out of scene. *(Mix)*	... Now let's see an actual demonstration.
43.	511	LS School grounds. Master and some of his pupils form a circle round a brazier.	Here we have a brazier—
44.	524	CU, Brazier with flames.	—a fire,—
45.	533	MS. A wooden base put round the brazier; a chimney stack put above the fire.	—a platform, ... a chimney to catch the hot air—
46.	547	MS. Balloon taken to the chimney.	—and the balloon.

Films in the Making

Sc. No.	35mm footage	Visual	Commentary
47.	555	MS. Balloon put over chimney.	... Filling the balloon takes some time.
48.	573	LS. Balloon being airborne.	When there is sufficient hot air in the balloon, it is released.
		(Fade out)	
49.	593	*(Fade in)* CU. Windsock on airfield.	Gliding depends very much on convection currents such as rise from certain areas on the ground. These currents are called 'thermals' by the pilots.
50.	611	LS. Launching of glider by winch.	Gliders can be launched by various mechanical methods, but once in the air, they are dependent on thermals—
51.	622	CU. Glider in air.	—for cross-country flying... Let's see how these thermals originate.
		(Fade out)	
52.	628	*(Fade in)* Animated Diagram: Village amidst fields. Thermal appears, upward movement is marked.	The sun does not heat the ground evenly. For instance, the roofs of houses get hot more quickly than the green vegetation of fields and woods. So, warm-air currents rise from towns and villages.
53.	655	Ditto: Wider landscape with 4 thermals.	Amongst other areas which produce thermal currents, are ripe cornfields and sunny or wind-protected slopes. How does a glider respond to such currents?
54.	673	Ditto: Closer shot with 2 thermals. Path of glider is drawing itself across scene.	Without the help of thermals, a sailplane loses height steadily... But in an up-current, the rising air *lifts* the glider again... By sailing from one thermal to the next and so on and on, gliders can cover hundreds of miles.
		(Mix)	
55.	709	Real glider, coming down and landing.	When the pilot can find no more thermals, he must return to the ground.
		(Fade out)	
56.	725	*(Fade in)* Title: CONVECTION AND WEATHER *(Fade out)*	

169

Sc. No.	35mm footage	Visual	Commentary
57.	736	*(Fade in)* An. Diagram. Thermal with cumulus cloud forming on top.	When a warm air current has reached a higher level, it cools because it expands. The water-vapour contained in the current condenses and a cumulus cloud might form.
58.	762	*(Mix)* Real Cumulus Cloud.	Clouds are a collection of water droplets—
59.	768	Cloud above rooftops; pan up to big dark cloud. *(Mix)*	—and when these droplets grow big enough, the cloud becomes darker, and the drops—
60.	778	Street scene in rain.	—may fall as rain. Convection currents, therefore, are one of the causes of showers and thunderstorms.
61.	794	*(Fade out)* *(Fade in)* Drawing of a silhouette of town in daylight.	Under certain conditions, a so-called 'inversion' occurs in the atmosphere.
62.	805	Ditto: inversion layer high up in air jumps in.	This means that an upper layer of warm air floats on top of a lower layer of cool air.
63.	815	Ditto: Labels 'warm', 'cool', jump in and out.	Warm air above, cool air below; this is the reverse of what normally happens.
64.	828	Ditto, as 62.	The warm layer may float at a height of 500 to 1000 ft, and it is liable to interfere with the convection currents in the atmosphere.
65.	842	Ditto. Scene below the layer becomes dark; night-effect of town with the windows lit up.	Sometimes artificial light is needed even in day time because smoke rising from the town forms a pall which keeps out the sunlight.
66.	857	Ditto: layer is now on the ground, half obscuring the town. *(Mix)*	Often, the inversion layer forms *on* or *near* the ground.
67.	866	Real town scene; church-tower, sunlit, seen through mist.	If it is so thin that you can see through it, it is called ground mist.
68.	873	Park scene in mist, no sunshine.	Thick mist reduces the sunlight.
69.	880	Street scene in thick fog.	If visibility is *very* poor, we speak of fog. Often, the town's smoke is trapped in this lower layer, and then we have *smog*.

Films in the Making

Sc. No.	35mm footage	Visual	Commentary
70.	899	Other street in thick fog.	The circulation of air currents is greatly diminished and sometimes it stops altogether.
		(Fade out)	
71.	913	*(Fade in)* Title: SUMMARY *(Fade out)*	
72.	922	*(Fade in)* Iron ball with Schlieren-effect, as Sc. 3.	The film has illustrated the various ways in which heat is carried by moving particles in fluids; that is: in gases—
73.	938	CU. Currents in water tank, as Sc. 6.	—and in liquids. When a fluid is heated, currents are set up.
74.	958	LS ditto; with Bunsen burner, as Sc. 5.	The cold, more dense fluid sinks, and the warmer, lighter fluid is pushed up. This process is called *convection*.
		(Fade out)	
75.	965	*(Fade in)* END TITLES	
	987	*(Fade out)*	

The filming of the non-technical actuality shots needs no comment. The scenes which had to be staged, partly with and partly without special effects, were produced as described below:

SCENES 2–4: The cannon-ball set-up. We used the Schlieren system (see pages 87–89) for the convection effect. At the time of shooting this film, there were not many research laboratories equipped with a Schlieren apparatus. Luckily, the Imperial College in London not only owns such an installation but was very accommodating in letting us use it. Consequently, we took our cannon-ball along and with the help of two laboratory technicians set it up within the optical system of the huge apparatus.

FIG. 93. *Transference of Heat.* A heated cannon ball served as 'leitmotiv' for the three films of this series.

When we heated the ball and switched on the Schlieren beam, no air currents could, of course, be seen with the naked eye. But when we looked through the viewfinder of the camera whose lens had now become part of the Schlieren optical system, we could see a beautiful multi-coloured flame-like movement rising from the ball, the colours indicating the density gradients of the air. The film picked up the image exactly as we saw it in the viewfinder. We took additional shots of hot air rising from a model of a chimney which we had also brought along and then experimented with a few other objects for future reference. Even the warm air, rising from the palm of a hand, could clearly be seen.

FIG. 94. *Rising Heat made visible by the Schlieren Process.* The heated cannon ball, shown in Fig. 94, was set up within the Schlieren optical system and a multi-coloured ghost-like flame was seen rising from the ball in the camera's viewfinder, positioned at point I of Fig. 30. The film picked the image up exactly as it appeared in the viewfinder.

The Gas Council film *Something Nice to Eat* (Director: Sarah Erulkar), produced at a later date, used the Schlieren method in a most engaging way in connection with the art and science of Cookery. Thus, this method whose main application is the sphere of aerodynamic research can be very useful in the most diverse fields of film-making.

SCENES 5–6: There are several ways in which to show invisible *currents in fluids* (see page 112). In this and the following scenes we used aluminium powder. The light metal particles, suspended in the water and lit from the back, showed up effectively as they floated with the currents.

SCENES 7–19: The glass model for these scenes had to be specially blown to our instructions. Its size was about 75 × 100 cm. Lighting was a bit of a problem due to the narrowness of the glass tubes and if we had to do this sequence again we would use a larger model.

Scene 16 is an insert showing a real radiator. A simple enough shot, one would think, but its filming almost brought about a nervous crisis. There was one single radiator in my house. It stood in the hall but offered no good camera angle and anyway, we wanted to show it in a living room. This radiator had not been used for years because the boiler had become defunct. We thought that no water could still be in the system and detached the radiator from the pipes. First nothing happened, but after a moment a suspicious gurgling noise started and all of a sudden a jet of a rusty brown fluid shot out of the pipe and in no time floor and carpet were awash. Before we could do anything, the flood stopped as suddenly as it had started.

Films in the Making

The cleaning-up operations took several hours and the carpet was spoiled for good. But Denys Parsons asserted in cold blood that according to all scientific probability, 'this could not have happened'.

SCENES 26–28: The description of the Schlieren system on page 87 makes it obvious that, effective as it is, it has certain limitations. Solid objects, for instance, appear in silhouette. In order to make air currents *within* three-dimensional models visible other methods have to be found.

Over the years, we had experimented with various media. One of them is smoke. It is suitable for all air currents which move within a contained space such as glass tubes or glass-enclosed models of rooms. It is fairly controllable and shows the air movement convincingly but has the disadvantage of quickly clouding up the interior of the model. Smoke can be produced by various means (see page 111) and transferred to the model by a flexible tube.

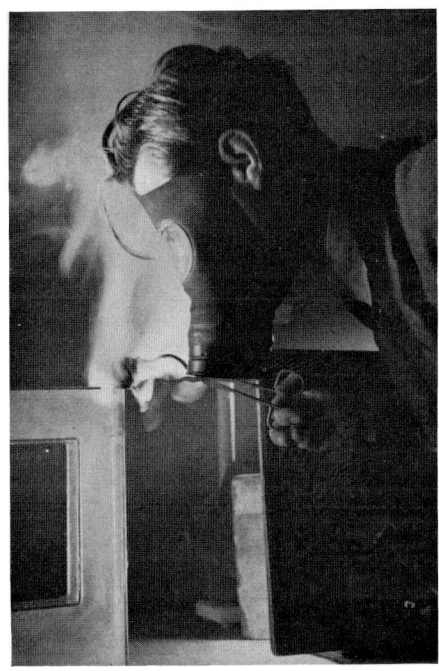

FIG. 95. Smoke was produced from burning celluloid to represent air currents.

Denys again had his own ideas about smoke manufacture. He took a short length of inflammable film, made a tight little roll of it, gripped it with a pair of tongs, went into the lavatory, set light to the film and when it burnt brightly dipped it into the bowl. As a result, dense white-yellowish fumes characteristic of burning nitrate film issued from the celluloid in the tongs which he then took in double-quick time to the model a few doors away. The idea seemed workable, but needed some more experimenting. Denys, his eyes smarting, refused to go on without a gas mask. He brought

173

The Work of the Science Film Maker

Fig. 96. The smoke is drawn by the heat of a candle through a glass model representing a ventilated mine shaft. The convection currents are thus made visible.

one along next morning and we completed the shooting, but a ghastly acrid smell pervaded the whole house for several days.

SCENES 30, 31, 34: Solid carbon dioxide (dry ice, page 111) is another useful material for showing up currents. If put into water, it gives off vapour which, by means of a small fan, can be made to float along. We had used dry ice once or twice in previous films; the vapour is quite white but has the same disadvantage as smoke in that it quickly settles as a dense layer, not very desirable if ventilation is the subject of the scene.

For the present film therefore, we were anxious to find another medium and in the end fell back on our Pepper's Ghost. The room model was put up in front of the camera and the moving air effect was produced by an electro-mechanical device, somewhat similar to that described on page 189. This effect was projected on to the model during shooting. The result resembled a kind of three-dimensional animated diagram but since the scene could be shot with a normally running camera there was a great saving in time and cost. The same method was used for Scene 34.

Fig. 97. Pepper's Ghost effect of air circulating in a model room.

SCENES 32 and 35: We used the Schlieren effect as in Scenes 2–4.

SCENES 37–42: These shots, referring to aeronautics, were taken at a school. In a junk shop I had found a gay French painting showing a number of Montgolfier balloons taking off from a parade ground. Guided by this picture, our model maker made a colourful paper balloon, about

Films in the Making

FIG. 98. A contemporary French painting was shown in the class room as an introduction to the balloon sequence. It also served as a guide for the making of the balloon model shown in the plate below.

1 m in diameter, plus the necessary 'launching pad', consisting of a brazier, a platform and a chimney.

In the classroom, the teacher first used the painting to explain the principles of hot-air ballooning. The next scenes showed the assembly of the launching pad in the school ground and the balloon being filled with hot air from the brazier. In due course, the balloon was released and it did, indeed, rise some 30 m into the air before the wind blew it down again. We secured a perfect shot of this.

FIG. 99. Our balloon model on the 'launching pad' in the school ground. It is in the process of being filled with hot air from a brazier inside the platform.

The next sequence referred to gliding. The actuality shots were taken in the grounds of a gliding club near London.

SCENES 52–54: An animated diagram was necessary to show the intricate movement of the warm air currents (thermals) rising from the ground and their effect on gliders. This sequence was subcontracted to Halas & Batchelor, the cartoon film-makers. The information on page 118 refers to some important points which have to be understood before commissioning animated material. We prepared a schedule containing rough sketches, directive comments and the timing of the action. This took the following form:

SCENE 52		*Timing*	
	Static background: a village within green fields and other features	Fade in Hold (background	3 ft

of a rural landscape.
Shape of thermal appears
(warm reddish hue)
Within it, 'ticks' moving upwards
suggest the hot air rising.

only)   12
Fade in thermal
with moving
'ticks' and hold   12

SCENE 53   Wider angle: Static background: a   Hold scene
            sunny slope on the left, 2 ripe cornfields   with thermals
            on the right of village. 4 thermals   in action   18
            'in action'.

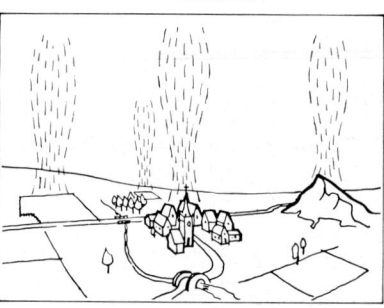

SCENE 54   Closer shot with 2 thermals rising
            from village and slope,
            The path of the glider draws
            itself across the scene.
            Total glider movement with thermal
            movement throughout the scene.
            Fade out for mix.

            Total animation:

Glider footage
from 1 to 2   8 ft
     2 to 3   8
     3 to 4 10
     4 to 5   6

                              32
                               4
                             ―――
                             81 ft

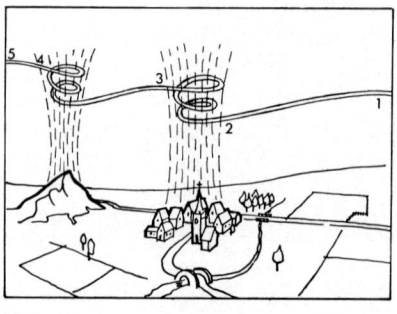

Films in the Making

Scene 54 showed the flight path. We could have used a more elaborate visual showing the glider itself drawing its path as a trail behind it. That would have been easy, had the glider flown in a straight line. But the upward spiralling of the glider within the thermals would have involved making a great number of drawings, each showing a different view of the glider during its twisting journey. The added cost would not have been worth it as the scene makes its point very well as it stands.

Scene 57 is almost a repeat of the animated diagram of Scene 52 with the difference that the thermal is seen 'growing' from the ground up to condensation level where a cloud forms.

SCENE 57	*Timing*	
	Static scene of village.	2 ft
	Thermal grows with rising 'ticks' inside it up to the required height.	12
	A cloud forms on its top (slow superimposition).	5
	Hold, incl. action of 'ticks'.	5
	Fade out for mix.	2
	Total animation:	26 ft

SCENES 61–66: The 'inversion' phenomenon was dealt with by static drawings, with the inversion layers and labels jumping in and out. There was no need for animation in this sequence.

SCENES 67–70: Reality shots: we were lucky because at the time of shooting there was plenty of natural mist and fog about and we were able to obtain some very effective scenes. Failing such good luck, one might have to resort to mist- and fog-filters (page 87).

SCENES 72–74: Summary: repeat shots of Scenes 3, 6 and 5.

Conduction

The first scenes after the title once more show the cannon ball on its tripod, heated by a Bunsen burner. In this film, we had to demonstrate atoms and molecules in motion. As this involved moving hundreds of tiny particles simultaneously, we had again to use an animated diagram for this sequence. The script for these introductory scenes reads:

Sc. No.	35mm footage	Visual	Commentary
2.	28	(Fade in) Iron ball on bunsen burner.	Conduction is the passage of heat through substances.
3.	40	(Match dissolve) Animated Diagram: Motion of atoms in the ball. Faster movements of atoms creeping up bottom to top.	... In this iron ball— —the atoms are in constant motion. This motion is an expression of their temperature. If particles get hotter by heating— —they get excited, bump into the cooler particles with greater energy and thus pass the heat on to them.
4.	68	(Match dissolve) Iron ball (as in 2); Hammer head appears and touches the ball.	If a hot body comes into contact with a cooler one, the same thing happens.
5.	78	(Match dissolve) Animated Diagram: The fast movement of the atoms in the ball creeps into the hammer.	Watch the hammer—and you will notice how the particles of the hot iron ball pass the heat on to those of the cooler hammer.
	96	(Fade out)	

Films in the Making

The instructions for the animation unit (Science Films Ltd.) were as follows:

SCENE 3. Animation		*Timing*	
	The circle is filled with dots, moving to and fro and bumping into each other (indicating kinetic energy of molecules). Starting at the bottom, the particle motion becomes more violent and spreads upwards. The number of particles does not alter, only their speed.	Particles at 'normal' speed: Fade in: Hold 'Double' speed motion starts and spreads upwards 'Double' speed motion in the whole ball, hold Track back for match-dissolve to Scene 4	2 ft 9 8 4 3
SCENE 4. Reality scene: a hammer appears and touches the ball.			
SCENE 5. Animation			
	'Double' speed motion in ball, 'normal' motion in hammer. The vigorous motion invades the hammer until it fills it. Note! Both circle and hammer must fit exactly the position they have in the reality scenes. Frames of reality scenes enclosed for reference and matching.	Fade in from Scene 4 and hold 'Double' speed motion passes into the hammer All particles at 'double' speed. Fade out. Total animation:	4 7 5 2 44 ft

The film proceeds by showing a number of experiments relating to conductivity. Various materials are examined as to their conductive properties. Rods of metals are arranged to diverge from a central heat source, and the rate of the heat flow is demonstrated by flash powder igniting, or flags popping up, when the heat reaches given points on the rods.

Another model compares good conductors and bad conductors. A flask filled with water is heated to boiling point and the steam escapes through a horizontal cylinder at the top of the model. On its way through this cylinder, the steam heats a copper bar, a porcelain bar and a column of motionless air contained in a glass tube. These bars branch vertically off the cylinder side by side, each ending in a glass funnel filled with pieces of ice. As the heat reaches the ice, it melts it and the water drops into beakers below. The demonstration shows that copper is a good conductor,

The Work of the Science Film Maker

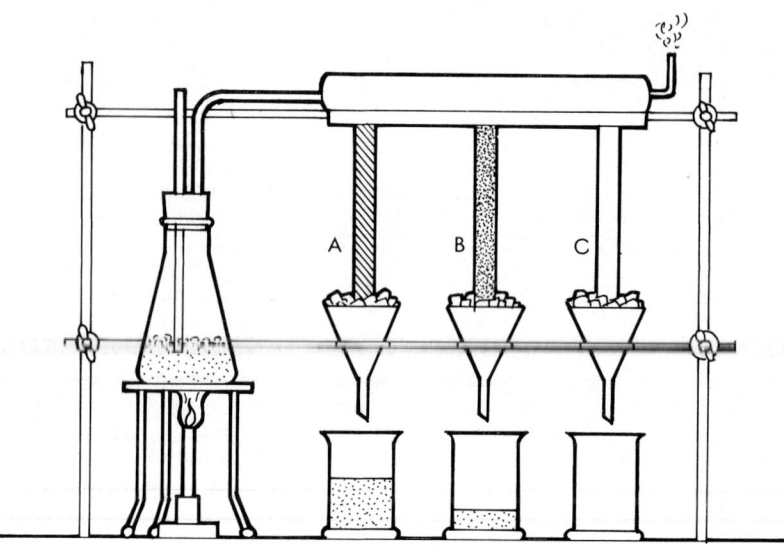

Fig. 100. *Table-top set-up: Good and Bad Conductors*. The steam produced in the flask on the left heats the horizontal cylinder at the top of the set. This in turn heats a copper bar (A), a porcelain bar (B) and a column of air in a glass tube (C). The funnels contain ice cubes which are melted by the heat of the bars. The water drops into beakers. The time it takes to fill the beakers shows the difference in the conductivity of the chosen substances.

the beaker is filled in 10 min. Porcelain takes much longer to conduct heat and the beaker is full at the end of 3 days. Air is a very poor conductor indeed; it would take some 6 months to fill the beaker. The times are indicated by a clock and by calendar dates. The point is thus made that conductors are divided into good conductors and poor conductors, called insulators.

The next sequence: 'Uses of Good Conductors' shows reality scenes of everyday articles, machines and heat exchangers.

A similar sequence shows 'Poor Conductors' used for conserving heat. Live scenes refer to various examples of insulators such as glass wool, lagging, wool, furs, feathers, and the materials used in house building.

Next, a table top set shows an igloo in an arctic landscape. We used artificial snow (see page 111). A micro-shot of snow crystals proves that snow contains a large amount of air and that it is therefore a good insulator.

At the end of this sequence, the script makes the point that a cave, dug in snow, can be used as a bivouac for mountaineers or explorers. For a realistic effect, we wanted this point demonstrated by a live scene. This

Fig. 101. (top): Scenic table top set of an igloo set in an appropriate arctic landscape.
Fig. 102. (bottom): Production still showing a 'snow cave being built outside a house after a heavy snow fall.

Films in the Making

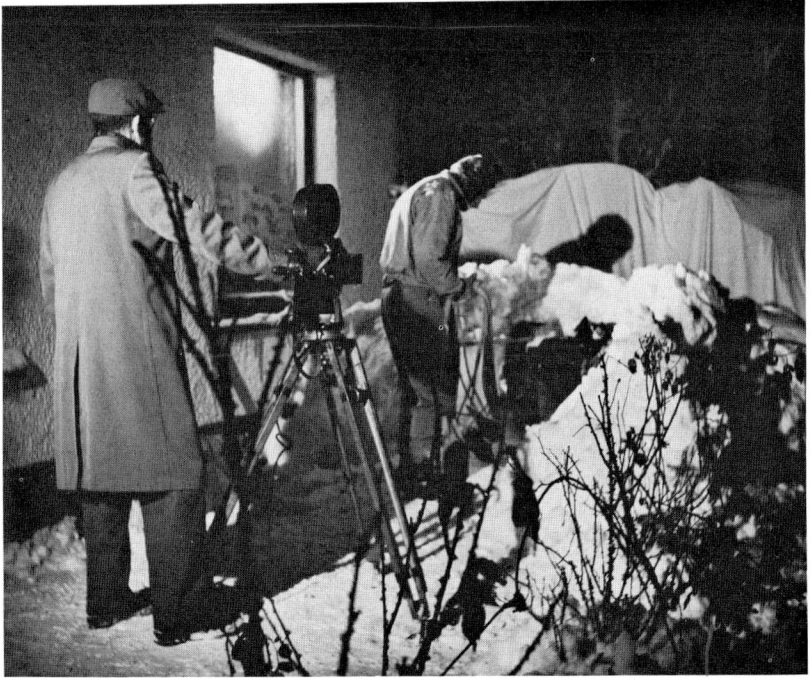

produced some headaches as to where and how to film it. If it is dealt with here in some detail it is to show how a piece of unexpected luck can help a unit over an awkward problem.

In London, a good layer of snow is too rare an event for figuring in a production schedule. There were no suitable stock shots available at any of the film libraries, and a journey to the Alps, or even to Scotland, was ruled out for budget reasons. We were on the point of resigning ourselves to another model scene. Suddenly, however, it started snowing and what's more, it kept snowing for days. At tea-time on the second day—it would of course be a Sunday—there was about 2 ft of snow on the ground. We shovelled a heap of snow on to the terrace of my house, sufficient for us to dig a cave in. The scene had to be shot after nightfall to obscure any unwanted detail of the surroundings. Even so, we had to cover the hedges at the back of the snow heap with white sheets. It was bitterly cold. We set up two spotlights in my living room which threw their beams through the window, lighting the outside of the cave dramatically. To light the inside of the cave took some time. We had to lay a cable and dig a side channel to accommodate the lamp. The light inside the cave was actually too bright to suggest a mountaineer's torch but we had no time for elaborate adjustments because an icy wind had sprung up. We began rehearsing. One of us, in an anorak, wrapped in blankets, lay down inside the cave and another person, dressed up in a mountaineering outfit, complete with pick axe and rope, fixed a ground sheet on top of the cave entrance and then crept into it closing the opening from inside by pulling the ground sheet down. We had to shoot the scene three times before we got what we wanted. A hot rum toddy put everybody on his feet again, and we were thankful that this irritating production item had solved itself so conveniently.

Radiation

The film opens again with our cannon ball. The commentary says that heat radiation is in the form of infra-red rays. We produced the radiation effect by the Pepper's Ghost method. In the present case, our mechanical device produced 'ticks' radiating from a central point. Superimposed over the ball during the filming, they seemed to emanate from the surface of the ball.

The commentary makes the point that infra-red rays are invisible but can be felt. The scene shows a hand held against the ball. If the hand is replaced by a galvanometer connected to a thermopile, the instrument absorbs the rays and sets up an electric current which registers the amount of radiation on a dial.

Heat can also be detected by photography if infra-red film is used (see page 83). The shots can be taken in complete darkness, the object illuminating itself by its own radiation. But we had to resort to faking this demonstration because we could not raise the temperature of the cannon

Films in the Making

Fig. 103. *Heat Radiation made Visible.* The cannon ball's radiation is symbolized by outward travelling 'ticks'. An electromechanical device caused the ticks to radiate from a central source. Superimposed by the Pepper's Ghost method, they seemed to emanate from the surface of the ball.

ball sufficiently. With a still camera loaded with infra-red film we photographed a cistern float, heated by a blow lamp to just short of red heat. We made an enlargement and filmed it on Eastman Color with a red gelatine in front of the lamp. The end result was a convincing impression of infra-red photography in the dark. At that time, there was no infra-red colour film on the market.

The film then discusses electro-magnetic wave motion, and with the help of coloured charts and live inserts, the visible and invisible wave spectra are demonstrated, showing the place of infra-red radiation on the waveband.

The commentary mentions that all electro-magnetic waves, including light and heat, travel at the same speed. We showed that the light from the moon would reach the earth in one and a third second. (For certain reasons, our adviser chose the moon instead of the sun as an example). The effect of the travelling moon-ray was easy to produce by the method of simulated animation.

The sequence 'Reflection of Radiation' again uses light as an analogy for heat. Flat surfaces of various materials pass the camera on a turntable, demonstrating the point in the commentary that bright surfaces reflect more light than they absorb while dark surfaces absorb more than they reflect.

The next scene shows a small concave mirror being put into a smoke box. Two small holes in one side admit two narrow parallel beams of light. The house lights are switched off and the beams are projected: the concave surface of the mirror brings them to a focal point in front of it. Infra-red rays can be focused in the same way, as for instance in a solar furnace which uses the sun as a heat source to produce power for industry and research.

We would have liked to show an actual solar furnace. But again we would have had to travel far, this time to the Pyrenees where the nearest operational solar furnace is installed. Therefore, a model had to do. We had heard of a firm that manufactured large concave metal bowls for some mysterious purpose. We traced this factory and found the bowls eminently suitable. Fig. 105 shows how we set up our 'furnace' in my garden. The tripod and the flask holder were rigged up and the flask, resting on a small metal support was then fitted in the approximate position of sharpest focus in front of the bowl and filled with coloured water. In spite of weak, typically 'British' sunshine, the water started to boil and, in a close-up, steam could be seen escaping from the flask. How did this miracle of nature happen? Simply by inserting a heating element in the bed of fireclay on which the flask rested and connecting it to the nearest mains socket in the house. This shot was followed by a colour photograph of the actual solar furnace at Mountlouis in the Pyrenees with its reflector, 10 m in dia.

The smoke box appeared again, this time with a small light bulb at the focal point. This demonstrated that reflectors can be used in reverse to *beam* light- and heat-rays. Practical applications of this principle were shown in live scenes such as car headlamps, radiant gas fires and an infra-red lamp.

'Absorption and Emission' is the subject of the next sequence. Two or three bench set-ups showed the difference between the amount of heat absorbed by and reflected from black and white bodies; thermometers and thermopiles were used to measure these differences. Again, a number of practical applications followed.

We then showed that all objects emit *and* absorb infra-red radiation. We filmed a boy, sitting in front of a radiant gas fire and also took a still of this scene. We enlarged it, cut the boy's figure out and mounted it on plywood. Then we had a model replica of the room made to scale and placed the model boy in exactly the same position as in the live scene. The commentary says that the boy and all objects in the room absorb the rays from the fire and get warm. But they do not get hotter and hotter

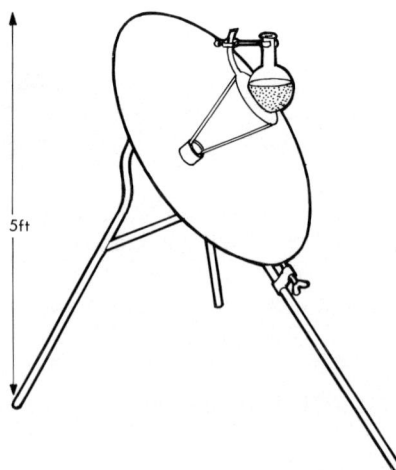

FIG. 104. *Model of a Solar Furnace.* A large concave metal dish was put on 3 legs fixed together to form a tripod. Since the British sun is too weak to make the water in the flask boil, the flask-holder ended in a bed of fireclay containing a heating element which was connected to the mains in our house. The flask had, of course, to be fitted in the approximate focal position of the concave bowl. On the screen, a CU shows clearly the water boiling and steam escaping from the flask.

Films in the Making

FIG. 105. Live scene of a boy in front of a gas fire. This dissolves into the model scene below.

FIG. 106. A cut-out from a photograph of the boy is placed in the same position and the radiation effect produced by Pepper's Ghost.

FIG. 107. (top) and 108 (bottom). An alternative method of showing the radiation- and re-radiation effect by the 'bump' method. The arrows are 'jumped' from the fireplace to the wooden figure.

because at the same time they re-radiate some of the heat. Only very hot objects, like the fire, radiate light rays as well.

All this was shown in long-shots and various close-ups by means of our model-cum-Pepper's Ghost technique.

The rest of the film uses charts, models and reality scenes to demonstrate the effects of radiation and re-radiation on the earth's surface and the way clouds act as a blanket to keep the earth warm. The last sequence deals with 'Radiation and Climate' and shows by a simple experiment why it is hot at the equator and cold at the poles. Live scenes from the tropics and arctics, obtained as stock shots from a film library, are interspersed with the experiment.

The usual summary concludes the film.

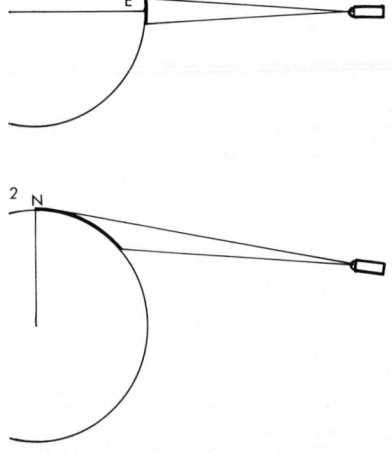

FIG. 109. *Radiation and Climate.* This is a simple and easily filmed demonstration which shows why it is hot at the equator and cold at the poles. A bent sheet of dark cardboard represents the surface of the Earth. A torch throws a beam indicating the sun's heat radiation.
1. At the equator (E) the heat is concentrated on a small sector of the globe.
2. At the North pole (N) the same amount of heat is dispersed over a much larger sector; each point on the surface receives correspondingly less heat.

Electro-Magnetic Waves

This teaching film for higher age groups, sponsored by the Educational Foundation for Visual Aids in association with Mullard Ltd. and shot in 35mm colour, was one of the toughest our team had to tackle. Envisaged first as a fifteen to twenty min teaching film for the sixth form Grammar School and first term University, it grew eventually to more than 40 min in length because of the amount of material which had to be included. The film was therefore divided into two self-contained parts.

Part 1: The Discovery and Generation of Electro-Magnetic Waves first deals in short sequences with the theories and experiments of the principle

Films in the Making

scientists working in this field, from Newton in 1680 to the Curies in 1902. The electro-magnetic spectrum is then dealt with by means of charts and models and the generation and detection of the frequencies from radio-waves to gamma rays is discussed. Concepts such as oscillating charges, waves and photons, magnetic and electric fields, the types of spectra, energy levels, etc., are demonstrated. A survey of the practical uses of electro-magnetic radiation in research, medicine and industry ends this part.

Part 2: Properties and Behaviour of Electro-Magnetic Waves introduces wave-motion in general as well as the specific topics of propagation, velocity, straight path, polarization, transmission and absorption, reflection, refraction and dispersion. It next deals with diffraction, interference, spectrum analysis, X-ray crystallography, radio beaming and polar diagrams. This leads to micro waves and to stimulated emission in masers and lasers. The film ends on the note that many of the newest developments are still in the laboratory stage and that the history of the electromagnetic waves is yet very much in the making.

The production of this film lasted, with several interruptions, for more than three years. The investigation and the writing of the four or five versions of the script took about twelve months but additions to, and alterations of, the script became necessary throughout the filming.

For scientific guidance for the film, we were fortunate in finding an ideal adviser. Dr. George Wilkinson of the Physics Research Department of King's College, London is not only an authority concerning the subject matter of this film but as a university reader he could assess all problems from the teacher's point of view. And very important: he believes in films as a teaching medium. He was willing to take on the scientific supervision of the film and he stuck to his guns in the ensuing meetings of the sponsors' film committee which took place after the 'rough-cut' screenings. It was due to his tireless and always good-humoured collaboration that the appropriate academic standard which must be expected from teaching films, was achieved.

After the approval of the final version of the shooting script (actually, no script is ever 'final'), it had to be broken down for the purpose of budgeting and scheduling. The script contained some 250 master scenes plus the related close-ups. The breakdown took a considerable time and ran into some twenty pages. The list on page 188 is a summary:

Animated diagrams and library material are charged by the foot and for reasons of economy it is essential to work out the footage as correctly as possible (see page 118).

Only a short selection of scenes and effects, shot for this film, can be discussed here. They are not set down in chronological order but grouped together according to the methods of filming. Again, we have to use words and static black-and-white illustrations for describing moving cinematic effects in colour which can manifest themselves only on the cine screen.

The Work of the Science Film Maker

	Locations	Set-ups	Master-scenes
Exteriors: in and near London	15		46
Interiors: exhibits, etc., in university labs., factories, museums.	19	29	41
Experiments and demonstrations specially set up for us.	8	10	28
Own studio: charts, etc., prepared by artist.	—	10	54
Animated models and effects.	—	17	44
Scientific apparatus, hired (partly with operators) or bought.	—	8	22
Subcontracted: animated diagrams.	—	—	10
Library material: stock scenes.	—	—	5

Total: 42 scattered locations,   250
       35 set-ups in the studio,
       11 diagrams and library shots

     The most important sequence in part 1 of the film is concerned with the generation of electro-magnetic waves by (a) free electrons, (b) ions, and (c) orbital electrons moving within atoms. Parts (a) and (b) were demonstrated by animated diagram, for (c) we used an effects technique of our own.

     The film explains that in an atom, the electrons revolve round the nucleus in set orbits which are grouped in shells. The scene shows an atom with 5 such shells, and we see that orbital electrons are sometimes displaced through impact with a free electron; they then jump to an outer shell, taking with them the energy picked up from the free electron. Usually, these displaced electrons return at once to their orginal orbit and in the process release the picked-up energy in the form of a series of wave packets, called quanta or photons, which radiate into space. The energy of the photon determines the frequency, and this, in turn, defines the type of radiation. It needs least energy to dislodge orbital electrons from outer and intermediate shells: the result can be infra-red-, light- or u.v. radiation. But *great* energy is needed to displace electrons from an inner orbit and the released energy is correspondingly of high frequency and strong penetrating power as in X-rays. Gamma rays, as emitted by radio-active substances, are of still higher frequency; they radiate not from the shell but from the nucleus of the atom.

     For making all these processes visible, we needed one basic background drawing showing an atom with a nucleus in the centre and 5 shells surrounding it. This drawing (approx 60 cm in dia.) was set up in front of the camera.

     The bombarding free electrons were animated by a rotary motor-driven device connected with a row of small bulbs which lit up one at a time in quick succession so as to give the illusion of a travelling particle. Fig. 112 shows the diagram of the mechanism. The emitted photons (in

Films in the Making

Fig. 110. *Generation of Electro-Magnetic Waves by Orbital Electrons.* This is a composite chart of the action described on page 188. An atom with 5 shells is the static background. On each shell (or orbit) a number of electrons, altogether up to about 90, are circling the nucleus. To simplify matters, only one electron is shown on each shell. If a free electron BE hits one of the orbital electrons, this jumps to an outer shell and back again. The energy picked up from the bombarding electron, is released and radiates into space in the form of photons. The nearer an electron circles round the nucleus, the higher is the frequency of the emitted radiation, marked on the drawing by wavy lines with arrow heads. The frequency determines whether the generated waves are infra-red (I), visible (L for light), ultra-violet (u.v.) or X-rays (X). Gamma rays (G) are emitted by the nucleus. In the filming, the jumping of the various electrons and the radiation effects were produced by Pepper's Ghost in the set-up shown in Fig. 111. The electrons were not put in place all at once, but successively in step with the commentary and the sequence was interspersed with other scenes referring to the various types of radiation.

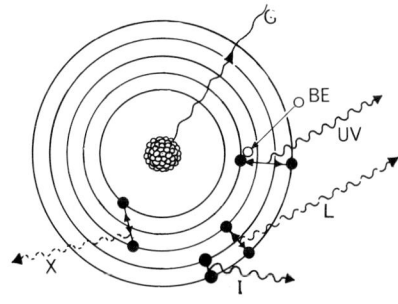

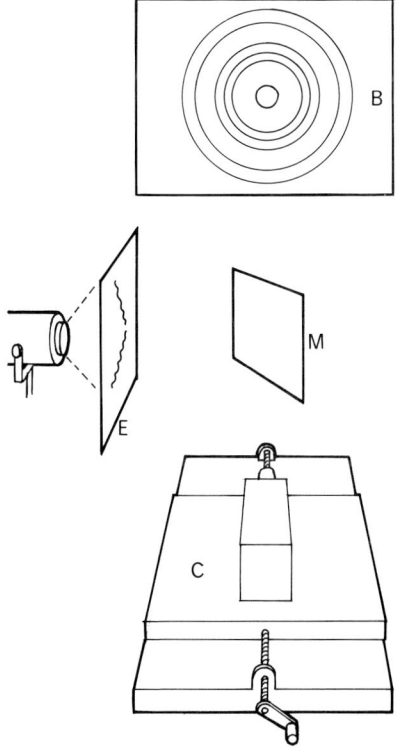

Fig. 111. *The Set-Up for the Wave-Generation Sequence (Fig. 110).* The board B is set up in front of the camera which is mounted on a horizontal bench C. On the side is the effects mechanism E. The effects are superimposed as Pepper's Ghost on the static background by the mirror M. This mirror is actually fitted right in front of the lens; the diagram shows it in a more forward position for the sake of clarity.

The Work of the Science Film Maker

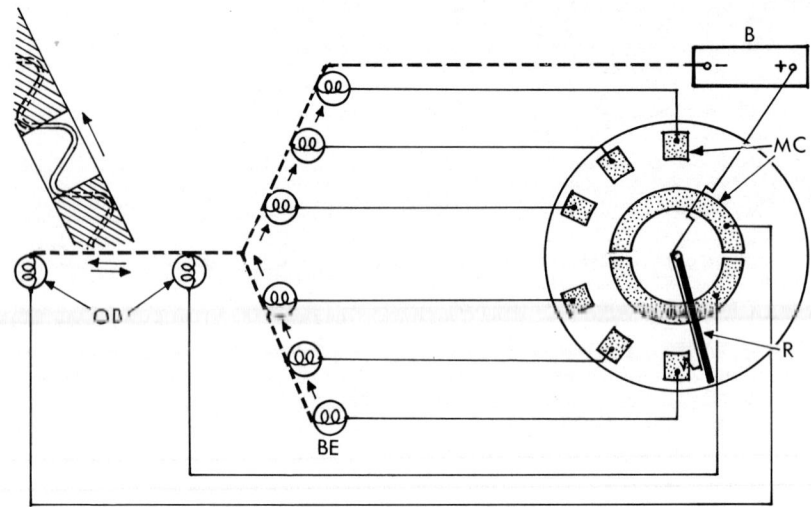

Fig. 112. *Circuit used for the Wave-Generation Effects* (*Fig.* 110). This motor-driven electro-mechanical device was used for the jumping and radiation effects of the various electrons but realignment was necessary for each scene. The movement of the bombarding electron BE was shown by a row of blue torch bulbs lighting up in quick succession. (Only a few of these bulbs are shown in the diagram). A rotating switch arm R, sliding across the metal contacts MC, activated both the BE bulbs and the 2 bulbs OB used for the orbit-jumping electron. The radiation effect (photon) was produced by a sliding mask (see Fig. 117) travelling out from between the 2 bulbs OB. B is the battery.

the shape of 'squiggles') were animated by a cut-out waveline with a sliding mask (see Fig. 116) all lit from the back.

By lining up the projected moving effects to match the static atom drawing, and by changing the positions of the jumping orbital electrons on the various shells as well as the colour of the photons, we were able to demonstrate the whole range of electro-magnetic radiation from the infra-red to the gamma spectrum.

The jumping of one of the orbital electrons to an outer shell (lower energy level), its return to the original position and the released energy in the shape of photons were shown as close-ups in an insert-sequence. Instead of ordering an animated diagram we did it again ourselves in the following way:

A static drawing was made, showing two straight lines representing the energy levels E_1 and E_2, with a white orbital electron on the bottom line which is of a higher level than the top line since it is closer to the nucleus. The drawing was pinned on to a board in front of the camera. The electron was a white drawing pin. A few feet were shot of this first scene (1). Fig. 114.

Films in the Making

FIG. 113. *Orbital Electron Releasing Photon.*
Illustration of the sequence used.
Scene 1.
Lines E_1 and E_2 (Energy levels) and black arrow with caption 'Energy' remain static throughout. White drawing pin on lower line represents electron.

Scene 2.
Yellow arrow flashed in by Pepper's Ghost for 6 frames.

Scene 3.
Drawing pin (electron) transferred to upper line indicating its jump from E_2 to E_1. 5 frames.

Scene 4.
Yellow arrow pointing in opposite direction signifies return jump of electron. 4 frames.

Scene 5.
Drawing pin put back to bottom line. 6 frames.

Scene 6.
A squiggle (photon), projected by Pepper's Ghost, travels from the centre of frame in the direction of the arrow. 14 frames.
Each scene was shot at sufficient length to allow for 5 repetitions of the complete action in the cutting.

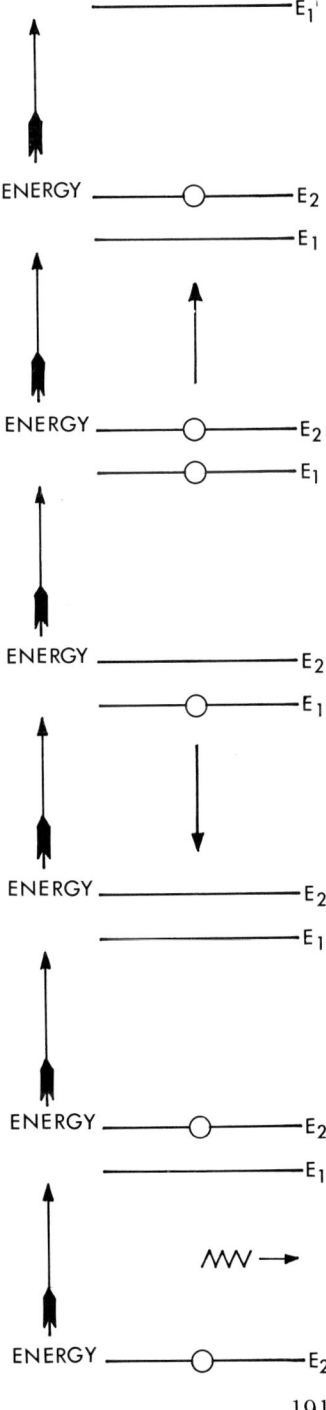

The Work of the Science Film Maker

A yellow arrow was flashed on to the drawing for a few frames by Pepper's Ghost, and the drawing pin (electron) put on the upper line signifying the jump (2 and 3).

This was repeated in reverse order, representing the return jump (4 and 5). With the electron now back on the lower line, a small white squiggle, the photon, travelled from the centre to the right and out of frame. A sliding mask (see page 194) was used for this (6). This was repeated several times to cover the commentary.

For the sake of convenience, the order of shooting was slightly different from the order in which the scenes followed each other on the screen.

Thus we had a simple set-up consisting of a line drawing with a drawing pin which was moved by hand between shots, and two effects produced by Pepper's Ghost. Apart from the squiggles, all material was static; the illusion of movement was achieved by the quick intercutting of the single scenes.

This little sequence ends by showing the formula (explained in the commentary):

$$hf = E_2 - E_1.$$

Waves or photons, radiated into space, had to be shown repeatedly in the film. The sources of emission, whether an atom, a light source, a dipole or an aerial were always represented by static drawings and the travelling waves were superimposed by Pepper's Ghost.

The lengthy radiation sequence was interspersed with scenes illustrating certain details of the various types of radiation. In the case of X-rays, for instance, we demonstrated what happens inside an X-ray tube. The film shows the outline of the tube with its cathode and anode inside it. A fusillade of high-speed electrons, emitted from the cathode, bombards the metal plate at the end of the anode causing a stream of other particles to burst from the metal, powerfully penetrating the confines of the glass tube. These are X-rays.

Here, we used Pepper's Ghost again. But since there were now two particle streams, we had to shoot first one stream and after re-aligning the

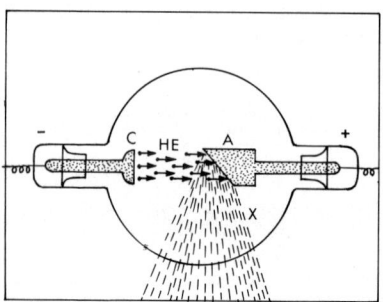

Fig. 114. *An X-ray Tube*. A stream of high-speed electrons (HE) emitted by the cathode (C) bombards a metal plate at the end of the anode (A) causing another stream of powerful particles to burst from the metal. These are X-rays. The two moving particle streams were superimposed on the static drawing of the tube by Pepper's Ghost in two successive shots, with the film wound back between them.

Films in the Making

effects and winding the film back in the camera, we shot the second stream, thus superimposing the shots on each other.

We also wanted to refer to the practical application of X-rays in medicine. The scene shows an X-ray apparatus with a small fluorescent X-ray screen in front of it. A hand is held against the screen. The houselights are dimmed. The X-ray tube is switched on and emits radiation presented by self-drawing lines. As they hit the fluorescent screen, an X-ray image of the hand appears on it.

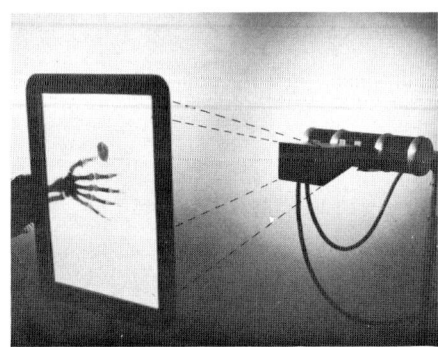

FIG. 115. Our X-ray mock-up as explained below. On the left, a person holds his hand behind the screen

This scene needed some special preparation. First we secured an X-ray of a hand from a hospital; then we made a transparency from it with a still camera. This slide was projected onto the X-ray screen from outside the camera range. A pale-green gelatine was put in front of the projector lens, suggesting fluorescence.

The X-ray apparatus was made up from metal tubes, cardboard and cables.

The travelling lines appeared again by courtesy of Pepper's Ghost and at the moment they hit the screen the slide projector was switched on and the X-ray of the hand lit-up.

Two or three live scenes followed showing patients being X-rayed in a hospital.

Another scene for which Pepper's Ghost was vital, shows one of the methods by which the *velocity* of electro-magnetic waves can be determined. The commentary explains: 'The dish aerial on the left sends out a microwave signal which is reflected by the target 150 km away in the air, to produce an echo. The oscilloscope screen shows the outgoing signal and incoming echo as two 'blips'. The distance between the blips shows the time taken by the signal for the round trip of twice 150 km: it is 1·003 msec.'

We filmed this scene as follows:

The static background was a drawing in colour, about 60 × 100 cm in size. It was pinned on to an upright board.

The moving effects were achieved in the following way: At right-angles to the camera was a large velvet-covered board with an inch-wide glass-

193

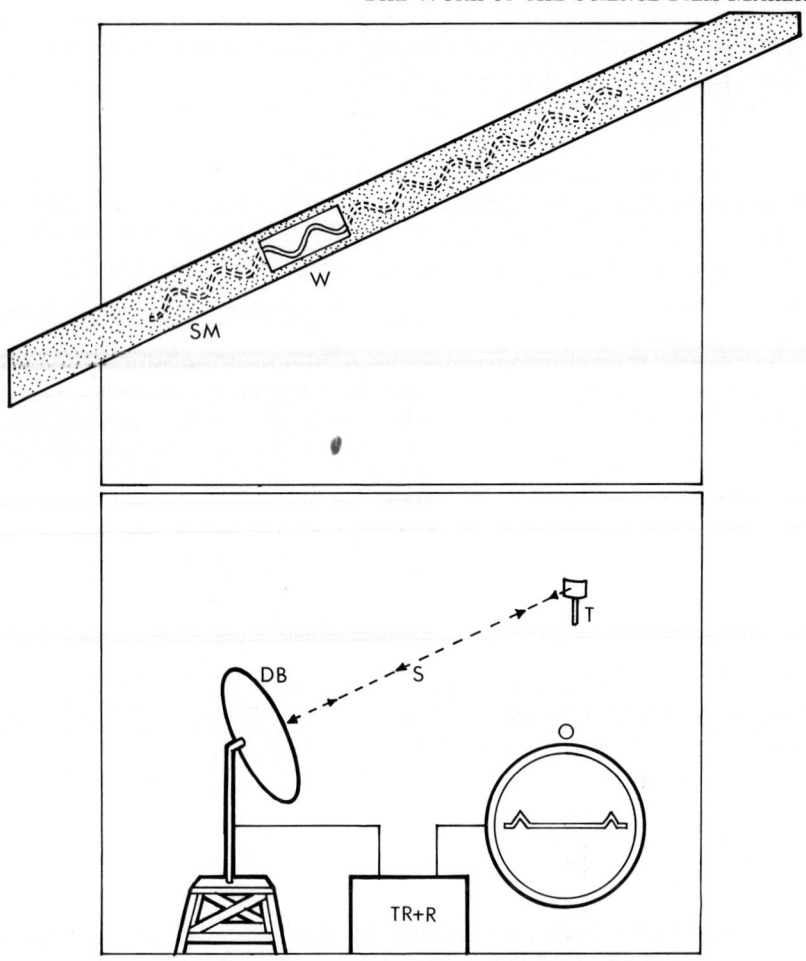

Fig. 116. *Determining the Velocity of Electro-Magnetic Waves.* This is a diagram of the Pepper's Ghost model with its moving effects.

Bottom: *Background Drawing.* DB marks the dish bowl aerial, T the target at a distance of 150 km, TR and R the energy source for the transmitter and receiver. O stands for the oscilloscope. Across it, a slit with 2 'blips' is cut out. To start with, this slit is unlit and invisible. All objects, named so far, are static. As to the moving effects, S is the travelling microwave signal, produced by a sliding mask (see below). Behind the oscilloscope which is now lit from the back, a second sliding mask uncovers the cut-out left to right in step with the signal, producing a trace. The first blip marks the outgoing signal, the second one the returning echo. The action of the signal and the oscilloscope trace is repeated several times. At the end, the wording: 1·003 millisecs appears in the oscilloscope.

Top: *Sliding Mask.* A board is covered with black velvet and a glass-covered slit in it is lit from behind. On the glass, a wave line is painted. The sliding mask SM is a strip of wood, also covered with black velvet. First it covers the slit completely, then it is slid along it so that the window W exposes 2 or 3 squiggles which seem to travel up and down and thus produce the effect of a travelling wave. This board was put up at right angles to the camera so that the travelling signal effect could be superimposed on the static background by Pepper's Ghost.

Films in the Making

covered slit, lit from behind. On the glass, a wave-line was painted. A sort of sliding mask arrangement, also covered with black velvet, contained a rectangular cut-out exposing 2 squiggles of the painted wave. This sliding mask was fixed diagonally and pushed by hand so that the cut-out (the squiggle) travelled to and fro between the aerial and the target. The squiggles represented the signals and were superimposed on the static drawing by Pepper's Ghost.

The circle on the right represents the oscilloscope. A cut-out slit across the circular drawing was lit from the back. A sliding mask uncovered the slit (which represents the trace with the two blips) in step with the return trip of the signal. All movements were slowed down to allow for the length of the commentary.

The film continues with a blackboard drawing, showing that twice the distance, divided by the time, equals the velocity of the electro-magnetic wave:

$$\frac{2 \times 150 \text{ km}}{1 \cdot 003 \text{ msec}} = 299 \cdot 793 \text{ km/sec} \quad \text{or} \quad V = \frac{2D}{T}$$

The next visual concerns beam width. The method of filming it were rather similar to those in the previous scene. The commentary points out that the shorter the wavelength, the easier it is to produce a signal with a narrow beam. Narrow beams mean, amongst other things, greater accuracy in detecting the position of moving targets. The scene shows on the left a radar bowl sending out a beam, and on the right a PPI (Plane Position Indicator) display with a time base. In the sky above is an aeroplane.

Fig. 117 top: a *wide* beam rotates past the plane. On the PPI display, the time base sweeps round in step with the rotating beam and causes a *large* blip. This means that the plane may be anywhere within the area of the wide beam.

Fig. 117 bottom: The radar bowl now sends out a *narrow* beam and there is a *small* blip on the PPI display. The plane's position is more accurately pinpointed.

Fig. 118 shows the set-up for the above scene.

The static background is a painting showing an aeroplane, a radar bowl, and a PPI display. This painting is fixed in front of the camera.

Left of the camera is the mechanism for the moving parts of the scene. On a large board, covered with black velvet, 2 rotating discs are fitted. They, too, are covered with black velvet. The wide and narrow 'beams' and the time base are white paper cut-outs, fixed on the discs and reflected through the Pepper's Ghost mirror onto the static painting in front of the camera. The line-up has to be absolutely accurate so that the pivots of the rotating beams and time base coincide with the centres of the painted

The Work of the Science Film Maker

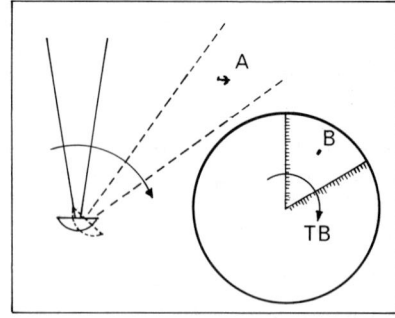

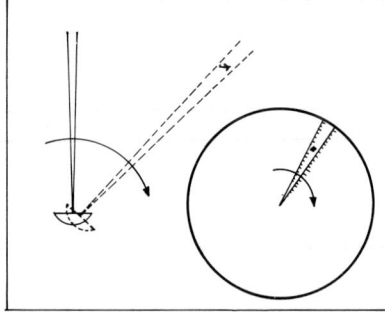

FIG. 117. *Widths of Radar Beams.* This Pepper's Ghost effect shows the importance of narrow radar beams. Top: The radar beam spots a plane (A). Since the beam is wide, on the screen of the plane position indicator appears a large blip (B) produced by the sweeping time base (TB). The position of the plane is not accurately defined. Bottom: The beam is narrow, the blip is small and the plane's position is accurately pinpointed. The filming of this effect is shown in Fig. 113.

objects. The rotating paper cut-outs are front lit. On the PPI display, holes for the large and small 'blips' are cut out of the board. These are lit from the back.

The motor of the mechanism was started. It was easy to make the paper cut-outs rotate in perfect synchronization. We had, however, to prepare a special switching arrangement for synchronizing the flashes of the blips.

Working with scientific apparatus

There are numerous occasions when museum- and scientific laboratory apparatus have to be used to achieve the right ends. On page 148 when discussing sound waves, I described how we demonstrated the propagation of longitudinal waves, but we had to use different methods with transverse waves.

We started off by showing ripples created by a pebble thrown into a pond. The commentary explains the character of the transverse wave motion in which the (water) particles only vibrate—or oscillate—*up and down* while their sideways pressure creates waves which travel out in ever widening circles.

A closer study of the oscillating movement is possible by means of wave

Films in the Making

machines. Various types exist in museums and research institutions. We chose one of the models in the Science Museum in London, consisting of a row of rods with coloured knobs at their ends. These rods vibrate up and down in their arranged order and the knobs clearly show the sinusoidal wave motion, of course only in a linear direction (not with spherical expansion). We blocked out the top and bottom of the apparatus and concentrated the light on the knobs. This machine enabled us to demonstrate

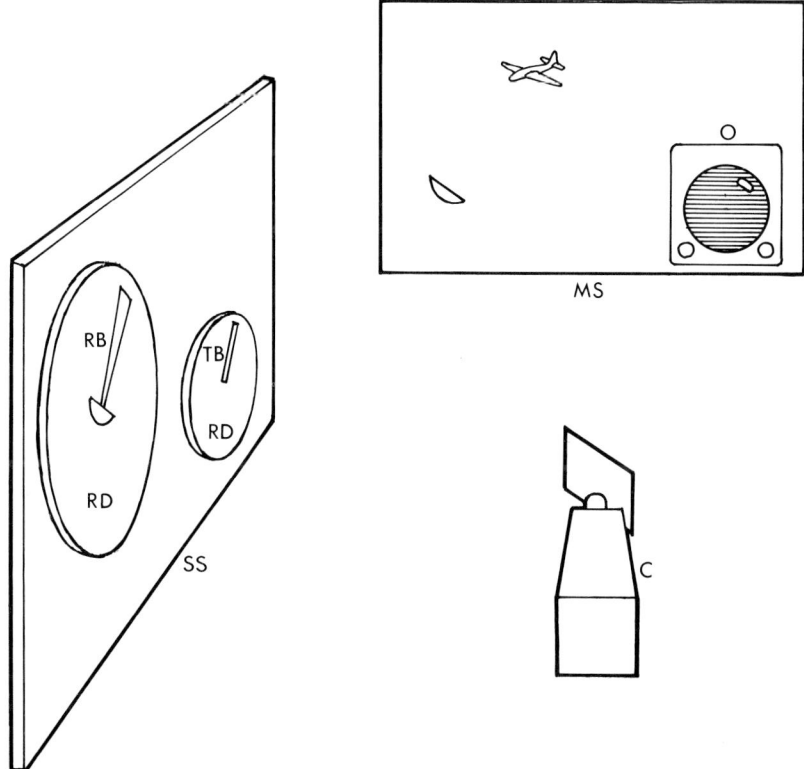

Fig. 118. *Producing the 'Beam Width' Effect*. The set-up resembles to some extent that described in Fig. 116. The main set (MS) consists of a static drawing set up in front of the camera (C) and showing a radar bowl. a plane and a P.P.I. display (O) which contains a cut-out hole in its screen for the 'blip'. The side set (SS) is a board covered with black velvet on which 2 rotating discs are fitted (RD). They are also covered with black velvet. On the larger disc a white paper shape is mounted representing the radar beam (RB). The white shape on the smaller disc (TB) stands for the time base. These white shapes are front lit. Of course, both the beam RB and the hole in the P.P.I. screen had to be changed for the second scene in which the narrow beam was shown. Using the Pepper's Ghost technique, the effects of the side set were superimposed on the main set by the mirror in front of the camera lens. The rotating discs on the side set were driven round by a motor which synchronized their speed. The synchronization of the back-lit 'blips' on the P.P.I. screen needed a special switching device.

not only the propagation of waves, but also wavelength and amplitude. The velocity of electro-magnetic waves was previously discussed on page 195; in the film that sequence follows this propagation sequence.

The refraction of light was demonstrated by means of an optical spectrometer. A tungsten lamp whose light is similar to that of the sun was put against the open end of the spectrometer tube and its light beam passed through a prism or grating, producing a continuous spectrum which could be observed through the eyepiece of the instrument. The image of the spectrum normally forms on the retina of the eye, but if the eye is replaced by a camera (with its lens removed), then the film in the gate takes the place of the retina. By rotating the prism or grating, the spectrum passes across the field of view and can be filmed: it appears as a luminous band of great beauty. The camera speed depends on the intensity of the image which, in turn, depends on the strength of the light source. In our case the camera could run at normal speed.

If instead of the tungsten light, a monochromatic light source is used, a line spectrum is produced which can be filmed in the same way.

Infra-red and u.v. spectrometers pose no problems to the camera. They are pieces of laboratory apparatus in which not the refraction process itself, but only its results can be shown, consisting in the first case of a line spectrum on a photographic plate, and in the second of a graph on a rotating sheet of paper. All these different types of spectrometers were filmed at King's College, London, under Dr. Wilkinson's guidance.

We also proved that prisms and lenses of different shapes refract the light differently. We threw the light beam from a special lamp-house with a slotted grid in front sideways on to a table top and put the prisms and lenses, one next to the other, across its path during the filming. The deflections of the beam, caused by each of these prisms, showed up clearly against the black background.

Problems with diffraction and interference photography

Diffraction and interference of light waves cause certain difficulties to photography due to the extreme narrowness of the light beams and the

Fig. 119. The refraction of a light beam by lenses of different shapes.

Films in the Making

minuteness of the obstacles and apertures by which they are affected such as, for instance, a single hair or a slit of a hair's breadth. A number of exhibits in science museums demonstrate the various phenomena of light diffraction within optical systems. Most of these phenomena are meant to be viewed with the help of magnifying or projection devices, but some of the resulting diffraction patterns are distinct enough to be filmed. For clearness sake it may, however, be better to re-draw the patterns on a larger scale and film these drawings in big close-up. This is what we did in conjunction with a Young–Fresnel apparatus which we hired from a firm of scientific instrument makers.

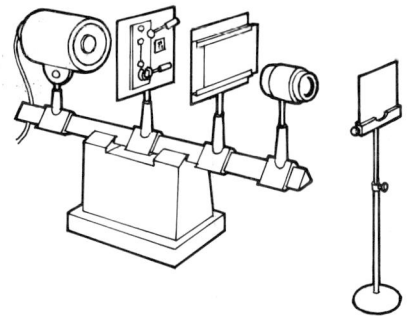

FIG. 120. *Young Fresnel Apparatus.* This simplified drawing shows the optical system of the apparatus. A beam of light from a point source passes through 2 slits of hair's breadth and a magnifying lens which throws an interference pattern onto the screen (Fig. 121. The commentary explains the significance of the experiment.

FIG. 121. CU. The diffraction pattern on the screen of the Young–Fresnel apparatus. (Not the projected image but a drawing).

Various other phenomena, connected with the diffraction and interference of light waves can best be shown by means of water waves. We chose a ripple tank for the demonstration. Fig. 123 shows how water waves behave if an obstacle is put in their path. We see that the waves bend slightly round it, but since in this particular case the size of the barrier is greater than the wavelength of the water wave, a 'shadow' is created. If the barrier is small in relation to the wave length, the waves bending round its edges reunite at once; the wave front is reestablished and there is no shadow.

This and various other relevant phenomena are also shown in this sequence.

The Work of the Science Film Maker

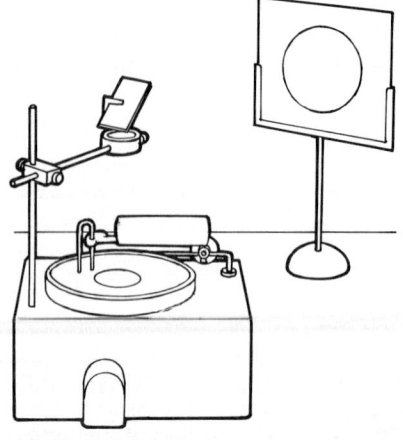

Fig. 122. *Ripple Tank*. The drawing shows the make of ripple tank (Griffin & George) which we used for the filming. The motor-driven agitator dips into the water contained in the bowl and creates ripples. Small metal shapes, put in front of the agitator, act as barriers to the ripples and produce diffraction phenomena whose patterns are projected onto the screen on the right. Figure 123 shows one such pattern.

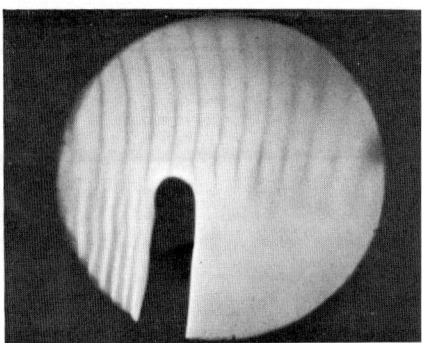

Fig. 123. CU. The image of the diffraction of a water wave as projected on to the screen of the ripple tank.

Ripple tank photography is riddled with gremlins and probably every cinematographer uses his own methods to deal with them. When we asked an expert at a university laboratory for *his* method, he was very indignant that we expected him to divulge it.

There are many types of ripple tank. Our adviser used a particular model which contained technical features useful for his demonstrations. But this model also had a built-in stroboscope; this was a nuisance because it counteracted the effect of the camera shutter which is itself a kind of stroboscope. So, the first thing we did was to disconnect the stroboscope of the tank. Then, looking through the camera while it was running, the camera operator regulated its motor speed (i.e., the number of frames exposed each sec) until the strobe effect was compensated for and the ripples appeared to move in the right direction away from the agitator. But when we saw the rushes, the waves were travelling *towards* the agitator. This was probably due to the fact that the image seen in the viewfinder of the camera was one or two frames out of step with the recorded image.

Films in the Making

If this assumption is correct, the remedy would be to adjust the camera speed so as to see backward-running waves in the viewfinder which would then be moving forward on the screen. We calculated that a camera speed of 25 fps with 50 cycles A.C. ought to do the trick, but it did not in our case. When we shot some more tests, the rushes showed the waves sometimes stationary and sometimes moving erratically.

As our time and money were limited we decided to hang on to the photographically best scenes although the waves moved backward in them. Projecting these scenes upside down made the waves move forward and, consequently, the negative was cut into the film, tail first. This saved us hours or even days of further experimenting.

A rough and ready way of demonstrating diffraction is available in any seaside resort which has a small harbour and a pier. Weather and tide permitting, the incoming waves show some forms of diffraction quite effectively. Behind large obstacles, such as a breakwater, the water is quiet but the slight bending of the waves round the edge of the mole is very noticeable. Behind the poles which support the pierhead, there is no area of quiet water, no 'shadow': the waves continue in an unbroken front. There are also the hydraulic and oceanic research stations. They are, of course, more reliable than the open sea for demonstrations because they provide controlled conditions. In their wave-generating tanks, excellent visible evidence of diffraction, interference and other phenomena can be produced. In addition, there are often large scale models of harbour installations and waterway systems in such places. These are visually attractive and clearly laid out, and they can thus effectively express the abstract arguments in practical terms.

We also constructed several models for this project. One aspect of interference will be discussed on page 221 in connection with Appleton's experiment. There we demonstrated what happens when two waves meet either 'in step' or 'out of step' with each other. We showed that in the first case the signal is reinforced, and in the second case it is cancelled out. This time, we used a different method: we built two models which illustrated the same phenomena by means of a striking, yet beautifully simple sleight-of-hand trick. Unfortunately, no static drawing can show the action of these models.

In another model which we made to illustrate the absorption of electro-magnetic waves by the earth's atmosphere, we used coloured knitting needles to represent the sun's rays. They jumped in in groups corresponding to the seven wave-bands of the electro-magnetic spectrum. The 'jump technique' (page 123) is very versatile and can convey a strong sense of action. If only very few different phases of a process are to be shown, the overlaying of cels is a feasible method. To show the penetrating power of alpha-, beta- and gamma-rays, for instance, only three cells were necessary, one for each particle group.

Electro-magnetic waves follow a straight path. This is a well-known feature of photography and we used two different scenes to prove it.

The first scene showed a sectional view of a pinhole camera with a candle in front of it. Two lines, representing light rays, drew themselves from top and bottom of the candle, converging in the pinhole and throwing an inverted image of the candle onto the back of the pinhole camera.

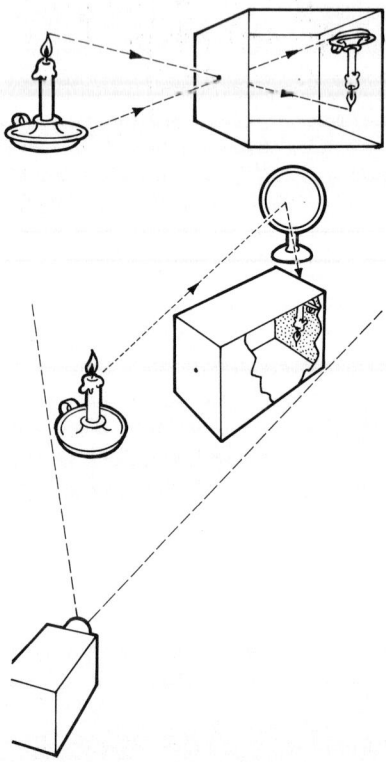

Fig. 124. *Pinhole Camera.* This standard textbook illustration demonstrates that light rays follow a straight path.

Fig. 125. In order to obtain the flickering effect of the candle flame the set-up illustrated in this drawing had to be adopted. The concave mirror projected a real inverted image on to a piece of frosted Perspex stretched across the back of the pinhole camera. By judicious lighting of the candleholder and flame, a well-exposed 'back-projection' image was obtained which showed the flame to be alive.

In order to achieve a live effect, we put a concave mirror behind the pinhole camera at such distance that it projected a real inverted image onto a piece of slightly frosted Perspex fitted across the back of the pinhole camera (tightly stretched gauze would do as well.) The mirror was shielded from direct photographic light and its frame and stand were painted black. The live effect of this scene depended on the agitation of the candle flame so that the flame in the mirror was seen to flicker as well.

In the second scene we showed the same effect by a practical example. We mounted a large, old-fashioned studio-camera on one side of a turntable with the lens pointing at a candle on the other side. By moving the turntable round, the candle disappeared behind the camera and re-appeared upside down on its ground glass. This was pictorially most convincing.

Films in the Making

The paths and the reflection of light rays can be shown by means of a smoke box (see page 183).

The last sequence of Part 2 is devoted to masers and lasers, and a particularly intricate piece of animation by Science Films, devised and supervised by Dr. Wilkinson, explains what happens inside a laser tube. In this case, professionally executed animation was absolutely essential.

One more scene is perhaps worth mentioning. At one point, the film refers to photo-synthesis. The explanation of this process would need a film by itself. We only wanted one symbolic visual combining the concepts 'nature' and 'science' to cover a short length of commentary, and eventually dreamed up the following scene.

We borrowed a window-frame from a builder and also two sheets of white hardboard. We also got hold of a small laboratory bench, a microscope and other biological paraphernalia, including green leaves from several plants.

We took all these props to a spot near London where a large cornfield extends up a slope.

We assembled the walls with the window at the edge of the field and put the laboratory equipment against it. First we filmed the microscope on the bench in close-up, then we tilted the camera up to the window and zoomed through it to reveal the full extent of the ripening cornfield with the green halms swaying in the breeze.

'Some motorists had stopped their cars to watch our antics and to ask the usual question: 'When will this film be on the telly?'

Two films on the history of modern science

Several years ago, the nations of the Western European Union agreed on a scheme which was a first attempt at international co-operation in the sphere of the educational film. Each country was to produce one or several films on a 'historical approach to an important aspect of science in which a scientist of the country concerned has made an outstanding contribution'. The Educational Foundation for Visual Aids in connection with Mullard Ltd, the electronics concern, having given much thought to finding appropriate subjects, decided to make two films as the British share in the scheme. The first, *Mirror in the Sky*, was to deal with the origin and development of radio-communications and had Sir Edward Appleton's discovery of the ionosphere as its centrepiece. This was to be followed by the film *Conquest of the Atom*, built round Rutherford's first atom-splitting experiments. These two subjects were chosen because in addition to complying with the terms of reference of the agreement, they were 'good examples of the interrelation of pure research and applied technology'.

The films under this scheme had to be suitable for international distribution; they had to fit into the curricula of classes for the 13–15 years age group but were expected to appeal to wider audiences as well. Synchronized speech and lengthy diagrams had to be avoided.

Of all the films with a historical slant, produced by our team, the above two are the most interesting ones for the purpose of this book. Radio-communications and atomic physics offer endless opportunities to the camera for filming invisible phenomena, objects and processes, and a great number of models and visual effects had to be specially prepared.

The subject also introduced one or two problems which are common to all films with a historical background. One of these problems was how to present the historical characters involved in the story.

Historical personalities

There are several ways in which scientists of the past can be presented in films and none of them is ideal.

Impersonation by actors should generally be left to the entertainment field. The factual film can rarely afford the means for engaging top actors or for reconstructing elaborate historical settings and events. To-day's school audiences, conditioned by much film- and TV-watching, have become quite sophisticated. They are bound to be critical of charade-like performances and more likely to prefer a factual straightforward approach.

Impersonation by implication is much safer. If a sequence is to suggest that an experiment is, or was, carried out by a particular scientists, a close-up shot of the hands of any person, doing this experiment with the equipment of the period or its replica, will automatically associate the scene with that scientist. Silhouetted figures or back-views of persons can achieve the same effect. There is a danger, though: this method can easily appear self-conscious or even phoney if carried on for too long or used too often.

Photographs and drawings, valuable as they are as historic documents, have the disadvantage of all static material. They can be made more interesting by camera movement such as tracking and panning. This can give emphasis to certain points of the commentary (see for example 'Hertz' on page 210).

Animated cartoon characters are sometimes used. Unless the whole film is made as a cartoon, this method should only be considered if the treatment of the story warrants such a switch into the realm of fantasy or caricature. Also, animation of figures is very expensive.

There is yet *another* possibility and perhaps the most appropriate one if it fits in with the film: a present-day scientist could take the place of the historic personality with a clear statement in the commentary that he stands in for the character in question. One could even choose a cute schoolboy for that part and might get an appreciative laugh from the audience.

Clearly, all these alternatives have their *pros* and *cons* and the choice

Films in the Making

depends entirely on the character of the film and on the size of its budget.

The study of corresponding programmes in television would be worth the time spent on it. Character impersonations in every possible form and style, some excellent, others downright bad, appear almost every day on the TV screen and they will tell better than any words what can be achieved with modest means and what must by all means be avoided.

The problem becomes even more complex when historic *and* living persons have to be portrayed in one and the same film. The next pages will show how we dealt with this question in the two films under review.

Historic equipment

An aspect, peculiar to historical films, concerns the authenticity of the material to be shown. This creates no big difficulty where ordinary items of every day life are concerned, such as pieces of furniture or clothes of a given period—all these can easily be hired. Moreover, slight inaccuracies would not greatly matter or even be noticed provided these items are used merely as incidentals.

The authenticity of scientific equipment, however, used in a given period or by a particular scientist for an experiment *can* matter very much and may necessitate thorough investigation. Some of the historic apparatus to be shown in a film may *have* to be either the original ones or accurate replicas.

The usual sources of information are museums, research institutes, learned societies, universities and the laboratories of industry. Collectively, these organizations are the custodians of the nation's scientific treasures accumulated over the centuries.

You can be almost certain to find any required scientific objects in one or the other of these places, but it may take some considerable time to locate them. The information on an exhibit's label or in the catalogue is normally reliable. In addition, the keeper in charge of a collection will, on request, give further details or explain points which are not clear.

Problems can arise when the authenticity of a historic object is attested by one expert and discounted by another. We are all familiar with such disputes which are given much publicity in the world of art.

The question of whether authenticity is really vital for the purpose of a film is one which depends entirely on the film's subject and argument. If the advisers agree that a demonstration can be carried out convincingly with a reasonably accurate replica, there is no point in a prolonged search for the original. Perfection, if carried too far, can have disastrous effects on the budget.

The two films were commissioned to Realist at the time Basil Wright was its executive producer. Denys Parsons had by then left the unit and our team had thus lost a most valuable member. On the sponsor's side, Dr. J. A. Harrison, the Director of EFVA, gave us the necessary overall guidance, particularly by combing out all 'fringe' material and in this way keeping us to the point whenever we were likely to go off at a tangent. Mullard Ltd supplied two educational advisers who assisted generously in matters of detail. In addition, a great number of specialists had to be consulted, either personally or in writing. Each of the investigation files of these films ultimately contained some 500 letters, memos and other documents. The commentary for *Mirror in the Sky* was written by Lord Ritchie Calder.

Both films are 20 min long. The first is in black-and-white, the second in colour. They were shot on 35mm negative and reduced to 16mm for distribution.

Mirror in the Sky

After a short introductory sequence indicative of the theme, the film opens with a demonstration of how Heinrich Hertz, in 1887, discovered radio waves. This achievement of pure research was followed up by Marconi with technological experiments carried out between 1895 and 1901, the year in which the 'impossible' happened and the first man-made radio waves, ignoring the curvature of the earth, crossed the ocean. The question posed is, how could they do this?

The next sequence deals with this question and explains the theory put forward by Heaviside and Kennelly in 1902. These scientists assumed the existence of an ionized layer somewhere in the atmosphere, a sort of mirror in the sky, which reflected the radiated waves back to earth. An animated diagram is used to demonstrate how ionization of air particles occurs.

Some twenty years later, the late Sir Edward Appleton investigated the electric properties of the atmosphere and in 1924 he succeeded in actually discovering such an ionized atmosphere, later called the ionosphere. The film describes the decisive experiment which proved that Heaviside's much derided theory was correct. During the following years, Appleton continued his research into the atmosphere, taking advantage of the newly invented pulse-technique. This further investigation showed that the ionosphere consists not only of one, but of several layers.

The film goes into the properties and behaviour of the ionosphere and its influence on radio-communications. Work in a radio-research station is shown and several practical applications are described. The most important of these is radar which is not only used for navigation and other practical purposes but was instrumental in bringing about the new science of radio-astronomy. The film shows the part radio-telescopes play in to-day's exploration of the universe and finishes on a montage of star clusters and galaxies.

Introduction: A signal across the ocean

Marconi's early research work reached its climax in St. Johns, Newfoundland, on the 12th December 1901 when he and his assistant

Films in the Making

Kemp, pressing the headphones of a primitive receiving set to their ears, heard the first faint signals radioed from the transmitting station which Marconi had previously built in Poldhu, Cornwall, at the other side of the Atlantic.

Basil Wright and I thought that this incident would make an interesting and even exciting opening to the film. It involved, however, using impersonators and building a small set. Yet we were wary of this approach for the reasons stated before. In the end, considering that neither 'acting', nor talking was necessary and that the whole scene was not intended as a factual demonstration but as a dramatic prelude, we came to the conclusion that this sequence justified our choice of treatment.

Guided by contemporary illustrations, we reconstructed the interior of

FIG. 126. Contemporary photograph of Marconi and his paraphernalia at his Receiving Station on Signal Hill, Newfoundland, 1901.

FIG. 127. Our studio set of the station re-constructed from the above photograph. Marconi (right) and his assistant Kemp listen to the first transatlantic transmission of the agreed code signal.

the hut in our studio; an iron stove in the style of the period was its main item of furniture. We then dressed the set with the receiving apparatus and other paraphernalia actually used by Marconi and lent to us by Marconi Ltd.

In addition, we built a small scenic model of Signal Hill, St. Johns, on which the hut was sited, and also a full-sized replica of the kite which Marconi had used to hold up the aerial. The opening scene, showing the

The Work of the Science Film Maker

actual coastline at St. Johns, was obtained from the National Film Board of Canada.

The following script extract shows how this sequence was visualised and filmed.

INTRODUCTORY SEQUENCE (SHOOTING SCRIPT)

(following main- and credit titles)

Sc. No.	Picture	Commentary
3.	Library shot of Newfoundland coastline.	This is a story of exploration and scientific research into the region far above the surface of the earth. It begins in Newfoundland—
4.	Scenic model: side view of the Signal Hill promonotory with its buildings.	—at Signal Hill, near St. Johns, in the year 1901.
5.	CU Kite flying below some clouds (Actuality shot showing a replica of Marconi's kite.)	A kite is flying—a kite that made history. It trails a wire—
6.	Overhead view of the Signal Hill model as seen from the kite's position, with the aerial wire reaching up from the ground.	—sent up from the ground to waylay a wireless signal.
7.	CU. Exterior of the hut's window with the wire leading into the building.	Behind the window of a barracks building—
8.	MS. Hut interior. Marconi at desk looks out of the window, then picks up earphone and starts listening. Kemp enters the hut, dressed in a wet overcoat.	—Marconi anxiously waits: a bleak stormy day;—
9.	CU. Marconi listening.	—a crude earphone—
10.	CU. Receiving set on desk.	—linked to a primitive receiving set;
11.	CU as 9.	—groping for the signal;—
12.	MS. Kemp warming himself at the stove. He throws more wood into the flames.	—hoping for what commonsense said—
13.	CU as 9. Marconi's head suddenly jerks.	—was impossible. Impossible... but true!
14.	Quick insert: Kemp at stove bends forward expectantly.	
15.	Big CU. Earphone at Marconi's ear.	(Sound effect: pip-pip-pip)
16.	Two-shot: The excited Marconi hands earphone to Kemp.	Hear for yourself!
17.	Big CU. Kemp's hand pressing earphone to ear.	(Sound effect: pip-pip-pip)
18.	Two-shot as 16, other angle. Kemp nods vigorously.	The Morse letter 'S'!—Again... and again...

Films in the Making

	(following main- and credit titles)	
Sc. No.	Picture	Commentary
19.	Two-shot, side view: Kemp hands earphone back to Marconi, who listens once more. Both are very agitated.	It is the pre-arranged signal which has travelled from the Old World to the New.
20.	Big CU. Marconi's hand comes into view holding watch. The time is clearly seen.	At 12.30 on the 12th December 1901—
21.	Specially made model of section of globe showing the Atlantic between the contours of England and Newfoundland. The word ATLANTIC is faded in across the ocean, suggesting a bridge. Fade out.	—wireless waves had bridged the Atlantic. To grasp the full meaning of this, we must go back to the very beginning of radio.

End of Introduction; a full account of Marconi's research follows later in the film.

Discovery of radio-waves by Heinrich Hertz

Hertz carried out his work in the laboratories of the Technische Hochschule (College of Technology), Karlsruhe, and I was afraid that we might have to go to Germany for the preparation and filming of the historic experiment. This, however, proved unnecessary because we found that an authority on Hertz was available practically on our doorstep in the person of Mr. Gerald Garratt who, at that time, was in charge of the telecommunication section at the Science Museum, London. This was a piece of exceptionally good fortune since Mr. Garratt was not only prepared to cooperate by vetting the script and by advising on numerous theoretical points but also by providing all necessary equipment from the Museum's collection. He spent many evenings on getting the various apparatus in working order after they had been locked away in glass cases for several decades. Some of the pieces had to be brought up from the country where they had been stored during the war. Thus, Mr. Garratt's assistance proved indeed invaluable.

One of the important aspects of Hertz's discovery from the film's point of view, is that he did not stumble upon the radio-waves by a lucky chance but that he deliberately set out to test and prove a given theory, much like Appleton did in his own field fifty years later.

In 1864, James Clerk Maxwell had predicted the existence of electromagnetic waves by mathematical calculation, and when 20 years later, Hertz decided to investigate this theory he had to start out on a great number of experiments. In these he used a variety of apparatus, all of which consisted essentially of a wave-generator at one end of the laboratory bench and a detector, a few feet away, at the other end. Eventually, in 1888,

Hertz found that the discharge of electricity across the spark gap of the generator caused a tiny spark to jump across the diminutive open gap of the detector. This showed that electricity can travel through space without a conductor in the form of waves, which were first called Hertzian waves and later, radio-waves.

A question arose as to which of Hertz's numerous experiments should be shown in the film, and on Mr. Garratt's advice we chose the two which were most telling for the purpose of the film's argument: (a) a reconstruction of one of Hertz's very first demonstrations which proved that electro-magnetic waves did, indeed, exist, and (b) a sequence to show that such waves can be reflected by a conducting surface.

The wave-generator for the first experiment consisted of an induction coil and oscillator with a spark gap, and the detector of a wire loop fitted to a wooden frame, also with a tiny spark gap.

After Mr. Garratt had set up his equipment in our studio, he peered at this spark gap through a magnifying glass as Hertz had done. We realized then, at once, how to present the person of Hertz at the beginning of the sequence without resorting again to acting. We took a photograph showing Mr. Garratt bent over the apparatus and handed it to an artist* with the request to make a drawing of this scene, replacing Mr. Garratt by a likeness of Hertz.

This drawing was to cover the first commentary sentence which introduced Hertz into the film. When we shot this drawing, we tracked slowly on to the spark gap in the background until it filled the screen. Then we set up the *actual* oscillator with the spark gap and, matching its exact position to that of the drawing, we took a similar tracking shot. These two scenes were later optically mixed and the resulting match-dissolve provided a smooth transition from the drawing to the actual experiment.

The experiment itself presented only one problem to the camera: how to make the tiny sparks in the detector clearly visible. We solved this by macro-photography. A 75mm lens was fitted to several extension tubes until we obtained the necessary magnification.

The last scene of this sequence shows the whole set-up from a high camera position with a curved white wave front emerging from the oscillator and travelling towards the detector.

For this scene we had to take two shots: a static shot of the equipment and a shot of the travelling waves for which we used a Crova disc effect. These two scenes were then superimposed in the laboratory.

Hertz also used parabolic reflectors to beam the waves. Accurate replicas of these reflectors were provided by Mr. Garratt for sequence (b).

---

* A. R. Thomson, R.A. His inspired illustrations in Sherwood-Taylor's *History of Science* had drawn our attention to him.

Films in the Making

FIG. 128. Reconstruction of one of Hertz's first transmission experiments. The wave-generating apparatus is seen in the background and the detector in the foreground. Tiny sparks could be observed through a magnifying glass in the spark gap of a wire loop. The first Hertzian waves travelled a distance of several inches up to 3 ft.

They had been polished so well by the Museum staff that we had to undo part of their work to get rid of the glare. The reflectors were set up several feet apart on a bench; one was the oscillator or 'transmitter', the other the resonator or 'receiver'. For our filmic demonstration we had to add a few items which were not part of Hertz's original equipment, such as a small electric bell and also a copper sheet which was suspended horizontally above the bench and could be raised and lowered. At the start this copper sheet was pulled up to the ceiling so as not to be seen.

The first scene showed the two reflectors facing each other squarely. The coil was switched on and a wave generated by the spark in the oscillator. This wave was beamed towards the receiver and indicated in the film by a white line which drew itself. The moment the line reached the receiver the bell rang.

Next, the reflectors were tilted upwards by means of invisible wires. The beamed wave-line shot diagonally towards the ceiling, by-passing the receiver. The bell stopped ringing.

Now, the copper sheet was lowered into the picture. Being a conductor it acted like a mirror and reflected the diagonal beam—the white line—towards the receiver. The bell started ringing again. (Fig. 129).

The white wave-lines were filmed at the same time as the actual scenes and superimposed on them in the camera by the Pepper's Ghost technique in the following way. An opal glass sheet was set up vertically at the side of the camera, at right angles to the lens and at a similar distance. At the given moments, the lines drew themselves on the glass sheet; we used the simulated animation method (pages 129–30).

As these lines had to travel into different directions, we had to reposition the gap on the glass sheet before each shot.

The camera filmed simultaneously these lines ghosted on to the semi-silvered mirror by Pepper's Ghost *and* the reflectors visible *through* the mirror.

As is well known, it never occurred to Hertz that radio waves could be put to practical use; he was interested only in *how* the waves behaved.

Marconi, however, was quick to realize the enormous commercial possibilities of Hertz's discovery.

Marconi's experiments

One of Mr. Garratt's marginal notes on the first draft of our script reads: 'Marconi's essential contribution in the early years was the *elevated aerial* and I feel strongly that the initial reference to Marconi should focus on this aspect of his work'.

FIG. 129. Hertzian Waves can be deflected and reflected. Reconstruction of another one of Hertz's early experiments: reflection by a copper sheet.

This comment was a clear pointer to the way this sequence should be handled. To start with, we obtained a photograph of the apparatus which Marconi used for his experiments in his father's garden in Bologna. Unfortunately, it was not Marconi but his assistant Kemp who was shown in the picture, so that we had once more to enlist Mr. Thomson's art. As before he prepared a drawing which was an exact reproduction of the photograph with Marconi taking Kemp's place.

The two drawings of Hertz and Marconi, similar in style and used in the same way at the beginning of each sequence to introduce these personalities, turned out to be quite successful as a device for linking the separate stories which dealt with the early history of radio.

The original apparatus shown in the photograph luckily was preserved in the collection of the Marconi Company. We were allowed to take it away for filming and we set it up in a garden which, though situated nearer to London than to Bologna, had quite a southern flavour about it.

The filming of this sequence followed the procedure adopted for the previous one. The drawing dissolves into an actuality scene in which the details of the equipment are shown one by one in a panning shot which ends with a close-up of a metal sheet that served as aerial and was fitted vertically about twelve feet from the ground between two poles. This arrangement represented Marconi's first attempt to overcome ground obstructions by putting the aerial in a high position.

The film now shows, with the help of maps and little models of aerial masts, how Marconi extended the range of his transmissions.

Films in the Making

By the end of 1900 he had increased his range to 320 km, and on 12th December 1901 he received the first faint signal across the Atlantic.

Using a specially made globe combined with simulated animation and the Pepper's Ghost technique as before, the film demonstrates why this was considered 'impossible' at that time. Since the earth is curved, the waves would shoot over the horizon into space. 'Marconi', says the commentary, 'acted not on science but on a hunch'. At Poldhu in Cornwall—helped by Ambrose Fleming, the radio valve pioneer—he constructed a powerful transmitting station, the first of its kind. Fig. 134.

Guided again by a photograph of the period, we made a model of the enormous aerial which Marconi had built in Poldhu. But this model looked unrealistic because even the thinnest wires or threads were too thick in proportion to the required size of the model. We therefore decided to use a drawing made on glass. Effectively lit, and put in front of a background onto which moving clouds were projected, it appeared almost more gigantic than the actual aerial could have done. Fig. 131.

This scene was followed by a flashback to the opening sequence showing Marconi and Kemp in their hut in Newfoundland receiving the signals. The experiment had succeeded but how it could succeed remained a mystery.

During the next 25 years, a world-wide system of wireless telegraphy had been created and we show the soaring arrays into which Marconi's first improvised aerials had grown. Broadcasting stations sprang up everywhere and the one at Bournemouth, England, played a part in solving the mystery of how radio waves can travel round the globe.

Ionisation (an animated diagram)

Before dealing with Appleton's experiments, the film had to explain Heaviside's theory. We felt that the phenomena involved in this theory called for an animated diagram. This meant devising a precise schedule and blueprint for the animation artists from which they could take their instructions and cues. The procedure is described in the chapter on animation.

The initial subject investigation for a film is mainly concerned with the overall information which is necessary for writing an outline or treatment. But when it comes actually to putting the subject on celluloid it is the *detail* which matters and almost every sequence might require further particularised research.

Our ideas about the ionisation of the atmosphere were somewhat hazy and we urgently needed additional information. This was given to us by two experts at the Physics Department of the Imperial College, London. The points they made were that much that is happening up in the air is still obscure and any visual presentation of it would have to be a mixture of facts and fantasy.

Fig. 130. Contemporary photograph of Marconi's wireless sender, as used by him in 1896. Note the copperplate aerial at the top.

Fig. 131. Glass painting of Marconi's giant aerial at Poldhu, Cornwall from where the first transatlantic signals were transmitted in 1901.

There are no 'atoms of air'. Air is mainly made up of nitrogen atoms (7 electrons) and oxygen atoms (8 electrons). The 'simpler' atoms, such as those of helium (2 electrons) and hydrogen (1 atom) are for all practical purposes non-existent in air. But in view of the difficulty of handling diagrammatically seven or eight orbiting electrons, the experts thought that the helium atom should be the one used in the demonstration with a few words in the commentary to explain this choice.

With its two negative electrons the helium atom is neutral because the nucleus has two positive charges. But when u.v. radiation collides with one of these electrons it knocks it out of its orbit. The atom with its one remaining electron has now become an electrically charged particle, i.e., an ion. The process of turning neutral atoms into ions is called ionisation it applies of course to all atoms including the N and O atoms of which air mainly consists.

The sequence suggested by the two experts was not arrived at in one session but by stages, in further meetings, by phone calls and letters.

Eventually, a schedule was worked out and the key drawings could be taken in hand. These were checked by the experts who either approved or corrected them and then the material was ready for the preparation of the cels and for the photography. The following shooting script was handed to the animators; it shows the sequence as it finally appeared in the film.

Films in the Making

Ionisation : Animation script

Sc. No and length	Shooting instructions	Visual	Commentary
45a Fade in 2 ft Hold 6 ft	Black dots, static; dense at bottom, thinning in middle, diffused at top.		The air in the upper atmosphere is rarefied.
45b Animation 20 ft	Squiggles ('photons') appear at top, travel down diagonally; speed top to bottom 3 sec. None should reach the earth but must disappear within dense layer of dots. Some squiggles disappear in upper half of frame and are replaced by white dots which oscillate as discussed.	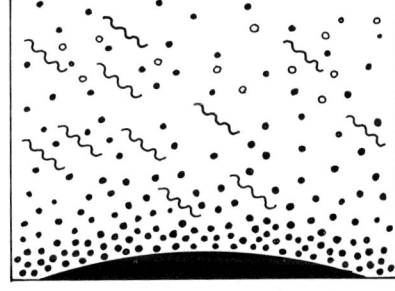	The thinly dispersed atoms are subject to intense u.v. radiation from the sun which causes them to lose some of their electrons. To see how this happens—
Mix 2 ft to 46a Animation 12 ft	Electrons A and B circle round nucleus as shown. They draw their orbit-lines, completing them in 7 ft. Electrons continue action for 5 ft.		—lets take an atom with a simple structure. 2 negative electrons circle round the positive nucleus.

215

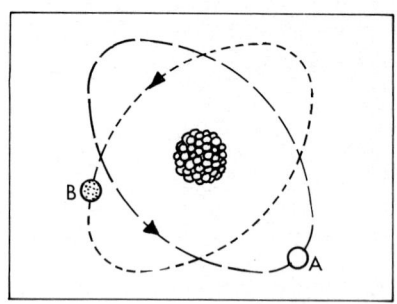

46b Animation 10 ft	Electrons continue orbiting. Squiggles appear and travel downwards as in 45b. They must not hit the Electrons. No more than 1 or 2 squiggles to be in frame at any time.	In this form the atom is neutral and does not interfere with radio waves... But if u.v. radiation—	

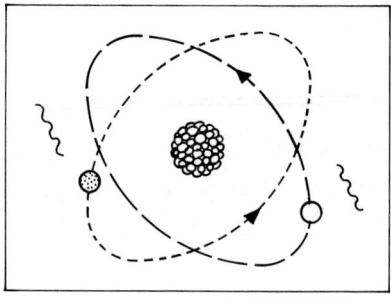

46c Animation 4 ft	Electrons continue orbiting. Another squiggle appears and (2 ft) hits Electron A. Squiggle disappears; Electron A shoots downwards out of frame (1 ft).	—hits an electron, it is torn out of its orbit.	

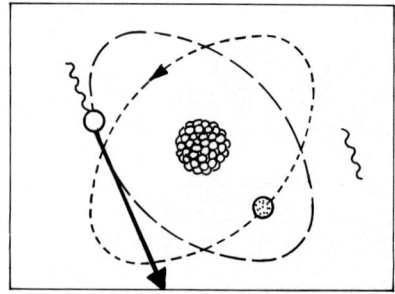

46d Animation 12 ft	Electron B continues circling. Further squiggles appear but miss the electron.	The nucleus with its remaining electron now has a positive charge and is called an *Ion*... Watch again!	

Films in the Making

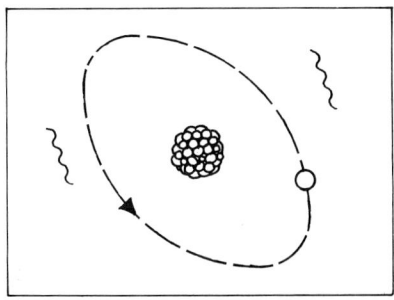

46e Animation 12 ft	Electron A reappears and both A and B orbit round nucleus as in 46b; after 7 ft repeat action of 46c.	

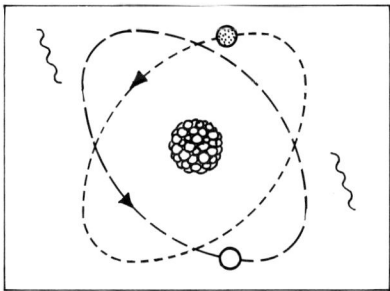

Mix 2 ft
to

47 Animation 20 ft	Field and action as in 45b, but a visible layer of animated white dots in upper half of frame is clearly visible at start of scene. Continue action throughout, making this layer denser. There are always more squiggles in upper half of frame than in bottom half.	Heaviside believed that these ions together with the liberated electrons form a layer which conducts electricity. It can be seen in the upper half of the picture.

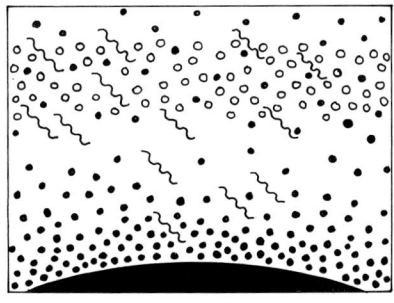

2 ft Fade out
_____

Total   104 (35 mm) ft.

End of animation sequence.

217

The Work of the Science Film Maker

The Heaviside sequence ends with the shot of the globe seen in previous scenes, this time set against a background on which the ionosphere curves as a dark band above the Atlantic. Self-drawing Pepper's Ghost lines follow the path of the reflected waves from England to Newfoundland. The commentary reads:

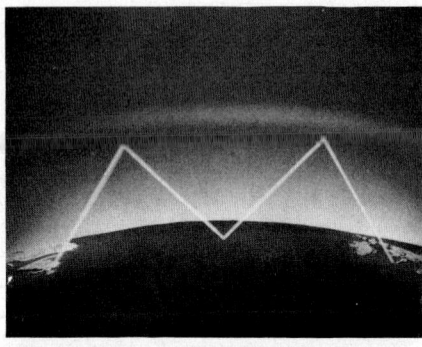

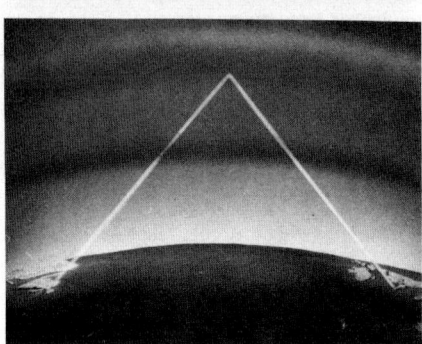

FIG. 132 (top) and FIG. 133 (bottom). In translantic transmission radio waves are reflected and bounced across the sea either by the Heaviside Layer (long waves) or by the higher Appleton Layer (short waves).
In these model shots the self-drawing lines were produced by the Pepper's Ghost method.

'[Heaviside] ... suggested that this ionised atmosphere, now called ionosphere, acted like a mirror, reflecting back the radio waves just like the copper sheet used by Hertz. Since land and sea also act as reflectors a wave, sent out from England, would bounce along until it reached America.... Heaviside's theory remained a theory for over twenty years, waiting for a man who could prove it. That man was Professor Edward Appleton'.

Discovery of the ionosphere by Appleton

Appleton, later Sir Edward, who was alive at the time of filming, is seen working at his desk while the commentary refers to his 'ingenious way of investigating the electric properties of the upper atmosphere'.

For the ensuing sequence which describes this investigation we chose a method of presentation which is very simple and effective wherever it is adequate for its purpose.

A glass sheet takes the place of the usual classroom blackboard and

Films in the Making

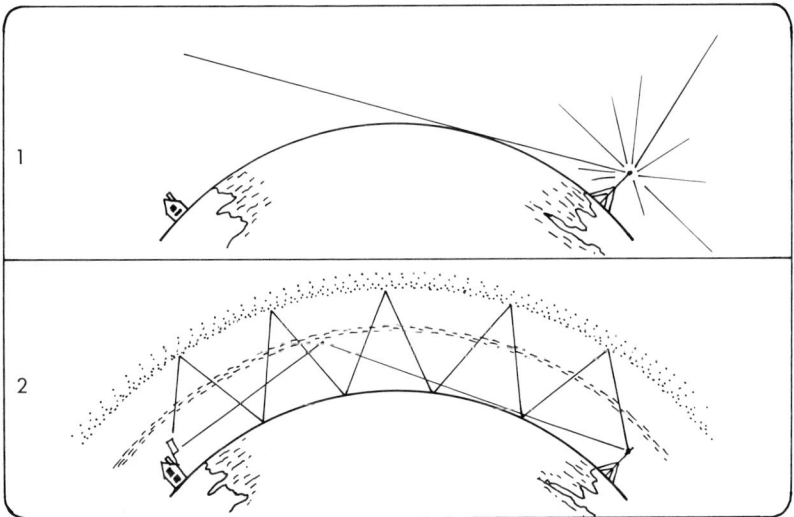

Fig. 134. *Spanning the Ocean by Radio.* A page from the story-board album handed to the sponsor with the script.
1. The conventional theory at the turn of last century: since radio waves travel in a straight line, signals sent out in Europe would get lost in space.
2. Heaviside's theory: the signals would be reflected by an electrically charged layer in the atmosphere and bounce across the ocean to be received in America. Marconi's successful transmissions had not been based on this theory (which did not exist at that time) but on a hunch.

the diagrams, etc., are drawn on it from the back. The glass is set up in front of a wall covered with black velvet. The demonstrator standing between the velvet and the glass is dressed in a dark suit and his face is covered by a black mask. The glass is lit sideways from the front so that the light misses the person behind it. If the demonstrator's hand is also covered by a black glove, the lines on the glass appear as if they draw themselves. It is, however, often preferable to leave the hand *un*covered, because seeing the hand in action helps to pin-point the area of interest, particularly in the long shots; it also makes the whole presentation less of an animated diagram.

The most outstanding example of this kind of demonstration is the film *La Mystére Picasso* in which this artist displays his technique of painting. This film was made many years ago but I remember it as vividly as if I had seen it yesterday. Picasso did not, of course, hide behind a black mask; on the contrary, he made the most of his picturesque personality. What was most striking, apart from seeing the master at work, was the appropriateness of this method to expositional treatment. The slightly unreal 'transparent' quality of the emerging picture—whether done in chalks or paint, in monochrome or colour—seems to have a psychological effect which

The Work of the Science Film Maker

causes the audience to follow the action with a heightened sense of expectancy and concentration right to the end.

This method is, of course, not suitable for all demonstrations; if for instance a large amount of written text is involved, the demonstrator would have to be a wizard in mirror-writing.

Figure 135 shows the glass drawing. The action was divided up into

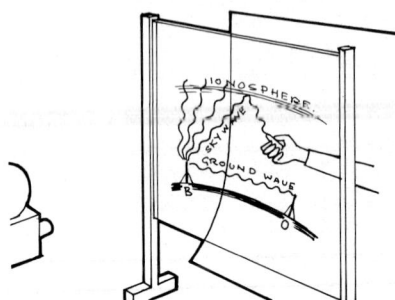

Fig. 135. *Glass Drawing showing the Appleton Experiment.* On a glass sheet, set against black velvet, a hand appears at the back of the glass and, using a white grease pencil, draws a diagram in step with the commentary as described on the previous page. This kind of presentation is much cheaper than an animated diagram and pictorially more interesting than the usual classroom method of writing on a blackboard.

several long-shots and close-ups. The corresponding commentary reads:

'There was a BBC transmitter at Bournemouth and a receiving station at Oxford. Waves, sent out by a transmitter, radiate in all directions. Some take a direct route along the ground to Oxford. Others shoot skywards and, assuming that there was a Heaviside layer, some of the sky waves would be reflected; having a longer route, they would arrive at Oxford later. The waves might still arrive *in step* with each other because the delay might be a *full* wavelength—wave crest will be opposite wave crest (shown in a big close-up; Fig. 136.2)—they will reinforce each other and a *strong* signal will result. (Shot of an ammeter with its needle swinging to a maximum reading).

But the delay may *not* be a full wavelength: then they are *out of step* (close-up, Fig. 136.1); part of a wave trough is now opposite to a wave crest, the waves conflict with each other and a *weak* signal results (small swing of the ammeter needle).

Therefore, if the wavelength at Bournemouth was gradually changed, the difference in distance between the two routes would result in the two waves arriving at Oxford alternately *in step* and *out of step* and *in* and *out* and so on. So, if the signal strength varied during the experiment, the presence of a reflecting layer would be proved'.

All experts agreed that this was a very difficult concept to explain to 13–15 year-olds whose knowledge of wave motion would be largely confined to water waves. In the end, the following scene was devised, filmed in CU and added to the glass-drawing sequence.

We prepared a long strip of transparent paper with the 2 wave lines drawn one above the other as in the preceding close-up shots. To start with, the crests of the waves are opposite to each other. To indicate that the

Films in the Making

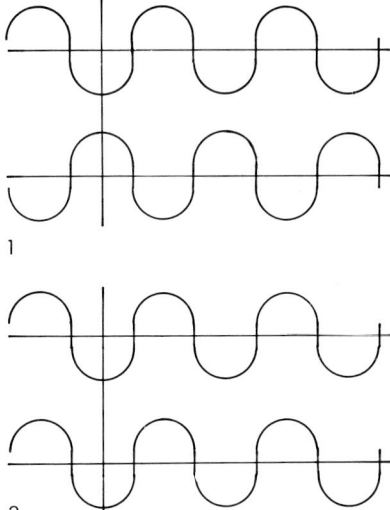

FIG. 136. *Ground Waves and Sky Waves I.*
1. CU showing radio waves arriving at a receiving station marked by a vertical line. If the ground- and sky-waves are 'out of step' with each other—i.e., if the wave crest is opposite or nearly opposite a wave trough—there is a weak signal or no signal at all.
2. If the waves arrive 'in step' with each other, crest opposite crest and trough opposite trough, a strong signal results.

wavelengths varied and also got out of tune with each other, the modulations were drawn closer and closer together but in an uneven degree so that the crest–crest position, after a while, became a crest–trough position. The paper strip was then pulled past the vertical line which in the preceding shots marked the Oxford receiving station (Fig. 137). This scene was visually similar to the previous scenes of this sequence with the exception that the hand had vanished and that the wave-lines appeared to move by themselves. At the end, this scene mixed into one showing the ammeter again, this time with its needle oscillating fairly rapidly between a high and low reading.

Having described the reasoning behind Appleton's experiment, the film now shows its actual performance. As it happened, the BBC had, at some time previous to our filming, produced a programme which was a reconstruction of the decisive experiment with Appleton himself taking part in it. Our sponsor, for reasons of authenticity as well as economy, came to an arrangement with the BBC by which the relevant part of the programme could be included in our film. This BBC-insert shows, slightly dramatized, what took place during the night of 6th December 1924. This is the gist of it:

Appleton and his colleague Dr. Barnett were waiting at the receiving station at Oxford. At midnight, Appleton lifted the telephone and called up Bournemouth: 'I'll count three and then you change the wavelength—fairly slowly and uniformly . . . When I count three again, you bring it back slowly to the original wavelength . . . Here we go: . . . one–two–three - - - change . . . one–two–three - - - change . . . (The ammeter needle swung

221

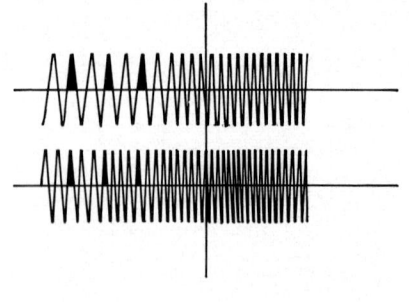

FIG. 137. *Ground Waves and Sky Waves II.* In order to show the variations in signal strength which Appleton experienced it was necessary gradually to vary the 'in step' position to the 'out of step' position (as shown in Fig. 136) and back again. A strip of transparent paper several feet long was prepared on which the waves lines were drawn, getting into and out of step repeatedly and this strip, lit from the back, was slowly pulled across the field of view of the lens. The above drawing shows how the wave lines look in one frame of this scene.

vigorously to and fro) . . . Yes, yes, it's there alright. We got a reflection!! . . .'

This variation of signal strength proved to Appleton the existence of a reflecting layer—a mirror in the sky.

But this was just a beginning. In 1931, Appleton made further experiments employing the pulse technique (a forerunner of radar). Bursts of radio waves were reflected off the ionosphere and the echoes were seen on the cathode ray tube or an instrument called the 'ionosonde'. Appleton often noticed two echoes on the tube, one from 60 to 70 miles up, the other from about 150 miles. (Fig. 138 of cathode ray tube trace). This convinced him that there had to be at least two reflecting layers. The film shows them as dark bands drawn on a sky backing and demonstrates, again by means of Pepper's Ghost lines, that the lower 'Heaviside layer', reflects long and medium waves, while short waves pass through the Heaviside and are bounced back by the higher 'Appleton layer'. (Fig. 133)

Further research

The next part of the film was concerned with the influence exerted on the ionosphere by u.v. radiation from the sun, with its day-and-night and seasonal variations in height and intensity, with magnetic storms caused by sun flares, with the forecasting of 'ionospheric weather', with radar, rockets and artificial satellites as means of exploring the upper atmosphere, with meteor activity and similar celestial details. The visual material in this part consisted of library scenes, and of further models and effects a description of which would be repetitive. We also took shots of some of the work carried out in a radio research station.

A few words must be said here about filming in modern electronics laboratories. From the pictorial point of view, they are the despair of every film-maker. The tracings of the electron beams on the screens of cathode ray tubes,* shown for the time necessary to cover a lengthy

---

* Special instrumentation film stock of high contrast, in 35mm, 16mm and 8mm are available in both black-and-white and colour for filming in CU the various kinds of oscillographs, glow tubes, ionosondes and PPI-screens, bubble- and cloud chambers, etc., also for

Films in the Making

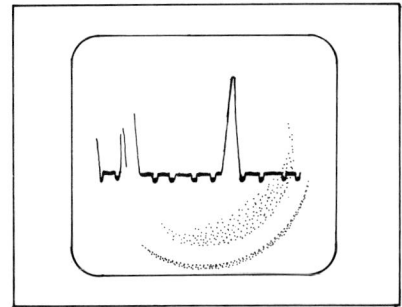

FIG. 138. *Cathode Ray Tube Trace.* Most cathode ray traces can be filmed without difficulty provided all stray light is kept off the tube. High-speed emulsions are useful. The above trace shows the tube of an ionosonde on which a burst of radio waves is seen to be reflected twice: one echo comes from the Heaviside layer (about 60 miles up) and the other one from the Appleton layer (about 150 miles up).

commentary, are as inspiring to watch as the movements of the hands round a clock face, unless the film manages to get its audience interested in their special significance. The same goes for graphs, charts and similar items. Control panels are even worse with their dead-pan facings on which nothing moves but an occasional flicker of a coloured bulb, the swing of a meter needle or the numbers on a counter. What a contrast to the industrial scene of the steam age with its vigorous activity of enormous wheels, pistons and columns of smoke!

You just have to make the best of visually unrewarding locations by keeping the commentary as short as is compatible with the need of giving information. Also, if possible, you should arrange the material so that the more interesting details are not all bunched together. Both visual and aural stimuli must not follow each other too quickly in a film which is designed for the intellect rather than the emotions; but they must not be too few and far between either. The first confuses, the second bores.

Radio astronomy

This section of the film was concerned with the 'new window to the heavens' which Appleton had opened, for which work, he had been awarded the Nobel Prize.

Fig. 139 compares the wide 'sky-light' above the radio-wave band with the narrow slit above the light-wave band, showing how our view of the universe has been extended.

By means of star photographs and sky maps obtained from various observatories the film contrasts the range of visual astronomy with that of radio-astronomy. The two biggest British radio-telescopes, the interferometer at Cambridge and the dish-telescope at Jodrell Bank were both still under construction. But while we eventually managed to get a satisfactory shot of the almost finished array at Cambridge and of the installations in its control rooms, we could film the Jodrell Bank telescope

---

high-speed and infra-red recording. There are about 70 different film types to choose from. For information about sizes, technical applications, etc., write to Instrumentation Product Sales, Eastman Kodak Company, Rochester, New York 14650 or its overseas branches.

The Work of the Science Film Maker

only in an incomplete stage. The consulting engineers had, however, built an extremely good model with every detail in scale. It had been exhibited at an industrial fair. We obtained permission to film this model, and with the help of a moving-cloud projector (such as was used in the Marconi sequence) we got a shot giving a lifelike impression of the completed telescope (Fig. 36).

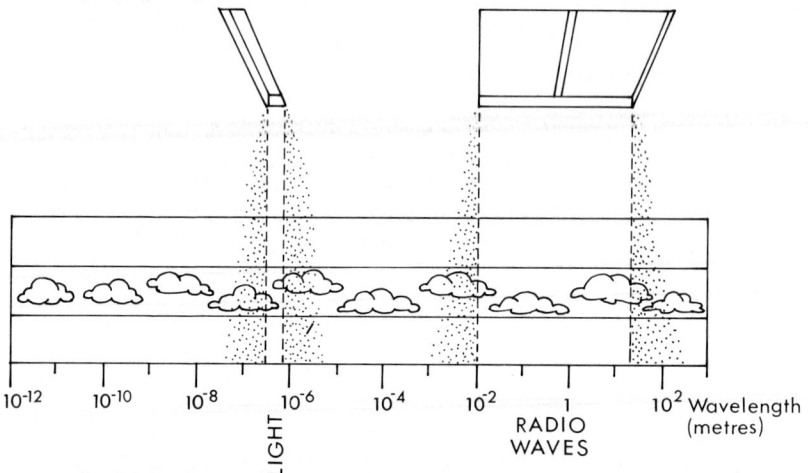

Fig. 139. *Radio-Astronomy.* The two 'sky-lights' of observation demonstrating the hugely enlarged range of vision afforded by radio-astronomy. The economics of factual film-making make the occasional use of static material in a film inevitable.

The end of the film consists of a series of photographs of galaxies and nebulae, all filmed by tracking into them and mixing one shot into the other, thus conveying the idea of a journey through outer space. The commentary concludes: 'In 50 years, wireless waves have bridged the oceans, conquered time and distance. Now, the story is reaching far further to explore the distant regions of the expanding universe'. Music plays the film out.

Conquest of the Atom

This film, also made for EFVA–Mullard, follows *Mirror in the Sky* in the *History of Science* series. Apart from its teaching purpose it sets out to demonstrate the methods of scientific discovery and the significance of scientific achievement in the civilization of our time.

The film was shot in colour and, as stressed before, some of the cine effects in colour cannot easily be conveyed in a book by black-and-white illustrations. Where the colour is of special significance, mention is made of this in the text.

The production procedure was rather similar to that of *Mirror in the*

Films in the Making

Sky and the following description confines itself largely to filming techniques which have not been mentioned before and which can be assumed to be of interest to the reader.

Synopsis

A brief introductory sequence shows the opening of Calder Hall, Britain's first atomic power station, in 1956. The film then goes back in time and refers to the Greek atom concept in which the atom was visualized as a sort of minute solid ball. This notion or 'model' was still considered valid at the end of the last century.

In 1897, J. J. Thomson investigated the behaviour of gas discharge tubes. Several of his experiments shown in the film—proved to him that the atom is *not* a solid and indivisible sphere but is composed of negatively and positively charged particles. The whole concept of the atom changed: the particle was now likened to a sort of currant bun, with the (negative) currants distributed in the (positive) mass of the bun.

In 1911, Rutherford proved that this idea was also wrong and that the atom really consists of a planetary system in which negative electrons circle round a positive nucleus. Later, in 1919, Rutherford succeeded in splitting the nucleus of an atom for the first time in history, turning the element nitrogen into oxygen. The film shows exact reconstructions of Rutherford's experimental methods.

The terms *electron* and *proton* for the negatively and positively charged atomic particles were firmly established at that time.

In 1932, Cockcroft and Walton bombarded the lithium nucleus with accelerated protons. They were successful in splitting it and thus turned lithium into helium. Sir John Cockcroft himself explains in the film how he and his colleague built and used the first man-made atom-smasher.

Also in 1932, Rutherford's pupil Chadwick discovered the *neutron*, a further step in the exploration of the atomic structure.

The rest of the film is concerned with the problem of nuclear fission. In a diagram as well as by three-dimensional models, the film shows how Hahn and Strassman, in 1938, used slow-moving neutrons to split the famous uranium isotope 235. Another model demonstrates how *nuclear energy* can be produced by controlled chain reactions in an atomic pile.

The film ends with a recapitulation of the events of the past and looks forward to the peaceful possibilities offered by *nuclear fusion*.

The 'shrinking atom'

After the introduction, the film showed Dalton's table of elements which dissolved into a 'billiard-ball atom' of screen-size proportion. This large sphere began to shrink and, within a second or so, became the size of a pin-head to suggest the smallness of an atom. Or rather: that is what the scene was supposed to show, but it did not quite succeed in doing so because of an inhibiting psychological phenomenon which is involved here.

Creating an illusion of diminishing size seems a straightforward matter, and indeed, the mechanics are simple enough. The easiest technique for producing concentrical contraction or expansion of shapes or objects is the animated diagram. In the case of two-dimensional discs it is possible to make a 'diagram' yourself by putting an iris shutter behind a transparent screen and lighting the set from behind. All but the shutter opening must, of course, be covered with black paper. Adequate modelling by light can make a disc look like a sphere. Closing the shutter during filming makes the disc gradually appear smaller. Such a set-up allows for straightforward shooting.

Whatever method you employ, though, the shapes or objects if shown in isolation will not appear to be shrinking but to be travelling away from the camera and disappearing into the distance. This effect can only be rectified by providing a 'point of reference' which makes the shrinking item look like remaining in the same vertical plane of the image. If a shrinking sphere could be seen lying on a table or hanging from a support, the illusion of diminishing size would be achieved. But this solution does not suit all circumstances, each case has to be considered individually. Without such a definite point of reference, the shape or object will always appear to move away from the camera. The same phenomenon in reverse applies to expansion.

J. J. Thomson finds the electron

There are many types of vacuum or gas discharge tube. J. J. Thomson used mainly Crookes tubes for his early studies of cathode rays. Crookes tubes contain a cathode and an anode at their opposite ends and are filled with a residual gas. The film showed first that when a voltage is applied, a blue glow appears in the tube; the glow itself is caused by rays passing from the cathode to the anode; the colour of the glow depends on the nature of the gas. In some of the shots the travelling rays were indicated by white dots moving lengthwise in the tube.

The film then showed a second tube with a shield in it. A hole in the shield let only a thin beam of rays through. With the room in complete darkness, this beam became clearly visible on a built-in fluorescent screen. A hand held a bar magnet against the tube and the beam was seen to be deflected *towards* it. This proved to Thomson that cathode rays do not consist of electro-magnetic waves (which cannot be deflected from their path by magnets) but of tiny electrically charged particles, later called electrons.

A third tube was then shown which contained a plate connected to a battery. A negative charge was applied and the beam was deflected *away from* the plate. Since like charges repel each other, Thomson inferred that the particles had to be negatively charged.

Films in the Making

Measuring the deflections, Thomson calculated that the weight of such a particle had to be one two-thousandth of the lightest known atom. He also used different gases in his experiments; as all produced the same result he concluded that these negative particles are constituents of all matter.

The three tubes used in the filming were made for us to the specifications of our scientific adviser by a firm of electronic valve manufacturers. The firm also lent us the power pack from which we obtained the 15,000 V needed for the operation of the tubes. One of the firm's engineers set up the whole apparatus in our studio in such a way that the camera could smoothly

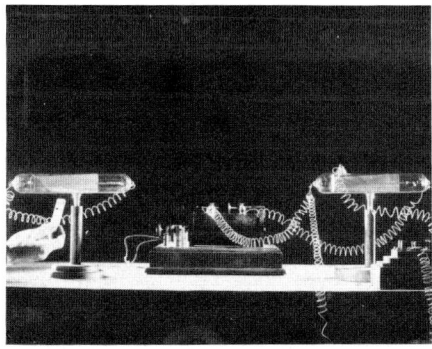

FIG. 140. Reconstruction of J. J. Thomson's experiment showing that a magnet (on the left) can deflect an electron stream.

move from one tube to the next by panning; he also supervised the filming from the technical angle. The beams themselves presented no problems since they were strong enough for straightforward photography.

The horizontally moving light-dots were superimposed on the actual scene during filming by the Pepper's Ghost method. The apparatus for producing these dots was set up at right angles to the camera; it consisted of a revolving drum with holes in it and a strong light bulb in its centre.

J. J. Thomson also used a 'positive ray tube' in some of his experiments to show that gases contain not only negatively, but also positively charged particles. This tube separates the two kinds. The round bulb on the right contains the anode and the cathode, but the cathode has a second cathode next to it which is connected to the first by a narrow canal. With a voltage applied to it, the tube starts glowing; as before there is a blue glow in the round bulb caused by the cathode rays travelling towards the anode. But there is also a red glow in the left part of the tube; this is produced by particles travelling in the opposite direction, from the anode towards the two cathodes, passing through the canal into the chamber on the left. Thomson found that these positively charged particles were much heavier than the negative ones. They are called 'canal rays' to differentiate them from the cathode rays.

Our electronic friends supplied the positive-ray tube but there were various reasons why it could not be made practical for straightforward

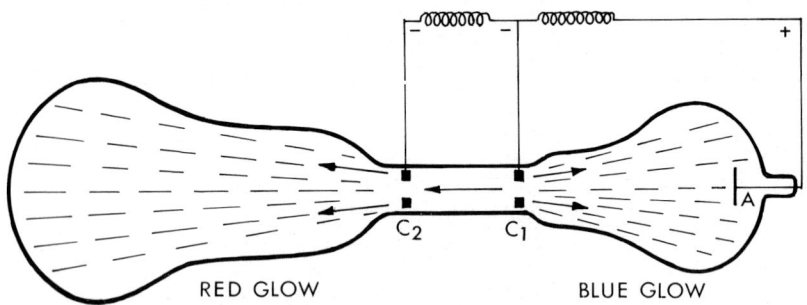

Fig. 141. *Positive Ray Tube.* The tube which J. J. Thomson used to prove that gases contain both negatively and positively charged particles. There are two cathodes, one at each end of the 'canal' in the middle. If a voltage is applied, the negative cathode rays travel from C_1 towards the anode and there is a blue glow in that part of the tube. The positive rays are emitted by the anode A and travel in the opposite direction into the left chamber of the tube causing a red glow in it. Thus, this tube separates the two kinds of particles by means of C_2. The tube shown here was blown to our expert's specifications by a firm of electronic equipment but, for various reasons, it could not be made practical. We had to produce the red and blue glow in the way described below. The particle streams were superimposed by Pepper's Ghost.

shooting. We therefore had to simulate the blue and red glows by means of coloured gelatines. The two colours necessitated double exposure: first the blue glow, and after rewinding the film in the camera, the red glow was filmed and the white particle streams obtained by the same method as before. None of the experts who later saw the film noticed that this was not an actual experiment but a fake.

The sequence ended by showing models of a number of 'currant-bun atoms', such as J. J. Thomson visualized at that time. 'After 2000 years', says the commentary, 'the atom could no longer be regarded as solid and indivisible; Thomson had opened the door to atomic science.'

Rutherford's 'Shooting Range'

This sequence deals with the discovery of the nucleus. The first few scenes show—by means of abstract coloured effects—how a radio-active source shoots off particles in all directions. If they hit a fluorescent screen they cause flashes. The flashes (scintillations) can be observed in a small tube, containing a radio-active source and a suitable screen. Such a tube is called a spinthariscope.

The commentary says that Rutherford, a pupil of J. J. Thomson, studied the nature of the particles emitted from radio-active substances, and found that some of them consist of what he later knew to be the nuclei of helium atoms. They carry two positive charges and travel up to 3 in. in air at tremendous speed. Rutherford called them *alpha-particles* and he wondered whether they could be used as a sort of probe for exploring the inside of an atom; a seemingly impossible idea. To find out, two of

Films in the Making

Rutherford's assistants, Geiger and Marsden, built an apparatus based on the principle of the spinthariscope.

Fig. 142 shows an exploded view of this apparatus. The radio-active source was enclosed in lead and a channel allowed the alpha-particles to travel only in the direction of the fluorescent screen to which a microscope was attached for the observation of the flashes. The main feature of the chamber was the scattering-foil, a thin leaf of gold fitted between the source and the screen so that the alpha-particles had to hit it. This illustration, taken from an old physics text-book, served as a guide for the building of our model.

The model was made from wood, cardboard, Perspex and tin foil. One side panel as well as the top of the chamber were detachable so that the camera could film the inside both from the side and from above. The stream of alpha-particles was again superimposed in the camera by our Pepper's Ghost.

The air in Rutherford's actual apparatus had to be removed for his observations; Fig. 145 shows the entire reconstructed set-up for his

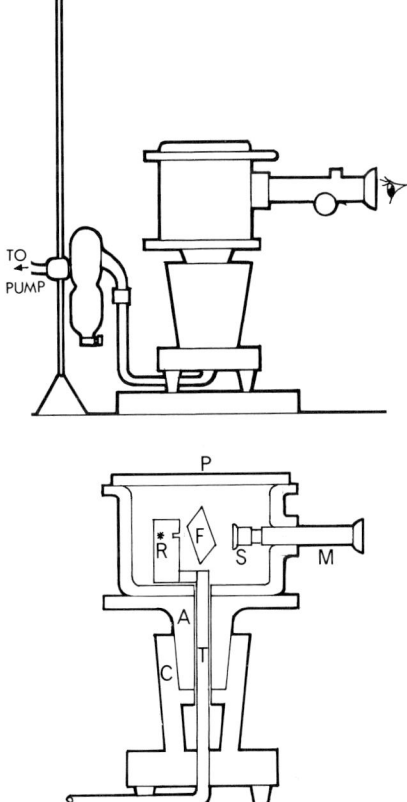

FIG. 142. *Geiger–Marsden Apparatus and an Exploded View of it.**
P Glass plate covering the rotating metal box;
R Source of radiation (alpha-ray tube filled with radon);
F Scattering foil (gold leaf);
S Zinc sulphide screen attached to
M Microscope;
A Circular platform rotating in
C Air-tight joint;
T Exhaust tube leading from rotating chamber to pump.
M and S rotate with chamber, R and F remain fixed. A description of the function of this apparatus is given on page 232. See also Figs. 143–145.

* The dummy model which was used in the filming was copied from this drawing taken from an old physics textbook.

The Work of the Science Film Maker

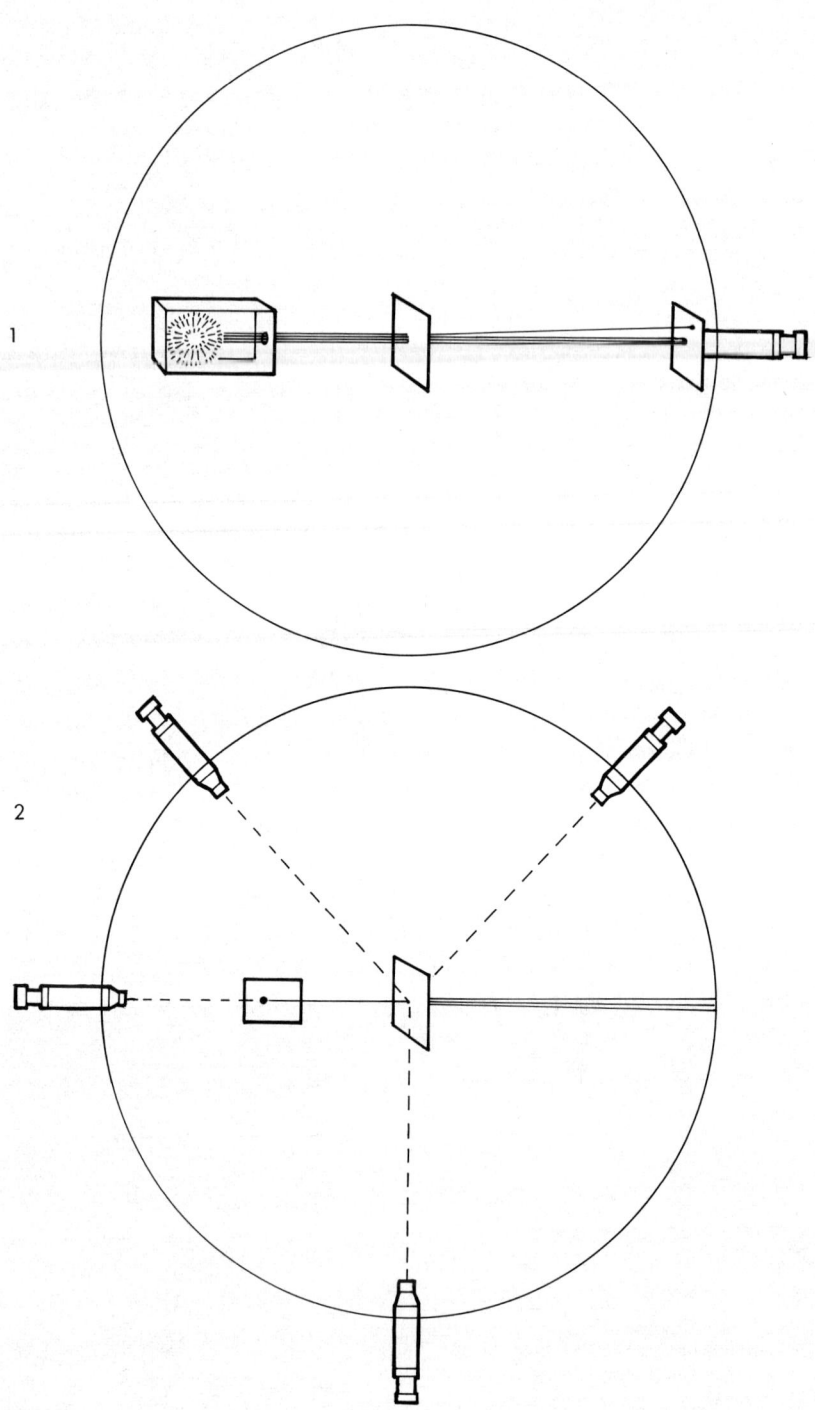

230

Films in the Making

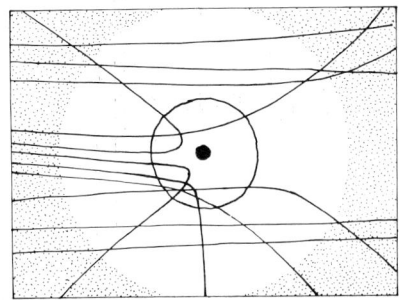

FIG. 144. *Bombardment of the Nucleus with Alpha-Particles*. This is a follow-up to Fig. 143. The drawing shows the atom with its nucleus in the centre. The tracks of the deflected alpha-particles are again shown as a composite picture. In the film, the particles are seen bombarding the nucleus one after the other. The drawing refers to Scene 32 on the next page; it is the last scene of a short animated diagram sequence.

FIG. 146. Reconstruction of part of Rutherford's laboratory in 1911. The model of the Geiger–Marsden apparatus is seen on the right.

experiment as it looked in 1911. On the right is the model of the Geiger–Marsden apparatus with the observer. The Toepler statical mercury vacuum pump which was used by Rutherford had been preserved in the museum of the Cavendish Laboratory in Cambridge and is seen on the left. This part of the film was shot in Cambridge under the guidance of Rutherford's assistant, Mr. George Crowe, who had long retired from his post but came specially to the Laboratory to assist us.

The Geiger–Marsden sequence began with Scene 24 of the script by explaining the apparatus and its function. The film then proceeded as shown in the extract of the script, next page (see also Fig. 143). The sequence ended by showing in animated diagrams three of Rutherford's atoms: the hydrogen, helium and lithium nuclei consisting of one, two and

---

FIG. 143. *Inside the Geiger–Marsden Apparatus (overhead view)*.

1. The inside of the model seen from above: on the left the source of the radiating alpha-particles, in the centre the scattering foil, on the right the zinc sulphide screen in front of the microscope. The stream of alpha-particles was superimposed by Pepper's Ghost.

2. This is a composite diagram showing the various successive positions of the microscope with the screen on which the flashes were observed. Both these diagrams refer to scenes 27–29b of the shooting script on page 232. The Pepper's Ghost effects showing the alpha-particles being deflected and even reflected by the scattering foil were produced by a rather specially constructed electro-mechanical device. Some experiments were necessary but finally the problem was satisfactorily solved. The cost was about half that of an animated diagram.

The Work of the Science Film Maker

Sc. No.	Visual	Commentary
24a.	A gold foil appears between the source and the screen.	A thin gold foil was now put in the path of the alpha-particles—
25.	CU. Person looking through eyepiece.	—and the result was watched.
25a.	Scintillations on plain green ground.	There were still flashes...
26.	As Scene 24: model of chamber with alpha-radiation. (Fig. 143).	...proof that alpha-particles can penetrate matter such as gold which is considered solid.
27.	The chamber from overhead.	Here the model is seen from above.
28.	As 25: The observer swings the eyepiece off the straight axis.	The microscope with the fluorescent screen could be turned, and from whatever angle the observations were made—
28a	Fewer scintillations	—flashes could be seen.
28b	As for 27: Some particles are deflected.	Obviously, a few alpha-particles were deflected from their straight course while passing through the gold foil.
29.	As 28: Eyepiece swung further round.	Even in this reversed position—
29a.	Very few scintillations.	—there were one or two flashes.
29b.	As 28b: some particles are thrown back at an acute angle by the gold foil.	Some particles were *thrown back* by the foil without passing through it at all. This could not be explained by Thomson's atom. Slowly a new idea formed in Rutherford's mind.
	Start of animated diagram:	
30.	Out of a pin-point grows an atom with a nucleus at its centre	Atoms had to have a *nucleus* at their centre which had to be positively charged.
31.	Alpha-particles are deflected by the nucleus	This nucleus would deflect some of the positive alpha-particles. (Here follows a reference to the weight of the nucleus.)
32.	The nucleus shrinks to small size. Action of the alpha-particles continues (Fig. 144).	The nucleus had to be very, very tiny because only 1 in 8000 particles was thrown off its course, the others went right past the nucleus.

Schedule for the diagram scenes 30–32 (as handed to the animators):
Colour code: background—cloudy blue
                atom   —yellow-red
                nucleus   —saturated red
                α-particles —pink.

			ft
Footages:	Sc. 30:	hold the pin-point atom for mix	2
		zoom-up until nucleus is half screen size	6
		hold	6
	Sc. 31:	action of α-particles	18

Films in the Making

Sc. No.	Visual		Commentary
Sc. 32:	nucleus shrinks		3
	action of α-particles continues		15
		Total:	50

three positively charged protons respectively, each with an equal number of orbiting negative electrons which balance the charge.

Rutherford splits the nucleus

This sequence as well as the following ones dealt with the achievements of those scientists whom Professor George Gamow calls the 'Nuc-Crackers'.* Rutherford, the first of these pioneers, asked himself: 'Could a nucleus be smashed by alpha-particles, and would the fragments form atoms of other elements'? He started experimenting.

The first scenes of this sequence showed what Rutherford was up against. Translated into the dimensions of our everyday world the problem was like trying to shoot from the moon a fly buzzing around in the dome of St. Paul's. Our film used a somewhat similar analogy (see Fig. 146, next page).

SCENE 37.   If the nucleus were the size of a hazelnut, the nearest electron would be about 150 ft away.
SCENE 37a. If the nut was lying on top of the Nelson's column—
SCENE 38.   —which stands in London's Tragalgar Square—
SCENE 38a. —the length of the column would just be the radius of the atom.— Of course we must think of the atom—
SCENE 38b. —as a sphere—
SCENE 38c. —and there are similar spheres all around it. The tiny dots in their centres were Rutherford's targets.

We commissioned a number of drawings and then did the animation ourselves. Scene 37 consisted of a picture showing a hazelnut against a blue sky. Scenes 38a to 38b were shot in reversed order, with the drawings mounted vertically upside down on a wall.

The sphere in Scene 38b (the scene which we filmed first) was a disc cut from a sheet of yellow gelatine overlaid on the drawing. After shooting a sufficient length, the gelatine overlay was removed and replaced by a thin sheet of glass with the circumference of the sphere chalked on to it as a circle. In register with the top of the column was a small hole in the glass with a pin protruding to which a cut-out column was fitted. This was identical to the column in the drawing and covered it completely. The scene was shot in single frame. The cut-out column was swivelled round its pivot and the chalk circle rubbed out bit by bit after each exposure. When

---

* Everybody interested in the subject of this book should not fail to read Professor Gamow's books. Lively, witty and lucid, they suceed in bringing difficult science concepts within the grasp of the non-scientist reader.

The Work of the Science Film Maker

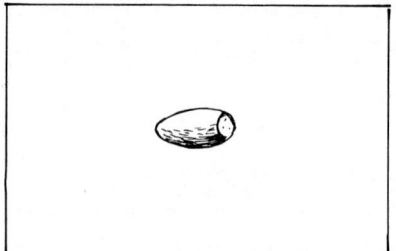

Fig. 146. *Rutherford's Problem*.
Scene 37.
A hazelnut represents an atom's nucleus. The nearest orbital electron would be some 150 ft away.

Scene 38.
Reality shot of Trafalgar Square. If the hazelnut would lie on Nelson's head, the column would be the length of the atom's radius.

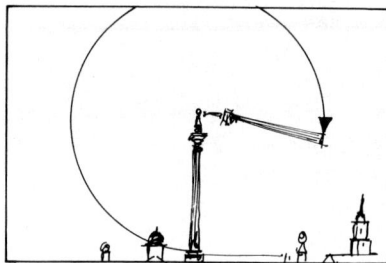

Scene 38a.
The column draws a chalk circle round the nucleus. This circle represents the size of the atom. Of course, we must think of the atom as a sphere.

This scene was shot in single frame and in reverse. A glass sheet with the circle was put on the drawing and a separate cut-out column, pivoted on Nelson's head, was animated round in small steps and the chalk circle rubbed out bit by bit. The scene was then printed tail to head, making the column seem to draw the circle.

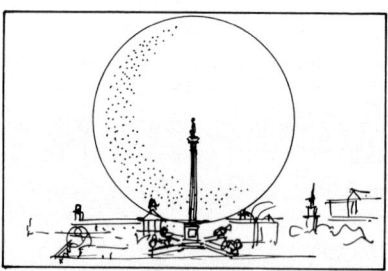

Scene 38b.
This was shot *before* 38a. A shaded yellow celluloid disc, the size of the circle in 38a, was laid over the drawing to give the impression of a sphere. After a few feet, the sphere was dissolved out to be replaced by the column and chalk circle needed for 38a.

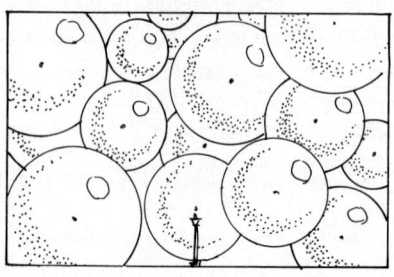

Scene 38c.
A multitude of spheres (atoms) fills the air. The tiny nuclei in their centres were Rutherford's targets.

Films in the Making

the film was projected in the normal way, the column appeared to draw the circle.

Shot 38c was another drawing with a multitude of yellow spheres appearing in depth.

The last scene mixed into a close-up shot of the actual nuclear disruption apparatus which Rutherford used. Consisting of a small metal cylinder, again with a microscope attached, it looked not unlike a spinthariscope; the main difference was in the two glass tubes at the top of the cylinder through which it could be filled with nitrogen gas. This apparatus was placed between two strong electro-magnets. Fig. 147 shows a corner in Rutherford's Laboratory as it looked in 1919, with the nuclear disruption apparatus standing on the table on the left.

In the following scenes, the film showed—by means of a model—what happened inside the cylinder. A radium source at one end of the cylinder emitted alpha-particles. Rutherford hoped that some of them would hit the nuclei of the nitrogen atoms. At the other end of the cylinder was a fluorescent screen which could be observed through the microscope. The question was: would there be flashes?—There were!—Since alpha-particles could only travel about half the length of the cylinder, these flashes had to be caused by something else. This 'something' proved to be protons, ejected from the nitrogen nuclei.

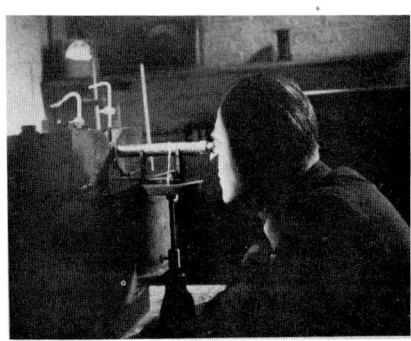

Fig. 147. The original Nuclear Disruption Apparatus, preserved in the Cavendish Laboratory, Cambridge, in which Rutherford turned nitrogen into oxygen.

The filming technique for this demonstration was the same as for the Geiger–Marsden apparatus, described on pages 229–31.

Following this demonstration, an animated diagram shows the transmutation in another form:

Nitrogen is number *seven* on the periodic table of elements.
This is hit by an alpha-particle with its two protons.
Now, there are 9 protons in the nucleus.
One proton is ejected again and if it hits the screen, there is a flash.
8 protons are left.
The nucleus with 8 protons is that of oxygen (see diagram next page).
Thus, in 1919, Rutherford turned nitrogen into oxygen.

THE WORK OF THE SCIENCE FILM MAKER

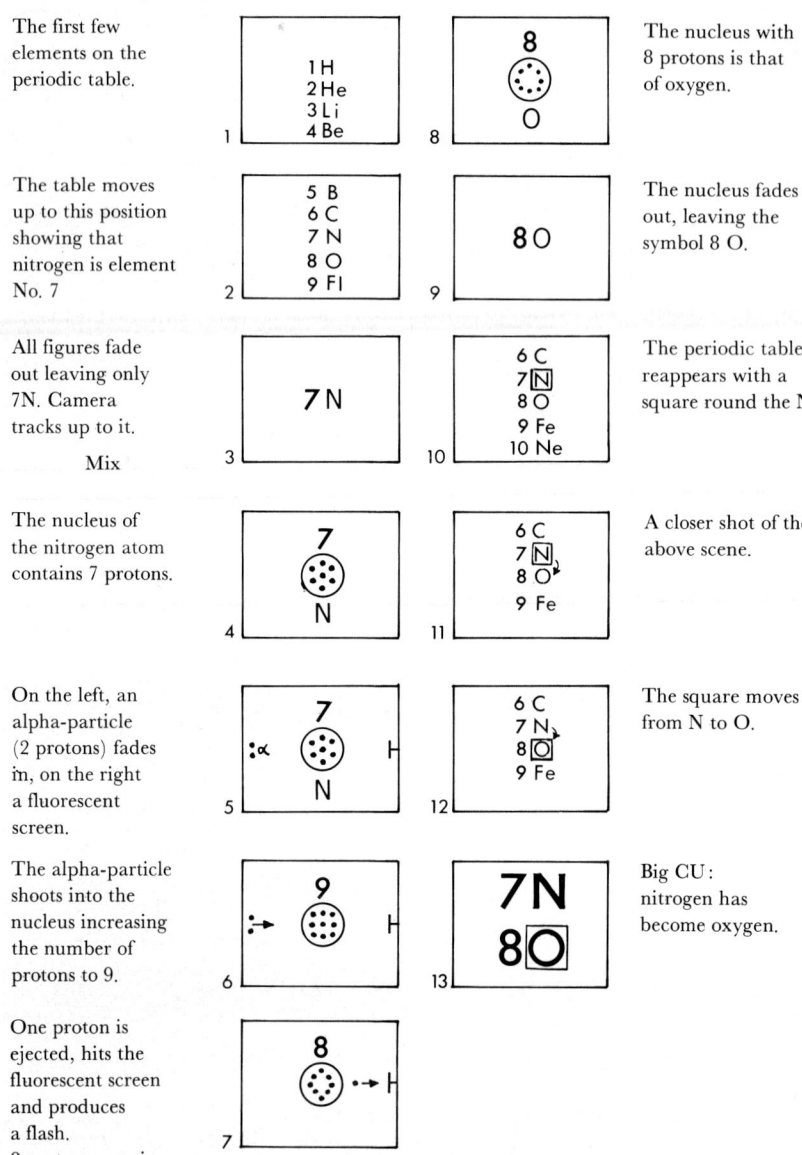

Fig. 148. *N into O*. Rutherford's first atom-splitting experiment, shown by an animated diagram which demonstrates by means of the periodic table of elements what happened during the experiment.

Rutherford and his colleagues succeeded in splitting several other atoms. But all of them were the atoms of *light* elements; alpha-particles were not powerful enough to crack *heavy* nuclei. Two of Rutherford's colleagues, Dr. Cockcroft (later Sir John) and Dr. E. T. S. Walton,

Films in the Making

developed equipment by which *protons* could be accelerated to high velocities. Could these protons be used to split the heavy atoms?

Cockcroft–Walton atom smasher

The sequence opened by showing Sir John Cockcroft at his desk, telling (at the start in sync., and continued off-screen) what happened when he and Dr. Walton worked in the Cavendish Laboratory in 1932. On the desk stood a small model of their laboratory and as Sir John explained the equipment and its working mechanism, he pointed to the corresponding details of the apparatus in the model which came alive in CU whenever some action took place. Fig. 150 shows a close-up of the apparatus; this will serve as a guide to Sir John's talk:

'That is a transformer (A). It was used to step up the electricity from the mains to a high voltage which was then further multiplied several times and rectified in this glass tower (B) to make it flow in one direction only. Finally, the electricity was stored in these condensers (C). A positive voltage of about 300,000 was reached.'

Sir John threw a small switch on his desk and a huge spark was produced in the spark gap (D) with a corresponding loud bang on the sound track.

'This voltage was applied to the accelerator tube. At its top was one of J. J. Thomson's discharge tubes (E) in which hydrogen atoms were pulled

Fig. 149. *Models of the Cockcroft–Walton laboratory in 1932. Sir John Cockcroft explains his experiment with the help of a small desk model.*

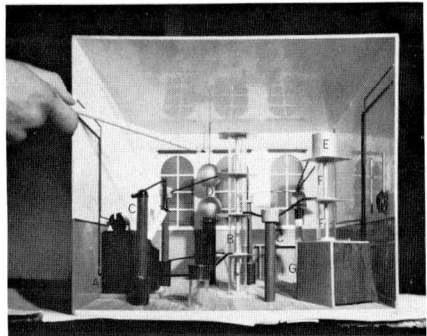

Fig. 150. During Sir John's talk, a big working model of the laboratory takes the place of the small desk model. All details are clearly discernible.

apart into electrons and protons. The protons travelled through a hole into the highly evacuated glass cylinders underneath (F) where the positive voltage accelerated them to energies of 300,000 V. Here is a closer view of the lower end of the accelerator tube.'

This lower end was behind the curtain of the observing cabin (G). Fig. 151 is a diagram of the accelerator tube showing what happened in this 'lower end'.

'The accelerated protons struck a lithium plate (H) at the rate of a million million a sec. The Lithium nuclei were the targets, but most of the protons passed between them. Only *one* proton in a thousand million scored a direct hit on a lithium nucleus, splitting it in two. The fragments flew off, some of them striking a zinc sulphide screen (I) at the side, thus causing flashes.

We observed the screen through the microscope and we could clearly see the flashes, each a visual proof that a lithium nucleus had been split.'

From the production point of view, this part of the film was one of the more difficult ones to devise and to prepare, but the work on it was most rewarding, not least because Sir John, the originator of this experiment, was himself taking part in this sequence. The apparatus was visually interesting and even exciting in its picturesque appearance and mechanics.

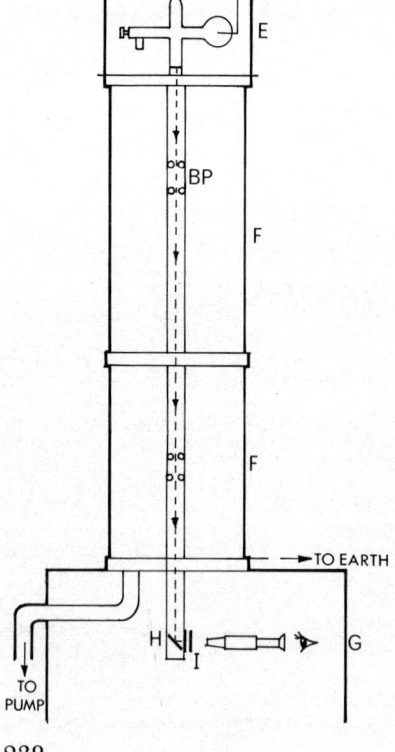

FIG. 151. *Cockcroft's Accelerator Tube.* This diagram explains how lithium was turned into helium in the accelerator tube which formed part of the Cockcroft–Walton apparatus at the Cavendish Laboratory shown in Fig. 150. Its function is explained in Sir John's own words.
E A Thomson discharge tube in which hydrogen atoms were pulled apart into electrons and protons.
F Evacuated glass cylinders.
BP Beam of accelerated protons.
G Lower end of tube in the observation cabin seen in Fig. 150. Only this lower end was shown as a Pepper's Ghost effect in the film.
H Lithium plate.
I Zinc sulphide screen observed through the microscope.

Films in the Making

We were convinced that only a three-dimensional model would do full justice to it. To find authentic sources on which to base the model was not too difficult. Quite a few photographs of the original equipment, taken around 1932, were still in existence. In addition, a small replica of the laboratory exists in the Science Museum which helped our model-maker in matters of detail.

We actually had to have two models: a small dummy to stand on Sir John's desk, and a large practical one for the actual demonstration. The reason was that in a small-scale model details do not stand up to close scrutiny. Though Sir John was very co-operative, the time he could give us was limited and we could only hope to film one or two establishing shots with him in the picture, and to record what he had to say. We did this in a large office of the Atomic Energy Authority.

The actual demonstration of the details in the big model was filmed a day or two later in our own studio. By then, Sir John's talk had been broken down and timed to give us the length of each scene.

The action of the protons in the accelerated tube made a separate model necessary. Again we used the Pepper's Ghost method during the filming.

For a sufficiently impressive spark effect (and its bang) we had to

FIG. 152. The unit on location in the building of the U.K. Atomic Energy Authority. Sir John Cockcroft sits at the desk.

make special arrangements with the National Physical Laboratory in Teddington, which produced a choice selection of sparks from which we could choose the one we liked best. This had of course, to be filmed in register with the spark gap of our model.*

The sequence ends, in keeping with the previous one, by showing, again in animation, the relevant part of the table of elements. The commentary concludes: 'What happened to the lithium atom in the experiment? We know that the lithium nucleus contains three protons. It is hit by another proton which embeds itself in the nucleus, making four protons. This breaks up into two new nuclei each containing two protons. In other words, they become the nuclei of helium. Thus, lithium was turned into helium; it was the first atom to be split by deliberate proton bombardment.'

Chadwick discovers the neutron

'One problem had been left unexplained' continues the commentary; 'We know that the hydrogen atom contains *one* proton and the helium atom *two*. Why is it that while the weight of the hydrogen atom is *one*, that of helium is not two but *four*? Professor Chadwick, later Sir James, found where this extra weight came from.'

This sequence offered no great problems. Chadwick's original experiment was set up again for us at the Cavendish Laboratory by George Crowe, Rutherford's and Chadwick's assistant already mentioned before. (Fig. 154)

The arrangement on the bench consists of (left to right) a cylinder with a radio-active source, a piece of beryllium, a disc of paraffin wax and the recording and amplifying equipment of an electric counter.

At the beginning of the experiment, only the cylinder is connected to the counter. Pips, heard in the headphones, indicate the presence of alpha-particles. If the beryllium is put in the path of the alpha-particles, the counter is silent because the beryllium stops these particles. But if the disc of paraffin wax is put between the beryllium and the counter, pips can again be heard. The puzzling situation is that on the left the alpha-particles are stopped by the beryllium and on the right some other particles are shooting out of the paraffin wax, producing pips. These particles were found to be protons. But what makes them leave the paraffin?

Chadwick discovered the answer. He found that there must be *uncharged* particles in the beryllium nucleus. Some of them were displaced by the alpha-particles and they in turn displaced protons in the paraffin wax. Chadwick called these uncharged (neutral) particles neutrons.

---

* Discharge phenomena in the shape of sparks or flashes are of such short duration that they may occur just when the camera shutter obscures the gate. There is no other way with an ordinary type of camera but shooting a number of the sparks in the hope that a few will register on the film. In total darkness one can, of course, open the shutter and wait for the spark, provided the camera has a single-frame device.

Films in the Making

FIG. 153. The discovery of the neutron by Professor Chadwick in 1932. The still shows George Crow, Chadwick's assistant, with the original apparatus at the Cavendish Laboratory where the experiment was reconstructed for us.

To demonstrate this action we again built a model which showed the principle in a flow chart manner.

The experiment as shown by our model: (a) cylinder, (b) radio-active source, (c) alpha-particles, (d) beryllium, (e) neutrons, (f) disc of paraffin wax, (g) protons, (h) microphone of the counter. (Fig. 154)

The movement of the 3 kinds of particles was again filmed with the help of Pepper's Ghost.

The animated periodic table of elements appears now again and shows how a number of heavier nuclei could be split by means of the neutron, changing one atom into another. Chadwick's discovery was another milestone in the conquest of the atom.

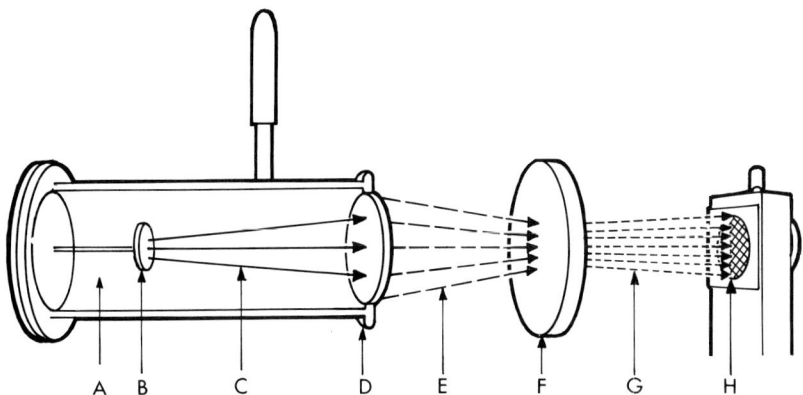

FIG. 154. *Chadwick's Discovery of the Neutron.* This shows in diagrammatic form what happened inside the apparatus shown on Fig. 153. The cylinder A contains a radio-active source B which emits alpha-particles (C). These smash into a disc of the metal beryllium (D). F is a disc of paraffin wax from which protons (G) emerge and cause pips in the counter H. What makes these protons leave the paraffin? Chadwick concluded that the alpha-particles which hit the beryllium nuclei dislodge some unknown particles (E) which then bombard the paraffin, in turn dislodging the protons. Because these particles are uncharged (neutral), Chadwick called them neutrons. For filming, the static coloured drawing was set up in front of the camera and the three particle streams C, E and G were then superimposed, one after the other, by Pepper's Ghost.

THE WORK OF THE SCIENCE FILM MAKER

The neutron in action

One of the heaviest atoms is that of Uranium. The film explains by means of blackboard equations that this element occurs mainly in two forms: ^{238}U and ^{235}U. 'Atoms of the same element', says the commentary, 'containing different numbers of neutrons are called *Isotopes*. Uranium-235 (92 protons and 143 neutrons) is unique in nature; the German scientists Hahn and Strassman investigated its behaviour. In 1938, they found that a bombarding neutron can split the ^{235}U nucleus, violently releasing energy, largely as heat. Such splitting is called nuclear fission.'

The film shows in slow motion what happens. An excellent animated diagram had previously been produced for the U.K. Atomic Energy Authority which we were allowed to use. This diagram shows how a bombarding neutron splits the nucleus in half. Radiation is emitted and two new atoms, barium and krypton, are formed. Two or three neutrons are released, each capable of splitting another ^{235}U nucleus.

The film repeats this action by demonstrating it once more in close-up, this time in a three-dimensional technique.

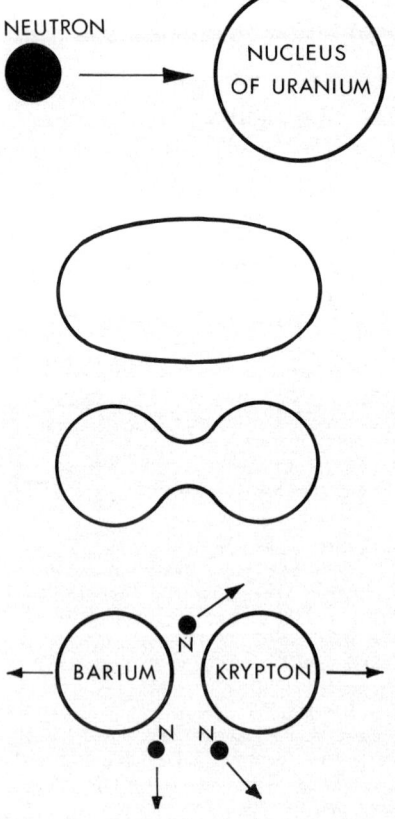

FIG. 155. *Splitting the Uranium 235 Nucleus*. This is a textbook drawing which was the guide to the construction and action of our model scene. A bombarding neutron splits the nucleus in half. Two new atoms, barium and krypton are formed. 3 neutrons are released capable of splitting further uranium nuclei. (See Figs. 156–157).

Films in the Making

Fig. 156 shows the situation after the splitting: the two newly formed atoms and the three released neutrons between them. Fig. 157 might give an idea of how we filmed this scene.

First we fitted some two hundred ping-pong balls on thin wires and suspended them in one big bunch from a curtain rail against a black velvet background. The 'protons' were left white, the 'neutrons' were painted pink. Then we tried to 'split' this bunch by various mechanical means, but the balls would not separate neatly and the wires got entangled. So we decided to shoot the scene backwards.

We started with the two separate bunches with the three balls in the middle as shown in Fig. 157 and then banged them all together to form one big cluster. This worked much better. At the moment of the impact, the cluster vibrated (a very desirable effect) and a single ball suspended on a thin black rod as seen in the illustration was pulled out of the cluster by a thread so that it moved sideways.

When the scene was optically reversed and projected in the normal way, the action took place in the desired order: first the single neutron hit the nucleus; this started to vibrate and then it split in half, leaving three further neutrons between its two parts.

The set-up should have been shot from below to hide the wires. This was, however, not possible because the ceiling of our studio was too low. We therefore put a mirror on the floor and filmed the reflections of the balls.

The lamps on the left of the camera with tracing paper in front were made to flicker rapidly at the moment the single neutron hit the nucleus to give the necessary effect of emitted energy. The Pepper's Ghost method was used again for superimposing the effect over the action.

No single-frame shooting was necessary; the whole of the scene could be filmed in a straightforward way after a day's preparation to which George Cooper contributed the main share, addressing the 200 ping-pong balls in very unparliamentary language.

The film continued by showing, once more in an animated diagram, how the three released neutrons might start a chain reaction by splitting further nearby ^{235}U nuclei. This could produce an explosion. In natural uranium, only 4 in 600 atoms are the fissile isotope ^{235}U. They are so far apart and fission neutrons are so fast, that most miss their targets. There can be no chain reaction.

But if a pile of graphite is built, it acts as a 'moderator' slowing down the neutrons and making them more effective. If a number of uranium rods are then inserted into the pile, a chain reaction can be induced. The temperature is controlled by another set of rods, usually of the metal boron which absorbs neutrons. The deeper these boron rods are inserted, the fewer are the number of fissions. In this way, a controlled chain reaction is produced and so yields a useful continuous supply of energy.

The diagram in Fig. 158 shows how graphite acts as a neutron-brake.

The Work of the Science Film Maker

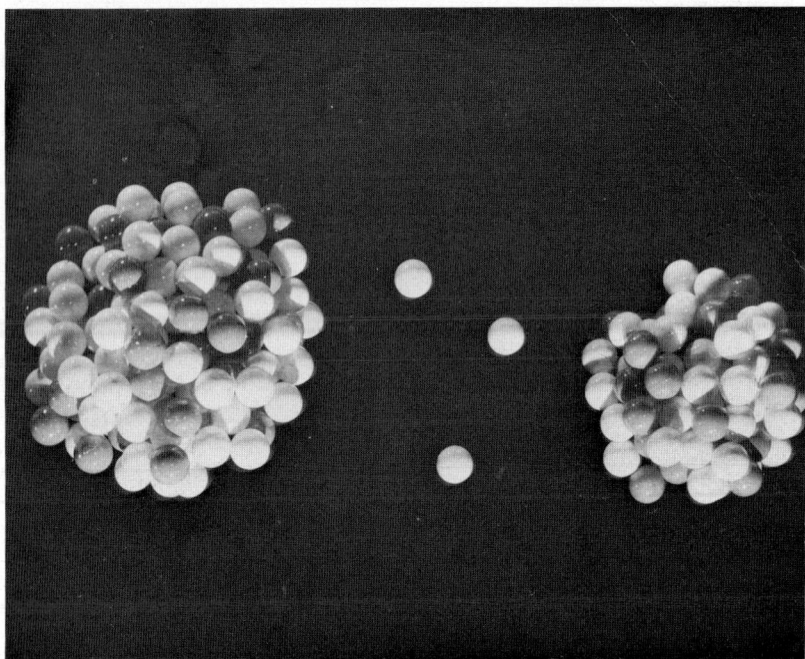

Fig. 156. Model of the Uranium 235 atom after the splitting. The three released neutrons are seen in the centre.

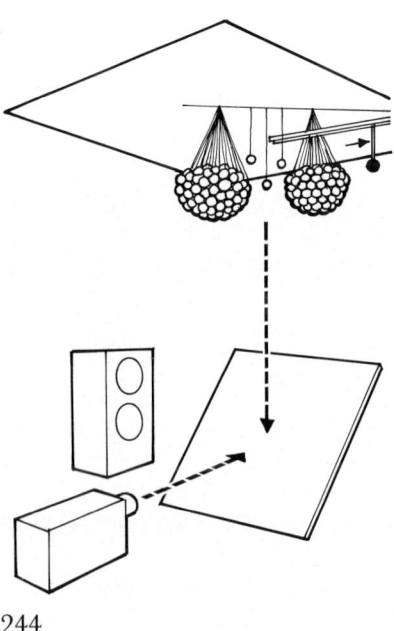

Fig. 157. *Model Set-up for the Atom-splitting Scene.* This needed some rather elaborate preparation. The filming was complicated by the fact that the ceiling of our studio was very low so that we had to shoot the action as reflected in an angled mirror on the ground. The mechanics of this model set-up are fully described on the previous pages. The drawing shows (simplified) the ping-pong balls (suspended from a thread running along under the ceiling) as they appeared *after* the splitting (See also Fig. 156). But since we had to shoot the scene backwards, for reasons explained in the text, this was in fact the starting position of the scene. The arrows from the balls and the camera point towards the mirror. The small arrow at the top indicates the bombarding neutron. The box-like apparatus at the side contained lamps which produced a flickering effect to suggest the released energy. This effect was superimposed on the balls by Pepper's Ghost.

Films in the Making

For the graphite pile we again made a model. The horizontal rods represent the uranium rods, the vertical ones the boron rods. They were moved in and out by the arrangement shown in Fig. 161. This sequence had to be filmed in single frame. The temperature changes were indicated by a red glow produced by gelatines in front of two lamps which were brought up and faded out on dimmers.

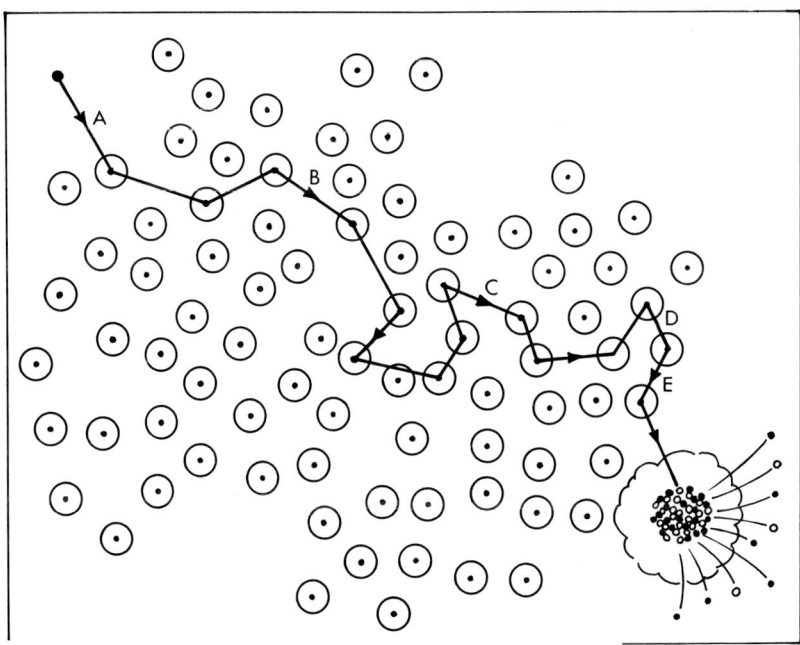

Fig. 158. *The 'Neutron Brake'*. This animated diagram shows how a neutron is slowed down in the Fermi-pile by up to 150 collisions with graphite particles. The initial speed of the neutron, at A, is 6–8000 miles per sec; this speed is reduced by successive collisions to 5000 miles at B, to 3000 miles at C, to 1000 miles at D and to 300 miles per sec at E. The Fermi-pile is shown in Fig 159 and in Figs 160 and 161.

The commentary said that the first atomic pile—or reactor, as it is now called—was built by the Italian physicist Fermi in Chicago in 1942. Our model dissolved into the actual reactor in Calder Hall, Cumberland; further shots taken in this atomic power station followed. 'Plants like this will meet our need for power for a long time to come. One ton of uranium can produce the power equivalent of one million tons of coal. We have come a long way since 1897.'

The final sequence began with a flash-back showing Thomson's and Rutherford's 'home-made' equipment and contrasted it with the enormous atomic machines of to-day. This led up to the Zeta reactor in Harwell

The Work of the Science Film Maker

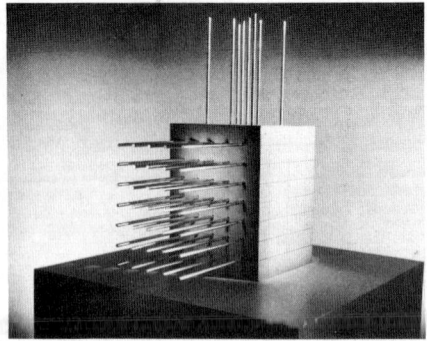

Fig. 159. Working model of the Fermi pile.

which does not *split* atoms but *fuses* them, turning hydrogen into helium at temperatures of over 5,000,000°. This is the way the sun produces its heat. A shot of solar flares, obtained from an observatory, provided an impressive visual of the sun's energy. The film ended with one or two more long-shots of atomic power stations. 'The atom has been harnessed, but we are still only on the threshold of the atomic age.'

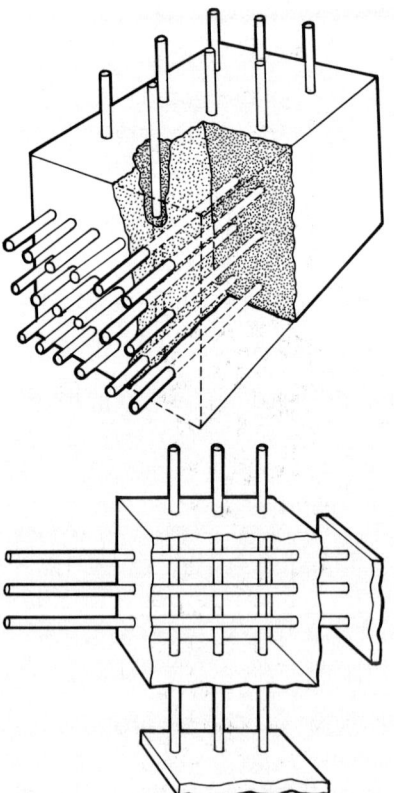

Fig. 160. *The Fermi Pile.* An exploded view of an early graphite (Fermi) pile contained in a scientific text book. It was used as a blueprint for the model shown in Fig. 159. The horizontal Uranium rods and the vertical Boron or Cadmium rods are moved in and out for temperature regulation. Our modern atomic reactors work on the same principle.

Fig. 161. This drawing shows in a simplified way the mechanism for sliding the two sets of rods in our model in or out simultaneously. The plates (right and bottom) to which the rods were fixed, were moved by hand and kept out of frame.

Films in the Making

Summary

The description of the films given in this and in previous chapters, and of the means employed in their making necessarily afford only a key-hole view of the immense pattern of production potentials open to the maker of science films.

A single phenomenon such as the behaviour of longitudinal waves can be demonstrated by the greatest variety of methods: by wave machines of different descriptions, by stretched string apparatus, helical springs, crova discs, shunting waggons, billiard balls, rows of children, and by several other ways and means. The range of experiments regarding transverse waves and their behaviour is possibly even greater. A thousand and one scientific phenomena might be explained by a similarly large variety of techniques. No book could attempt to give anything like an exhaustive survey of this field.

Teachers are accustomed to demonstrating certain facts in certain ways; they may have used them for years. These may not necessarily be the most effective ones from the filmic point of view. We ourselves should, therefore, explore all possible approaches of illustrating a given subject. We can then discuss them with our advisers and choose the filmically most forceful and educationally most convincing method.

Obvious sources of information are the museum catalogues, those of manufacturers of scientific apparatus and models, and of visual aid and school equipment. Other sources are books and articles on the relevant subjects, on schoolboys' experiments, magicians' tricks and stage devices. This seems an alarmingly large array of reference material but it looks formidable only at the start; as we gain experience, we will soon get to know to which special sources to turn.

Since acquiring specific knowledge is the essence of the investigation which precedes scripting, the problem really boils down to the question of how much trouble you are willing to take or can afford to take in terms of the budget. The time spent on this relatively cheap pre-production stage has a decisive bearing not only on the effectiveness of the presentation but also on the length of the most expensive part of the production: the shooting period.

Thousands of films are in existence dealing with physics, geology, zoology, bacteriology, astronomy, bio-physics, chemistry, botany, medicine, pathology, physiology, psychology and any other -ology we may think of. These films use micrography, X-ray crystallography, spectroscopy, infrared photography, high-speed cinematography and other specialized techniques in order to demonstrate, illustrate, inform, instruct, teach, or comment. Some of these films are general, many are specific; some are excellent, many are dull.

It is hoped that the examples described in these pages may help to indicate ways of heightening the visual interest in your films and therefore make them more effective in their intention to explain the mechanisms which make the world tick.

Some 350 years ago, in 1624, Francis Bacon published his book *New Atlantis*.* In the chapter describing the Palaces of Culture, he pictures with amazing prescience our present-day visual techniques. Only the shortest of extracts are given here but they could hardly be more to the point if written to-day.

'... Wee make Demonstrations of all Lights and Radiations: And of all Colourations of Light; All Delusions and Deceits of the Sight, in Figures, Magnitude, Motions, Shadowes. Wee have also Glasses and Meanes to see Small and Minute Bodies... Wee imitate Motions of Living Creatures by Images of Man, Beasts, Birds, Fishes and Serpents... Wee represent all manner of Feates of Iugling, and Illusions... And surely, you will easily believe that wee, that have so many things truelly Naturall, could in a World of Particulars deceive the Senses, if we would disguise those things, and labour to make them more Miraculous....'

---

* Re-issued 1924 by Clarenden Press, Oxford.

5

Film-making Procedure

As MOST OF the films discussed here are sponsored, the relationship between producer and sponsor plays a dominant part in almost every production. It is difficult to generalize about this because the species of the sponsored film lacks sufficient common characteristics for classification. Sponsors are rarely individuals; they are government departments or corporations such as local authorities, industrial or commercial firms, professional associations, welfare societies, educational bodies, etc., and according to their size and spheres of interest, the structure of these bodies and their internal and public relations policies vary considerably. So do their attitudes towards film, their use of this medium and the demands they make on it.

Sponsors

In the main, there are three categories of sponsor: those who are film-minded and regularly commision films as part of their communication- and training-programme; those whose views on films are rather indifferent but who now and then have a film made for reasons of expediency; and lastly, there are those who commission a film for the first time and are completely at sea as to how they have to set about it.

A sponsor of the first category might deal with the film producer through his public relations department or through a films officer who is responsible to the management either directly or via a specially appointed films committee. Sponsors of the second and third category usually have no distinct machinery to deal with films and the producer's contact is either the managing director himself or one of the executives. There are other set-ups and the film-maker therefore has to deal with a variety of people of different standing and responsibility whose knowledge of the film medium and whose attitude towards it can contrast sharply.

Whatever the circumstances, the producer–sponsor relationship is somewhat delicate. The answer to a film-maker's prayer would be an arrangement by which he has to deal with a single person, say, the films officer who has full authority, had once been a film technician himself, knows the rules of the game, gives clear instructions in his brief, provides at the right time the facilities for which the sponsor took responsibility, and who is available for consultation and constructive criticism but otherwise leaves the film-maker alone to act as he thinks fit. If a film-maker is lucky enough to meet such a person, a good relationship is ensured and the resulting film will benefit.

But often, conditions fall short of the ideal. The reasons might be personal or factual. The most frequent irritations are caused either by too casual or too meddlesome co-operation on the part of the sponsor or by long delays in arriving at decisions due to the sponsor's administrative set-up or in supplying the promised facilities. The sponsor, on the other hand, might feel that the film-maker is wide of the mark of what was agreed or has in matters of interpretation turned into a stubborn blockhead.

Film committees can create problems of a different kind. Such committees are usually composed of departmental heads who know everything about their special province but very little about film-making. It is difficult enough even for people who are familiar with the language and techniques of the film fully to understand a description in words of visual happenings on the screen, and it is certainly unreasonable to demand a considered opinion from filmically untrained persons. Yet, scripts have, as a rule, to be circulated amongst the committee members for approval and are returned with their comments and corrections which often not only contradict each other but also show how difficult it is for laymen to make sense of a film document. What the film-maker really wants to know is whether there are structural faults in the shape of the film, vital omissions or wrong arguments. Defects of this kind are rarely detected, they seem to be obscured by the form in which a film script is written. But small and irrelevant matters such as blunders in terminology or unimportant details often catch the reader's eye and are pounced upon and often discussed at interminable length.

If the films officer and the members of the committee are in sympathy with each other, all problems can be sorted out amicably. But if they are at loggerheads, things can become rather difficult for the film-maker and there may be much extra work and discomfort in store for him.

Finance

Where the sponsor is a commercial concern the film is often regarded as a medium for projecting the firm's image and is expected to bear some of the hallmarks of the company's advertising policy such as a certain panache, sophisticated design of the artwork and titles, modernistic music and other matters which are hoped to catch the eye of the press and of festival judges. This is alright as long as sufficient money is conceded for technical features which are essential to the argument of the film. A

Film-making Procedure

producer was once refused a little extra sum for improving a sequence and making its difficult concept easier to understand; but ten times as much money must have been spent on the reception which followed the press show. It is hoped that, in good time, a better appreciation of priorities will emerge in the boardrooms of commercial sponsors.

Amongst the most difficult sponsors are those who expect a Rolls-Royce type of film on a mini-car level of finance. This happens most often with newcomers to the field of film-sponsoring but also with experienced sponsors who should know better. This attitude is largely the outcome of the fierce competition which nowadays prevails in the market of the sponsored film. Certain film units advertise their services at a fixed cut-rate charge per foot. The absurdity of such offers should be obvious to everyone who knows the least bit about film-making. If there are signs that a sponsor is 'shopping around', a producer should be very careful about the amount of time, effort and money he puts into securing the contract. Nobody can make an adequate and conscientious job on an inadequate budget.

A really experienced sponsor will know how much a film of the type he wants to have made must cost and he will then choose not the cheapest man he can find but someone whom he can trust to make a good film within the means available.

Many sponsors have their productions handled by firms of consultants who advise them on matters of finance, presentation, distribution and the choice of producer. Most film consultants are highly qualified people who have been film producers themselves and are capable of guiding and supervising a production in the best interest of both the sponsor and the film-maker.

Technical and educational advisers

Unless the film-maker is himself an expert in the field which is covered by his film, a science film cannot be made without a technical adviser. In the case of a teaching film such a person might either supply both technical and educational expertise or an educational adviser ought to be appointed as well.

Advisers are usually nominated by the sponsor. But the sponsor is apt to want a big name on the credit title of the film. An expert at the top of his profession is sure to be a very busy man and therefore unlikely to be available for discussing details. He may even live in another town. Often, his contribution to the film consists of vetting the script and coming to the show in which the film is to be approved. This means that for all practical purposes, he is as good as non-existent and the film-maker has to find for himself a qualified and easily accessible person able to assist him.

Another difficulty is that scientists and technologists are reluctant to commit themselves on matters which are not strictly within their own, often very specialized, field. For films which relate to more than one particular branch of science, not one but several advisers have to be consulted. As spheres of specialized knowledge often overlap, there may be clashes of opinion and the film-maker is left with contradictory advice.

Besides the 'prestige adviser' an expert must therefore be found in whom both the sponsor and the film-maker can have confidence both for his qualifications and his sustained co-operation and who can act as an arbiter in the case of divergent opinions. This adviser should preferably be at a level in the academic hierarchy which leaves him time to be available both during the scripting period and during the actual production. Of course, such a person has to be paid adequately for practically becoming part of the production team.

It would be of advantage if an adviser also has a grasp of the fundamentals of film-making. Beware of perfectionists, however. They will try to find ever better ways of dealing with certain details and this may seriously interfere with the progress of a production. This has happened in more than one case. Once the green light has been given by the adviser, he should be content to let the matter rest there.

When meeting an expert for the first time, it is just as well to give the impression that you are not completely ignorant of the subject with which the film deals. Therefore, you should not approach experts before making a short preliminary study of the subject and its background. Experts should not be made to feel that they have to waste time explaining basic facts.

Since experts, in whatever field, are apt to disagree on certain points, science films are often somewhat controversial. They may be praised by one set of reviewers and criticised by others. They receive awards at one festival and fall flat at another. The film-maker must take a philosophical view of this; a science film can rarely be 'his' film, it is the product of the sponsor's intention, the adviser's expertise and the film-maker's skill. It is one of the penalties which the maker of science films has to pay that films are often judged on points over which he had no control. On the other hand, he feels amply rewarded if he sees that he has interpreted a difficult and complex theme in a way that can be understood by the audience for which the film was designed.

Production routine

The secret of a good film production routine is efficient organisation First things must come first, a certain order of priorities must be established.

An attempt is made here to show this order in diagrammatic form. But first, a few preliminary notes.

The end result of film-making is not a mass-produced article like a packet of detergent or a car. A film, in spite of all the technology involved in its making, is an individual piece of work; no film is exactly like another,

Film-making Procedure

and no film is made exactly like another. The course of film production cannot therefore be traced by means of a flow-chart such as is often prepared in certain industries for standardized manufacturing processes. We can, however, present diagrammatically the progressive stages of film-making as they follow each other, with the reservations that different film units might arrange things in a somewhat different order from the one shown here, and that each film poses different problems; some stages shown in the diagram might not be needed at all.

With this proviso, we can consider the following chart as typical for making a factual or science film, produced either in 35mm or 16mm and drawing on all or most of the cinematic resources, including composed music. Such a film would be in the five-figure bracket.

The production phases are numbered on the chart and these numbers correspond to those of the notes in the next. These notes which follow the chart, elaborate on matters of detail.

The proportions of the working periods, as shown here are arbitrary. The asterisks denote the main points of contact with the sponsor or his representatives.

Pre-production

This is a phase in its own right not only due to the nature of the work involved but also from the financial point of view. It is usual for a sponsor to commission first the investigation and scripting of a film at an agreed fee, plus expenses. If the script is accepted, the contract or letter of agreement for making the film is signed after the approval of the budget.

1. *The brief.* This may consist of one short paragraph or of a lengthy document, handed to the producer at the briefing session in which the project is discussed. Whatever else the brief contains, it must cover the following points: *contents, purpose* and proposed *style* of the film, the intended *audience* and the *completion date* (if any). With regard to *finance*, sponsors are sometimes disinclined to quote a ceiling figure at that stage in the hope of getting a bargain. It should be pointed out to them that one can neither develop ideas nor form a framework for a film without knowing how much money is available. Even a rough estimate can only be made after some preliminary investigation. As this often involves considerable time and expense an investigation fee should ordinarily be agreed beforehand.

2. *Investigation.* The methods of investigation and the sources of information have been described at various points of the book. You should not omit to carry a still camera and a director's viewfinder when visiting prospective locations.

3. *Investigation report.* For certain categories of film, sponsors expect a written investigation report. Whether the sponsor will go ahead with the project or abandon it may depend on this report. With science subjects,

The Work of the Science Film Maker

Chart for production routine

The numbers showing the various stages of a production refer to the corresponding paragraphs on the previous page and on the following pages.

(A) *Pre-production*

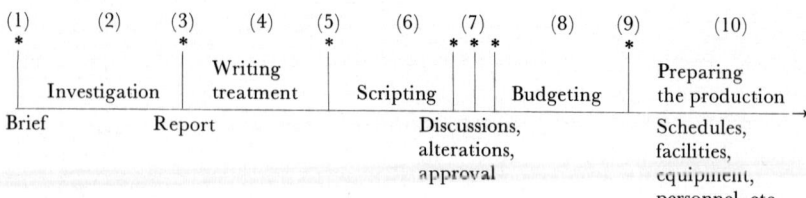

(B) *Filming and Editing*

(11) Production Management

> Location 'logistics', permits, etc.;
> Laboratory contact, delivery and viewing of rushes;
> Ordering models, art work and 'special' opticals;
> Arranging for studio, art director, props, sound crew, composer;
> Subcontracting animation, micro-material, etc.;
> Dealing with emergencies.

(12) Shooting

(13) Work in the Cutting Room   (14)   (15)

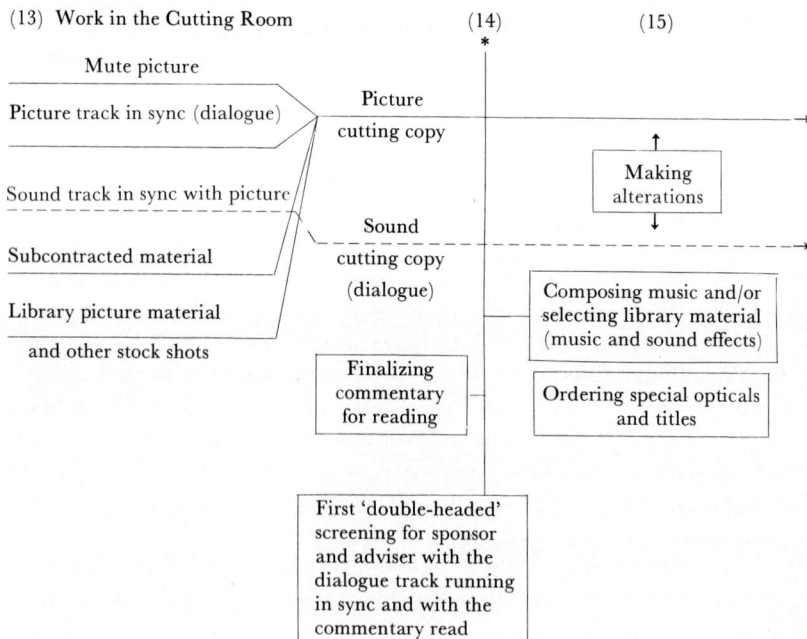

(C) *Recording, Track-laying, Dubbing*

(16) General practice

Film-making Procedure

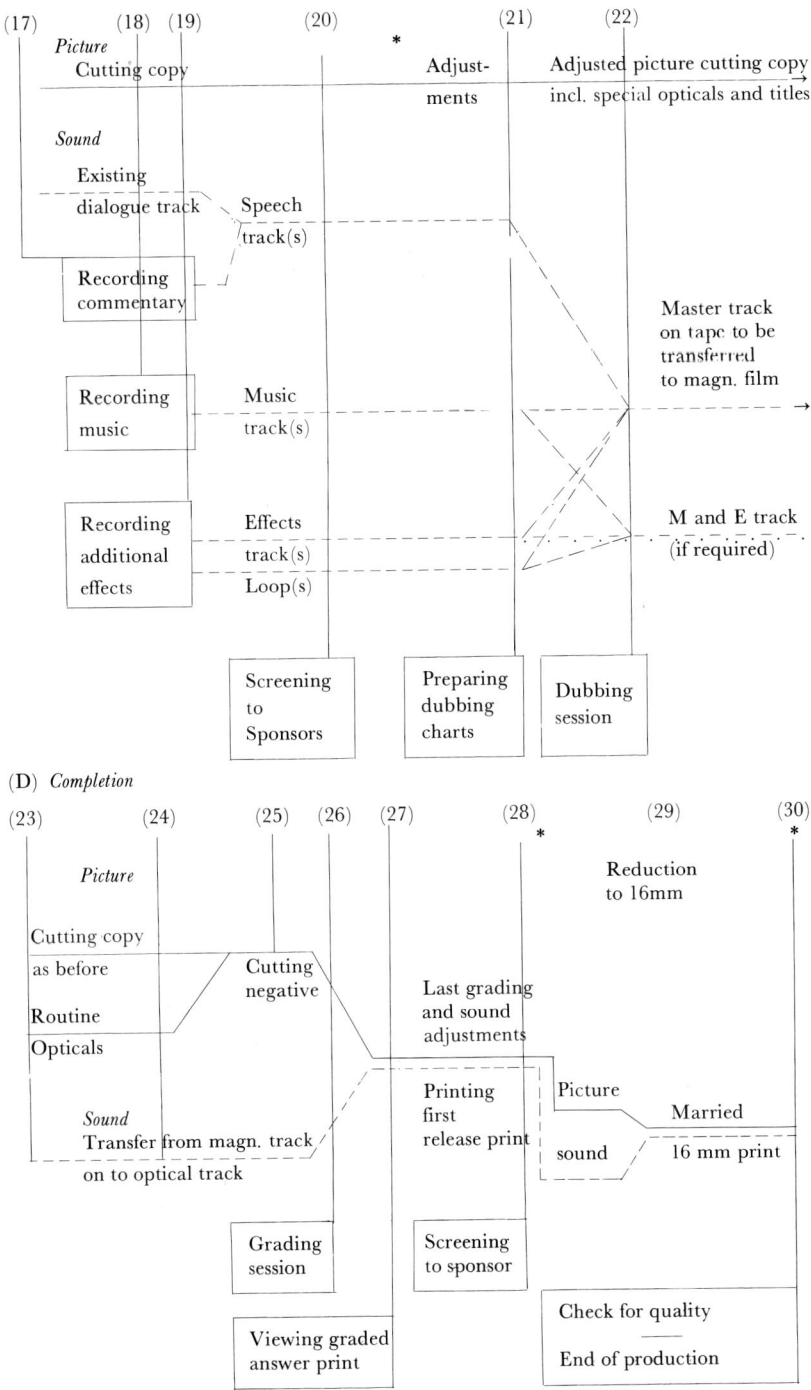

it is essential to have the report vetted by the technical adviser before submitting it.

In the case of a simple straightforward subject, a separate investigation report is normally unnecessary and you can proceed straight away with writing an outline or treatment which should include notes on the investigation as an introduction.

4, 5. Treatment. The treatment is an outline of the contents and shape of the film, written in narrative prose, to give the gist of the story and argument. It is also very much a diplomatic affair: you must try to make the proposed form of the film attractive to the sponsor without suggesting ideas which you will find impracticable to follow up in the scripting or shooting stage. Again, the adviser should approve the treatment. It is helpful if you prepare a storyboard consisting of rough sketches and diagrams and perhaps including photographs culled from books or trade journals, etc. One picture can be worth a thousand words.

As a rule, the submitted document is returned by the sponsor with his and his committee's comments and counter-proposals, or they are discussed in a meeting.

6. Scripting. Scripting means breaking down the treatment into single scenes with the visuals shown on the left side of the page and the sound on the right. The adviser will probably have to be consulted repeatedly. Some fundamental points about scripting have already been discussed; in addition, extracts from scripts have been reproduced in several chapters. It was also pointed out that a description in words can rarely convey a true impression of the final appearance of the film; yet, some sponsors are apt to regard every word of the script as gospel and will later be baffled if the resulting film looks somewhat different from what they expected. It is sensible, therefore, to call the submitted script, or at least its first version, not 'shooting script' but *master script*.

In a master script, such events and technical processes with which the sponsor is familiar or which are very complex or not easy to control do not need to be fully itemized. This leaves room for manoeuvre and does not commit the film-maker too much at this stage. A master script will also be more easily understood by non-experts and it is sufficient as a base for budgeting.

7. Approval of script. The script, whatever its form, will probably be bounced backward and forward several times between sponsor and producer and discussed in meetings; so there is still time to break summarily treated items down further if required. The question of facilities to be provided by the sponsor should be raised and settled in a way which excludes divided responsibilities. It is most irritating to find during a heavy shooting schedule that agreed arrangements have gone awry because someone had thought that somebody else had dealt with them.

Writing the script and its approval may take anything from a few

Film-making Procedure

weeks to many months. At this stage the producer has to turn into a tight-rope walker, keeping the balance between the sponsor's justified demands and his own intention to make a lively and informative film acceptable not only to the sponsor but to the intended audience.

8. *Budgeting*. Budgeting is a matter of long experience and a producer without that experience must call in a fully qualified accountant or other administrative person who knows all the ropes of film finance.

Correct costing for a film is essential to make sure that a job can not only be taken on at a given price but can also be *completed* at that price *and* leave a profit. Only a few guidelines can be given here.

The cost of a production can usually be divided into predictable and less predictable expenditure. One of the most unpredictable items is the production *time*, as expressed in the technicians salaries. Salaries are usually the biggest item on the budget. A hundred factors may combine to get a production into the red on this count alone. Scientific experiments, uncontrollable events and special effects can run away with both time and film stock. Again, only experience can be a fairly reliable guide, and an adequate safety margin must be provided for. Other items bound up with the production time are equipment- and car-hire, location expenses, cutting-room hire, personnel insurance, overtime, etc. Film consumption and consequently the laboratory charges are also variable items.

Verifiable expenditure includes all sub-contracted material (animation, etc.), and all such items for which a quotation can be obtained beforehand or which are charged at known rates: model- and set-construction, library scenes, sound recording, dubbing and track-transfer, studio hire, the commentator's and composer's fees, the orchestra, negative insurance, etc.

There are other points which must be considered beforehand. Scientific experts may co-operate free of charge or may require considerable fees. Specialized film technicians might command salaries that are higher than normal. Danger- or dirt-money could be demanded by certain members of the unit. Music- and other royalties depend on the kind and areas of distribution, etc.

The sum of the above items shows the actual outlay incurred in the production. To this must be added the overhead- and profit-figures which depend on the size of the company. This figure should be large enough to cover the almost inevitable loss made during the scripting stage. Most sponsors, deplorably, are not willing to pay fees adequate to the time and effort spent on investigation and scripting. The pre-production job is therefore accepted by the film-maker at a more or less nominal charge with a view to securing the actual production. The grand total shown in the budget represents the contract price of the film.

Certain safety clauses must finally be added to the budget stating expressly what it does *not* cover. In the main, these clauses will list such items as prolonged weather delay, delay due to causes outside the control of the producer, or increases in stock- and laboratory-charges during production.

Any additional work required by the sponsor during the course of production should be undertaken subject to a supplementary budget.

9. *Submitting the budget.* The completed budget should correspond with the requirements of the brief in content, format and the production level of the film, and cover the period from the start of the work up to the delivery of the first release print.

The submitted budget should break down the expenditure under main headings so that the sponsor knows what he is paying for and can, if he wishes, prune items which he finds too expensive, or ask for cheaper alternatives. There is bound to be a meeting at this stage in which the sponsor is apt to regard the producer as a robber, and it is therefore just as well to have the evidence for all charges well documented or to bring the financial adviser along as a supporting force.

As to payment, the norm is to be paid in three instalments: at the start of production, at the acceptance of the cutting copy and on completion. It may be said in parentheses that some sponsors put the widest possible interpretations on the prepositions 'at' and 'on'.

The budget is of great importance if any future disagreement should arise. As many sponsors do not bother to draw up a proper contract, the budget, backed by the script, could be the only document clearly stating the producer's commitments. It should therefore be prepared and checked with greatest care.

10. *Preparing the production.* This is an organizational job which should ideally be handled by a production- or unit manager. If the size of the contract does not justify engaging one specially, the producer, director and assistant director will have to divide these administrative chores between them.

The first step after the film has been commissioned is to arrange for the necessary facilities and to prepare a master *shooting schedule*. The fixed poles in such a schedule are (a) events which occur once or at certain times only, (b) the periods least inconvenient to factories or laboratories to suffer the invasion of a film unit, and (c) the availability of facilities or of scientists who have to operate apparatus or instruments or who are to appear in the film. Everything else has to be woven round these dates. Since the shooting period is the most costly stage of a production, the aim must be to devise a compact schedule in which the various priorities dovetail neatly and which leaves a margin for possible delays: a tall order if ever there is one. Yet, with a well-devised shooting schedule, half the battle is won.

Further matters which should be dealt with before the production starts concern the ordering of film stock, hire of equipment which is not part of the unit's own outfit, engagement of outside technicians and

Film-making Procedure

artists, and forewarning the laboratory of the work to be undertaken. A number of other items will be dealt with under the next heading.

Filming and editing
11. Production management. Naturally, not all arrangements can be made in advance and the management of the production, combining organizational and administrative work, must keep pace with the progress of the film. The main items are shown in the diagram but there will be dozens of additional chores, too numerous to be listed. Some of them, however, warrant special mention.

Rushes
Foremost in importance is the question of rushes. In the case of colour films, it is usual—for reasons of economy—to have the rushes printed in black-and-white and to be supplied with a colour pilot of each scene in the shape of a short strip, showing differently graded frames. These pilots are printed haphazardly and may show the number board or the middle of a zip-pan instead of decisive features of the scene. Colour pilots are, therefore, not always reliable guides as to the colour quality, and since colour can play an important role in scientific subjects, it is advisable to have the rushes of key scenes and animated diagrams printed in colour. The cutting copy will consequently assume a rather checkered appearance. This point should be discussed with the sponsor at the budgeting session since an untrained audience of committee members could become rather confused by such a checkerboard and may misjudge the film as a whole. With this in view, the sponsor might agree to, or even ask for, a full-colour cutting copy.

All negative material is processed and the rushes are printed overnight. To view the rushes as soon as possible is vital. It is best if the director and cameraman themselves see the rushes; if this is impossible as in the case of their absence on location, someone competent at headquarters must attend to the viewing and report the result as quickly as possible by phone. Where important material is at stake it would be unwise to leave a location or to strike a set before all work has been inspected and approved.

Studio hire
Not many science films are likely to require a large studio but now and then the necessity may arise. A studio hire agreement, even if supported by a detailed quotation, is full of pitfalls, too numerous to be gone into here. It is therefore highly advisable to engage a production manager at least for the period of hire. He negotiates with the studio manager, devises the working schedule and generally keeps tabs on things with a particular eye on the question of overtime. He works hand in hand with the art director

and checks the buyer's prop lists. Finally, he will try his best to make the production run smoothly and on time.

It is hardly possible to keep within the quotation submitted by a studio. There are too many gremlins at work and many bewildering items will appear on the bill. 10–20% should therefore be added in the budget to the quoted cost.

The commissioning of models and animation was discussed in the relevant chapters.

Production management must also deal with emergencies. They must not happen but they may happen. A member of the unit might fall ill, facilities, experts or actors may not be available as arranged or shooting schedules may have to be re-devised due to constant bad weather.

12. Shooting. The technical side of shooting and editing has been discussed in previous chapters. Only points regarding procedure will, therefore, be dealt with here.

It cannot be said often enough that the secret of a successful shooting period lies in adequate preparation and organization and in obtaining *and* keeping the goodwill of people who are expected to co-operate whether they are professors, lab assistants, works managers, or foremen. Hospital staff, particularly, must be handled with kid gloves. When shooting in other people's domains, the key words are speed, tact and tidiness.

With difficult and non-repeatable subjects, specially on location, it is necessary to take a good number of 'saving' shots (alternatives and cut-away scenes) as well as plenty of close-ups. Overlapping footage for editing and optical work must be allowed for.

A still camera should always be carried even if stills were not commissioned. Reference photos are often needed for a variety of purposes and production stills are always welcome. An additional Polaroid camera is useful for on-the-spot checks of the lighting as well as for continuity purposes.

If natural sound effects are to be included in the film, a battery-operated tape-recorder will be of value. Certain brief sound effects such as shouted orders, bangs, etc., can easily be synchronized, even lip-synced, later on. But any elaborate do-it-yourself recording might provoke the wrath of the trade unions.

A walky-talky is very helpful on such locations where the director, the cameraman and the filmed persons are out of earshot of each other. Local regulations for the use of such outfits vary and a permit must usually be obtained.

A record (continuity or dope sheet) has to be kept of each scene in addition to a camera sheet. It must give the date and camera details and describe setting and action. The film resulting from a day's shooting will be collected by the laboratory the same evening for processing. When working on location, the exposed negative must be put on a train or a plane; most

Film-making Procedure

laboratories have facilities for collecting rushes from stations and airports at any time of the day or night. Each batch of rushes must be accompanied by a camera sheet (negative report sheet), available from the laboratories; it has not only to show the routine data but also special instructions such as 'night effect', 'develop to high gamma', etc.

13. *Work in the cutting room.* Editing can follow shooting or can run parallel with it. A certain amount of overlapping is unavoidable. It might, for instance, be necessary to assemble a sequence as soon as it has been shot in order to appraise its effect. If no editor has yet been engaged the director or his assistant will have to attend to such bits of preliminary editing.

The first phase of editing is concerned with the assembly of the mute picture track in accordance with the script. This includes not only the scenes filmed by the unit but also all sub-contracted and library material. The resulting track forms the mute picture cutting copy.

If dialogue has been shot in sync and the sound track approved by immediate playback the picture and sound rushes must be synchronized as soon as the sound has been transferred from the master tape to magnetic film. The syncing-up is done either on a Moviola or on the cutting bench by means of a two-way synchronizer connected to a track reader. After the synced-up rushes have been screened, the visuals are inserted into the mute cutting copy at the appropriate points, whilst the sound is laid alongside it on the synchronizer, often simply called a 'two-way' or 'four-way'. The sound scenes are joined together by lengths of spacing to form the first version of the speech cutting copy. Synchronization must be maintained throughout the length of the tracks.

In step with the assembly of the cutting copy, the commentary contained in the script must be adjusted to fit the length of each scene (or vice versa: the scenes must be kept long enough to fit the words). Frequent pauses should take care that the commentary is not just a monotonous drone. Before screening the cutting copy for the sponsor, the reading of the commentary should be well rehearsed, not at the moviola but in a theatre. If one or two scenes are not yet available, a corresponding length of film with the words: 'scene missing' (but *not* just a piece of blank film as is sometimes used) must be inserted so that the commentary can be read over it.

14. *First screening for sponsor.* As much depends on the first impression the film makes on the sponsor and his committee, the show must be well prepared. The technical advisers should be present. A pleasant, up-to-date and intimate trade theatre should be chosen which is known for good projection of both picture and sound. The time is also important. Nothing is more certain for your 'judges' to take a jaundiced view of your film than seeing it early in the morning in a large, cold and dilapidated theatre in which only six out of a hundred seats are occupied.

The theatre should have a commentator's box with a mike so that the voice comes from the screen and not from behind the audience. If the commentator has already been chosen, it is a good idea to let him do the reading. This involves an additional rehearsal and some extra cost but it gives a better polish to the show.

At the start, the audience should be told that the film is incomplete, without optical effects and music, and that the fades and dissolves are still indicated by grease-pencil lines. The show can be compared to a first fitting of a suit made to measure. The booking for the theatre must be long enough for a probable second screening and the ensuing discussion.

15. Alterations—securing music, special opticals, titles. Certain alterations in picture and commentary and perhaps some more shooting are bound to be required as a result of the show. Before going ahead with these, the film should be shown to the composer so that he gets an impression of the sequences which are to be covered by music and can note their approximate lengths. Later on, a proper music cue sheet, giving the description and the exact length of each scene, must be prepared for him.

When the budget does not allow specially composed music you have to select appropriate music from libraries. The same goes for sound effects which have not been recorded specially (see page 264, section 19).

Since most of the picture will have been shot at this stage, the necessary scenes for any special optical effects are now available and can be handed to the optical department of the laboratory. Likewise, the wording and form of the main- and credit-titles should be approved by the sponsor. Sub-contracting the lettering and the shooting of the titles to a specialized film unit is dearer but safer than doing the job yourself. Without a proper title bench, the lines tend to slope one way or the other. Title cards should be carefully checked before they are filmed, names are often mis-spelt.

The rushes of the opticals and titles have to be cut into the picture track as soon as they have been checked on the screen. All the negatives of sub-contracted and library-material should be sent to the laboratory at once for safe keeping.

Recording, Track-laying, Dubbing
16. General practice. Work on the picture track continues throughout the production; the special effect opticals and titles have to be cut in as they become available. Sound comes into its own at this stage. Apart from some incidental wild recording with a small tape-recorder which you might do yourself, everything to do with sound: recording, mixing, dubbing and transfer is a matter for specialist sound technicians whenever professional or commercial use of the film is envisaged.

Sound recording on location is done on standard magnetic $\frac{1}{4}$ in. tape. If picture and sound are shot in sync one of the synchro pulse systems is normally used. Big film studios and dubbing studios do not use tape but record direct on 35mm or 16mm sprocketed magnetic film. The

Film-making Procedure

original tape or film is retained as a master, or a master track on film is produced from it. For editing, all sound must be transferred from tape to magnetic film.

For 16mm and 8mm, magnetic striping is available. A commentary can be recorded or music added on such a stripe after the picture has been completely edited and a print made of it. Only one sound copy can be produced at each recording; this process is, therefore, of limited use to the professional film-maker except when only a single copy is needed of a foreign-language version or for another purpose. The same applies to such 8mm sound filming as can be done with the Filmosound 8 camera. Scenes shot in this way permit no editing other than splicing them together, changing them around or throwing them out as a whole.

All magnetic sound should be played back for checking immediately after recording. Later, when no longer needed, the sound can be erased from the dubbing tracks and the master. Thus, magnetic tape and magnetic film can be used again and again.

For the quantity production of the release prints, the magnetic track has to be re-recorded on photographic film to produce an optical sound negative which will then be married to the picture in the printing process.

17. Recording the commentary. The commentary can be recorded as soon as the picture is completed. Its final wording must be approved by the sponsor, and a copy of the text sent to the commentator a few days before the recording. Each reel should be rehearsed at least twice. First, the director reads the text to the screened picture whilst the commentator watches the film and marks the pauses and points of emphasis in his own copy of the script. Each commentator has its own system of marking his script, so do not try to do it for him. Next, the commentator reads the script, cued by the director. The form of cueing should be agreed upon. Some commentators prefer to be alone in the booth and to get the cues by light signals, others like to have the director sit next to them and be cued by touch.

If the commentary is spoken to the picture, slips of the tongue cannot be corrected at once; faulty sections have to be re-taken wild straight away after the end of each reel, together with any other parts with which the director or recordist are not satisfied. Watch out for hisses and paper rustle! All re-taken parts of the script must be marked in the editor's copy so that at the breakdown of the material in the cutting room, the NG-takes can be put aside at once. If this is not done, such scenes have a strange tendency to find their way back into the cutting copy.

The marking up and breaking down of the commentary is most efficiently done with the help of a synchronizer and a track reader. The track is assembled alongside the picture cutting copy and the re-takes have to be inserted where they belong.

Where a dialogue track exists already, the commentary can be cut into it to form a single *Speech Track*. Some sound mixers prefer, however, separate dialogue- and commentary-tracks for the dubbing because they can adjust sound levels better that way, particularly if the dialogue- and commentary-sequences follow each other immediately. Thus, before laying the tracks, the mixer who will later dub the film should be consulted.

18. Recording music. Film music usually accompanies the picture as an emotive component. When it has been specially composed or arranged, it must be played by an orchestra engaged for the recording. Sometimes it is recorded wild, and the picture must then be adjusted to it on the cutting bench.

More often, the music is recorded *to* the picture. The orchestra is seated in the recording studio with their backs to the screen on which the cutting copy of the film is running. The conductor faces the screen and keeps time with the picture by watching the film and the footage-counter at the bottom of the screen. Since the music was written to the script and the score has been cue-marked, timing the music is not too difficult. Sufficient time must, however, be allowed for rehearsals.

If while the tracks are being laid you find that slight adjustments are necessary, the sensible thing is to lengthen or shorten scenes in the picture rather than to tamper with the music which is an organic whole. If cuts in the music really become necessary, the editor must use his discretion. It is best to cut from a loud sound to another loud sound and to leave the quiet passages alone. In case you have to lengthen the music, some bars can be duplicated by recording them again. A good mixer can help to smooth out any rough edges caused by such changes in the music.

When music is obtained from libraries, the pieces selected from the discs and takes must be transferred to magnetic film and the track is then laid as usual. The laying of music tracks is best done on the Moviola which reproduces the music more or less faithfully. Sometimes, both composed music and library music are used in one and the same film and may have to be dissolved into each other. In such a case, two music tracks have to be laid.

19. Dealing with sound effects. The technical side of recording sound effects, either on location or in the studio, has been discussed before. Any additional effects, still needed at this stage, can best be shot at the time the commentary or the music are recorded. All effects material, whether recorded or selected from libraries, must now be assembled. There are three ways of doing this.

(a) Usually, a separate effects track is laid. If effects overlap each other or if more than one effect has to be heard at the same time, two or even more effects tracks become necessary. Often such sections are pre-dubbed so that at the final dubbing session only one effects track is running.

(b) If in the whole film, only one or two isolated effects are required, such as a bang or a short exclamation, they can be accommodated on the music track—but *not* on the speech track—if there is at least a three-foot clearance on either side *and* if the mixer agrees to it. This would obviate the

Film-making Procedure

need for a separate effects track. If there is no music, an effects track *must* be laid if foreign language versions may be needed.

(c) Continuous sound caused by water and wind, by traffic or machinery, or such rhythmic sound as the ticking of clocks or the wheel noise of trains does not need to be recorded at the required length. 10 to 15 ft are enough to make a loop which the mixer can fade in and out as needed. More than one loop can be prepared since modern dubbing studios can accommodate up to 12 tracks and loops. Sound tracks must not be of the same length as the picture track, they can end after the last sound has faded away.

20. *Pre-dubbing screening to the sponsor.* As soon as the film cutting stage is completed and all tracks are assembled, there must be another show for the sponsor. The details mentioned in section 14 apply here as well. Since trade theatres can at the most run two sound tracks with the picture this show, too, will not give a final impression of the film. It is usual to screen the picture with speech and music, leaving the effects track out. The director or editor will have to do the necessary mixing by twiddling the knobs on the theatre console. Some rehearsing is therefore vital. If the sponsor wishes to hear the effects as well, the film must be run twice, the second time combining music and effects or speech and effects. Again, some discussions are likely to follow the screening.

21. *Preparing the dubbing charts.* When the last adjustments have been made, *dubbing charts* on forms provided by the dubbing studio must be prepared for each reel. The purpose of dubbing is to combine all sound on one single track, and the charts contain the instructions needed by the mixer. They consist of long and fairly wide sheets of paper, divided into several columns. The first column is for the picture track, the following ones for the speech track(s), the music track(s), the effects track(s) and the effects loop(s) in that order. Since a track is usually made up of sound and silent passages, bold lines, drawn in each column, indicate where the track is 'live' and thin lines where it is 'dead'. The exact footage, as measured from the start mark, is entered at the beginning and end of each live sequence. Then the cues for the mixer have to be written down in each column at the appropriate points. If effects have to be manipulated by the mixer their nature must be indicated in the effects column.

22. *Dubbing.* At the dubbing session, the mixer sits at his console with all controls within easy reach and with the dubbing chart spread out before him. One reel of no more than 1000 ft (35mm) is dubbed at a time and the dubbed track is immediately played back to the picture. If not considered satisfactory, the reel is immediately dubbed once more.

The 'rock-and-roll' method now in use in all the major dubbing studios makes it possible for the mixer to stop all tracks simultaneously when a mistake occurs and take them back several feet without losing sync, erasing the fault in the process. He then retakes the erased section and continues dubbing without a break. The result is a perfect track at the first run.

An experienced mixer can work wonders with the tracks. He can often eliminate clicks, crackles and hisses which had not been noticed before, can lower or raise the levels of sound passages and thus achieve sound perspective as well as an integrated sound pattern throughout the film; he can create resonance and echoes and he can introduce all sorts of electronic effects. Often, he can improve some badly recorded sound (obtained perhaps from an outside source) so that it becomes usable. The worst mistake a film producer can make is to have his film dubbed in any but a top ranking sound studio.

The final result of the dubbing is a magnetic master from which the sound is at once transferred to 35mm or 16mm magnetic film for all subsequent screenings.

If the sponsor intends to produce a foreign-language version for distribution abroad, he needs an 'M & E' track combining only the music and effects. This M & E track, can later be dubbed on to the foreign commentary. M & E tracks can be made at any convenient time after the dubbing.

Some sponsors wish to attend the dubbing rehearsal and/or the dubbing itself and ask for a few days between the rehearsal and the actual dubbing for last-minute considerations. This means two separate studio bookings and some extra cost which the budget must provide for. The presence of the sponsor at these sessions can be a nuisance but it also has an advantage. If the sponsor passes the tracks, he cannot raise objections later on.

The picture cutting copy and the dubbed track have to be put in sync in the cutting room, and can then be screened double-headed at all further working stages.

Completion
23. *Routine opticals.* The creative work on the film has come to an end and most of the remaining stages take place in the laboratory.

The routine opticals (fades, wipes, dissolves) can now be made; it is inadvisable to have them done before dubbing. The rush prints of the opticals have to be cut into the cutting copy which is then complete and can be handed to the laboratory for negative cutting. Where the A and B roll method is adopted, the cutting copy must be marked up for making the auto-opticals.

24. *Optical sound track.* The sound must now be transferred from the magnetic master onto photographic sound stock in order that the optical sound negative necessary for marrying picture and sound may be obtained.

25. *Negative cutting.* This is a highly skilled job. Some film-makers or sponsors entrust it to a negative cutter in whom they have particular

Film-making Procedure

confidence. This involves shifting the whole negative material from the laboratory, and if one roll of negative is found missing at the cutting stage (and it has happened more than once), one party puts the blame on the other before both of them start on a frantic search. From this point of view it is best to leave the negative cutting in the hands of the laboratory which has competent negative cutters and which can then be kept fully responsible for all material.

26. *Grading.* After the picture negative is cut it must be graded so that all scenes are well matched in tone and colour; some scenes need lightening, others darkening, still others must be printed for effect (moon-light, etc.). Although the grader will know what needs to be done, it is a good idea for the director and the grader to go through the cutting copy together.

27. *Answer print.* A few days later, the first married answer print, often called a grading print, will be ready and should be viewed by the director in the presence of both the grader and the sound printer. Several adjustments are still bound to be necessary, both in the grading and in the sound. Then, the first release print can be ordered.

28. *First show copy.* If found satisfactory, this print, often called first show copy, must be screened for the sponsor's approval. Only in exceptional cases should the sponsor ask for further changes at this stage. A few grading- and sound-adjustments can still be made but any alterations which would involve changing the overall length of the film would necessitate much additional work for which the sponsor must be prepared to pay.

The first 35mm release print will be used by the sponsor for press shows and film festivals.

29. *Reduction to smaller film gauges.* If the film was produced in 16mm there is, of course, only need for reduction if 8mm prints are required.

Methods of reducing 35mm negatives to 16mm vary; they depend on the number of prints required and on one or two technical factors.

For the picture, either a 16mm negative for contact-printing is made from the 35mm negative via a fine-grain positive (also called lavender) or, in the case of colour, via an interpositive. Or the 16mm prints are made direct from the 35mm negative by way of optical printing.

The job of reducing sound from 35mm to 16mm cannot be done by every sound studio but must be handed to a specialist firm. The type of sound negative which is required is determined by the method used for the quantity production of the 16mm prints. The sound can be transferred either from the 35mm optical sound negative or from the magnetic master. The decision has to be left to the studio concerned.

The first of the resulting 16mm release prints should be checked for quality of both picture and sound. Sound suffers more than picture in the reducing process but any distortion should not exceed the permissible tolerance. An efficient transfer technician will see to this. A sponsor who has a film made for the first time, should in any case be told in advance that he cannot expect 35mm quality from a 16mm print, but that a lay-audience will certainly find nothing amiss with it.

30. End of production. The handing over of the first 16mm print ends the production. The laboratory and sound studios must be informed that all material held by them, including all trims, etc., is now the property of the sponsor and that the producer's liability has ended. The cutting copy and positive trims should be kept in the producer's vault for a reasonable period and then disposed of in accordance with the sponsor's instructions.

6

Audio-visual Aids

AUDIO-VISUAL AIDS have in recent years advanced with the force of an avalanche despite the apathy of many teachers towards these new educational media and against the opposition of the more conservative elements in the profession who regard this development as an interference with their functions as educators. True enough, AVA require an entirely new approach to teaching.

The AVA scene

The range of these media is immense. A visitor to an AVA trade fair or showroom who is not familiar with this sphere is likely to be overwhelmed by the profusion of mechanical and electronic hardware which extends from single pieces of equipment to complete learning systems, language laboratories, computers and closed circuit television.

This development will still gather momentum to the dismay of the doubters and antagonists. But these 'classroom robots' are not meant to replace or encumber the teacher, they are there to assist him. Sir Brynmor Jones, Vice-Chancellor of Hull University, who headed the committee reporting on audio-visual aids in higher education states in one of his lectures: '... It cannot be stressed too strongly that the value and importance of the teacher, especially the intelligent, imaginative and perceptive teacher, remain unchallenged ... Technical media are but instruments in his hands. ...' Elsewhere in his lecture, Sir Brynmor said that 'present-day students have become accustomed from childhood to learn from audio-visual media as readily as we of the older generation did from books ... The young are becoming as 'picturate' as they are literate. ...'

And indeed, film and television have to a great extent usurped the status of the written word in both everyday life and in the educational field. This development can surely not be unwelcome in view of the shortage of teachers. The influx of students into universities and other places of learning exceeds nowadays by far the physical capacity of these institutions. Thus, the use of audio-visual aids is not just a matter of individual preference or dislike but is often dictated by the need to cope with a situation which becomes rapidly unmanageable all over the world. Closed circuit television has provided one of the answers to this problem, particularly since it is eminently suitable to draw other audio-visual media, such as the film, into its orbit. As a consequence, the Open University is now an established learning institution in the UK.

This book is only concerned with the part that the film plays in this educational revolution. Although the film as a teaching medium existed long before the term audio-visual aid was ever heard of, it is now considered to be a distinct part of the AVA scene.

Amongst the various kinds of teaching films, it is the 8mm loop which has sprung into prominence in recent years. This type of film has become one of the most flexible tools for the teacher, who can now illustrate and bring alive specific topics within his lesson by the flick of a switch.

Few teachers have so far made their own loops, most of them are commercially produced. They come from two sources: some film sponsors have taken account of the changing pattern of educational methods and provide, together with their films, subsidiary or complementary teaching media such as film strips, wall charts, teachers' handbooks and, last but not least, 8mm cassettes. Such multi-media packages are often called audio-visual units and they can be very useful provided the loops are designed and shot as separate entities. Sometimes, sequences from the main film have been dubbed and spliced into loops, a method which is widely adopted in the USA but does not recommend itself for various reasons.

However, only a small percentage of the total output of loops are made as part of sponsored packages. The majority come from film companies and publishing houses which not only produce loops but also sell them.

Many loops deal with scientific concepts and thus belong to the category of science films.

8mm film in education

The makers of 35mm or 16mm films have little need to concern themselves with the question of how their films will be projected later on. Everything is standardized and films made in either format can be screened by any projector of the same format. Furthermore, all these films can be reduced to the smaller gauges; this has become normal procedure for non-theatrical distribution.

The situation in the 8mm field is different because production and application are to a much greater degree dependent on each other. Unfortunately, there is a complete lack of standardization and conditions are, to say the least, extremely puzzling. This is the more regrettable since the 8mm film could, in principle, solve many of the problems connected with the use of film in education. Similar bizarre situations are nowadays

Audio-visual aids

created in various other technical fields in which technology seems to outpace its own progress, coming up with ever better and brighter ideas and products which sometimes make the previous ones obsolete before they have even been put to the test.

The confused and ever-changing pattern in the 8mm field would make it futile to try and examine its technical details in a book of this type. Whatever is true to-day may be out of date to-morrow. Even the monthly trade journals have quite a job to keep abreast with developments and to find space for the flood of correspondence, conference reports and articles arising out of this condition. Suffice it to say that the arguments revolve mainly round the following problems:

(a) the three film formats: single 8, standard 8 and Super 8;

(b) the multiplicity of cassettes, cartridges and projectors few of which are compatible;

(c) the sound complication. Contrary to the 35mm and 16mm fields in which projectors are equipped with both optical and magnetic sound heads, 8mm projectors can so far only accommodate either of these two alternatives.

(d) the wealth of prototypes on the hardware side contrast sharply with the shortage of workable mass-produced equipment.

(e) the existence of technical inconsistencies and conflicting opinions.

All this goes to show the extent to which production and application are interlinked in the 8mm field.

As commercial film units produce their 8mm films in 16mm or even 35mm, the question of which 8mm format is to be used does not arise until the stage at which the films must be reduced and cassetted. But this does not make the problem any easier. Schools and teachers are disinclined to spend considerable sums of money on films and equipment which may become obsolete in the near future. In order to cope with this situation, a large group of film-makers market their loops now in both standard 8 and Super 8. This means a heavy additional capital outlay and is therefore unlikely to become permanent. Either one or the other format must eventually be adopted provided that the whole problem is not overtaken by new developments.

There are several systems already in existence which aim at a more intimate linkage with closed circuit television; one of them, EVR, uses a format of 8·75mm. At present, these systems are confined to reproduction rather than to production but there is no guarantee that this will remain so. Any film-maker who considers producing 8mm films professionally will have to take a good look at the conditions prevailing at the time.

Although the bulk of 8mm films will continue to be produced by commercial companies, it is probable that, as the idea of the teaching film catches on, more and more teachers, lecturers, doctors, scientists and film groups in schools and universities will start to make their own films.

The position for these semi- and non-professionals is slightly different because most of them will produce their films direct on 8mm stock and they must, therefore, make up their minds *before* they start. Only those who already own a suitable camera and projector are relieved of this dilemma.

A teacher who intends to build up a useful library of loops cannot rely solely on his own production potential but he will have to acquire commercially made loops as well. This means he should, for his productions, choose the most versatile combination of camera, film, cassettes and projector. All three formats have advantages and disadvantages and again, it will be necessary to consider the position at the time the choice has to be made.

Information can be obtained from organizations such as the National Audio-Visual Aids Centre in London which have been set up for the purpose of advising and assisting people interested in this field.

Loop films (Cassettes)

The idea of splicing a length of film into a loop is very old. The early 35mm loop film back-projection cabinets were as tall and bulky as small wardrobes; they were set up in trade fairs to show the making or working of industrial products. With the advent of the 16mm film, the cabinets became smaller and they began to appear in shop windows as well. Loops were still chiefly used—as they often are to-day—as a means for marketing and selling. Only when technical improvements had put the 8mm film on the map as a medium of mass communication could the value of film for teaching be fully realised. Loops could now be added to the existing forms of educational films.

The teaching loop has its origin in the demand from both teachers and students for *very short* films which deal with only one single idea or with one repetitive process and which can quickly and easily be screened and re-screened in one and the same teaching period as the need arises. The single-concept cassette films, produced as loops of 2 or 4 min length, is the answer to this. These loops are viewed by means of a small projection unit which should be suitable for both front- and back-projection and should be equipped with a frame-stopping device.

The demands made on loops by teachers can best be illustrated by some comments made at conferences and in the press; these refer to the mechanical handling as well as to the purpose and nature of the loops. '... We do not want to set up a 16mm sound projector to show a 2 min situation when you could push in a cassette and have everything at your fingertips at less cost'. 'Loops must be reach-me-downs, not borrowed and booked weeks ahead from central libraries, but kept right beside the projector'. 'Loops are not only for teaching but for learning, for use by the children themselves'. 'Loops should relieve the teacher of the need to

Audio-visual aids

demonstrate procedures which it is difficult for a class to see simultaneously. They can be devoted to experiments which cannot be conducted in schools. They can show dynamic processes such as cell division, etc.' 'A loop can be instantly related to a particular teaching point while it is fresh in the pupil's mind, even in the last two minutes before the bell goes'. 'If a particular point is not clear, the film can be repeated immediately'. 'What we want is a loop which *suggests* and leaves ideas in the children's mind but also *information* loops which relates the work to be done in the classroom by teacher and child to the situation outside.'

Whilst there are wide areas of agreement about the use of the loop, there are also differences of opinion. Teaching methods and classroom conditions vary. Britain has about 50,000 schools with a corresponding number of teachers. 'It is not likely', says a teacher who himself makes loops 'that any one film will meet with unanimous approval. But making *bad* films can be avoided. The production companies should make a special study of the conditions under which films may have to be shown, the size of classes, the different types of schools and so on.' Since loops are silent, many of them qualify for international distribution. Ideally, this would require not only a nation-wide but a world-wide knowledge of teaching methods and conditions.

It is true that the quality of many films leaves much to be desired, both technically and with regard to their academic value. Teachers are united on this point. John Halas, one of the pioneers of the loop film and head of a company which has made several hundred loops, estimates the numbers of titles existing at present in Britain at 3000, in USA at 10,000. He thinks that of this total, only a small percentage is of adequate quality. And the manager of a large laboratory states that at least half of the total footage which comes to him for processing is technically 'rather poor'. It is also strange to see how much the conceptual side of film-making is disregarded by people who ought to know better. At a recent trade fair a loop was shown at the stand of a cine-camera manufacturing concern to publicise their newest product. This loop looked as if one of their apprentices had knocked it off during his lunch break.

The point is that making loops is a job which has to be taken seriously. John Halas believes that more thought has often to be given to the making of a 2 min loop than to a 10 min film. The co-operation of leading educators and scientists is vital. Whilst *all* loops must be terse, clear and coherent, the presentation of the subject depends on the contents. Simple, straightforward subjects may only demand straightforward shooting; other loops, particularly those for science teaching, might require special camera techniques and effects, animation, graphics and other sophisticated methods. Thus, what the books says about the conception, visualization and treatment of science films in general holds good for the science loop, too.

One of the arguments advanced against using loops is that the money for them is just not available. All teachers agree that loops should be cheaper, but how can this demand be combined with that for higher quality? No satisfactory answer to this question can be given as long as the situation remains as chaotic as it is. But will it remain so? We are only at the beginning of the 8mm era and much of the muddle found at present in this field is due to the process of growing up. Clearer and more stable conditions plus better planning must make it possible to reduce production cost. Also, in good time, more money is bound to be made available for schools by official sources. The market for the 8mm loop is even now steadily expanding all over the world; let us see to it that the right type of loops will be produced now to meet the demand which the future will bring.

Appendix

Guidelines for the evaluation of science films

THE SELECTION OF SCIENCE films for screening to specialized audiences, in schools, on television or at conferences and festivals, must to a large degree be based on the information handed out in advance by sponsors and producers describing the content, style and purpose of their films and the audience for which they are intended. The appraisal and cataloguing of such films by educational and scientific viewing committees, however, is often hampered either by total absence of such information or by incomplete and haphazard documentation, often ignoring vital aspects of a film. At the Montreal congress of the ISFA, Sir Arthur Elton deplored the fact that 'many sponsors spend lots and lots of money on making a film but find it impossible to put down on paper the essential information that other people could use in compiling their film catalogues.'

In order to provide assessments of films which are universally valid certain fixed standards regarding the data to be supplied by the sponsor and the appraisal procedure itself are necessary. It might be of interest to many readers to examine the system which a distinguished film organization, the Canadian Film Institute, has developed for the evaluation of popular science films. The following description is taken with the kind permission of the ISFA from their report of the Montreal congress. It has been slightly shortened by omitting a few details concerned with administration.

The Canadian system is, of course, not the only one. Other countries have different evaluation methods but they all have to rely to a great extent on the information supplied by the sponsors or producers.

THE EVALUATION OF SCIENCE FILMS
AS PRACTISED BY THE NATIONAL
SCIENCE FILM LIBRARY,
CANADIAN FILM INSTITUTE

General principles

The films to be evaluated are viewed by a group of people in order to take advantage of the fact that the combined memory, observation, knowledge and experience of a group are wider than those of an individual. Thus the evaluation is likely to provide a better guide to the *user* of science films than an individual review.

An *Evaluation Report Form* is used when judging films in order to maintain, as nearly as possible, consistent standards of assessment. Uniformity of style is achieved by recording physical data on a Data Sheet and by using a standardized layout in the published material.

EVALUATION PROCEDURE

Evaluation sessions are usually held on films relating to a selected theme. The organization of such an evaluation session is usually entrusted to a Chairman who is particularly interested in that theme.

Constitution of the Panel

An Evaluation Panel should consist of: experts in the subject matters of the films; people with experience in using films; teachers of the subject; representatives of the intended audience, together with someone competent to judge the quality of the production. Some of these functions may be combined in one person—for example, subject specialists may also be teachers, or teachers may be experienced in film matters.

A good panel should consist of at least five persons, but seven is a better number. As stated above, the Chairman is responsible for the formation of a balanced panel.

THE FILM DATA SHEET

Title: The title to be entered is the title of the evaluated or previewed version of the film. Alternative and other language version titles should also be given where possible. If the film is one of a *series* this should be stated.

Subject: The film may cover one or more subjects and/or sub-divisions of those subjects. These should all be entered if necessary.

Producer and sponsor: Care should be taken to differentiate between these two items. The Producer is the organization or individual actually responsible for the physical processes involved in making the film; the Sponsor initiates the project and supplies the funds. For example: *The Revealing Eye* was produced by the Shell Oil Film Unit for Shell Oil Ltd— *not* produced by Shell Oil Ltd.

Technical adviser: The technical adviser is the person or organization responsible for advising the producers on the accuracy of the subject matter of the film. Where no technical adviser is credited 'None' should be entered in this space.

Summary of content: The summary should describe succinctly, but accurately

Appendix

and objectively, the content of the film and should be long enough for the reader to understand precisely the content of the film. It should provide the theme and setting of the film and the relative length of the different sections. No evaluative words or phrases, either commendatory or condemnatory, should be included in the summary.

Purpose of film: This should be a one sentence statement of the general aim of the film.

Availability: If the film is available from more than one source—e.g. one source for hire and another for sale—all these should be given.

EVALUATION REPORT FORM

For *Title* and *Subject* see Film Data Sheet above

Aim
The purpose of the film may or may not be stated, but an attempt should be made to discover it and the extent to which this purpose has been achieved should be indicated. Occasionally, a film may satisfactorily achieve a purpose different from the stated purpose and this should be mentioned.

General opinion of the film
This should be an attempt to describe the overall quality and value of the film, together with other matters considered of importance to film users.

Special techniques
All special techniques or effects used should be recorded.

Type of film:
Under type (or style of treatment) the method used in presenting the subject is described by means of key words. A film may be classified as of more than one type. Definitions of the key words given on the Evaluation Report Form are listed below.

Record	Film in which phenomena are registered or represented as they normally occur.
Training	Film designed to help in acquiring a technique for a specific purpose.
Instructional	Film to aid the acquisition of knowledge.
Historical	Film made to reconstruct or describe events of a past era.
Biographical	A biographical film lays emphasis upon the relation of a particular person or persons (living or dead) to a particular set of events.
Demonstration	Film representing phenomena arranged specifically for the camera.

The Work of the Science Film Maker

Information Factual film of typical life and scenes, principally of interest value, not necessarily instructional.

Descriptive A film presenting a group of facts in a coherent form, but without showing the group's relation to, or interaction with, groups exterior to itself.

Inspirational A film which inspires or encourages the viewer to follow a particular course of action.

Factual A factual film lays emphasis upon the events with which it deals.

Interpretive Film used to interpret scientific facts to a lay audience.

Integrational An integrational film presents a group of facts and shows how they may be inter-related to form a complete item of knowledge.

Motivational A film which offers a reason as to why particular course of action should be followed.

(These key words are derived from the UNESCO publication: *A Manual for Evaluators of Films and Filmstrips*)

Factual content

This is an extremely important section and care should be taken that subjective judgements do not colour the assessment of accuracy. For example, an assessment of a film on Jungian psychiatry undertaken by psycho-analysts holding Freudian theories might be biased. A film may legitimately illustrate the theories of a particular school of thought as it may deal with generally accepted facts. (This does not suggest that films which set out to advertise a particular theory, product, process or person under the guise of objective truth may not be exposed as such.)

It should also be noted that in this, as in the following section, one or more of the items may be checked. For example, a film on rocket techniques may be 'up-to-date' at the time of evaluation but may also be 'liable to become out-of-date within a short time'. Films which deal with basic, and well-accepted processes or theories would be indicated as 'dating not important'.

Presentation

The way in which the information is presented is as important as the subject matter itself, for if the information is dull or lacking in clarity, an audience will fail to assimilate the information the film is intended to convey.

Poor photography or a bad sound track can ruin an otherwise satisfactory film and the same consideration applies to any other techniques used in the film. Care should be taken, however, to ensure that any criticisms raised are legitimate, concerning faults inherent in the film, and not faults arising from a poor print or bad projection. This latter information should be specified under 'technical quality of print'.

Appendix

Commentary
The degree of accuracy of the commentary should be indicated as well as the method of presentation. Please note that an overly verbose commentary which attempts to include too much information often renders a film as ineffective as a commentary which is either dull or does no present sufficient information.

Audience
It is important to consider all possible types of audience, bearing in mind the film user and his needs. Possible audiences, other than these specified, may be added.

Technical quality of print
This means the *print* quality and *not* the cinematic quality of the film.

Panel
The name or names of the panel, commission or persons responsible for the Evaluation should be recorded.

Film libraries and catalogues

One of the first things the film-maker ought to discover before he starts on a production is whether his intended subject is already covered by other films and, if so, where he can hire them for viewing. Such information is not always easy to come by. The total number of films relating to science, technology, medicine, education, etc., is enormous and is growing from year to year. Moreover, there is no central body which assists in the planning of a systematic coverage of the factual field; the individual sponsors and producers too often choose their subjects to suit their own purpose, regardless of what there might already be on the market. The result is a surfeit of films about some subjects and no film at all about others.

The only fairly reliable method of finding out about existing films is to study the various film lists and catalogues issued by the 16mm film libraries and by other sources. The fact that there are dozens of such catalogues in circulation and that many films have fancy titles which do not readily indicate what they are about does not make the job of tracing all films on a given subject any easier. The following particulars may provide some guidance through this special maze of mass communication.

'The British National Film Catalogue', published by *The British Industrial and Scientific Film Association*, 193–197 Regent Street, London W 1, is the most nearly comprehensive list of non-fiction and short films made in the United Kingdom since 1963. It is arranged in subject order by Universal Decimal Classification. Each entry lists (when available) the title, distribution, production company, running time, whether sound or silent, colour or b/w, gauge, production credits and gives—very important—a synopsis.

The catalogue is in the form of four quarterly issues and one annual hardback cumulative volume published in the spring of the following year. Back volumes can still be obtained. B.I.S.F.A. also keeps a retrospective reference file reaching much further back. The catalogue can either be obtained by subscription or borrowed from a public library.

The British Film Institute, 81 Dean Street, London W 1, some years ago published a catalogue of their science films library containing the data and synopses of some 500 films in the B.F.I. library, but this list has unfortunately not been brought up to date. Enquiries will elicit the titles and data of the more recent additions to the library and other useful information.

The Central Film Library, Government Building, London W 1, is the distributor of all films produced by the Central Office of Information and of many films made by various sponsors in Britain and abroad. With approximately 1500 titles, it is the largest lending library of non-fiction films in this country. It has published two catalogues. The main catalogue lists general subjects but also a great number of films about science, hygiene and medicine; the catalogue of films for industry contains industrial films and also many films of a technological and scientific nature. Both catalogues have a classified table of contents and an index of film titles.

Of special interest to atomic physicists are the films made and distributed by *The United Kingdom Atomic Energy Authority*, London SW 1, which will send its catalogue free on request.

The British Medical Association, London WC1H 9JP, lists under subject headings some 500 medical films which can be borrowed by doctors and other qualified persons. They include teaching films which are part of the ENCYCLOPAEDIA CINEMATOGRAPHICA, kept at the *Institut für Weissenschaftlichen Film*, Göttingen, Germany.

The National Committee for Audio-Visual Aids in Education (N.C.A.V.A.E.) and *The Educational Foundation for Visual Aids* (E.F.V.A.), both in London, have not only issued a catalogue listing their own productions, but E.F.V.A. has also published a number of catalogues containing many educational and scientific films, including cassette films, by other sponsors and producers. The catalogues are arranged according to subjects. Part 5, for instance, lists films on physics, mathematics, astronomy and chemistry. Enquiries should be made to E.F.V.A. Library, Paxton Place, Gipsy Road, London SE 27.

Appendix

Mention should also be made of the film catalogues of the *British Association for the Advancement of Science*, London SW 1. The annual Science Fairs of the B.A. are a stimulating hunting ground for the film-maker in search of scientific apparatus and visually attractive models and gadgets which lend themselves to filming.

Then there are the catalogues of the commercial film producers and distributors, amongst them:

Encyclopaedia Britannica Inc, London SW 1 (with offices in the USA and many other countries)
The Rank Film Library, Perivale, Greenford, Middlesex
Sound Film Services Ltd, London SW 19
Boulton-Hawker Films Ltd, Hadley, Ipswich, Suffolk

Some of these firms handle the distribution not only of their own films but also of films made by other sponsors and producers.

In 1969 Alec M. Hughes identified for the National Council for Educational Technology over 1,400 films concerned with physics. *The Institute of Educational Technology of the University of Surrey* selected from these some 200 titles for screening to a panel of lecturers and students. Based on panel members comments 70 have now been listed in a special supplement of *Physics Education* (Institute of Physics, 47 Belgrave Square, London, sw1) as suitable for university teaching.

Industrial sponsors are too numerous to be mentioned here in full; only the most important ones, who have a regular output of films and who distribute them through their own libraries, are listed below:

The Gas Council, London W 1
A.E.I. (Associated Electrical Industries Ltd), London SW 1
I.C.I. Millbank, London SW 1
Unilever Ltd, London EC 4
Mullard Film Service, London WC 1. (Films on electronics, etc.)
Philips Ltd. Distributor: Sound Services Ltd, London SW 19
Ford, Dunlop and the *British Iron and Steel Federation* have their film libraries at Merton Park, London SW 19
Shell, Esso, BP and all other oil companies distribute their films through the *Petroleum Films Bureau*, London W 1.

As regards foreign educational and science films, some are available in this country through the *Central Film Library* which also distributes the films made by *USA Government Departments*. Details are found in the main catalogue of the library.

The films of the *National Film Board of Canada* can be obtained either from the Canada House Film Library, London SW 1, or from several commercial distributors who list them in their catalogues.

The French Institute in London keeps a lending library of French films and has published a single 'Catalogue des Films Scientifiques'. Enquiries should be addressed to *Service du Cinema, Institut Francais du Royaume-Uni*, London SW 7.

Scientific film associations and societies

Science film-makers are likely to wish to join one of the societies which have as their object the promotion of scientific film making, the exchange of information, the regular screening of new films, the arranging of meetings and lectures and which concern themselves generally with film communication. Such societies exist in many of the larger towns and at many universities and colleges. Their activities vary but most of them are available for consultation and advice; many have book libraries.

In Britain, the three most important organizations are:

The Royal Photographic Society of Great Britain which has a 'Scientific and Technical Group' and its 'Motion Picture Group', 14 South Audley Street, London W 1
The British Kinematograph, Sound and Television Society, 110 Victoria House, Vernon Place, London WC 1
The British Industrial and Scientific Film Association (B.I.S.F.A.), 193 Regent Street, London W 1
B.I.S.F.A. is affiliated to the *International Scientific Film Association* (see below).

To be a member of one of these societies, read their publications and attend their meetings, lectures, and film shows keeps one up to date with what is going on in the various spheres of factual and science film production.

Societies outside the United Kingdom include:

International Scientific Film Association. Secretariat: 38 Avenue des Ternes, 75–Paris 17e. (General Secretary: Mme Suzanne Duval.)
International Scientific Film Library, 31 Rue Vautier. Bruxelles 4, Belgium. (This is not a lending library but an archive. Films can be viewed on the spot by arrangement.)
U.N.E.S.C.O., Radio and Visual Services, Place de Fontenoy, Paris 7e.

The I.S.F.A. also has member societies in the following countries. Their addresses can be obtained from the Paris Secretariat.

Argentine,
Australia,
Austria,
Belgium,
Brazil,
Bulgaria,

Japan,
Mexico,
Netherlands,
Nigeria,
Philippines,
Poland,

Appendix

Canada,
Czechoslovakia,
France,
German Democratic Republic (East Germany)
German Federal Republic (West Germany)
Hungary,
Israel,
Italy,
Rumania,
Spain,
Switzerland,
Uruguay,
USSR,
USA,
Venezuela.

Educational and popular Science films referred to in this book

(*S:* Sponsor, *D:* Distributor, *P:* Production company, *PR:* Producer, *DIR:* Director, *C:* Cameraman)

The following credits are taken from the producers' hand-outs and catalogues which are not always exhaustive. I apologize for any omissions on these grounds.

PAGE 62   *A Light in Nature*   *S:* Shell; *P:* Shell Film Unit London; *D:* Petroleum Films Bureau London; *PR:* Stuart Legg; *DIR:* Ramsey Short; *C:* Alan Fabian. Colour, 35 min.

PAGE 66   *The Revealing Eye*   *S/P/D* as above, compiled by Walter Storey. B/w and colour, 19 min.

PAGE 66   *Magic Light* (German title: *Mit Licht Schreiben*) *S:* Agfa/Gevaert Ltd; *D:* Rank Organisation London; *DIR:* Hugo Niebeling. Colour, 2 versions, 20 and 40 min.

PAGE 67   *The Structure of Protein*   *S/D:* Unilever Ltd London; *P:* De La Chevre Films Ltd London: *DIR*: George Seager and John Armstrong; *C:* David Holmes. Colour, 17 min.

PAGE 67   *Carbon*   *S:* Morgans Crucible Co Ltd; *P/D:* A. Gilkison Associates, London; *DIR:* Peter de Normanville; *C:* Wolfgang Suschitzky. Colour, 25 min.

PAGES 68, 104   *Physics and Chemistry of Water*   *S/D:* Unilever Ltd London; *P:* World Wide Pictures Ltd London; *DIR:* Sarah Erulkar; *C:* Charles Smith. Colour 21 min.

PAGE 68   *The River Must Live*   *S:* Shell; *P:* Shell Film Unit London; *D:* Petroleum Films Bureau London; *PR:* Douglas Gordon; *DIR:* Alan Pendy; *C:* Wolfgang Suschitzky. Colour 21 min.

PAGE 69 *Between the Tides*   *S/P/D:* British Transport Films London; *PR:* Edgar Anstey; *DIR:* Ralph Keen; *C:* Donald Craigen. Colour, 22 min.

PAGE 69   *Exploring Chemistry*   *S:* Unilever Ltd London; *P:* Rank Organisation London; *D:* Unilever and Central Film Library London; *DIR:* Robert Carter; *C:* David Muir. B/w, 35 min.

PAGE 69   *Visual Aids*   *S:* Ministry of Defence; *P:* Stewart Films Ltd

283

THE WORK OF THE SCIENCE FILM MAKER

London; *D:* Sound Services Ltd London; *DIR:* Richard Need. Colour, 22 min.

PAGE 77 *The Microscope*   *SD:* Shell; *P:* Realist Film Unit; *DIR:* Denys Parsons; B/w, 15 min.

PAGE 78   *How the Motorcar Works*, Part 1: *The Engine*   *S:* Shell; *P:* Shell Film Unit London; *D:* Petroleum Films Bureau London; *DIR:* John Armstrong; *C:* Alan Fabian. Colour, 17 min.

PAGE 88   *High Speed Flight*, Part 1: *Approaching the Speed of Sound* *S/P/D:* as for above; *PR:* Sir Arthur Elton; *DIR:* Peter de Normanville; *C:* Sidney Beadle. Colour, 28 min.

PAGE 88   *Schlieren*   *S/P/D/DIR:* as above; *C:* Ron Whitehouse. Colour, 20 min.

PAGES 58, 105   *The Second Law of Thermodynamics*   *S/D:* I.C.I. London; *P:* Millbank Films London; *DIR:* George Griffith; *C:* Peter Grimwood. Colour, 23 min.

PAGES 106–7   *Your Childrens' Meals*, part of the 'Your Childrens'' series, see below *Your Childrens' Eyes*.

PAGE 111   *River to Cross*   *S:* Central Office of Information for Ministry of Transport; *P:* Basic Films Ltd London; *D:* Central Film Library London; *PR:* R. K. Neilson Baxter; *DIR:* John Shearman; *C:* Michel Currer-Briggs and Arthur Englander. B/w, 20 min.

PAGE 114   *Distillation*   *S:* Shell; *P:* Shell Film Unit London; *D:* Petroleum Films Bureau London. B/w version 1940: *PR:* Arthur Elton; *DIR:* Peter Bayliss. 15 min. Colour version 1966: *DIR:* Rodney Giesler; *C:* Ron Bicker, 15 min.

PAGE 130   *Experiments with the Bubble Model of a Metal Structure* *PR/D:* Macqueen Film Organisation Ltd, Sevenoaks, in co-operation with Sir Lawrence Bragg, F.R.S. and Dr. W. M. Lomer (Cavendish Laboratory, Cambridge).

PAGES 133–6   *Your Childrens' Eyes*   *S:* Central Office of Information; *P:* Realist Film Unit London; *D:* Central Film Library London; *PR:* John Taylor; *D/C:* Alex Strasser. B/w, 15 min.

PAGES 142–64   *Science in the Orchestra* Part 1: *Hearing the Music*, Part 2: *Exploring the Instruments* Part 3: *Looking at Sounds*   *S/P/D:* as for above; *PR:* Brian Smith; *DIR:* Alex Strasser; *C:* Adrian Jeakins. B/w, 35 min.

PAGES 164–86   *Transference of Heat*, Part 1: *Convection*, Part 2: *Conduction*. Part 3: *Radiation*   *S/D:* The Gas Council London; *P:* Realist Film Unit London; *DIR:* Alex Strasser; *C:* Adrian Jeakins, B/w version 1948. Colour version 1963, 22 min.

PAGES 186–203   *Electro-magnetic Waves*, Part 1: *Discovery and Generation*, Part 2: *Properties and Behaviour*   *S:* Mullard Ltd London with Educational Foundation for Visual Aids; *P:* Realist Film Unit London; *D:* E.F.V.A. London; *PR/DIR:* Alex Strasser; *C:* Adrian Jeakins.

Appendix

Colour, 40 min.
PAGES 206–24   *Mirror in the Sky*   S/P/D; as above; PR: Basil Wright; DIR: Alex Strasser; C: Adrian Jeakins. B/w, 22 min.
PAGES 224–46   *Conquest of the Atom*   S/P/D/PR/DIR/C: as previous film. Colour, 22 min.

Film running time to Footage

Time in minutes	35mm @ 24 fps feet	35mm @ 24 fps metres	16mm @ 24 fps feet	16mm @ 24 fps metres	SUPER 8mm MUTE @ 18 fps feet	SUPER 8mm MUTE @ 18 fps metres	SUPER 8mm SOUND @ 24 fps feet	SUPER 8mm SOUND @ 24 fps metres	Time in minutes
1	90	27·43	36	10·97	15	4·57	20	6·10	1
2	180	54·86	72	21·95	30	9·14	40	12·19	2
3	270	82·30	108	32·92	45	13·72	60	18·29	3
4	360	109·73	144	43·89	60	18·29	80	24·38	4
5	450	137·16	180	54·86	75	22·86	100	30·48	5
6	540	164·59	216	65·84	90	27·43	120	36·57	6
7	630	192·02	252	76·81	105	32·00	140	42·67	7
8	720	219·46	288	87·78	120	36·57	160	48·76	8
9	810	246·89	324	98·75	135	41·15	180	54·86	9
10	900	274·32	360	109·73	150	45·72	200	60·96	10
15	1350	411·48	540	164·59	225	68·58	300	91·43	15
20	1800	548·63	720	219·45	300	91·43	400	121·91	20
25	2250	685·79	900	274·31	375	114·29	500	152·39	25
30	2700	822·94	1080	329·18	450	137·15	600	182·87	30
35	3150	960·10	1260	384·04	525	160·01	700	213·35	35
40	3600	1097·26	1440	438·90	600	182·87	800	243·84	40
45	4050	1234·42	1620	493·76	675	205·72	900	274·30	45
50	4500	1371·57	1800	548·63	750	228·59	1000	304·78	50
55	4950	1508·73	1980	603·49	825	251·44	1100	335·26	55
60	5400	1645·89	2160	658·36	900	274·32	1200	365·74	60
120	10,800	3291·78	4320	1316·71	1800	548·63	2400	731·51	120
180	16,200	4937·67	6480	1975·07	2700	823·11	3601	1097·57	180

To obtain standard 8mm footages:
Mute deduct 20% off above footages shown for Super 8mm
Sound deduct 10% off above footages shown for Super 8mm

By courtesy of Rank Processing Laboratories, Denham.

Bibliography

REFERENCE BOOKS
The Focal Encyclopaedia of Film and Television Techniques, Focal Press, London (1969). An exhaustive work listing both general and specialized terms and techniques.
J. V. MASCELLI, *American Cinematographer Manual*. American Society of Cinematographers, Hollywood 28, USA. English distributor: Samuelson Film Services Ltd, London NW 2. An indispensable pocket-size handbook containing innumerable tables and data. Frequent new editions.

HISTORY AND ART OF CINEMATOGRAPHY
I. MONTAGUE, *Film World*. Penguin, London (1964). Deals with the four aspects of film: as science, as art, as commodity and as vehicle. A valuable and readable general introduction to the subject.
R. STEPHENSON and J. R. DEBRIX, *The Cinema as Art*. Penguin, London (1968). An interesting investigation into 'film space', 'film time', 'film reality' and other filmic phenomena.

GENERAL FILM TECHNIQUE
C. C. CLARKE, *Professional Cinematography*. American Society of Cinematographers, Hollywood 28, USA. (1968). A textbook which deals comprehensively with most aspects of production methods and equipment.
W. H. BADDELEY, *The Technique of Documentary Film Production*. Focal Press, London (1970). A comprehensive textbook with special application to the factual field.
D. DAVIS, *Filming With 16mm*. Iliffe, London (1960). A complete guide to 16mm cinematography with an extensive glossary.
J. V. MASCELLI, *The Five C's of Cinematography*. Cine/Grafic Publications, Hollywood 28, USA (1965). English distributor: Samuelson Film Services Ltd, London NW 2. Deals with continuity, composition, camera angles, close-ups and cutting. Profusely illustrated.

Bibliography

J. D. FISHER, *The Craft of Film*. Attic Publishing Ltd, London (1970). A 'filing-system of basic information', in sections and ring-bound for adding new material.

SPECIALIZED FIELDS

D. TOWNSEND, *Filming in Colour*. Fountain Press, London (1960). Intended for amateurs, this is a short and informative guide to the theory and practice of colour cinematography.
Infra-red and Ultra-violet Photography, Kodak Advanced Data Book M3. From Kodak dealers or Sales Service Division, Eastman Kodak Co. Rochester, New York, USA. A complete list of all handbooks and data books will be sent free by Kodak on request.
R. FIELDING, *The Technique of Special Effects Cinematography*. Focal Press, London (1970). Deals comprehensively with optical effects.
F. P. CLARK, *Special Effects in Motion Pictures*. Society of Motion Picture and TV Engineers Inc. N.Y., New York 1007 (1963). Deals mainly with mechanical and atmospherical effects.
J. HALAS and R. MANVELL, *The Technique of Film Animation*. Focal Press, London (1969). Richly illustrated, it is concerned with every type of two- and three-dimensional animation.
J. BURDER, *The Technique of Editing 16mm Films*. Focal Press, London (1968). A book on the practical aspects peculiar to narrow gauge cutting room work.
E. WALTER, *The Technique of the Film Cutting Room*. Focal Press, London (1969). A comprehensive book on the mechanics of film editing.
K. REISZ and G. NULLAR, *The Technique of Film Editing*. Focal Press, London (1969). Enlarged edition of a classic work on the aesthetics of film editing.
BRYNE-DANIEL, *Grafilm*. Studio Vista, London (1970). Discusses the use of graphics in film.
A Note on The Schlieren Method. Shell, London (1959). A short and lucid booklet on the technique of 'Schlieren' cinematography.
A. S. DUBOVIK, *Photographic Recording of High-Speed Processes*. G. H. Lunn, London (1968).
R. F. SAXE, *High-Speed Photography*. Focal Press, London (1966). Both the above contain chapters on advanced cinematographic high-speed techniques.
Underwater Photography, Movies and Stills. Stanley Paul, London (1964). A handbook for skin-divers.
A. NISBETT, *The Technique of The Sound Studio*. Focal Press, London (1970). Although written mainly for sound technicians, it contains useful chapters on sound editing, tape- and disc-recording, sound effects, etc.

G. WOLF, *Der Wissenschaftliche Dokumentationsfilm und die Encyclopaedia Cinematographica*. Johann Ambrosius Barth, Munich (1967). Mainly about the aims and contents of the scientific film archive being built up by the Institut für den Wissenschaftlichen Film, Göttingen, Germany. This Institute periodically publishes contributions to science film literature.

G. RIECK, *Technik der Wissenschaftlichen Kinematographie*. Johann Ambrosius Barth, Munich (1967). Mainly about the stop-motion- and high-speed-methods employed in the Göttingen Institut.

TEACHING

L. HERMANN, *Film and Teaching*. Crown Publishers, New York (1965).
Film in Higher Education and Research (Edited by P. GROVES). Proc. Conf. Pergamon Press (1966). Both the above contain comprehensive assessments of the film as an educational medium.
A. G. ROMISZOWSKI, *The Selection and Use of Teaching Aids*. Kogan Page, London (1968). A practical guide to all audio-visual aid techniques.

DIRECTORIES AND YEARBOOKS

Kemp International Film and Television Directory. Kemp's Publishing, London. Covers production facilities, film distributors, etc., in the UK and overseas.
Motion Picture, TV and Theatre Directory. Motion Picture Enterprises Publications Inc. Terrytown, New York, USA. Covers services and products in the USA.
World Directory of Stock Shot and Film Production Libraries (Edited by J. CHITTOCK) (Compilation by M. J. LEDOUX Curator of the Royal Film Archive of Belgium) Assisted by UNESCO. Pergamon Press (1969). Contains information on material, an alphabetical index of film libraries, etc., covering fifty eight countries and UNO.

PERIODICALS

The following British monthly magazines print news as well as reviews of the most important factual films currently released:
Audio-Visual. The Maclaren Group Publications. PO Box 109, Croydon CR9 1QH, Surrey.
Visual Education. The official magazine of the National Committee for Audio-Visual Aids in Education, 33 Queen Anne Street, London W1M 0AL. This journal also reviews cassette films.
Business Screen, 402 West Liberty Drive, Wheaton, Illinois 60187, USA.

Glossary of Film Terms

A and B rolls In 35mm: for making of *auto-opticals* the picture track between dissolves, wipes, fades, etc., is usually put alternately on two rolls so that the optical printer can print such *opticals* automatically. In 16mm: checkerboard arrangement of the scenes on two rolls for preventing the joints from becoming visible on the screen. Also for producing *auto-opticals* as above.

Academy size The standard frame size of 35mm sound film as opposed to the frame size of silent film and wide screen formats. Gate aperture 22mm × 16mm. Screen proportion: 1·33 to 1.

Anamorphic lens A distorting lens used in shooting to compress an image horizontally on the film and on the projector to 'unsqueeze' it again for certain wide screen formats.

Answer print The first print of a film supplied by the laboratory to check the *grading*; also called *grading print*.

Auto-opticals Automatically produced *opticals* which obviate the need for interpositives and *dupes*; they usually require the division of the negative into *A and B rolls*.

Baby legs A very short-legged tripod for low-angle shots supporting the camera 1–2 ft above ground. See also *Top hat*.

Backing A surface at the back of a set. It may consist of black velvet, or painted canvas, or wall-papered hardboard, or a scenic view on a back-projection screen, etc. A white cycloramic (coved) backing suggests 'infinity'. See also *Cloud projector*.

Bi-pack A photographic method in which two negatives are exposed simultaneously in a *process camera* fitted with a beam-splitter. Its application is nowadays mainly in the field of trick-photography.

Black velvet This material is vital for many split-screen and other effects because it is wholly light-absorbing. Several pieces of various sizes should be part of every film unit's stock-in-trade.

Blimp A sound-proof case fitted round the camera. See *Sync shooting*.

Break-down The separating and sorting of the day's *rushes* in the cutting room.

Camera sheet   The term used for the *negative report sheet* which is sent to the laboratory with the *rushes*.
Catathermic filters   Heat-absorbing glass sheets put between light-source and subject to protect it from excessive heat. Often necessary in macrophotography.
Cel   Short for 'celluloid sheet' as used in animation. Nowadays, colourless plastic sheets have replaced celluloid but the term *cel* has remained.
Chinagraph   A white or coloured grease-pencil which writes on glass and plastic, mainly used in the cutting room to make *sync-marks*, etc., on the cutting copy. Also called wax crayon.
Cinex   See *Rushes*.
Clapper board   *A number board or take board* used in *sync shooting*. A few feet are shot at the start of each take. A hinged batten is then banged down onto the clapper board making a 'plop' in the sound track by which picture and sound can be synchronized in the cutting room. The clapper board shows all data necessary for the identification of the scene: name of film unit and cameraman, the title of the film, the date, the scene- and take-number.
Cloud projector   A projection device by which static or moving cloud effects can be thrown onto a background screen. See also *Backing*.
Colour pilots   See *Rushes*.
Computer-made films   A computer can 'make' films (although so far only animated diagrams) if fed in the usual way with programmed instructions. The process is a mixture of photographic and electronic methods and is still in the experimental stage. Once it reaches the stage of commercial film production, it will save much time.
Continuity sheet   Or *dope sheet*. Gives all relevant data of a filmed scene (setting, dresses, action, etc.) for the use of the editor; of great importance for avoiding continuity mistakes in shooting and editing.
Cross-cut   A method of editing in which scenes not of the same visual sequence are intercut with each other in order to suggest parallel action, or to achieve a *montage* effect.
Cue sheet   (1) A form containing all data (length, source, film distribution, etc.) on the music used in a film. When a production is completed, in England it must be sent to the Mechanical Copyright Protection Society Ltd (commonly called the Music Bureau) which deals with all copyright questions, fixes the charges for library music and other copyright material and accepts payment of royalties.
(2) The term is loosely used for sheets of instructions given to composers, animators and sound mixers.
Cut-away   See *Insert*.
Cutting copy   The working copy of a film which is assembled scene by scene in the cutting room.

Glossary of Film Terms

Dolly A four-wheeled trolley supporting the camera, needed for smooth tracking shots in studios or factories. Rails or tracks have usually to be laid unless the distance is very short. The trolley is pushed or pulled by hand. For frontal tracking, a zoom lens is now often used instead of a dolly but for side tracking (with the camera shooting at a 90° angle) a dolly is still essential. See also *Velocilator*.

Dope sheet See *Continuity sheet*.

Double exposure An exposed negative can be re-wound and exposed again to superimpose a second image on the first. Much used in trick cinematography but nowadays done usually in the optical printer rather than in the camera.
Unintentional double exposure is the result of inadvertently reloading an exposed negative into the magazine.

Double-headed The projectors in laboratories and trade theatres are fitted with double spools so that the mute picture and the sound cutting copy can be projected together in *sync*. This is often necessary during the editing stage, when viewing sync rushes or showing cutting copies to the sponsor.
If a second projector is interlocked with the first, it is possible to run a film triple-headed: picture, music and commentary or sound effects. In this case, the director will have to fade the tracks up and down or mix them on the theatre's console.

Dubbing The same as *re-recording*. In a dubbing session, the separate sound tracks (speech, music, sound effects) are combined on to one track, called a 'dubbed track' which is later *married* to the picture.
Also: replacing speech in one language with that in another.

Dupe Short for 'duplicate negative'. A 'dupe' is taken from an original negative via a fine grain print (see *Emulsion types*) or, in colour, via an 'interpositive'. *Dupes* are necessary for all optical work.
Also: all library- or stock-shots are dupes. There is a slight lessening of quality inherent in duping owing to the obtrusive quality of the emulsion grain.

Edge numbers All optical film stock, negative and positive, picture and sound, has consecutive numbers printed along one edge, one foot apart. They are essential for editing. Magnetic stock has no edge numbers. To safeguard against losing the *sync* one can have identical numbers printed on the picture and magnetic track opposite each other, also one foot apart. This should be done *before* the first cut is made in any of the tracks.

Emulsion types
PICTURE STOCK *Negative* and *positive* film for all gauges exist in many black and white and colour grades. The slower the film speed, the finer the grain.

Reversal, both in black and white and colour, is often preferred in 16mm because it shows less grain and suffers less wear and tear than a 16mm negative, But a 16mm colour reversal film gives less exposure latitude than a colour negative.
Ultra-high-speed emulsions are necessary in poor light conditions and for extreme high-speed photography.
Infra-red emulsions exist now in black and white and colour.
Lavender: a fine-grain positive stock used for duping.
Internegative and *interpositive* colour stock is used by the laboratory for optical work and process photography.
Light-struck stock: see *Leader*.
SOUND STOCK, all gauges. See also *Sound track*.
(1) Recording film with a photographic emulsion for 'optical sound'.
(2) Recording film with a full-width or striped magnetic coating.
Erase To obliterate sound from a magnetic tape or film so that it may be used again. This is often done on the spot by the recordist if a take is considered *NG*.
The likelihood of unintentional erasure is one of the objections put forward by the opponents of magnetic sound for 8mm casette films.
Film types See *Emulsion types*.
Fine-grain print See *Emulsion types*.
Flare Light from the sun or a lamp can hit the lens and fog part of the image. A lens hood should always be used. Flares from shiny objects in the set can be avoided by touching up the shiny part with a matting powder or spray, or by slightly altering the position of the lamp, object or camera. Flares from the sun or from street lights, which appear as radiating streaks, are often deliberately produced for effect by smearing petroleum jelly on the lens.
Flashback An earlier scene shown again as a reminder. A flashback sequence often relates to an event which happened before the action of the film begins.
Focus pulling, or *following focus*. In short-film making, this is the job of the assistant cameraman.
Fog A blackening or darkening of part of the image due to flare.
Edge fog is usually caused by light seeping into the magazine or camera.
Four-way See *Synchronizer*.
Gamma The contrast value of a negative, expressed in such figures as 0·5, 1·0, 1·5, etc. *Gamma time:* time of development. *High gamma:* pushing the development beyond the normal time in case of underexposure. *Gamma infinity:* maximum contrast obtainable. In further development the contrast decreases again.
Gel Short for 'gelatin sheet' such as is put in front of a lamp to alter the power or colour of the light.
Grading Determining the printing light for each negative scene

Glossary of Film Terms

of the rushes in the laboratory according to its tone, colour and density. At the completion of the film, the whole negative is regraded; the result is the grading- or *answer-print*.

Grey scale   A board with a scale of grey shades, filmed at the beginning of each roll of colour film as a guide for the laboratory.

Guide track   A temporary sound track, usually shot on a location in which conditions for quality recording are unsuitable due to extraneous noise from machinery, traffic, etc. The track serves as a guide for the final recording of the sound in the studio.

Hold   'Hold for 10 frames!', 'Hold for 3 ft': instruction to optical printer to print a single frame of a scene more than once to make up a required length. If this single frame is part of a live scene, we speak of 'freezing the action'. In animation: to shoot the stated number of frames or feet.

Hold it   Call to cameraman not to 'roll it' yet (not to start the camera).

Holography   A process by which a subject is 'photographed' (without a lens) by the coherent light emitted by a laser. After the *hologram* is processed, a three-dimensional image of the subject can be seen in the light of another laser beam. This process is still in its infancy and, as yet, without importance in practical cinematography.

Inky Dinky   A very small spotlight, useful for table-top sets to light several miniature objects or models individually.

Insert   A close-up of a static object such as a chart, book, clock, etc., inserted in a sequence to emphasize a point or create an aside. Many film units have small 'insert studios' where such shots can be taken at any convenient time.

Intercut   See *Cross cut*.

Intervalometer   An instrument for regulating the exposure intervals in time-lapse photography. It must be used in connection with a power unit which in turn is plugged into the mains supply. The device also controls the illumination. Exposures from about 1/50 sec to about 60 sec can be obtained at intervals of 2 or more sec up to several hours.

Jump cut   The result of an unworkmanlike piece of editing or negative cutting to eliminate a defect, or some unwanted action, by cutting a few frames or feet out of a scene which contains movement. This produces a jump in the action. The proper way is to have a quick dissolve made between the two parts of the scene. Deliberate jump cuts, created for effect, are of course permissible.

Lap dissolve   An ordinary dissolve. The term derives from the overlapping by superimposition of the fade-out and the fade-in.

Lavender   See *Emulsion types*.

Leader   A short length of film preceding the first scene, necessary for threading up the film. Ready-made 'Academy' leaders are used for show copies; they are a length of black film on which the start mark and nine countdown numbers are printed. For the *cutting copies*, cheap 'light-struck' film (also called 'leader stock') can be used on which the start marks are drawn. It is also used as *spacing*.

For *dubbing*, the start marks on the cutting tracks must be 15 ft in front of the first picture frame. For the later synchronization, one of the magnetic tracks must have a 'plop' (one frame of loud sound) 3 ft in front of the first frame. A corresponding frame must be marked on the picture track.

Library shot   A scene, sound effect or piece of music bought from a film library. If the scene is taken from another film shot by the unit itself, or obtained from another film unit, it is called *stock shot*.

Lip sync   Short for 'lip synchronization', when lip movements of actors in the film correspond with the delivery of their speech.

This is automatic in all synchronous shooting. It has, however, to be obtained by artifice in all types of post-synchronization of speech with the pictures done in the studio. Several methods exist to 'lip-sync' a *guide track*, a *wild track* or a foreign language track.

Loop   A film 'loop' is obtained by joining the ends of a length of film together for continuous running. Loops are mainly used for showing repetitive action, or for repeating some self-contained action several times, often with the live commentary of a teacher. The loop has to be guided over rollers or some improvised device at the back of the projector. Sound loops are used for repetitive or continuous effects.

Loop films: the name for 8mm cassetted film loops for classroom use. They form part of audio-visual aids.

Marker   A length of film (for instance an NG take) inserted temporarily into the cutting copy to indicate a missing scene.

Married print   The term is normally used for the *first* copy in which picture and sound have been combined in the laboratory. Naturally, all further copies are married prints as well.

Master   *Picture*: When a large number of release prints are required, a master fine-grain positive is first produced from the negative. From this, many *dupes* can later be taken. With reversal stock, the original should be treated and preserved like a negative. It must never be projected if more than two or three further prints will be needed.

Sound: The original magnetic tape or film from which all necessary working tracks are produced by transfer.

Master script   A document in the form of a film script but not broken down to so much detail as a shooting script.

Match dissolve   A dissolve in which the outlines of objects or the placing of people at the end of the first scene and the start of the second one are in *register*.

M & E track   Short for 'music and effects track'. Such a track has

Glossary of Film Terms

to be produced by the dubbing studio if it is anticipated that foreign language versions may be needed later on. The foreign commentary can then be dubbed on to the M & E track without difficulty.

Mock-up   (1) A replica of a machine or apparatus, or a set-up used as a temporary stand-in for experiments, etc.
(2) A small-scale three-dimensional scenic set of an actual location for plotting camera- and actor's movement, lighting, etc.

Montage   A term coined by the French film avant garde in the twenties to denote a quickly moving sequence consisting of heterogeneous material assembled to convey impressions of thought processes, dreams or mental conditions or sensations. Nowadays the term indicates any fast-moving *cross-cut* sequence.

Moviola   Trade name of a popular editing machine but now often used as a synonym for any such machine. There are several types in existence, either upright or of the bench type. The principle is the same in all of them; the picture can be viewed in a window or on a small monitoring screen whilst the sound emerges from the speaker.
The film can be run backwards and forwards, at normal and slow speeds, and stopped on any particular frame.

Multicam   The term is mainly used in TV and means that four, five or more cameras are set up at various vantage points to cover an event from every angle by running all cameras simultaneously. This method is time-saving but with photographic film it is so expensive that it can only be used in exceptional circumstances (State occasions, Olympic Games, etc.). For TV, which uses *videotape*, it is of great advantage.

Negative effects   An original film negative should never be projected. If, for pictorial or other reasons, a negative screen image is required, a *dupe* has to be made. In television, reversing the polarity makes negative appear positive on the TV screen and vice versa. A polarity reversal switch permits the instant transmission of negative newsreel material, etc.

Negative report sheet   See *Camera sheet*.

NG takes   Short for 'no good' (defective) takes and marked NP, 'not to be printed', on the camera sheets.

Number board   A *clapper board* without the clapper device for mute shooting.

Opticals   Scenes processed in the optical printer of the laboratory, such as fades, dissolves, superimpositions and special effects.

Outline treatment   or *synopsis*. Usually the first stage of scripting.

Pan   (1) Short for 'panorama shot'. A sweeping movement of the camera from one point to another. A fast swing from object to object is called a *zip pan*. A vertical pan is a *tilt*.
(2) A large studio flood lamp ('sky-pan').

Perforation The holes at the edges of the film into which the claw(s) of the camera engage(s). The distance from one hole to the next is known as the 'pitch'. The pitch is standardized for each of the film gauges but some high-speed cameras require 'long-pitch' perforation.
Pilot See *Rushes*.
Playback The playing of an existing, or *pre-recorded*, soundtrack in a studio to match sound and action as, for instance with lip movements. Where an orchestra appears in a scene, for better sound quality its performance is sometimes pre-recorded and then played back in the studio where the players play again in front of the camera but are not recorded.
All magnetic sound recording is played back straight away for checking.
Polaroid camera A still camera which produces a positive print in b/w or colour within seconds. Very useful for photographing locations selected for shooting and for checking continuity.
Post-production script A shooting script describes how a film is visualized; it is a document of intent. A post-production script, on the other hand, is a blueprint of the finished film: a record of performance. It sets down all visuals and sound and gives the progressive footage. It is kept for reference. The shooting script and PP script sometimes bear little resemblance to each other.
Post-recording The opposite of *pre-recording*. Often, conditions at the time the picture is shot are unfavourable for quality recording and this has to be done later in the studio in sync with the picture. See also *Guide-track*.
Practical Any *props* such as lamps, water taps, gas rings, etc., which have actually to function in the filmed scene.
Pre-recording A recording of speech or music made under the best conditions for later synchronizination of sound and action. See *Playback*.
Props (1) Short for 'properties'. Any objects used for dressing the set or needed in a scene.
(2) Short for 'property man', the studio hand who looks after the props.
Process camera A camera which is not used for the principal photography but for processing (re-photographing) the filmed material for effects, etc. Mainly to be found in film laboratories or animation and effects studios.
Ratio, shooting (or cutting) A considerable wastage of film stock inevitable in filming. The proportion of this wastage to the stock actually used in a film is the 'shooting ratio' (5:1, 10:1, etc.) which depends on the subject, the level of production and so on. The envisaged shooting ratio for an intended production should be stated in the budget submitted to the sponsor.
Register To put an object 'in register' with another, filmed previously, means to put a frame of the previous scene into the

Glossary of Film Terms

camera gate and to align the contours of the new object exactly with those of the object on the image in the gate. This is often necessary for superimpositions and special effects.

Release prints   Mass-produced prints made for distribution.

Re-recording   See *Dubbing*.

Re-take   Two or more takes of each scene are usually filmed. If none of these takes is found satisfactory when viewing the rushes, the scene has to be re-shot. The scene-number for the shot remains the same but the new takes must be clearly marked RT on the *clapper board*.

Revamp   To alter the appearance of a set or set-up for a further shot, without changing its basic layout.

Rock-and-roll   A time-saving dubbing method (see page 265).

Rough-cut   A first assembly of the filmed material before editing proper starts.

Rushes   Short for 'rush prints', the first prints of the filmed material, usually processed overnight in the laboratory and ready for viewing on the day after shooting. A report on the quality of the rushes is usually available by phone sooner than the prints themselves. After viewing, the rushes are sent to the cutting room for editing.

Of each scene, a short strip of about 16 frames is printed at different printing lights for the director or cameraman to check contrast or colour quality. Such a strip is usually called 'cinex' in b/w or 'pilot' in colour.

Scene number   The scene number, as marked in the script, should be written clearly on the *clapper board* for easy identification of the shot.

Scratch commentary   A temporary recording of the speech for a preliminary show to the sponsor. (Can be spoken by a member of the film unit.)

Show print   A *Release print*.

Sound track   (1) The visible modulations traced by the sound on the photographic base in optical recording.

(2) The narrow band running alongside a film's perforation which carries the sound, either as described above, or invisibly, as on all magnetic tracks. The magnetic stripes on 16mm and 8mm prints consists either of a chemical coating or of a laminated strip pressed on to the film.

In 16mm prints, an optical and magnetic track can run side by side.

(3) As opposed to the picture track of a cutting copy: a roll or reel of magnetic sound film onto which the sound has been transferred after recording for the purpose of editing. Also referred to as 'sound cutting copy'. See *Double-headed* and *married print*.

Spacing   Any film stock which is used for connecting scenes (picture or sound) which are not immediately consecutive.

Spider A wooden, metal or canvas support for the tripod which prevents it's legs from slipping on smooth floors, or damaging carpets.
Standard gauge A 35mm film with 16 or 24 frames per foot.
Stock shot See *Library shot*.
Stripe See *Sound track*.
Strobe Short for 'stroboscopic effect'. 'Strobing' manifests itself on the screen in many ways: car wheels appear to turn the wrong way round, ripples in water to run backwards, upright pillars flicker in a *pan* and the movement of an object animated across the screen in single-frame filming often appears jerky. Strobing results from the phenomenon known as 'persistence of vision'. (Where a remedy is possible, it is mentioned in the text.)
Substandard gauges The 16mm film with 40 frames per foot and the 8mm film with 80 frames per foot.
Sync Short for 'synchronization'. To 'run in sync' means that the picture and sound track are running exactly at the same speed so that the sound exactly matches the action. Wild sound has to be synchronized with the action in the cutting room by manipulation. See *Sync shooting*, *Sync mark*, *Lip sync*.
Sync mark Corresponding marks made frequently (with a wax crayon) on the picture and sound tracks will prevent 'losing the sync'. The start marks, often called 'gate marks', on the *leaders* are the first sync marks on a cutting copy.
Synchronizer An instrument used in editing in which two or more drums with toothed wheels, the width of the film, rotate in synchronism. The teeth engage in the perforations of the tracks which are pulled over the wheels by turning a knob or handle. The device is used to synchronize picture and sound. A track reader can be connected to it which picks up and amplifies the sound from the tracks.
According to the number of tracks which the instrument can accommodate, it is briefly referred to either as a *two-way* or a *four-way*. Film frame- and footage-counters are incorporated.
Synchro pulse See *Sync shooting*.
Sync shooting Short for 'synchronous shooting'. In this picture camera and the sound recording instrument are interlocked so that they run at the same speed. There are several systems: The *synchro pulse* system is used in connection with $\frac{1}{4}$ inch tape recorders; it is most suitable for location work. The picture camera sends electrical pulses to the tape recorder where they are recorded on one half of the tape whilst the sound is recorded on the other half. Each pulse is a sort of electronic sprocket hole and serves to keep the sound in perfect synchronization with the picture in much the same way as linked sprocketed systems do.
In sprocketed systems the picture- and sound-equipment are kept in

Glossary of Film Terms

sync by synchronous a.c. motors. For sync shooting the picture camera has to be *blimped* so that the camera noise is not picked up by the microphone. See also *Clapper board*.

Synopsis   See *Outline treatment*.

Take-board   A number board. See *Clapper board*.

Take number   This follows the scene number on the *clapper board*. Each take of a scene is given a consecutive number which has to be entered on the *camera sheet*; the takes to be printed are ringed or marked 'P', the others 'NP' or 'NG'. See also *Retake*.

Thermograph   Infra-red photograph of a subject illuminated by its own heat radiation.

Top-hat or **Hi-hat**   A very short, rigid, camera support of metal. See also *Baby legs*.

Track Reader   See *Synchronizer*.

Treatment   Usually the second stage of scripting, following the synopsis or outline and preceding the writing of the shooting script. See also *Master script*.

Trip-gear   A device used in time-lapse photography to trigger off the exposure. It is usually part of the *intervalometer*.

Triple-headed   See *Double-headed*.

Two-shot   A mid close-up of two people.

Two-way   See *Synchronizer*.

Velocilator   A sophisticated type of *dolly*. There are many models. Some can elevate the camera and swing it around by means of a powered lifting device, others can move sideways or diagonally (a crab dolly). Velocilators of one kind or another are a standard part of the equipment in large studios. They can also be hired for location work.

Video recording   Recording a picture, or picture-and-sound, electronically on videotape for replay on a television screen. Videotape is much used in TV productions and video recording is useful for including scenes in closed-circuit TV.

Wild track   Any soundtrack which is not recorded in sync with a picture.

Zip-pan   See *Pan*.

Index

A & B rolls 100, 266, 289
Action stills 123
Adviser, educational 165, 206, 247, 251–2
 technical (subject) 118–9, 145, 187, 205–6, 209, 227, 251–2, 256–7, 261, 276
Aerial survey 81, 87
Aerodynamic research 89, 172
Aeronautics 168–9
Agfa-Gevaert 66
Air currents (*see also* Thermals) 165–177
 eddies 153
 particles 147
Alpha particles 228–36, 240–1
Aluminium powder 172
Ames, Adalbert 31
Analogies 58, 130–38, 152
Angle of sight 27, 30, 38
The Animals 69
Animation 18, 58, 67, 68, 92, 100, 116–30, 203–4, 233–4, 256
 bench (rostrum) 119
 cel(s) 117–19, 129–30, 201, 214
 diagrams 48, 101, 105, 117–19, 142, 175–77, 178, 187, 213–17, 226, 231, 235–6, 243, 259
 figure 122, 126–29
 model 48, 126–29
 schedule 175–77, 179
 simulated 129–30, 183, 211, 213, 218
Answer print 267
Anvil Films 59, 163
Apparatus, scientific 196, 199
Appleton, Sir Edward 203, 206, 209, 218–23
Arnold, Malcolm 143, 163
Art director 143–4, 259
Atom(s) 177–79, 188–92, 214, 225–46
 fission, see Nuclear fission
 pile (reactor) 225, 243, 245–6
 power station, see Calder Hall
Audience 13, 23, 36, 49, 62, 69, 70–1, 98, 113, 117, 134, 136, 164, 203–4, 220, 252–3, 275–79

Audiospectrometer 160–63
Audio-visual aids 21, 69, 165, 269–74

Baby legs 43
Barndoor 46
Barnett, Dr. 221
Barnett, Lincoln 137
BBC, BBC-TV 49, 59, 69, 92, 221–2
Between the Tides 69, 283
The Birth of the Robot 126–28
Black body 47, 165
 velvet 150, 153, 154, 195–97, 219, 289
Blimp 53
Blur *see* Softness
Bragg, Sir Lawrence 59, 130–32
Bragg, Sir William 56
Brief 253, 258
British Film Institute 20, 280
British Transport Films 69
Britten, Benjamin 142
Brownian Movement 101
Bubble raft 69, 130–32, 134, 284
Budget, budgeting 100, 187, 247, 250–1, 253, 257–8, 260
Bump technique *see* Jump technique

Cabinet of Dr. Caligari 31
Calder Hall power station 225, 245
Camera angle 41
 sheet 261
 speed 90–1, 93–7
Cameraman *see* Film cameraman
Canadian Film Institute 275
Carbon 67, 283
Carbon dioxide, solid *see* Dry ice
Cassette film *see* Loop film
Cathode ray tube(s) 160, 162–3, 222–23, 226–28
Cavendish Laboratory 231, 235, 240
Cel *see* Animation
Central Heating 166–67, 172
Central Office of Information (COI) 107, 134, 142, 144, 280
Chadwick, Sir James 225, 240–1

300

Index

Chloride, cupric   112
Cinemacrography   73–4, 81
Cinemicrography   55, 62–5, 66, 68, 72–4, 93, 96, 97
Civilisation   49
Clark, Frank P.   103, 112
Clark, Lord   49
Clarke, C. C.   83
Classroom films   *see* Teaching Films
Climate   186
Close up   25, 26, 39–41, 51, 73, 103, 111, 119, 163, 260
Closed circuit television   22, 61, 269
Cockroft, Sir John   225, 236–40
Cockroft-Walton "atom smasher"   237–40
Colour in film   18, 24
  code   48
  pilot   259
  shooting   47–8, 86, 89, 259
  temperature   47
Commentary   23, 50, 70, 113, 116, 135, 223, 261, 263
Commentator   49, 257, 261, 263
Compilation film   26
Composer   257, 262
Composite image   *see* Effects (split screen)
Conduction   177–82, 284
Conquest of the Atom   203, 224–46, 284
Continuity   51
  sheet   260, 290
Convection   165–77, 284
Convection   *see* Air- and Water currents
Cooper, George   141, 159, 243
Crookes tube(s)   226–28, 237
Cross cutting   25
Crova disc   154–56, 210, 247
Crowe, George   231, 240–41
Curie, Marie and Pierre   102
Cutting copy   259, 261–64, 266, 290
  room   261–67
Cuvette   74

Dalton, John   225
Darwin, Ch. R.   132
Day-for-night photography   86, 99
Dialogue   *see* Speech
Dimmer   46, 78, 120
Director   *see* Film director
Dissolve   26, 43, 72, 100, 262, 266, 293, 294
Distillation   114, 284
Dolly   *see* Velocilator
Dope sheet   *see* Continuity sheet
Double exposure   77, 79, 80, 291
Double-headed screening   265, 291
Drag   116
Dry ice   111, 174

Dubbing (Re-recording)   51, 53, 54, 147, 163, 257, 263–66, 291
  chart 265
Dupe negative   26, 34, 92, 100, 149, 291

Ear, anatomy of   151
Edge number(s)   99, 150, 291
Edison, Thomas A.   19
Editing   19, 24, 25–7, 43, 50, 59, 90, 92, 98, 123, 140, 261–67
  schedule 163–64
Educational film   *see* Teaching film
Educational Foundation for Visual Aids (EFVA)   186, 203, 205, 224, 280
Effects   *see also* Filters, Optical printing, Models
  atmospheric   101, 111–12
  cloud   213
  flashing   152, 243
  fog   87, 111
  kaleidoscopic   75
  mattes   *see* Mattes
  moonlight   48, 81, 86
  radiation   46
  scenic   *see* Models
  snow   180–81
  special   39, 58, 72–3, 98–100, 103, 144–148
  split screen   72, 80, 99
Effects loop   54
  track (*see also* Sound track)   54
Einstein, Albert   137
Electro-Magnetic Waves   186–203, 284
Electro-magnetic waves   183, 186–203
  absorption   187, 201
  beaming   187
  beam width   195–97
  behaviour   187, 193–203
  diffraction   69, 187, 198–201
  dispersion   187
  emission   187, 192
  energy level   190–91
  gamma rays   188–89
  generation   186–93
  interference   187, 198–201
  micro waves   187, 193
  polar diagrams   187
  propagation   187, 198
  properties   187, 193–203
  reflection   187, 203
  refraction   187, 198
  spectrometer   198
  spectrum   186, 198, 201
  spectrum analysis   187
  straight path   187, 202–03
  transmission   187
  velocity   183, 187, 193–95
  X-rays 188, 192–93

301

Index

Electron(s)   188–92, 214–17, 222, 225–28, 238
Electron microscope   58, 64, 74
Elton, Sir Arthur   70, 275
Emulsion (film)   73, 96, 100, 291–92
Evaluation (appraisal)   275–79
  (research)   13, 91
Evolution   132
Exploring Chemistry   69, 283
Exploring the Instruments   152–59, 284
Exposure factor   73
  meter   45, 73, 84, 96
  time   73, 93
Eye, anatomy of   133–36

Facilities for filming   250, 256, 258, 260
Fade(s)   26, 262, 266
Faraday, Michael   19
Fermi, Enrico   245–46
Field, Mary   67
Field of view   27–31, 37, 39–41
Film Centre International   70
Film cameraman   140, 259
  consultant   251
  director   50, 68, 99, 118, 139–40, 259, 263, 267
  editor   *see* Editing
  gauge, 35mm   37, 91, 99, 262, 267–68, 271
    16mm   37, 39, 91, 99, 113, 140, 262–63, 267–68, 271
    8mm   37, 39, 91, 99, 113, 263, 267, 270–74
  laboratory   47, 48, 73, 86, 92, 96, 98, 259–62, 267–68
  language   18, 19, 21, 23, 24, 25–27, 37, 117, 250
  library material   52–3, 257, 262, 264, 279–82
  loop (*see also* Loop film)   265, 294
  maker, non-professional   141
  producer (*see also* Sponsor)   139–40, 249–51, 271–2, 276
  reality   26, 38, 90
  space   25
  speed   103
  studio   140, 144, 257, 259–60
  time   25, 41, 90
Filter(s)   45, 47, 73, 84, 86–7, 89
  cloud   86
  dichroic   47
  diffusion   42, 87
  fog   87, 177
  haze   87
  heat-absorbing   74, 96
  neutral density   42, 46, 86
Fine-grain negative   100, 267
Flame(s)   112

Flash, electric   240
Flatland by A Square   137
Fleming, Ambrose, 213
Flow phenomena   112
Focal length   37, 39, 41
Focus, focusing   39, 83, 119
  deep   42
  depth of   39, 41–2, 73
  differential   42
Fog, artificial   *see* Effects, Filters
  photography in   87
de Forest, Lee   19
Forgeries   81
Franklin, Benjamin   105
Freezing of frames or action   97–99

Gamow, Professor G.   233
Garratt, Gerald   209–12
Gas Council, London   164, 281
Gauze   42, 75, 159
Geiger, Professor Hans   229
Geiger-Marsden apparatus   229–33
Gel (Gelatine sheet)   47, 81, 183, 228, 233, 245
Glass shot   129–30, 213–14, 218–20
Gliding   169, 175–76
Gobo   46, 146
Grading   48, 267
Grain (emulsion)   34
Granada TV   132
Graphics   113–14, 117–19, 223
Grayson, Dorothy   144
Grey scale   48
Grierson, John   20
Griffith, D. W.   25
Guide track   *see* Recording

Hahn, Professor Otto   225, 242
Halas, John   117, 175, 272
Harrison, Dr. J. A.   205
Hass, Hans   92
Haze   87
  penetration   81–3, 87
Hearing the Music   145–52, 284
Heat absorption   184–85
  conduction   165, 177–82
  convection   165–77
  emission   184–85
  radiation   107, 165, 182–86
  reflection   183–4
  transference   164–86
Heaviside layer   218, 222
Heaviside, Oliver   206, 218
Hertz, Heinrich   206, 209–12
High Speed Flight   88, 284
High speed (slow motion) camera   91, 96–7
  cinematography   58, 61, 66, 72, 90

Index

Historic characters 204
   equipment 204–05
Historical subjects 203–48
History of Science by Sherwood-Taylor 210
Holography 67, 293
How the Motorcar Works 78, 284
Hydraulic research station 201
Hydrocarbons 114
Hyperfocal distance 42

Image 27–41, 45, 80
Imperial College, London 171, 213
Infrared camera(s) 83
   cinematography 58, 66–7, 81–7, 182–83
Institut fuer den Wissenschaftlichen Film, Goettingen 74, 280
Instruments of the Orchestra 142
Interference pattern 146
International Scientific Film Association 282
Inter-negative, -positive 100
Interpretive film 67–70
Intervalometer 93, 293
Investigation (subject) 23, 40, 187, 205–06, 213, 247, 253–56
Invisible, The 21, 55–8, 60–67, 72–74, 81, 84, 88, 97, 101, 116
   Filming the Invisible: examples 144–248
Ion(s), Ionization 188, 213–17
Ionosonde 222
Ionosphere 203, 206, 218–222
Isotopes 242–244

Jeakins. Adrian 141.163
Jeans, Sir James 137
Jitter 116, 119
Jones, Sir Brynmor 269
Jump cut 43
   (bump) technique 122–28, 201

Kahn, F. 134
Keen, G. K. 89
Kemp (Marconi's assistant) 206–09, 212–14
Kennelly, Professor A. E. 206
King's College, London 187, 198
King Solomon's Garden 69
Kodak 84, 122

Laboratory (film) *see* Film laboratory
   (science) 40, 87, 89, 134, 140, 222–23
Lamps, types of 45–7, 84, 88, 93, 198
Laser 187, 203
Lavender (film stock) 26
Lecture (*see also* Teaching film) 58, 61
Lecturer 58, 61, 140
Lens 37, 73, 74
   diopter 73
   distorting 75
   fish-eye 27–9
   long focus 30, 31, 37–9, 73
   quartz 84
   short focus (wide angle) 31, 37–9, 42, 75, 77
   supplementary 73, 75
   telephoto 30, 37–9, 75
Lens angle *see* Field of view
   aperture (stop) 41, 42, 73, 84
Library material *see* Film library
A Light in Nature 62–5, 283
Light, lighting 37, 44–8, 74, 78, 93, 96, 226
   rays (*see also* El.-magn. waves) 111, 183–84, 202
London Symphony Orchestra 142–64
Looking at Sound 160–64, 284
Loop (cassette) film 13, 20, 164, 270–04
Losey, Joseph 50, 53
Lycopodium powder 112
Lye, Len 117, 126

Macro-photography
   see Cinemacrography
Man 92
Magic Light 66, 283
Magnetic board 122
Magnetic stripe 263
   tape 262–63
   track 19, 262–65
Man measures the Universe (Unesco) 55
Manvell, Roger 117
Marconi, G. 206–09, 212–13
Marconi Ltd. 207, 212
Marey, E. G. 66
Married print 15, 267
Marsden, E. 229
Maser 187, 203
Mask(s) 79–80, 146
Master-script 256
   track (*see also* Sound track) 263, 266–67, 294
Mathieson, Muir 142–64
Matte(s) 21, 72, 79–80, 99
   box 45, 75, 80, 87
Maxwell, James Clerk 209
McClaren, Norman 117
Medical Research Council 61
M & E track 266
Melde string apparatus 157, 160, 162
Metaphor *see* Analogy
Micro photography *see* Cinemicrography
The Microscope 77, 284
Ministry of Defence 69
Mirror, semi-transparent 74, 77–8
   shot (*see also* Pepper's Ghost) 72, 74, 75, 77–9, 88, 202

303

Mirror in the Sky 203, 206–24, 285
Mix *see* Dissolve
Model(s) 58, 67–8, 100–12, 134, 144–248
 anatomical 103
 animated 105, 122–29
 architectural 103
 commissioned 105, 109–10
 do-it-yourself 102, 105–09, 111
 engineering 78, 102
 mathematical 69, 105, 109
 miniature 93, 101, 103
 molecular 105
 ready-made 102
 scenic 101, 109, 198
 scientific 103–05
 toys 105, 126
Model maker 109–10, 144, 174
Molecule(s) 177–79
Montage sequence 37, 41, 145, 295
Montblanc 54
Montgolfier balloon 168, 174–75
Morgan Crucible Company 67
Morrison, Professor Philip 34
Moviola 119, 261, 264, 295
Mullard Ltd. 186, 203, 206, 224, 281
Multicam 59, 295
Multiple printing 96
Multiplexer system 78
Music (film) 23, 51–4, 116, 263–64
 cue sheet 262
 royalties 257
 track (*see also* Sound track) 54
Music (as a subject 142–64
Musical note, fundamental 160–62
 harmonics 160–62
Muybridge, Edweard 66
La Mystère Picasso 219

National Audio-Visual Aids Centre,
  London 272
National Film Board of Canada 208, 281
National Physical Laboratory, Teddington
  88, 111, 240
Negative cutting 266–67
Neutron(s) 225, 240–46
New Atlantis by Francis Bacon 248
Newton, Sir Isaac 186
Nuclear fission 225, 242–46
Nucleus *see* Atom
Nuffield Science Teaching Project 69

Oak dust 112
Optical illusion 31
 printer, printing 73, 80, 92, 96, 97,
   98–100, 146, 150
Opticals 262, 266, 295
Optics *see* Lens
Outline *see* Treatment

Over-running of camera 43, 73, 90,
  93–7, 103
Oxberry animation camera 118

Panning 38, 43, 204, 212, 295
Paraffin wax 112
Parsons, Denys 144, 160, 163, 173, 205
Pepper's Ghost technique (*see also*
 Superimposition) 77–9, 130
 applications 174, 182, 186, 188–97,
   211, 213, 218, 222, 227, 229, 239, 241,
   243–44
Persistence of vision 35, 117
Perspective 30–3, 37, 39, 103, 126
Phi phenomenon 35
Philipp, K. 74
Photon(s) 188–92
Physics and Chemistry of Water 68, 283
Picasso, Pablo 219
Picture track 15–8, 24, 254–5, 261–2
Pinhole camera 202
Playback 51–2, 261, 263, 265, 296
Pola screen (polarising filter) 87, 105
Polaroid camera 260, 296
Porter, Professor George 56, 58, 105
Postgate, Oliver 120
Potassium permanganate 112
Pre-production stage 247, 253–58
Prism 75, 78, 156, 198
Procedure of film-making 249–68
Process cinematography 72
Production management 140, 258–59
 routine 252–68
 schedule 188
Projection 90, 91, 92
Proton(s) 225, 235–41

Quantum *see* Photon

Radiation 182–86, 284
Radar 206
Radio-activity 188, 228–30
Radio waves (*see also* E.-magn. waves)
  206–224
 astronomy 206, 223–24
 communication 206, 213
 discovery 209–12
 reflection 210–11, 218, 220
 telescope(s) *see* astronomy
Realist Film Unit 141, 164, 205
Recording (sound) 19, 163, 257, 262–64
 guide track 163, 292
 post 163
 pre 52, 163
 wild 50, 51, 53, 163, 263, 299
Reflections (in glass, etc.) 75, 86, 151
Reflectors (light) 45
Refractive index 87–9

Index

(in) Register 146, 296
Re-recording *see* Dubbing
Research films 13
The Revealing Eye 66, 283
Reversal film 100
Reversed motion, intentional 58, 92, 98–9, 107, 119, 147, 150, 201, 233–35, 243–44
  stroboscopic 35, 200–201
Ripple tank 199–201
Ritchie-Calder, Lord Peter 206
River to Cross 111, 284
The River must Live 68, 282
Rock-and-roll 265
Rodker, Francis 128
Royal Institution of Great Britain 56, 58–60, 105
Royal Society 62
Rushes (rush prints) 26, 48, 79, 259, 261, 297
Rutherford, Ernest 203, 225, 228–36

Sargent, Sir Malcolm 142
Scene, length of 37, 113, 19,
Schlieren method 66, 87–9, 166, 168, 171–72, 283
Schüfftan process 78, 101
Science (scientific) film(s) 13, 14, 21, 22, 37, 39, 41, 46, 47, 48, 50, 52, 54, 61, 69, 72, 78, 99, 101, 142–248, 251–53, 270, 275–79, 282
Science in the Orchestra 103, 142–64, 284
Science Museum, London 209, 239
Screen-space, -time *see* Film-space, -time
Script, scripting 23, 25–7, 62–5, 135, 144, 165–71, 187, 208–09, 232, 252, 256–57
Second Law of Thermo-Dynamics 58, 105, 284
Secrets of Nature 93
Seeing 55–58
Sequence (film) 36
SHELL, Shell Film Unit 62, 66, 68, 70, 78, 88, 114, 128, 281
Shock waves 88–9
Shooting 25, 46–8, 259–61
  period 258
  schedule 258, 260
  script *see* Script
Show copy 15, 267–68
Shutter (camera) 34, 35, 226, 240
Single concept film *see* Loop film
Single frame photography (*see also* Time lapse) 91–3, 105, 116, 119, 150, 233–34
Skip printing 92
Slow motion *see* High speed cinematography
Smith, Brian 144

Smith, Professor C. Maynard 132
Smith, Percy 93
Smoke, 109, 111, 167, 173–74
  box 111, 183–84
  candle 87, 111
Snow, artificial 111
Softness of image 41, 42, 75
Solar furness (model) 183–84
Something Nice to Eat 172
Sound (as a subject) 142–64
  loudness 161–62
  physics of 142–64
  pitch 156–61
  production of 145–52
  propagation of 146–48
  speed 148–51
  wave(s) 148–51
Sound (on film) 18, 19, 24, 49–54
  effects 23, 51, 53–4, 153, 260, 262, 264–65
  mixer 263–66
  recording *see* Recording
Sound track 15, 254–55, 261, 264, 297
  effects 264–65
  magnetic 92, 262–64
  magnetic stripe 263
  master 263
  M & E 266
  music 264
  optical 92, 266–67
  speech 263–66
Spark(s), electric 88, 237, 239–40
Spectrum *see* El.-magn. waves
Special techniques 58, 72–138
Speech, (*see also* Commentary) 23, 50–1, 261
Spinthariscope 228–29, 235
Split-screen *see* Effects
Sponsor 20, 23, 52, 69, 70, 119, 125, 136, 142, 187, 205, 249–51, 253–59, 261, 263, 265–68, 270, 275, 276
Squash 116
Still camera 253, 260
Stobart, Tom 139
Stop-motion *see* Time-lapse
Stop printing 97
Story board 119, 219, 256
Strassmann, Professor F. 225, 242
Stroboscopic effect(s), strobing 35, 43, 119, 128, 200–01, 298
Structure of Protein 61, 67, 283
Studio *see* Film studio
Subject expert *see* Adviser
Superimposition (*see also* Pepper's Ghost) 80, 99, 109, 118, 145, 149–50, 156
Symbol 113, 116
  as code 114
Symbolic content 37, 41, 109

305

Index

Sync shooting, (*see also* Recording)   49, 51, 52, 53, 262, 298
Synchronization   261, 298
Synchronizer   261, 263
Synopsis   *see* Treatment

Taylor, John   141
Taylor, Professor Charles   31
Teaching film(s)   21, 22, 48, 52, 70, 113, 126, 142–248, 251, 269–74
 notes (handbooks)   70, 144, 270
Television   19, 20, 21, 22, 26, 54, 58, 59, 69, 97, 99, 113, 123, 141, 144, 205, 269
Thermal photography   *see* Infrared cinematography
Thermals (*see also* Air currents)   169, 176–77
Thomson, A. R.   210, 212
Thomson, J. J.   19, 225–28
Three-dimensional cinematography   27
Time-lapse cameras   91–93
 cinematography   58, 66, 83, 90, 91–3, 139
A Time to Play   45
Titles   78, 109, 113, 121, 262
 animated   122
Titler   120–21, 262
Top hat   43
Track   *see* Sound track
 laying   262–66
Tracking   43, 120, 204, 210
Transference of Heat   164–86, 284
Treatment (film)   22, 23, 213, 256, 299
Tripod   43
True Life Adventure   93

U.K. Atomic Energy Authority   239, 242
Ultra-violet microscopy   74
 cinematography   58, 66–7, 84
 rays   87
Under-running of camera   86, 90–3, 96, 98, 153, 162–63
UNESCO   55, 278, 282
Unilever   67, 68, 69, 281
Unipod   43
The Universe of Light by Sir William Bragg   56

University Film Foundation, U.S.A.   140
Unshackled (roving) camera   43

Velocilator   43, 299
Ventilation   167–68
Vibration (caused by sound)   102, 145–46, 160, 162
Video-recording, -tape   19, 59, 299
Viewfinder   40, 253
The Violent Universe   69
Vision, human   27–35
Vision-mixing   19, 59
Visual   23, 24, 145
Visual Aids   *see* Audio-visual Aids
Visual Aids   69, 283
Visualisation   23, 24, 26, 27

Walky-talky   260
Walton, Dr. E. T. S.   236–40
Warrendale   26
Water (as subject)   68–9
 currents   165–77
 waves   196, 199–201
Waters of Time   49
Wave(s), longitudinal   148, 247
 standing   154
 transverse   196, 247
Wave machine(s)   148, 197, 247
Weather   170, 177
Wild shooting   *see* Recording
Wilkinson, Dr. George   187, 198, 203
Wipe   26, 266
Wood alcohol   112
Wright, Basil   49, 141, 205, 207

X-rays   *see* El.-magn. waves
 apparatus (model)   193
 crystallography   187
 cinematography   58, 64–5, 92

Young–Fresnel apparatus   199
Your Children's Eyes   134–36, 284
Your Children's Meals   106–07, 284

Zajek, Dr. E.   31
Zip-pan   43
Zoom lens   39, 43

THE LIBRARY OF COMMUNICATION TECHNIQUES

THE TECHNIQUE OF
DOCUMENTARY FILM PRODUCTION *by W. Hugh Baddeley*
A wealth of information on how to plan, budget and produce documentaries.
Price £2·50   2nd rev. ed., 268 pp., 63 diag.

THE TECHNIQUE OF
FILM AND TELEVISION MAKE-UP   *by Vincent J-R. Kehoe*
New ideas and information on products, both British and American.
Price £3·50   2nd rev. ed., 280 pp., 8 colour plates, 123 black and white photographs, 182 diag.

THE TECHNIQUE OF FILM MUSIC   *by Roger Manvell and John Huntley*
For everyone interested in motion pictures as well as professional music-makers.
Price £3·00   300 pp., 73 photographs, 103 diag.

THE TECHNIQUE OF
TELEVISION PRODUCTION   *by Gerald Millerson*
A survey of the mechanics, art and techniques used in T.V. studio work.
Price £3·00 Case   9th ed., 440 pp., 1150 diag.
    £2·00 paperback

THE TECHNIQUE OF FILM ANIMATION   *by John Halas and Roger Manvell*

Price £3·00   3rd ed., 360 pp., 191 photographs, 56 diag.

THE TECHNIQUE OF FILM EDITING   *compiled by Karel Reisz and Gavin Millar*
A compendium of the views of Britain's leading directors and editors.
Price £3·50   2nd ed., 412 pp., 325 photographs, 21 diag.

THE TECHNIQUE OF THE SOUND STUDIO:
FOR RADIO, TELEVISION AND FILM   *by Alec Nisbett*
Recently revised to cover all aspects of television sound techniques.
Price £3·50   3rd revised ed., 560 pp., 242 diag.

THE TECHNIQUE OF
THE TELEVISION CAMERAMAN   *by Peter Jones*
Devoted wholly and specifically to the work of the television cameraman.
Price £3·25 3rd ed., 244 pp., 120 diag.

TECHNIQUE OF THE MOTION PICTURE CAMERA
by H. Mario Raimondo Souto
The first comprehensive study of the modern film camera in all its forms.
Price £3·50 2nd rev. and enlarged ed., 322 pp., 191 diag.

THE TECHNIQUE OF EDITING 16mm. FILMS *by John Burder*
Will equip people for the needs of the cutting-room today.
Price £2·50 3rd ed., 152 pp., 169 diag.

THE TECHNIQUE OF TELEVISION ANNOUNCING
by Bruce Lewis
A manual for those who appear, or aspire to appear, "on camera".
Price £2·25 264 pp., 43 diag.

THE TECHNIQUE OF LIGHTING FOR
TELEVISION AND MOTION PICTURES   *by Gerald Millerson*
How light behaves and effects portraiture and environment.
Price £4·00 472 pp., 8 pp. colour plates, 206 b & w photographs, 471 diag.

THE TECHNIQUE OF THE FILM CUTTING ROOM
by Ernest Walter
Shows the logic in the sequence of editorial activities.
Price £3·50 296 pp., 130 diag.

THE TECHNIQUE OF
SPECIAL EFFECTS IN TELEVISION   *by B. R. Wilkie*
Covers everything from bullet and bomb effects to dripping gutters.
Price £3·50 392 pp., 169 photographs, 51 diag.

THE TECHNIQUE OF
SPECIAL EFFECTS CINEMATOGRAPHY   *by Raymond Fielding*
Describes every special effects technique in use throughout the world.
Price £3·50 3rd rev. ed., 426 pp., 283 photographs, 222 diag.